TASK/TOPIC	PBE MENU SELECTIONS	R> COMMAND	PAGES
Combine two tables	(1)/R:BASE commands/Combine		379
Compare columns		*special operators*	89
Compressed print			169
Convert R:BASE 5000 data		CONVERT	556
Copy a form	(2)/FORMS/(3)		190
Copy a report	(2)/REPORTS/(2)	REPORTS	182
Copy a table	(1)/R:BASE commands/Combine/PROJECT	PROJECT	368
Count rows	(6)/Look at data/COMPUTE	COMPUTE COUNT	140
Create a command file	(8)/RBEDIT	RBEDIT	443
Create a database	(1)/RBDEFINE	RBDEFINE	20
Create a form	(2)/FORMS/(1)	FORMS	188
Create a rule	(1)/RBDEFINE/(2)/(4)/(1)	DEFINE RULES	257
Create a view	(1)/RBDEFINE/(2)/(2)/(1)	RBDEFINE, VIEW	392
Create an application	(2)/EXPRESS/(1)	EXPRESS	410
Create variables		SET VARIABLE	289
Cross-tabulation	(6)/Look at data/CROSSTAB	CROSSTAB	143
dBASE interface	(8)/ImportExport/GATEWAY	GATEWAY	576
Define a function key		Shift-F1	442
Define rules	(1)/RBDEFINE/(2)/(4)	DEFINE RULES	257
Define user access		GRANT, REVOKE	267
Delete a column	(1)/R:BASE commands/REMOVE/COLUMN	REMOVE COLUMN	232
Delete a file	(8)/Operating system/ERASE	ERASE	433
Delete a form	(2)/FORMS/(4)	REMOVE FORM	232
Delete a report	(2)/REPORTS/(4)	REMOVE REPORT	182
Delete a row	F2 (in EDIT mode)	F2 (in EDIT mode)	56
Delete a rule	(1)/RBDEFINE/(2)/(4)/(3)	REMOVE RULE	236
Delete a table	(1)/RBDEFINE/(2)/(1)/(3)	REMOVE TABLE	236
Delete a variable		CLEAR VARIABLES	293
Delete a view	(1)/RBDEFINE/(2)/(2)/(3)	REMOVE VIEW	399
Delete an application	(8)/All commands/ERASE	ERASE	433
Delete multiple rows	(5)/DELETE	DELETE	111
Display data on screen		OUTPUT SCREEN	124
DOS access	(8)/All commands/ZIP	ZIP	137
DOS commands	(8)/Operating system functions	*Any valid DOS command*	33

Understanding R:BASE

Understanding R:BASE®

Alan Simpson
Karen Watterson

San Francisco Paris Düsseldorf London

Cover art by Thomas Ingalls + Associates
Cover photography by Victor Budnik
Series design by Julie Bilski
Chapter art and layout by Charlotte Carter

Library of Congress Card Number: 88-61066
ISBN 0-89588-503-4
Manufactured in the United States of America
10 9 8 7 6 5 4 3

To Susan ——— *A.S.*

To Fred ——— *K.W.*

Acknowledgments

Many thanks to all the people whose skills and talents produced this book, including, in roughly chronological order, Jon Strickland, editing; Dan Tauber, technical review; Bob Myren and Jocelyn Reynolds, word processing; Aidan Wylde, typesetting; Maria Mart, proofreading; Charlotte Carter, paste-up; and Sonja Schenk, screen production.

Special thanks to literary agents Bill and Cynthia Gladstone for their support.

Sincere thanks to our spouses, Susan and Fred, for keeping us alive and well through all the long hours and short deadlines.

Table of Contents

Introduction

R:BASE for DOS and R:BASE for OS/2 together represent the fourth major version of the R:BASE database-management system for microcomputers. Like their predecessors, R:BASE 4000, R:BASE 5000, and R:BASE System V, R:BASE for DOS and R:BASE for OS/2, version 2.1 are powerful and flexible tools for storing, organizing, analyzing, and retrieving information on a microcomputer. However, the new R:BASEs offer a significant improvement over their predecessors. For the beginner, R:BASE for DOS and R:BASE for OS/2 offer a powerful Prompt By Example mode, and are better integrated for managing and analyzing data spontaneously, without any programming.

For intermediate and advanced users, the new R:BASEs offer more powerful tools for rapid development of customized business systems, including powerful report, form, and application generators. The new R:BASEs include a pseudo-compiler to make your applications run faster, and both support Structured Query Language (SQL) commands. You'll learn about using the new pseudo-compiler in Chapter 18, while SQL commands are introduced gradually, starting in Chapter 3, so don't worry if you've never heard of compilers or SQL!

The addition of SQL commands to R:BASE is an important feature, because SQL is an emerging standard in the world of relational databases. A standard such as SQL tends to reduce training costs, and guarantees database and application compatibility among different kinds of systems.

WHO SHOULD READ THIS BOOK

This book is written for the absolute beginner in R:BASE. To encourage rapid learning and complete mastery, this book focuses on practical examples of putting R:BASE to work immediately. Once you've learned how to manage data in R:BASE databases effectively, the book will instruct you in the more advanced topics of custom applications development, using a sophisticated accounts-receivable system as the practical example.

There are so many new features in R:BASE that even readers with previous experience in R:BASE 5000 or R:BASE System V will be able to profit from this book. While some of the basic concepts presented in the earlier chapters in the book may seem "old hat" to experienced R:BASE users, the new R:BASE tools and techniques will quickly become apparent as you read on.

TIPS FOR TYROS

There are a few tools and techniques that you can use in your work with R:BASE that will foster your learning. First, and perhaps most important, is the simple saying

> When in doubt...
>
> Escape key out

The Escape key (Esc on most keyboards, or the right button on your mouse) will usually allow you to escape from any jam that you might get yourself into. If you ever feel lost while working with R:BASE, press the Esc key a few times until you find yourself in more familiar territory. This is safer and easier than turning off the computer or rebooting with the Ctrl-Alt-Del keys.

Another point to keep in mind is that you can usually find additional help in R:BASE by looking for instructions at the top or bottom of your screen. Frequently, you'll be able to press the F10 key to get further help on your screen. (On a three-button mouse, the middle button corresponds to F10.)

Finally, look for the plastic keyboard templates that came with your R:BASE package. Place the appropriate template over the function keys on your keyboard. It may not mean much to you when you first place it on your keyboard, but as you work through the exercises in this book, the template will remind you of the purpose of the various function keys.

THE STRUCTURE OF THIS BOOK

This book is designed as a tutorial, not as a reference manual. It begins with the simplest and most basic concepts and builds upon acquired knowledge and skills toward complete mastery.

The Fast Track section at the beginning of each chapter summarizes the chapter's contents, listing the steps or keystrokes needed to complete specific tasks and pointing you to the page where you can find a more detailed explanation. In some cases, the Fast Track entry will be all you need to get going. In other cases, you can use the Fast Track to pick out the points you are interested in and then go directly to the information you need. Note that Fast Tracks cover the chapters' primary topics; they do not always cover every option discussed in the text.

The first nine chapters discuss all of the basic database-management techniques. These techniques include storing, organizing, analyzing, searching, and updating information in a database table. Chapters 10 through 14 discuss more advanced techniques involving multiple database tables.

Chapters 15 and 16 discuss the development of custom business applications with the R:BASE application generator and programming language. Chapter 17 brings together all the material from previous chapters and present a fully customized accounts-receivable system as an example.

Chapter 18 shows you when and how to use CodeLock and Developer's EXPRESS. CodeLock is used primarily by application developers to encrypt their work. This prevents others both from making inadvertent changes to the original program and from copying it. Developer's EXPRESS contains R:BASE's new pseudo-compiler, which you can use to make your applications run faster.

Chapter 19 discusses techniques for transferring data between R:BASE databases and other software systems, such as word processors and spreadsheets.

An appendix is also included, providing tips for installing R:BASE on single- and multi-user systems.

HARDWARE REQUIREMENTS

R:BASE for DOS and R:BASE for OS/2 are large programs that need a large amount of computer hardware to go with them. The requirements for R:BASE are listed in the following sections.

R:BASE FOR DOS

R:BASE for DOS requires the following software and hardware:

- PC-DOS 2.0 or higher (3.1 for local area networks running on the PC, PC/XT, or PC/AT, but DOS 3.3 or higher for local area networks running on the PS/2). Note that PC Convertibles require DOS 3.2 or higher and that PS/2s require DOS 3.3 or higher.
- An IBM PC, PC/XT, PC/AT, PC Convertible, or PS/2 or 100% compatible computer.
- A hard disk. R:BASE consumes approximately 4 megabytes (MB), so you may find a 20 MB hard disk preferable to a 10 MB hard disk. If you are using a PS/2 system, it is possible to run R:BASE from two floppies; however, a hard disk is highly recommended.
- At least 512K of RAM for single-user operation or 640K for network operation. (R:BASE needs a minimum of 436K available RAM.)

R:BASE FOR OS/2

R:BASE for OS/2 requires the following hardware and software:

- OS/2 1.0 or higher.
- An IBM-AT or PS/2 Model 50 or higher or 100 percent compatible.
- A hard disk. R:BASE consumes approximately 4 MB, so you'll probably want at least a 20 MB hard disk and one 5¼-inch floppy disk drive, or a hard disk and one 3½-inch disk drive.
- At least 1 MB RAM available after OS/2 or OS/2 with Presentation Manager have been loaded.

In addition to these requirements, R:BASE can use any printer and any mouse that works with your system.

For networking, R:BASE supports the IBM PC Network and 100%-compatible networks including 3Com EtherSeries, Novell, IBM Token Ring, and others.

R:BASE is not copy protected, and it can be run directly from any hard disk without the use of a key disk in the floppy drive.

PURCHASING SOFTWARE ON A DISK

If you would like to use the databases and software systems presented in this book (such as the accounts-receivable system), but don't want to type them in yourself, you can purchase a disk containing all the appropriate files. See the last page in this book for an order form.

Part 1

Working with a Single Table

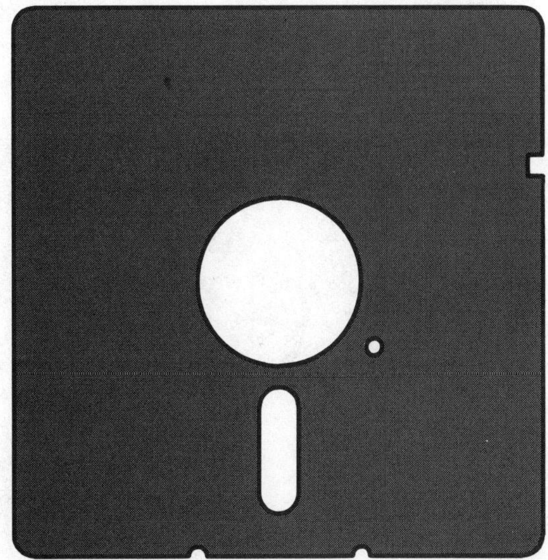

Chapter 1

Designing Your First Database

FAST TRACK

WHILE THE TERM *DATABASE MANAGEMENT* MAY SOUND like just another mysterious computer buzzword, managing a database is as commonplace as storing a Manila folder in a file cabinet. Rolodexes, tickler files, file cabinets, and even shoe boxes full of index cards are all databases. They all hold information (data) in an organized fashion. Each time you use one of these databases to look up information, store new information, create a sorted list, calculate numbers, or make changes, you are *managing* the database.

A computer database management system also allows you to store information in an organized way. However, rather than writing the data on paper and storing it in a file drawer, you store the information on a disk, where it is easily accessible through a computer. Once you've stored information, you can easily retrieve it, sort it, search through it, perform calculations, and make changes and additions.

The greatest advantage to using a computer to manage a database is speed. For example, suppose you had a shoe box full of index cards with names and addresses, stored in alphabetical order by name. If you wanted to print mailing labels for all the California residents, sorted in ZIP-code order (for bulk mailing), you'd have quite a bit of work ahead of you. The process could take hours. If this information were stored on a computer instead, your work would be limited to typing a few commands at the keyboard. The time required to pull out all the California residents and put them into ZIP-code order would be two or three seconds. Then you could go to lunch while the computer printed the mailing labels.

Of course, R:BASE can do much more than print mailing labels, as you'll see throughout the coming chapters.

R:BASE DATABASES

An R:BASE database can be a collection of many different types of information. Most of this information is stored in *tables,* which consist of neatly organized rows and columns of information. For example, take a look at the table of names and addresses in Figure 1.1. This table consists of six *columns* of information, labeled Last Name, First Name, Address, City, State, and Zip. The table consists of five *rows* of information, sorted into alphabetical order by last name. An R:BASE table can consist of as many as 800 columns and tens of thousands of rows.

Notice how each column in the sample table contains a specific item of information; that is, each last name, first name, address, city, state, and ZIP code occupies a separate column. Generally speaking, when structuring an R:BASE table, you want to break the information into as many separate, meaningful columns as possible, because this gives you the greatest flexibility in managing a database.

For example, notice how the table in Figure 1.2 combines the city, state, and ZIP code into a single column named CSZ. This sample table has some distinct disadvantages over the first one. Suppose you wanted to sort this table into ZIP-code order or pull out all the California residents? You couldn't do either operation with this table, because the state and ZIP code are combined within the CSZ column. As you'll see in the many examples throughout this book, it's always a good idea to place each item of information in its own column.

MANAGING A DATABASE

Once you've defined a structure for a table, you need to begin managing it. You may do any of the following tasks:

- Add new information to the table.
- Sort the table into a meaningful order.
- Search the table for specific types of information.
- Calculate sums and averages from information in the table.
- Print the information in an organized fashion.
- Edit (change) information in the table.
- Delete superfluous information from the table.

These tasks are no different from those performed with a shoe-box database. However, with the shoe box, you have to do all the labor;

CUSTOMER TABLE

Last Name	First Name	Address	City	State	Zip
Adams	Anthony	123 A St.	Berkeley	CA	94710
Baker	Betty	345 B St.	New York	NY	12345
Carlson	Marianne	P.O. Box 123	Houston	TX	54321
Carrera	Fred	3211 Fox St.	L.A.	CA	92991
Davis	Julie	671 Alpine Way	Newark	NJ	87654

Figure 1.1: A sample table in a database

Last Name	First Name	Address	CSZ
Adams	Anthony	123 A St.	Berkeley, CA 94710
Baker	Betty	345 B St.	New York, NY 12345
Carlson	Marianne	P.O. Box 123	Houston, TX 54321
Carrera	Fred	3211 Fox St.	L.A., CA 92991
Davis	Julie	671 Alpine Way	Newark, NJ 87654

Figure 1.2: A table with city, state, and ZIP code entries in one column

with R:BASE managing the table, you just do the thinking and a little typing. R:BASE does all the work—quickly, efficiently, and without errors.

DATABASE DESIGNS

There are many ways to structure or *design* a database. For example, the table in Figure 1.1 is useful for keeping track of basic mailing information. But a business manager using this table might also want to keep track of appointments or credit charges for each of the individuals in the list. In this case, two tables could be used in a database, as shown in Figure 1.3.

This database design keeps track of a *one-to-many* relationship between individuals in the Customer table and charges recorded in the Charges table. For every one customer in the Customer table, there may be many rows of charges in the Charges table. The two tables are *related* to one another based on their common Last Name column.

The advantage of the one-to-many design is that it allows you to find basic information quickly, such as the address of Mr. Adams, as well as find and total the charges that he has incurred during any period of time. By breaking the information into two separate tables, you avoid repeating the address, city, state, and ZIP code with every charge transaction that occurs and thereby avoid wasting a lot of disk space (as well as data entry time).

CUSTOMER TABLE

Last Name	First Name	Address	City	State	Zip
Adams	Anthony	123 A St.	Berkeley	CA	94710
Baker	Betty	345 B St.	New York	NY	12345
Carlson	Marianne	P.O. Box 123	Houston	TX	54321
Carrera	Fred	3211 Fox St.	L.A.	CA	92991
Davis	Julie	671 Alpine Way	Newark	NJ	87654

CHARGES TABLE

Last Name	Date	Amount
Adams	6/1/88	123.45
Adams	6/8/88	92.00
Adams	7/8/88	456.78
Davis	6/2/88	99.99
Davis	8/1/88	544.00

Figure 1.3: Two related tables in a database

A one-to-many relationship among tables can be used in other settings too. For example, note the structure of the basic inventory database in Figure 1.4. It consists of three tables: Master Inventory, Sales, and Purchases.

The Master Inventory table contains a single row for each item in the store (or warehouse). The Sales and Purchases tables record individual sales and purchase transactions. The tables are all related to one another through the Item Number column; that is, each table contains a column for recording the item number. These three tables can provide much business information. For example, through a procedure known as *updating,* R:BASE can instantly recalculate the Master Inventory table to determine the current quantity of any item in stock by using the data in the Sales and Purchases tables.

The sample inventory database structure is sometimes called a *master file–transaction file* relationship. The Master Inventory table keeps track of the status quo of each item in stock, while the two transaction tables, Sales and Purchases, maintain a history of every individual sale or purchase.

MASTER INVENTORY TABLE

Item Number	Item Name	In Stock	Price	Reorder
10001	Apples	100	.45	50
10002	Bananas	150	.65	40
10003	Cherries	50	.39	55

SALES TABLE

Item Number	Units Sold	Date
10001	5	6/1/88
10003	10	6/1/88
10001	5	6/1/88
10001	17	6/1/88

PURCHASES TABLE

Item Number	Units Bought	Date
10003	10	6/1/88
10002	20	6/1/88

Figure 1.4: A sample structure for an inventory database

LEARNING THE ROPES

Before we get too carried away with database-design theory here, it's a good idea to learn all of the techniques for managing a single table first. Once you've learned to handle one table, you will easily expand your skills to design and manage databases with multiple tables. Beginning with Chapter 2, you'll learn how to create and manage an R:BASE database with a single table. In the process, you'll develop a powerful mailing-list management system.

Chapter 2

Creating Your Database

FAST TRACK

To start R:BASE 15
type **PATH C:\rbfiles, CD \dbfiles**, and **RBASE** from your operating system prompt.

To begin creating a database, 20
select the *Define or modify a database* option from the R:BASE Prompt By Example Main menu. Then select RBDEFINE, and select option 1 *Define a new database*, from the Definition EXPRESS menu.

To get help while working 27
with the database, press the F10 key. Then press any key to remove the Help screen.

To ensure database security and integrity 29
by setting up protective passwords and data-entry rules, select Passwords and Rules from the Tables menu, respectively.

To access familiar DOS or OS/2 33
commands, select *R:BASE and operating system utilities* from the Prompt By Example Main menu and then *Operating system functions* from the next menu.

To exit from R:BASE, 34
select *Exit from R:BASE* from the Prompt By Example Main menu. Always exit R:BASE before turning off your computer.

IN THIS CHAPTER, YOU'LL LEARN HOW TO CREATE an R:BASE database. If you have R:BASE readily available, you may want to try these examples as you read. If you haven't already done so, you'll need to install R:BASE on your computer first. If you are using a single-user microcomputer, refer to the first part of the *Single-User and Multi-User Installation and Startup Guide* that comes with your R:BASE package for installation instructions. If you will be using R:BASE for DOS on a network, refer to the second part of the guide for installation and start-up instructions. Manuals will be available from Microrim for installing R:BASE for OS/2 on a multiuser system as OS/2 versions of LANs (local area networks) become available.

STARTING R:BASE

The first step in using R:BASE is, of course, to start the computer. If you have a computer with a hard disk and are using R:BASE for DOS, you will see the DOS C> prompt on your screen. If you have installed R:BASE for DOS according to Microrim's instructions, you will now want to take the following steps:

1. Type **PATH C:\rbfiles** and press Enter.
2. Type **CD \dbfiles** and press Enter. (If, by chance, you haven't already created the dbfiles subdirectory, DOS will display the error message "Invalid directory." Remedy the situation by typing **MD \dbfiles**, and then try typing **CD \dbfiles** again.)
3. Type **RBASE** and press Enter.

Some of you will have created a batch file that accomplishes these steps. If you have, simply run it instead.

If you are using R:BASE for DOS on a PS/2 system that has two 1.44MB, $3^{1}/_{2}$-inch floppies and no hard disk, you'll want to start your computer with your startup disk to get the A> prompt. Then follow these steps:

1. Type **PATH A:;B:** and press Enter to provide paths to both disks.
2. Type **B:** and press Enter to make B: the default drive.
3. Put your copy of System Disk 1 in drive A and a formatted data disk in drive B, and type **RBASE – 3** to inform DOS that you want to run R:BASE from a 3½-inch floppy system. Then press Enter.
4. When prompted, replace System Disk 1 with your working copy of System Disk 2.

Again, many of you will have created a batch file on your startup disk that will accomplish steps 1 through 3. Keep in mind that using R:BASE in the dual-floppy configuration means that you won't be able to use R:BASE's BACKUP and RESTORE commands (this doesn't affect your ability to use DOS's commands with the same name) or the R:BASE ZIP ROLLOUT command. Similarly, you'll have to run R:BASE's utility programs such as FileGateway, RBEDIT, UNLOAD, and CodeLock from the DOS prompt rather than from within R:BASE. (Each of these topics will be discussed in detail later on.)

If you are using R:BASE for OS/2 and have installed R:BASE according to Microrim's instructions, start your computer. If R:BASE is already available on your program selector, choose it. If not, select the

OS/2 COMMAND PROMPT

option. At the OS/2 prompt, take the following steps:

1. Type **PATH C:\rbfiles** and press Enter.
2. Type **CD C:\dbfiles** and press Enter. (If, by chance, you haven't already created the dbfiles subdirectory, OS/2 will display an error message. You can remedy this by typing **MD /dbfiles** and then typing **CD C:\dbfiles** again.)
3. Type **RBASE** and press Enter.

(Be sure you don't have an OS/2 batch file named RBASE.CMD on the path, or it will be run instead of RBASE.EXE.) Many of you will have established a batch file to accomplish the three commands listed above.

If you are using R:BASE for DOS in a multi-user environment, you will probably have a batch file installed at each work-station that will start R:BASE for you. Run the batch file. Contact Microrim for specific details about installing R:BASE for OS/2 on your OS/2 local area network.

Once the R:BASE system is running, you'll see the Prompt By Example Main menu, as shown in Figure 2.1.

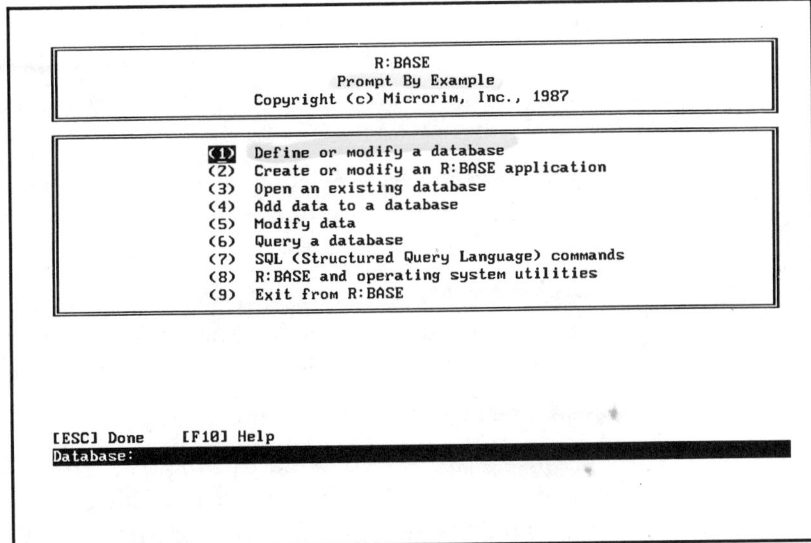

Figure 2.1: The R:BASE Prompt By Example Main menu

The menu displays nine options. You can select a module by moving the highlighter with the up arrow (↑) and down arrow (↓) keys on your keyboard. (If the keys don't work at first, press the Num Lock key once, and then try again.) You can also make a selection by typing the number of the choice you want, or using a mouse. To activate the highlighted choice, press the Enter (or Return) key, marked with the ↵ symbol on the IBM keyboard.

EXPLORING THE PROMPT BY EXAMPLE (PBE) MAIN MENU

The Prompt By Example Main menu lists the major activities you are likely to perform on your database. Once you select a menu item, R:BASE will display another menu, and perhaps additional ones, where you'll be prompted to make more decisions. As you do, you'll see an R:BASE command being built that corresponds to your answers to the prompts. Finally, you'll instruct R:BASE to execute the command. Here's a brief summary of the choices on the PBE Main menu:

- *Define or modify a database* lets you set up or define a database.
- *Create or modify an R:BASE application* takes you into R:BASE's Application EXPRESS, where you can create custom menus for your own database. You'll learn more about Application EXPRESS in Chapter 15.
- *Open an existing database* lets you select a previously defined database from the current directory. You'll be opening your own database in Chapter 3.
- *Add data to a database* lets you add rows to your tables. If a database isn't already open, you'll be prompted to select one. You'll be adding data to your own Mail database in Chapter 3.
- *Modify data* lets you edit existing data.
- *Query a database* lets you view existing data. You'll be able to specify the order in which you see the data and exactly which data should be displayed, if you so desire. Chapters 4 and 5 discuss querying a Mail database.
- *SQL (Structured Query Language) commands* gives you access to ten SQL commands, some of which are also available from other PBE menus.
- *R:BASE and operating system utilities* allows you to use DOS or OS/2 file- and directory-management commands, see a list of all R:BASE commands available via PBE, access R:BASE's Help mode, run R:BASE's mailing label program, and so on.

- *Exit from R:BASE*, of course, returns you to your operating system.

Since we're going to create a new database in the next section, option 1 seems the logical choice. This option should already be highlighted, unless you've experimented with the cursor arrows or typed a number to select another option. Notice the status line at the bottom of the screen. It's telling you that you can receive help by pressing the F10 function key. Verify that option 1 is selected and press the F10 key. You'll see a screen that explains what happens if you select option 1. Press any key, as prompted, to return to the PBE Main menu.

Verify that option 1 is highlighted, and activate your selection by pressing the Enter key. You should see another menu containing four choices; this is the *Define or modify a database* menu shown in Figure 2.2. This menu is a horizontal one, and the choices aren't numbered. With this sort of R:BASE menu, you can highlight selections either by using the arrow keys or by typing the first letter of the menu item you want.

The first option, RBDEFINE, should already be highlighted, so press Enter to select it. The next screen will explain what selecting

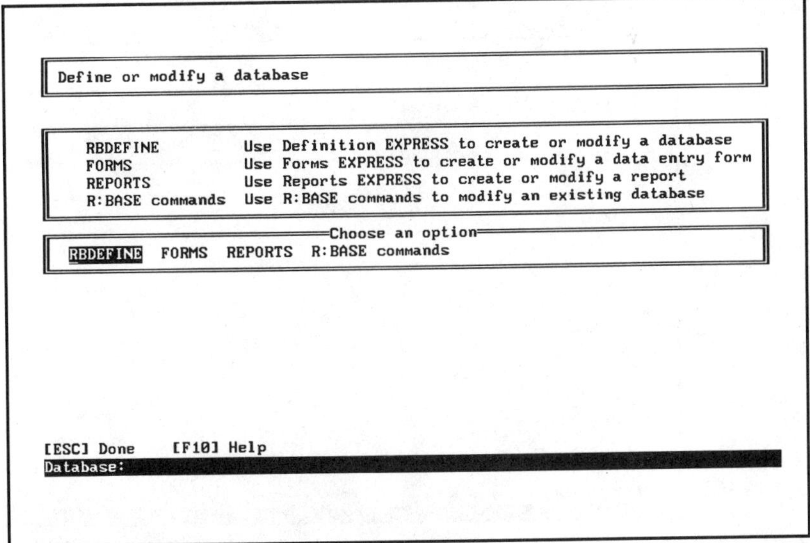

Figure 2.2: PBE's *Define or modify a database* menu

RBDEFINE means. Press any key to continue, as prompted. You should be rewarded with the Prompt By Example Action menu, as shown in Figure 2.3; as you develop your own databases with R:BASE, this menu will become very familiar to you.

The box below the menu contains the command (in this case the single word RBDEFINE) that will be entered if you choose to execute the command. The Prompt By Example Action menu also gives you the opportunity to edit the command, start all over, get more help, or return to the Prompt By Example Main menu.

Before going any further, tap the Esc key once. The Esc key, as you may remember from the introduction, allows you to back up through the menu system. Having tapped the Esc key once, you should see Figure 2.2 again. If you tap Esc a second time, you should be back to the Prompt By Example Main menu (Figure 2.1). If you have a heavy hand and have tapped too many times, you may see a lonely R> prompt. To return to PBE mode, simply type **PROMPT**.

CREATING A DATABASE

At this point, the Prompt By Example Main menu should be displayed again on your screen, as in Figure 2.1. Since we really are

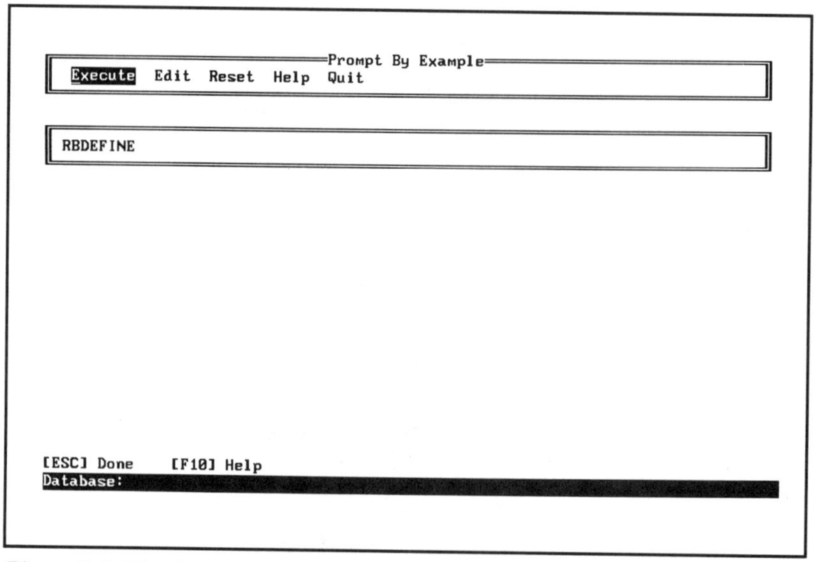

```
Prompt By Example
Execute  Edit  Reset  Help  Quit

RBDEFINE

[ESC] Done    [F10] Help
Database:
```

Figure 2.3: The Prompt By Example Action menu

going to create a database this time, press Enter when option 1 is highlighted, and continue as in the previous section. This time, when you see the Prompt By Example Action menu, press Enter to execute the RBDEFINE command.

You'll see the Definition EXPRESS Main menu appear on the screen, as in Figure 2.4.

Since we want to create a new database, make sure that option 1 (*Define a new database*) is highlighted, and press Enter. R:BASE replies by asking that you

Enter your database name (1–7 characters)

We'll begin by creating a relatively simple mailing-list database. It's best to use a name that is easy to remember, although you may have to use an abbreviated form since the database name is limited to a maximum of seven characters. For this example, type in the name **Mail** and press Enter.

After you name the database, a new screen appears, as shown in Figure 2.5. Notice that the screen is asking for the name of the new table. As we discussed earlier, an R:BASE database may consist of several tables, and so each table must have a unique name. A table

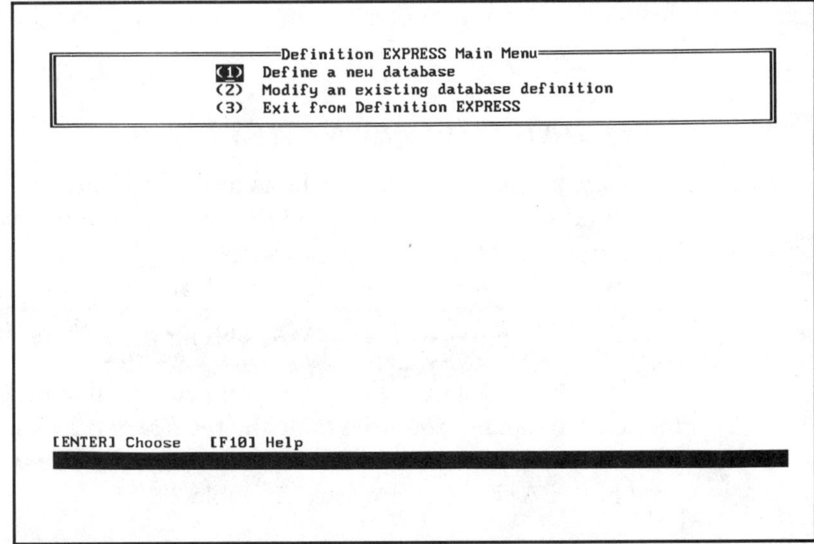

Figure 2.4: The Definition EXPRESS Main menu

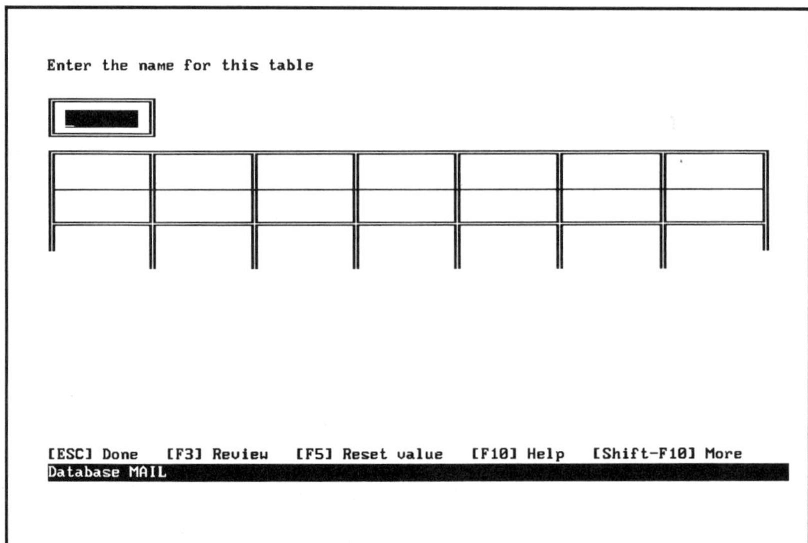

Figure 2.5: A screen for defining a database table

name may contain a maximum of eight letters. For this example, we'll create a table of names and addresses. Type in **Names** as the table name. (If you need to make a correction as you type, use the arrow keys or the Backspace key to reposition the cursor and retype the name.) When the correct name is typed in, press the Enter key. The screen will look like Figure 2.6.

DEFINING COLUMN NAMES

For the first table, we'll name the columns L:Name, F:Name, Company, Address, City, State, Zip, and Ent:Date. Notice that we've abbreviated some of the column names and used a colon rather than a space in some of the names (for example, Ent:Date stands for Entry Date). This is because column names are limited to a maximum width of eight characters, and they may not contain blank spaces.

When defining a table structure, you need to fill in more than just the column names. You need to define the *type* of data and the maximum *width* of the data to be stored in the column. The types of data used in R:BASE tables are listed in Table 2.1.

All of the columns in our first table, except for Ent:Date, will be TEXT data. Ent:Date will be DATE data. Figure 2.7 shows the exact structure that we'll use for the Names table.

Notice that we've assigned the Zip column the TEXT data type. This may seem odd at first, since we often think of ZIP codes as numbers; however, they have some characteristics that make them unlike actual numbers. For example, some ZIP codes contain hyphens, such as 92038-2802. Some foreign ZIP codes contain letters, such as A123I. Because these examples are not true numbers, R:BASE would not know how to handle these data if they were entered into a numeric column. In order to play it safe, we've defined the Zip column as TEXT data.

To define the table structure, you simply type in the name of the first column in the first box on the screen, and press Enter. For this example, type in the column name **L:Name** and press Enter. The column name box now contains the column name, and a menu of data types appears, as shown in Figure 2.8.

To select an option from the menu of data types, use the arrow and Enter keys as with previous menus. In this example, the TEXT option is already highlighted, so just press the Enter key.

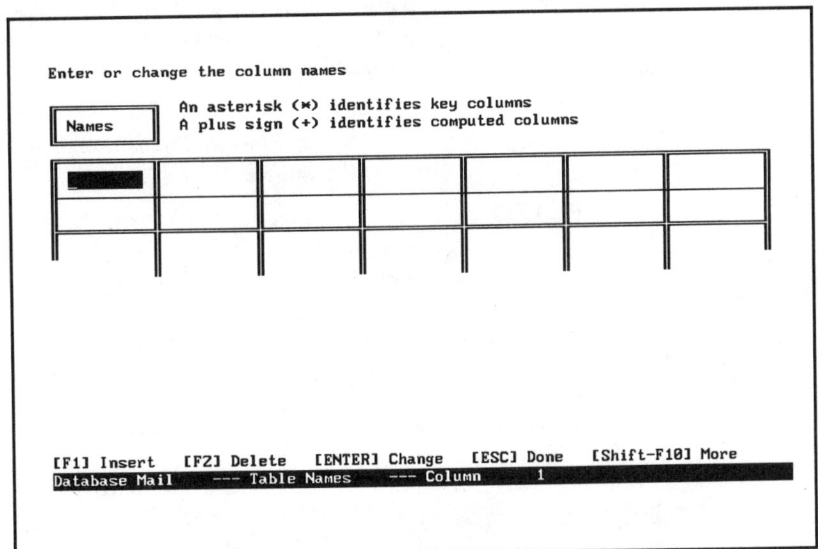

Figure 2.6: The table name entered on the screen

Table 2.1: R:BASE Data Types

DATA TYPE	USED TO STORE
TEXT	Any textual information that has no numeric value, such as names and addresses. Maximum length for a TEXT column is 1500 characters.
CURRENCY	Dollar amounts, such as the price of an item or an hourly wage.
INTEGER	Whole numbers that do not have any decimal places. Sometimes used for identification numbers, such as account numbers or part numbers.
REAL	Real numbers that may contain decimal places. Used to store numeric quantities such as -123.45 or 6543.2123.
DOUBLE	Very large numbers, outside the range $\pm 9 \times 10^{\pm 37}$. (Generally used only in scientific and engineering applications.)
DATE	Dates, usually stored in MM/DD/YY format.
TIME	Time, usually displayed in HH:MM:SS format (e.g., 12:31:46), in either a 24-hour clock or an AM/PM 12-hour clock.
NOTE	Like a TEXT column, holds non-numeric textual information. However, maximum length of a NOTE column is 4050 characters.
COMPUTED	A column that receives its value from the computation of other columns. For example, if a table contains two columns named Qty and UntPrice, a COMPUTED column named Total could contain the results of multiplying Qty times UntPrice.

Next, the screen asks for the maximum width of data in this column and suggests a width of eight characters. Many last names are longer than eight characters, so we'll assign a maximum width of 15 characters to this column. Type in the number **15** (using the number keys at the top of the keyboard), and press Enter.

Column Name	Type of Data	Maximun Length
L:Name	TEXT	15
F:Name	TEXT	15
Company	TEXT	20
Address	TEXT	25
City	TEXT	15
State	TEXT	5
Zip	TEXT	10
Ent:Date	DATE	

Figure 2.7: The structure for the Names table

Next R:BASE displays the question

Do you want this column to be a key? Yes No

Key columns are used to speed processing in some operations, but are of no concern to us now. Just press the Enter key to select No. At this point, the contents of the first column are defined, and the highlighting moves to the second column, as shown in Figure 2.9.

You can now define the structure of the second column, or you can use the arrow keys to back up and make corrections to the first column. If you are following along on-line, go ahead and fill in the definitions for the remaining columns using the information in Figure 2.8. The exact steps to follow are summarized below:

1. Type in **F:Name,** press Enter, select TEXT, press Enter, type in **15,** press Enter, and select No.
2. Type in **Company,** press Enter, select TEXT, press Enter, type in **20,** press Enter, and select No.
3. Type in **Address,** press Enter, select TEXT, type in **25,** press Enter, and select No.

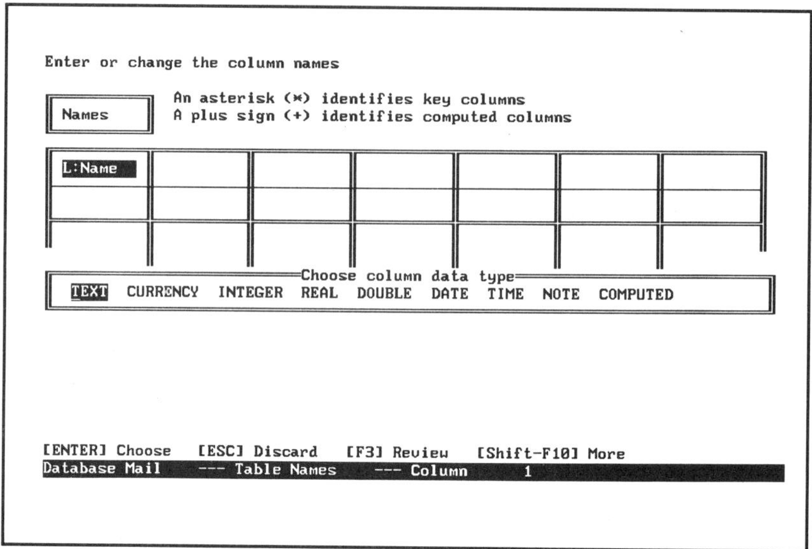

Figure 2.8: A column name entered onto the screen

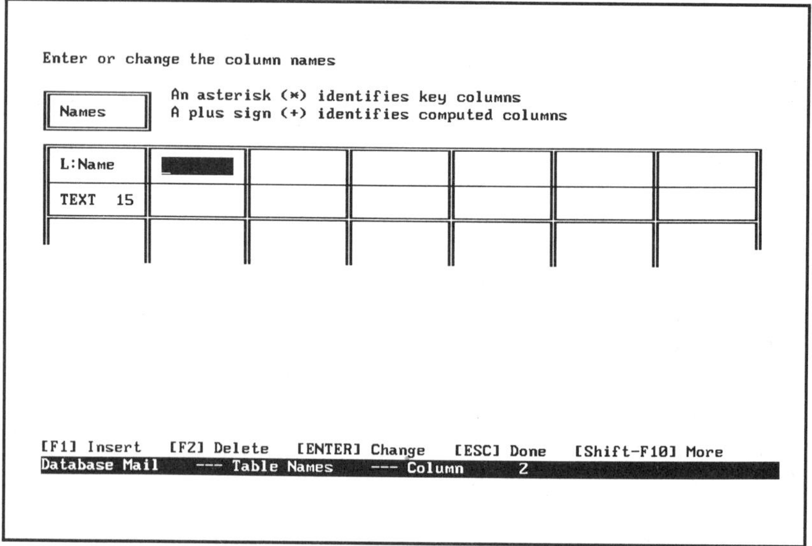

Figure 2.9: The first column defined in the Names table

4. Type in **City,** press Enter, select TEXT, press Enter, type in **15,** press Enter, and select No.

5. Type in **State,** press Enter, select TEXT, press Enter, type in **2,** press Enter, and select No.
6. Type in **Zip,** press Enter, select TEXT, press Enter, type in **10,** press Enter, and select No.
7. Type in **Ent:Date,** press Enter, select DATE, press Enter, and select No.

It is not necessary to define a width for the Ent:Date column, because R:BASE uses a predefined width for dates.

Once all of the column names have been entered, the screen will look like Figure 2.10. Notice that the L:Name and F:Name columns have disappeared from the screen. This is because there is not enough room for all the columns to be displayed. Rest assured, however; these columns are still in the table.

MAKING CHANGES

You can easily make changes and corrections after entering column names. The keys that you use to help with modifications and their effects are listed in Table 2.2.

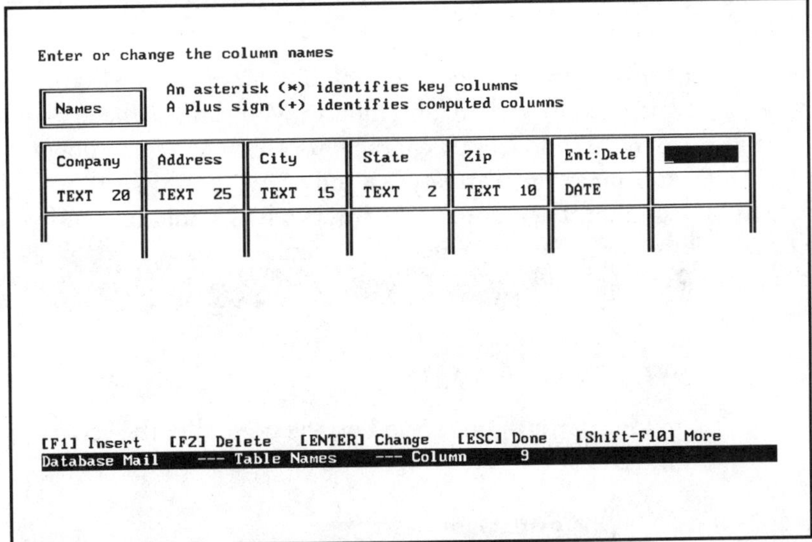

Figure 2.10: The Names table defined on the screen

Table 2.2: Keys Used to Modify Table Structure

KEY NAME	EFFECT
Home	Moves highlighting to the first column
End	Moves highlighting to the last column
←	Moves the cursor left through the highlighted area, character by character, then to prior column, if one exists
→	Moves the cursor right through the highlighted area, character by character, then to the next column if one exists
Tab	Moves highlighting one column to the right
Shift-Tab	Moves highlighting one column to the left
F1	Inserts a new column to the left of the highlighted position
F2	Deletes the highlighted column
↵	Defines the structure of the highlighted column
F10	Gets help

For example, if you accidentally leave out the State column name and need to back up and fill it in, you can use the left-arrow (←) key to move character by character or Shift-Tab (hold down the Shift key and press the Tab key) to move by columns to highlight the Zip column. Then press F1 to insert a blank column, and you can fill in the new column name and structure as usual. Pressing the End key returns the highlighting to the last column name in the table.

GETTING HELP

One of the options listed on the bottom of the screen on the status line is

[Shift-F10] More

Hold down the Shift (uppercase) key and press F10. One of the choices now offered is to press the F10 key to get help. Pressing this key will display some helpful advice, here as well as on most R:BASE screens. After reading the Help screen, press any key to return to the task at hand.

SAVING THE TABLE STRUCTURE

Once you've defined your table structure and made any necessary corrections, press the Esc key to save your work. The Database Definition menu appears on the screen. Selecting option 1, Tables, displays the Tables menu, shown in Figure 2.11. This menu allows you to add more tables to the database or to refine an existing database. We'll discuss these more advanced features in later chapters. For now, select option 4 (*Return to the Database Definition Menu*). You should now see the five-item Database Definition menu.

CREATING PASSWORDS

It's never too early to think about database security. If employee wages or salaries are part of your database in an employee table, you

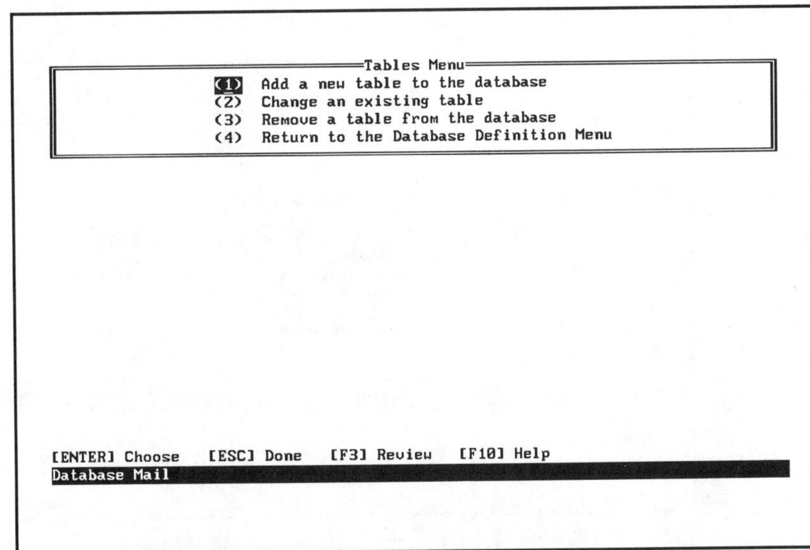

Figure 2.11: Additional options for defining a database

may not want everyone who uses the database to be able to see them. Perhaps you have a clients table which includes sensitive information such as unlisted phone numbers meant for your eyes only. R:BASE provides you with a number of tools to establish varying levels of database security. Passwords are the most straightforward of these tools.

R:BASE allows you to set up three levels of password protection: owner, modify, and read. The *owner password* affects the entire database and allows those who know it to use all R:BASE commands. *Modify* and *read* passwords are established on a table-by-table basis to fine-tune users' access to specific data. The *owner password* is the database's most important password. Once an owner password is established, only individuals who know that password will be able to make structural changes in the database. Furthermore, more specific *table passwords* can only be set up once an owner password has already been established.

Select option 3, Passwords, from the Database Definition menu. R:BASE will prompt you to choose a table or view. Since the status line indicates that F10 is available with help, go ahead and press the F10 function key. Your screen should look like Figure 2.12.

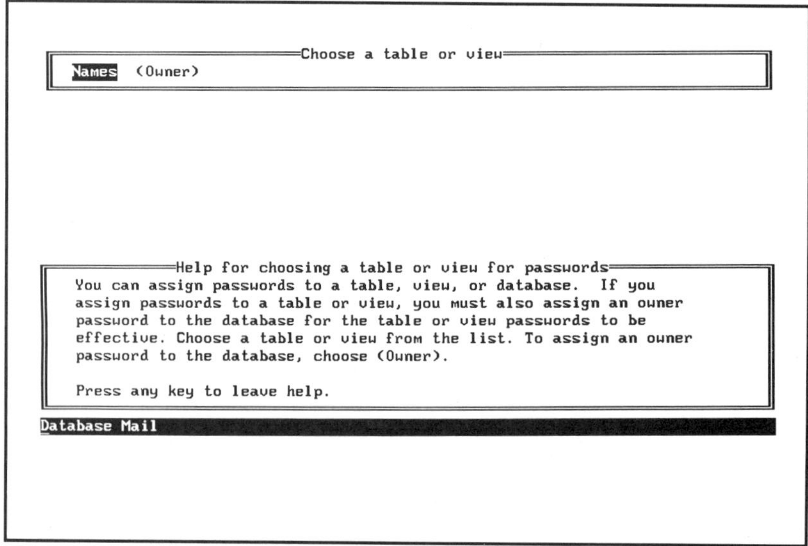
Choose a table or view
Names (Owner)
Help for choosing a table or view for passwords
You can assign passwords to a table, view, or database. If you assign passwords to a table or view, you must also assign an owner password to the database for the table or view passwords to be effective. Choose a table or view from the list. To assign an owner password to the database, choose (Owner).
Press any key to leave help.
Database Mail

Figure 2.12: The Help screen for setting up passwords

You must now create an owner password for your database. Press Esc to erase the help screen, and select *(Owner)*. R:BASE now prompts you to enter the database owner password. Notice that the default is NONE. Type **TEST** and press Enter.

Now you can set up passwords for the Names table, so select Names from the *Choose a table or view* menu, as shown in Figure 2.13. On the screen you will see prompts for the two different kinds of passwords that can be established for a table: Read and Modify. If you set up a *read password* for the Names table, only people who know that password (or one at a higher level) will be able to view data in the Names table. Setting a read password gives a table's data the greatest level of protection. A *modify password*, on the other hand, allows users who know it to modify as well as view a table's data. Like the owner password, the read and modify passwords are also hierarchical; a modify password must already be established in order to set up a read password. Rather than set up read and modify passwords now, press Esc twice to return to the Tables menu. We'll return to password protection in Chapter 10.

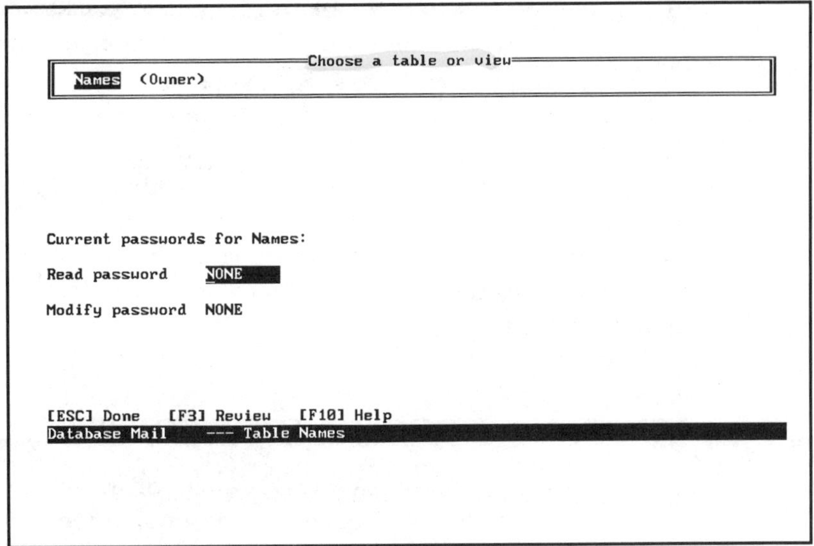

Figure 2.13: Establishing passwords for the Names table

ESTABLISHING RULES

Passwords can be crucial to database security, but rules are useful, too. Rules are usually established to prevent bad or incomplete data from being entered into a table. In the case of the Names table, we might want to set up a rule that prevents the user from entering an Ent:Date earlier than 1988. Or we might want to establish a rule that prevents the L:Name field from being left blank. Let's try doing the latter.

Select option 4, *Rules*, from the Tables menu. The Rules menu will appear; since we want to create a rule, select option 1, *Add a new rule*. A complex screen should appear, with a prompt near the bottom asking you to enter the error message for your rule. The error message is what the user will see if he or she breaks the rule. Since our rule is going to force users to make some sort of entry for L:Name, the error message might be something like, "You must enter a last name!" Type your message in the highlighted box and press Enter when done.

R:BASE should now be asking you to choose a table. Since our rule is going to affect the Names table, make sure Names is highlighted and press Enter. You should now see a screen that asks you to choose a column to validate. Our rule is going to affect the L:Name column, so select it. Your screen should now look like Figure 2.14.

You are now prompted to select an operator. The one you want is EXISTS, since you want to ensure that an L:Name exists for each entry in the Names table. Highlight EXISTS and press Enter. (If you're feeling breathless at this point, relax; this will become second nature in no time!)

We don't need a more complex rule that would include a logical operator, so select (Done) from the current menu to return to the Rules menu.

EXITING DEFINITION EXPRESS

You've defined a database and a table for it. You've set up an owner password for your database and established a rule to help ensure data integrity, and now it's time to leave Definition EXPRESS. Let the menus guide you out. First select 4 (*Return to the*

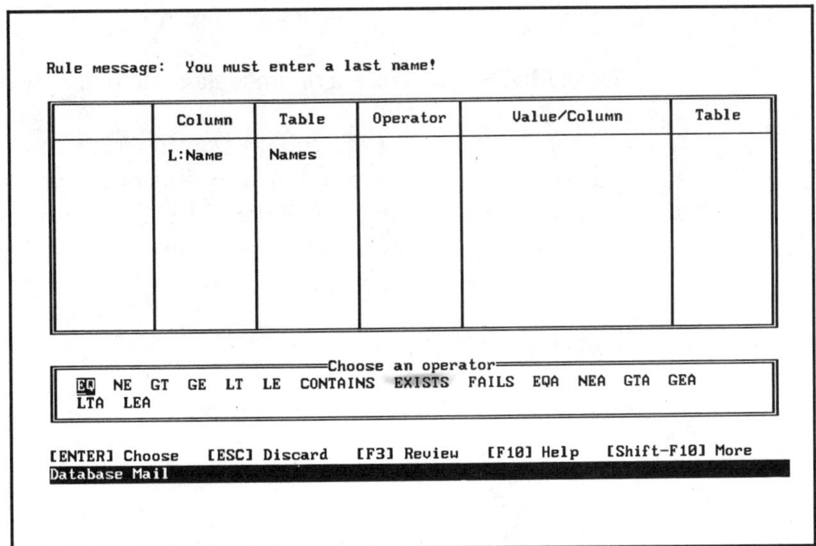

Figure 2.14: Establishing a rule for the Names table

Database Definition Menu) from the Rules menu. Then choose 5 (*Return to Definition EXPRESS Main Menu*) and glance at the new menu. Note that R:BASE allows you to modify a database. The Mail database is by no means cast in concrete; you'll learn how to add or delete columns, change data types and column names, and so on in Chapter 9. For now, select option 3 (*Exit from Definition EXPRESS*). Finally, press Esc at the Define or modify a database menu to return to the Prompt By Example Main menu.

USING DOS OR OS/2 FUNCTIONS

By selecting option 8 from the PBE Main menu, and then choosing *Operating system functions* from the next menu, you can use various DOS commands without leaving R:BASE. This is entirely optional and is provided only as a convenience. Selecting this option displays the menu shown in Figure 2.15.

Suppose you wish to view a list of all files that begin with the letters MAIL on the current directory. To do so, you could select DIR

(Directories). R:BASE will display the prompt

Press [ENTER] for current or enter alternate directory name:

You can enter a directory path and use your operating system's wild-cards to create a file-name template as well. In this case, we want to see all the files with the first four letters MAIL on the current directory, so type in the following line, taking advantage of one of your operating system's wild-cards, the asterisk (*):

MAIL*.*

Press Enter twice. The screen shows the files

MAIL1.RBF
MAIL2.RBF
MAIL3.RBF

along with their respective sizes. These files, together, form the Mail database you just created.

The prompt "Press any key to continue" appears near the bottom of the screen. Press any key, and then press Esc to return to the Prompt By Example Main menu.

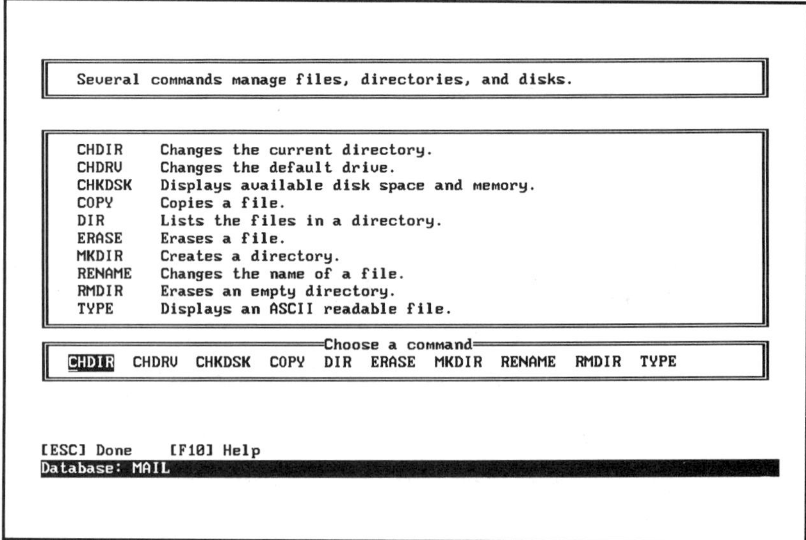

Figure 2.15: The DOS Functions menu

EXITING R:BASE

To exit R:BASE entirely and return to your operating system, select option 9, *Exit from R:BASE.* When instructed, press any key to continue, then press Enter to select the Execute option. You will see the DOS or OS/2 prompt from which you started appear on the screen.

You should *always* exit R:BASE and return to the prompt before turning off your computer. Failure to do so might result in loss of data or corrupted (unusable) files.

DATABASE LIMITATIONS

There are a few limitations to the size of an R:BASE database. A single database can have a maximum of 80 tables assigned to it. Each individual table may have a maximum of 80 columns. However, a database also can contain a maximum of 800 columns. Therefore, a database can contain a maximum of 10 tables if each contains 80 columns, or 20 tables if each contains 40 columns. This is a very large maximum, and it is unlikely that you will run out of room in an R:BASE database.

Numbers stored in currency columns can take on values in the range ± $99,999,999,999,999.99. Integer column numbers can have values in the range ±999,999,999. Real numbers can accept values in the range $\pm 1.0 \times 10^{\pm 38}$, with six digits accuracy. Double precision numbers can store values in the range $\pm 1.0 \times 10^{\pm 308}$, with 15 digits accuracy.

Alphanumeric data stored as text can be up to 1500 characters long. If longer fields are needed, you can store data in NOTE fields of up to 4,050 characters.

The maximum number of rows in a table or database is limited only by the maximum file size allowed by your version of the operating system, and by the amount of disk storage available on your system.

You have now created your first database, and it's ready to start storing information. Let's move on to the next chapter, where we'll start entering and editing data in your database.

Chapter 3

Entering and Editing Data

Fast Track

To build commands 40

in your first R:BASE sessions, use the *Prompt By Example* mode, which appears when you first start R:BASE. Prompt By Example (PBE) mode helps you build command lines through menus.

To enter your commands 40

once you become a more experienced R:BASE programmer, use R:BASE's *command mode*. When you're in command mode, you can enter R:BASE commands directly at the R> prompt. To move into command mode, press the Esc key at the PBE Main menu; return to PBE from command mode by typing **PROMPT** at the R> prompt.

To open a database 40

before working with it, use either the OPEN command or the *Open an existing database* option from the Prompt menu.

To add new data 44

to a table, select the *Add data to a database* and Load options from the PBE menu or enter the command LOAD *file name* WITH PROMPTS, where *file name* is the name of the table to edit.

To change data 52

on a table, select the Modify data option from the PBE menu or issue the command EDIT ALL FROM *file name*, where *file name* is the name of the table to edit.

To control the cursor and highlighter 54

while editing data on a table, use the arrow, PgUp, PgDn, Tab, Ins, and Del keys, as summarized in Table 3.1.

To undo a previous editing change, 56
use the F5 key to restore the original version, provided that the highlight is still on the edited field.

To delete a row 56
from a table in Edit mode, use the F2 key.

To exit from R:BASE, 57
select *Exit from R:BASE* from the PBE menu, or type in the command **EXIT** at the R> prompt, and press Enter.

NOW THAT YOU'VE CREATED A DATABASE WITH AN empty table in it, you can start storing information. In this chapter, we'll discuss techniques for opening an existing database, adding new data to it, and changing (editing) existing data.

If you exited R:BASE in the last chapter (so that your operating system prompt is showing), start R:BASE again as you did in the last chapter. You should see the Prompt by Example Main menu.

THE R:BASE COMMAND MODE

Before we get into the specifics of opening a database and adding data to it, let's discuss two alternative techniques for working interactively with a database: the *command mode,* which displays only the symbol R> on the screen, and the *Prompt By Example (PBE) mode,* which displays instructions for entering commands.

The *command mode* is generally used by individuals who are experienced enough with R:BASE to enter commands without any help. In command mode, you type in a *command* or a *command line,* which gives R:BASE specific instructions on how to perform a task.

The *PBE mode,* which is currently on the screen, helps the less experienced user build command lines with instructions and simpler menu selections. We'll use the PBE mode in this chapter and the next, and then start using the command mode as you become familiar with command syntax.

If, at any time, you find that you've inadvertently switched to the command mode (and only the R> prompt appears on your screen), you can switch back to the PBE mode by typing in the command

```
PROMPT
```

next to the R> prompt, and pressing Enter.

As an example, press the Esc key now. The Prompt By Example menu is replaced by R:BASE's command mode R> prompt. Now type **PROMPT** and press the Enter key to return to the familiar PBE Main menu.

OPENING A DATABASE

The first step in using any database is to *open* it so that R:BASE has access to it. Select option 3, *Open an existing database.* PBE displays a screen (Figure 3.1) that explains the options available to you when you open the database. The bottom menu shows the names of all databases currently available on disk. (Figure 3.1 shows the names Mail and Test, although your screen may show more or fewer file names.) To open the Mail database, move the cell pointer to the name Mail, and press Enter. The screen now displays the command

OPEN MAIL

followed by another prompt that asks you whether you want to open the database in Write/Read or Read only mode. The previous screen had explained that opening a database in Write/Read mode lets you add data to the database as well as edit and view the data, while Read mode only allows you to view the data. Select the default mode, Write/Read, and press Enter.

The next Prompt By Example menu displays the revised command

OPEN MAIL WRITE/READ

that your selection has built. Your PBE options at the top of the screen are now

Execute Edit Reset Help Quit

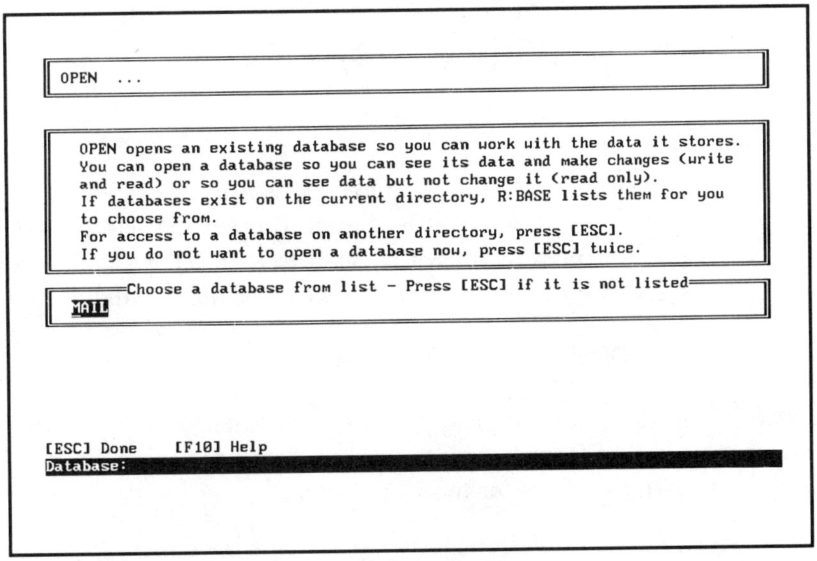

```
OPEN ...

OPEN opens an existing database so you can work with the data it stores.
You can open a database so you can see its data and make changes (write
and read) or so you can see data but not change it (read only).
If databases exist on the current directory, R:BASE lists them for you
to choose from.
For access to a database on another directory, press [ESC].
If you do not want to open a database now, press [ESC] twice.

Choose a database from list - Press [ESC] if it is not listed
MAIL

[ESC] Done     [F10] Help
Database:
```

Figure 3.1: Instructions for opening a database

To *execute* the OPEN Mail command, press Enter to select the Execute option. R:BASE displays

```
OPEN MAIL WRITE/READ
Database exists
Press any key to continue
```

R:BASE is simply telling you that you've opened an existing database and that you can press any key to continue.

When you press a key to continue, R:BASE returns you to the PBE Main menu. Before we continue with option 4, let's quickly try a simple exercise for entering a command without the aid of the prompts.

OPENING A DATABASE FROM THE COMMAND MODE

Let's take a moment to try entering the command to open the Mail database without the aid of the prompts. At the bottom of the Prompt By Example Main menu, on the status line, notice the instruction

```
[Esc]   Done
```

If you press the Esc key now, you'll see only the prompt

```
R>
```

on your screen. Go ahead and press Esc.

The command you executed to open the Mail database in the prompt mode was OPEN Mail WRITE/READ. To perform this same task in the command mode, type the command

```
OPEN MAIL WRITE/READ
```

next to the R> prompt, and press Enter. Again, R:BASE will display the *Database exists* prompt and then redisplay the R> prompt so that you can enter more commands.

HELP MODE AND SYNTAX DIAGRAMS

Take another minute to type **HELP OPEN** (and press Enter) at the R> prompt. What you see on the screen is an example of R:BASE's Help screens, as shown in Figure 3.2.

You might think of Help as a condensed version of Prompt By Example. Help screens give you basic information about an R:BASE command and then display that command's syntax diagram. In general, *syntax* refers to the proper arrangement of words in a sentence. In the world of computers, however, *syntax* refers to the proper arrangement of terms in a command.

R:BASE syntax diagrams read from left to right. R:BASE words are shown in uppercase, while arguments, or parts of a command that you must supply because they are specific to your database, are shown in lowercase. In the case of the OPEN command, the words *OPEN*, *WRITE/READ*, and *READ* are R:BASE terms. *Dbspec*, on the other hand, is a sample argument which stands for the database name. Since *dbspec* is lowercase, you should supply your own argument in its place (in this case, the name of your database).

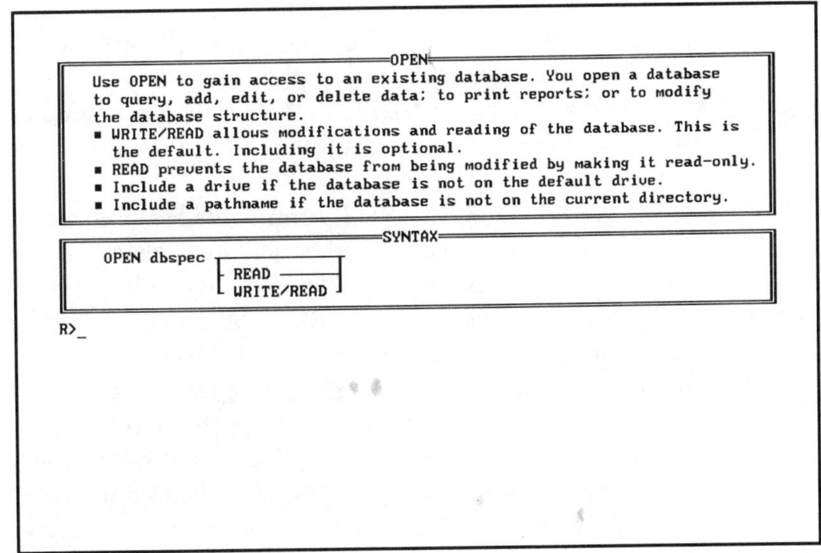

Figure 3.2: R:BASE's Help screen for the OPEN command

There's one more feature of syntax diagrams that is important to understand. Mandatory parts of a command are displayed along a continuous horizontal axis, while optional parts of a command are shown as spurs off the main left-to-right axis. With this knowledge, you can deduce that WRITE/READ and READ are optional parts of the OPEN command. In fact, the box that describes the OPEN command tells you that WRITE/READ is the default. That is, if you simply type OPEN MAIL, you are in effect typing OPEN MAIL WRITE/READ.

Let's return to the PBE mode. To do so, type in the command

```
PROMPT
```

and press the Enter key. The Prompt By Example Main menu will appear on the screen.

ADDING DATA TO A TABLE

Now that you've opened the database, you can enter data into it using any one of a variety of techniques. We'll start with the simplest technique in this chapter.

From the PBE menu, highlight the *Add data to a database* option, and then press Enter. This brings up the instructions and options shown in Figure 3.3.

The APPEND and INPUT commands are used when transferring data from one table to another and are irrelevant for our present needs. The ENTER command is used only with *custom forms,* which we'll discuss in Chapter 8. The SQL (Structured Query Language) command INSERT is similar to the LOAD command we're going to use. For now, highlight the LOAD command and press Enter. (If you hadn't already opened the Mail database, PBE would have you do so now.) This brings up some new options, as shown in Figure 3.4.

In this example we want to type in new data from the keyboard, so select the Keyboard option from the menu. Next the screen displays the names of all tables in the currently open database. In this

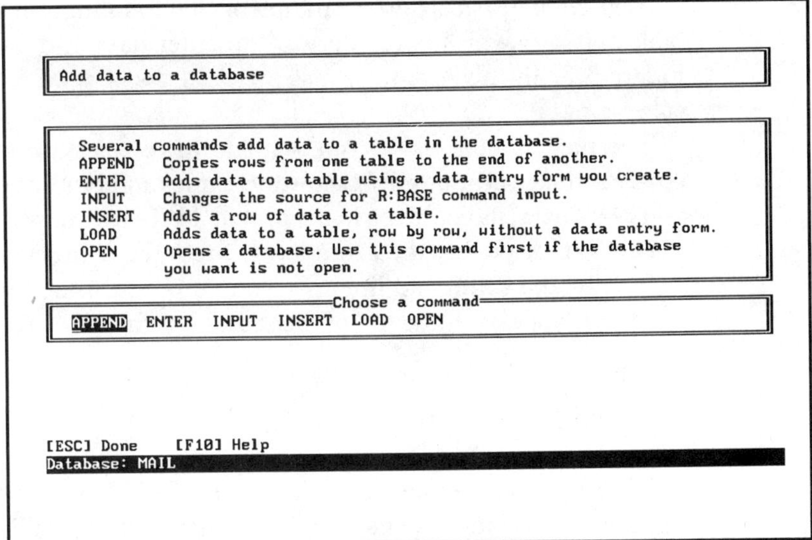

Add data to a database
Several commands add data to a table in the database.
APPEND Copies rows from one table to the end of another.
ENTER Adds data to a table using a data entry form you create.
INPUT Changes the source for R:BASE command input.
INSERT Adds a row of data to a table.
LOAD Adds data to a table, row by row, without a data entry form.
OPEN Opens a database. Use this command first if the database you want is not open.
Choose a command
APPEND ENTER INPUT INSERT LOAD OPEN
[ESC] Done [F10] Help
Database: MAIL

Figure 3.3: Instructions and options for adding new data

```
LOAD   ... USING ...

LOAD adds data to a table from the keyboard or from a file without
using a data entry form. You can type the data at the keyboard or read
it from an R:BASE input file created with the UNLOAD command or by
editing an ASCII delimited file.

Choose an input source
Keyboard  File

[ESC] Done    [F10] Help
Database: MAIL
```

Figure 3.4: Instructions for specifying source of incoming data

example, the database contains only the single table Names. Press Enter to select the Names table.

Next the screen displays the names of all the columns in the Names table and asks which ones you want to enter data into, as shown in Figure 3.5. In this example, just press the Esc key to select all the column names.

The next screen asks if you want to have *prompts* appear when entering data (these prompts show the names and types of columns as you enter data, as you'll see in a moment). When typing in new data, it's a good idea to use the prompts, so press Enter to select Prompt.

Finally, the command line that you've built through your menu selections appears at the top of the screen, as follows:

```
    Execute    Edit    Reset    Help    Quit
LOAD Names WITH PROMPTS
```

Select Execute to execute the LOAD Names WITH PROMPTS command. (As you may have guessed, you could have typed this command directly next to the command mode R> prompt, rather than selecting options from prompts, to achieve the same goal.) The screen displays the message

```
Press [ESC] to end, [ENTER] to continue
```

Press the Enter key to start entering new data. R:BASE will display the name and type of each column. You just type in the data that you wish to store for a single row, pressing Enter after each item. For example, suppose you wish to store the following information in the first row:

L:Name:	Smith
F:Name:	Sandy
Company:	Hi Tech, Inc.
Address:	456 N. Rainbow Dr.
City:	Berkeley
State:	CA
Zip:	94711

Ent:Date: 6/1/88

When R:BASE displays the prompt

L:Name (TEXT):

you type in the name **Smith** and press the Enter key. You can use the Backspace key to make corrections before pressing the Enter key, but don't worry about mistakes yet. They're easy to correct later.

When R:BASE displays the prompt

F:Name (TEXT):

type in the first name, **Sandy**, and press Enter. Continue entering data until you've typed in all the information for the first row. The screen will look like Figure 3.6.

Once you've entered the data for a single row, R:BASE again displays the prompt

Press [ESC] to end, [ENTER] to continue

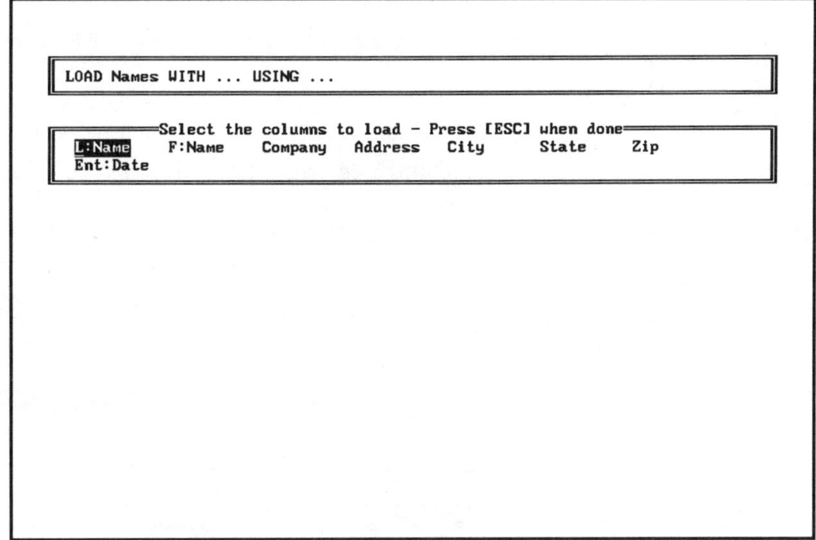

Figure 3.5: The screen for selecting columns to load

```
R>LOAD Names WITH PROMPTS
 Begin R:BASE Data Loading

 Press [ESC] to end, [ENTER] to continue
 L:Name    (TEXT      ):Smith
 F:Name    (TEXT      ):Sandy
 Company   (TEXT      ):Hi Tech, Inc.
 Address   (TEXT      ):456 N. Rainbow Dr.
 City      (TEXT      ):Berkeley
 State     (TEXT      ):CA
 Zip       (TEXT      ):94711
 Ent:Date  (DATE      ):6/1/88_
```

Figure 3.6: The first row typed in on the screen.

Press Enter to add another row to the table. If you're following along online, try entering the following rows into the table:

Jones, Mindy, ABC Co., 123 A St., San Diego, CA, 92122, 6/15/88

Miller, Marie, Zeerox Inc., 234 C St., Los Angeles, CA, 91234, 6/01/88

Adams, Bart, DataSpec Inc., P.O. Box 2890, Malibu, CA, 92111, 6/15/88

Miller, Anne, Golden Gate Inc., 2313 Sixth St., Berkeley, CA, 94711, 6/01/88

Baker, Robin, Peach Computers, 2311 Coast Hwy., San Diego, CA, 92112, 6/15/88

Again, don't worry about typographical errors—they will be easy enough to correct later.

TESTING YOUR RULE

Remember how you set up a rule in Chapter 2 so that no entries could be made in the Names table unless a last name was entered? To test the rule, you need to try to break it.

Your screen should now be prompting you to press either [ESC] to end or [ENTER] to continue, so press Enter. Now, however, when prompted to enter an L:Name, press Enter. By doing this you tell R:BASE there isn't any data for that field. Enter the remainder of the data as in Figure 3.7:

Steve, Zenophobes Ltd., 345 Main Street, Seattle, WA, 98100, 6/3/88

Surprise! Once you enter the last item, R:BASE beeps at you and displays your error message. Although R:BASE didn't display the error message immediately after you broke your previously established rule by pressing Enter for a last name, it did catch your error at the end of your data entry, and didn't load the incomplete data.

Now you should be looking at the prompt

Press [ESC] to end, [ENTER] to continue

Press Esc. Then press any key when prompted to do so. This will bring back the *Add data to a database* menu. Press Esc to return to the PBE Main menu. The Names table currently has six rows in it.

```
R>LOAD Names WITH PROMPTS
 Begin R:BASE Data Loading

 Press [ESC] to end, [ENTER] to continue
 L:Name   (TEXT     ):
 F:Name   (TEXT     ):Steve
 Company  (TEXT     ):Zenophobes Ltd.
 Address  (TEXT     ):345 Main
 City     (TEXT     ):Seattle
 State    (TEXT     ):WA
 Zip      (TEXT     ):98100
 Ent:Date (DATE     ):6/3/88
-ERROR- You must enter a last name!

 Press [ESC] to end, [ENTER] to continue_
```

Figure 3.7: Testing your rule

When we edit the table, you will be able to see all the rows and make changes as well.

USING THE LIST COMMAND

For now, you have to accept it on faith that R:BASE really did add your data. However, there's an easy way to verify that it did. Press the Esc key to enter command mode. You should see the R> prompt.

Now type LIST and press the Enter key. R:BASE responds by displaying the tables in the Mail database, as shown in Figure 3.8. Notice that there are two tables: the Names table you set up in Chapter 2 and a RULES table. The Names table, R:BASE says, has eight columns (L:Name, F:Name, Company, Address, City, State, Zip, and Ent:Date) and six rows. The rows are your data—the six names and addresses you just entered.

What about the RULES table, though? This is a special table that R:BASE creates and maintains to keep track of any rules you've established. It also happens to have six columns, but only two rows. Why two

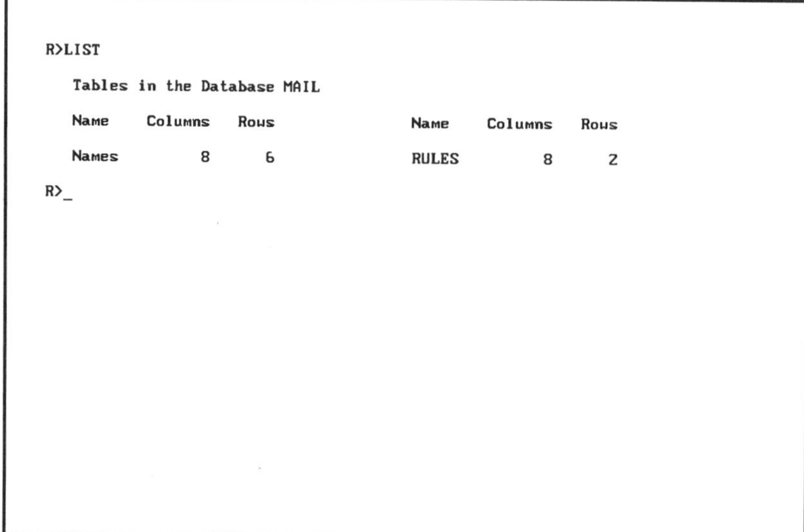

R>LIST
Tables in the Database MAIL
Name Columns Rows
Names 8 6
Name Columns Rows
RULES 8 2
R>_

Figure 3.8: Finding out about the tables in your database

rows when you've only set up one rule? Because each rule almost always requires at least two rows of storage in the RULES table.

Try a variation of the LIST command by typing **LIST Names** and pressing the Enter key. Where the LIST command alone gave you an overview of your entire database, LIST followed by a table name gives you the structure of the specified table only, as shown in Figure 3.9.

Your screen contains a good deal of information about the Names table. It reminds you that you haven't established Modify or Read passwords for it, and that there aren't any locks on it. *Locks* are security devices, like passwords but encountered only in multi-user systems; they are discussed in the Appendix. The rest of the screen conveys information about the columns in the Names table: their names, data types, lengths, and so on. None of the columns in the Names table has been defined as a key column, nor have any computed fields been established; hence the lack of data under the headings Key and Expression. R:BASE tells you here, too, that the Names table has six entries in it.

If you're curious about other variations of the LIST command, type HELP LIST. Otherwise, let's return to the PBE menu by typing **PROMPT** at the R> prompt.

```
R>LIST Names

   Table: Names              No lock(s)
   Read Password: No
   Modify Password: No

   Column definitions
   # Name      Type      Length          Key    Expression
   1 L:Name    TEXT      15 characters
   2 F:Name    TEXT      15 characters
   3 Company   TEXT      20 characters
   4 Address   TEXT      25 characters
   5 City      TEXT      15 characters
   6 state     TEXT       2 characters
   7 Zip       TEXT      10 characters
   8 Ent:Date  DATE

   Current number of rows:        6

R>_
```

Figure 3.9: Getting specific information about the Names table

EDITING A TABLE

In computer terminology, the term *edit* means to make a change in the database. For example, if you find that you've misspelled a name or entered the right data in the wrong column, you would need to edit the Names table. Similarly, if some of the people listed in the Names table moved and changed their addresses, you would need to edit the table to change the existing addresses.

There are many commands and techniques that you can use in R:BASE to edit a database. For our first example, we'll use the simplest method.

Before you edit a database, it needs to be open. In this example, we've already opened the Mail database. To move into the *edit mode* from the PBE menu, select option 5, *Modify data* from the menu. Doing so will display the instructions and options shown in Figure 3.10.

For general editing, you'll want to select the EDIT option (do so now). You'll be given the options for tabular editing or editing with a custom form. Since the Names table doesn't have any special data-entry forms set up for it yet, select Tabular Edit. Next you'll be asked to specify the name of the table to edit. Select Names.

The next screen lets you select particular columns to edit. In this example, select All so that you have access to all the columns. Next,

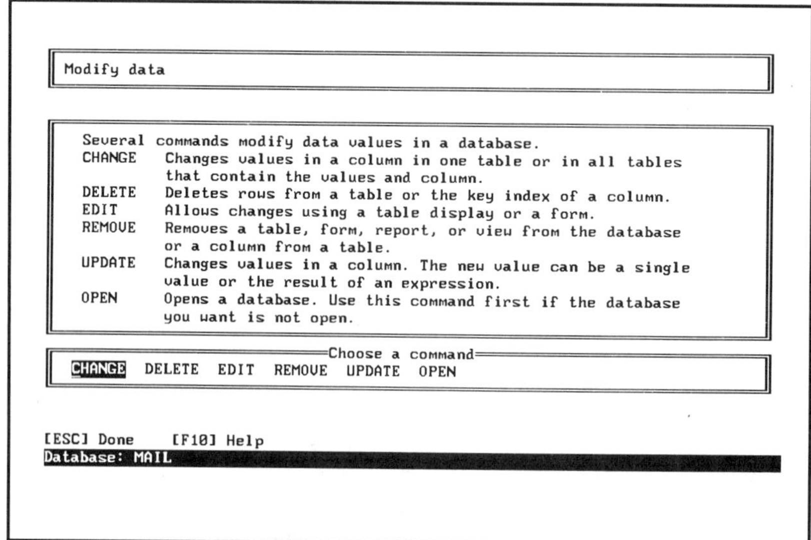

```
Modify data

Several commands modify data values in a database.
CHANGE    Changes values in a column in one table or in all tables
          that contain the values and column.
DELETE    Deletes rows from a table or the key index of a column.
EDIT      Allows changes using a table display or a form.
REMOVE    Removes a table, form, report, or view from the database
          or a column from a table.
UPDATE    Changes values in a column. The new value can be a single
          value or the result of an expression.
OPEN      Opens a database. Use this command first if the database
          you want is not open.

                    Choose a command
CHANGE  DELETE  EDIT  REMOVE  UPDATE  OPEN

[ESC] Done     [F10] Help
Database: MAIL
```

Figure 3.10: Options for editing a database

you'll be given an opportunity to display the data in sorted order. Press the Esc key for now to skip this option.

You'll next be given a chance to limit the number of rows displayed on the screen while editing. To have access to all the rows, press the Esc key. When you are done, the top of the screen will display the command line you've created, along with your current options, as follows:

```
     Execute    Edit    Reset    Help    Quit
EDIT ALL FROM Names
```

The command line tells R:BASE to display all the columns in the Names table on the *edit screen* so that you can make changes. When you select Execute to perform the command, you'll see the data appear as in Figure 3.11. This is an *edit screen*, which allows you to make changes to the data in the table. Table 3.1 lists keys that you can use to help edit the table.

Let's try a couple of editing exercises. Suppose you want to change the ZIP code in the first row from 94711 to 94721. First, you need to move the highlighting to the Zip column. You could either press the Tab key six times, or you could jump to the last column by holding down the Ctrl key and pressing the right-arrow (→) key, then pressing Shift-Tab (hold down the Shift key and press the Tab key). The Zip column in the

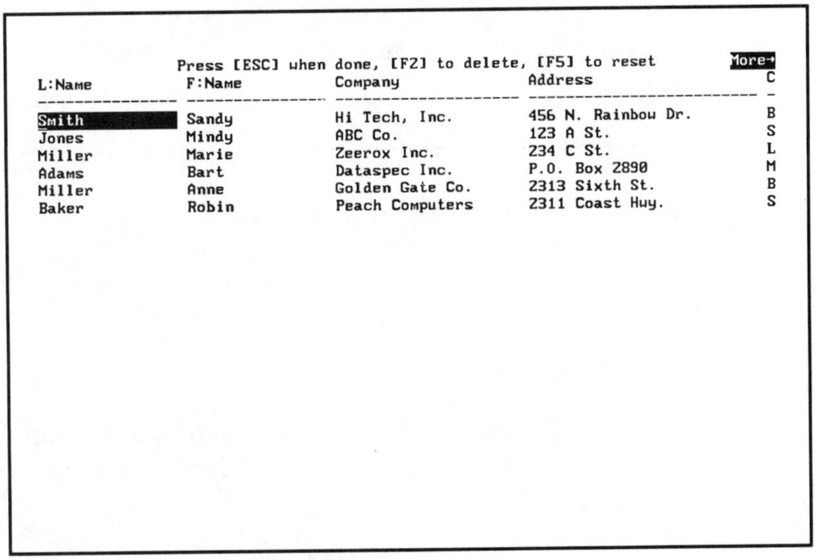

```
                  Press [ESC] when done, [F2] to delete, [F5] to reset          More→
L:Name            F:Name            Company               Address                   C
---------------   ---------------   -------------------   ----------------------    -
Smith             Sandy             Hi Tech, Inc.         456 N. Rainbow Dr.        B
Jones             Mindy             ABC Co.               123 A St.                 S
Miller            Marie             Zeerox Inc.           234 C St.                 L
Adams             Bart              Dataspec Inc.         P.O. Box 2890             M
Miller            Anne              Golden Gate Co.       2313 Sixth St.            B
Baker             Robin             Peach Computers       2311 Coast Hwy.           S
```

Figure 3.11: The Names table, ready for editing

Table 3.1: Keys Used with the EDIT Command

KEY	FUNCTION
↑	Moves highlighting up one row
↓	Moves highlighting down one row
Tab	Moves highlighting one column to the right
Shift-Tab	Moves highlighting one column to the left
→	Moves the cursor one character to the right
←	Moves the cursor one character to the left
Ctrl →	Moves highlighting to the last column in the row
Ctrl ←	Moves highlighting to the first column in the row
Home	Moves highlighting to first entry of the first record
End	Moves highlighting to the last entry of the last record
PgUp	Shows the previous screenful of data
PgDn	Shows the next screenful of data
Del	Deletes the character over the cursor
Ins	Inserts a space at the cursor position
F2	Deletes the currently highlighted row
F5	Restores the original contents of the current field

first row will be highlighted, as shown in Figure 3.12.

Next, you can move the cursor three spaces to the right by pressing the right arrow key three times. The cursor will appear below the 1 in the ZIP code, as in the following:

```
94711
```

Just type the number **2** (using the numbers at the top of the keyboard) to change the 1 to a 2, so the ZIP code looks like this:

```
94721
```

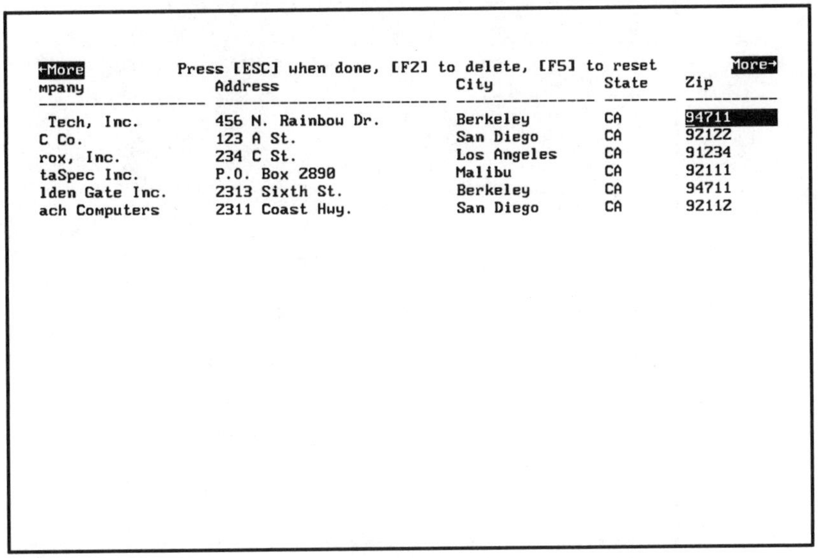

```
←More            Press [ESC] when done, [F2] to delete, [F5] to reset          More→
mpany              Address                  City             State    Zip
------------------ ------------------------ ---------------- -------- ----------
 Tech, Inc.        456 N. Rainbow Dr.       Berkeley         CA       94711
C Co.              123 A St.                San Diego        CA       92122
rox, Inc.          234 C St.                Los Angeles      CA       91234
taSpec Inc.        P.O. Box 2890            Malibu           CA       92111
lden Gate Inc.     2313 Sixth St.           Berkeley         CA       94711
ach Computers      2311 Coast Hwy.          San Diego        CA       92112
```

Figure 3.12: The Zip column highlighted in the Names table

Now let's change Golden Gate Inc. to Golden Gate Co. First, move down four rows by pressing the ↓ key four times. Then, move left to the Company column by pressing Shift-Tab four times (hold down the Shift key and press the Tab key four times). The Company column will be highlighted, as shown in Figure 3.13.

To move the cursor over to the Inc. portion of the Company, press the → key, or just hold it down, until the cursor is under the letter I, as follows:

Golden Gate Inc.

Next, type in the word **Co.**, so that the item appears like this:

Golden Gate Co. .

We just need to delete the extraneous period now. Do so by pressing the Del key. Now the item reads

Golden Gate Co.

```
←More            Press [ESC] when done, [F2] to delete, [F5] to reset          More→
Company              Address                     City             State     Zip
-------------------  --------------------------  ---------------  --------  --------
Hi Tech, Inc.        456 N. Rainbow Dr.          Berkeley         CA        94721
ABC Co.              123 A St.                   San Diego        CA        92122
Zeerox Inc.          234 C St.                   Los Angeles      CA        91234
DataSpec Inc.        P.O. Box 2890               Malibu           CA        92111
Golden Gate Inc.     2313 Sixth St.              Berkeley         CA        94711
Peach Computers      2311 Coast Hwy              San Diego        CA        92122
```

Figure 3.13: The Company column highlighted

Editing data in this fashion is easy, once you get used to the keystrokes used to control the highlighting and the cursor. If there are other errors in your table, try correcting them now. Refer to Table 3.1 for a list of the keys to use for editing.

If, while editing a single field of data, you find that you've made a mistake, you can "undo" your edit *as long as the highlight is still on the same field.* To restore the original contents to the field being edited, press the F5 key on your keyboard.

DELETING ROWS FROM A TABLE

You can also delete a row from a table while the edit screen is showing. To do so, use the ↑ and ↓ keys to move the highlighting to the row that you want to delete (don't do so now, however). When that row is highlighted, press the F2 key. R:BASE will double-check before deleting the row, giving you a chance to change your mind. Press Enter to delete the row, or Esc to change your mind.

EXITING R:BASE

You have now added some rows to your database using the *Add data to a database* option from the PBE menu, and you've edited (changed) some items of information using the *Modify data* option from the PBE menu. To make sure that everything is safely stored on disk before turning off the computer, you need to exit R:BASE and get back to the operating system prompt.

First, press Esc twice to leave the Edit mode and return to the PBE menu. Move the highlighter to the *Exit from R:BASE* option on the PBE menu and press Enter. The Exit command appears at the top of the screen. Press any key, as instructed, then select Execute, and R:BASE will store your new data on disk and return to the operating system.

In this chapter we've touched on the fundamentals of working *interactively* with a database, focusing on techniques for entering and editing data in a table. In the next chapter, we'll look at how you can sort that data into a variety of different orders.

Chapter 4

Sorting Your Data for Easy Use

FAST TRACK

To specify columns to sort on in PBE mode, 62
select the *Query a database* option from the PBE menu, and then define the sort using the menus that appear as you build your command line. (See also sorting from the R> prompt, below.)

To sort in descending order, 66
select the Descending option in PBE mode or add the =D option to your command line.

Long commands 66
that exceed the width of the screen are split automatically by R:BASE and wrapped around to the next line. R:BASE uses the plus symbol (+), to indicate wraparound.

To perform sorts within sorts, 68
specify the columns to sort on in order of most important to least important.

To specify columns to sort on from the R> prompt, 69
use the ORDER BY clause with the SELECT or EDIT command.

To recall an incorrect command line 79
and correct it after receiving an error message, use the →, Ctrl and →, End, Del, Ins, and Tab keys.

To recall previous commands 79
from R:BASE's command buffer, press the PgUp and PgDn keys.

To abbreviate R:BASE commands, 80

use the first three letters of the command. Column numbers (displayed with the LIST *table name* command) can be used instead of column names.

To create a new table 81

from an existing one, with data stored in a particular order, use the PROJECT command.

IN THIS CHAPTER WE'LL DISCUSS TECHNIQUES FOR displaying data in a sorted order. The rows in a database can be sorted into any order you wish, such as alphabetical by name, ZIP-code order for bulk mailing, chronological order, or numerical order. Your sorts can be in ascending order, such as A to Z in alphabetical sorts, smallest to largest in numerical sorts, or earliest to latest in date sorts. Optionally, sorts can be in descending order, for example, Z to A, largest to smallest, or latest to earliest. Furthermore, you can combine sort orders to achieve "sorts within sorts."

We'll begin working more with the R:BASE command mode (indicated by the R> prompt) in this chapter. While the PBE mode is certainly adequate for building command lines in R:BASE, it's a good idea to practice entering commands at the R> prompt. You may eventually want to learn to program in the R:BASE programming language; and even if you don't, the command mode is a bit faster than the prompt mode.

If you've exited R:BASE since the last chapter, enter the command that starts R:BASE on your system, and open the Mail database as discussed in the last chapter. You'll see the familiar PBE menu on the screen.

SORTING FROM PBE

We saw in the last chapter that the EDIT command allows you to select columns to sort the table on (although we skipped over the sort option then). Actually, several different commands in R:BASE allow you to specify sort orders. In this chapter, we'll discuss sorting with the EDIT command and the SELECT command. Unlike the EDIT command, the SELECT command only displays the data on the screen; it does not allow you to make changes. Nonetheless, the SELECT command is useful for getting a quick view of your database.

Suppose that you want to see a list of all the rows on your database, sorted into alphabetical order by last name. Begin by selecting the *Query a database* and then *Look at data* options from the PBE menu.

In this example we'll use the SELECT command to view data. Verify that the highlighter is on the SELECT option (Figure 4.1) and press Enter. R:BASE will ask for the name of the table to display. (If you haven't opened the mail database yet, you'll be prompted to do so now.) Select Names. R:BASE will ask for the columns to display. Select All.

Now R:BASE displays a screen for selecting columns to sort on, as shown in Figure 4.2. To display the data in alphabetical order by last name, highlight the L:Name option and press Enter. R:BASE will ask if you want the data sorted in Ascending order (A to Z) or Descending order (Z to A). Select Ascending. R:BASE then gives you the opportunity to select more sort columns. In this case, just press the Esc key.

R:BASE displays a screen for *searching* the database (a topic we'll discuss in the next chapter). Press Esc to bypass this screen.

Now you can see at the top of the screen that you've built the command, as follows:

```
Execute  Edit  Reset  Help  Quit
SELECT ALL FROM Names ORDER BY L:Name
```

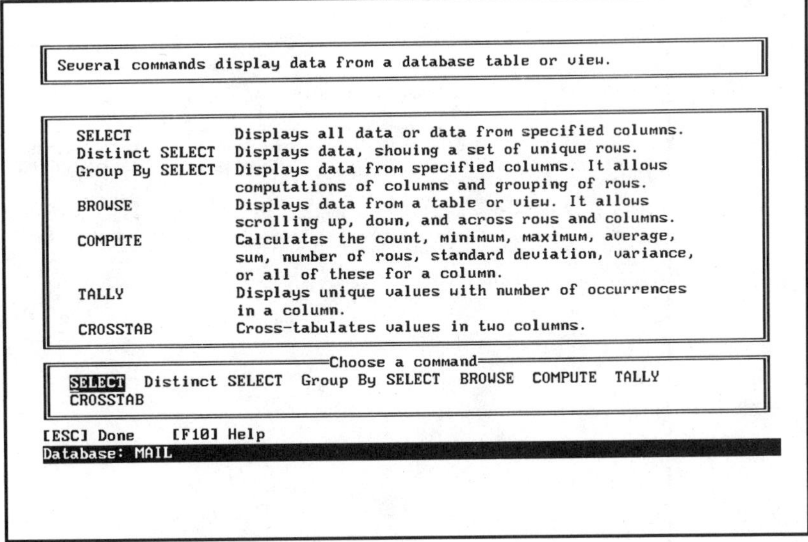

Figure 4.1: Options for viewing data

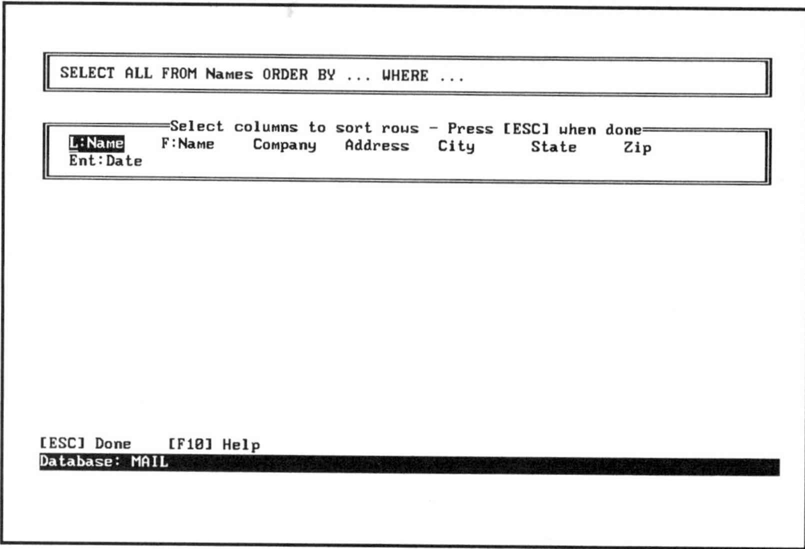

Figure 4.2: The screen for specifying columns to sort on

The command tells R:BASE to display all the columns from the Names table, sorted on the L:Name column. Press Enter to select the Execute option. R:BASE displays as many columns as will fit on the screen, sorted by last name, as shown in Figure 4.3.

```
SELECT ALL FROM Names ORDER BY L:Name
 L:Name          F:Name          Company               Address
 --------------- --------------- --------------------- -------------------------
 Adams           Bart            DataSpec Inc.         P.O. Box 2890
 Baker           Robin           Peach Computers       2311 Coast Hwy.
 Jones           Mindy           ABC Co.               123 A St.
 Miller          Anne            Golden Gate Co.       2313 Sixth St.
 Miller          Marie           Zeerox, Inc.          234 C St.
 Smith           Sandy           Hi Tech, Inc.         456 N. Rainbow Dr.
Press any key to continue_
```

Figure 4.3: The Names table sorted by last name

SPECIFYING COLUMNS TO DISPLAY

The SELECT command displays only as many columns as will fit on the screen; therefore, you probably will not be able to see all your data. You can, however, specify particular columns to display in a SELECT command and even specify the order (from left to right) that they will appear on the screen. Let's look at an example and sort the rows into descending order by date along the way. First, press any key to return to the *Look at data* menu.

Choose the SELECT command and the Names table, as in the last example. R:BASE shows a menu for selecting columns to display, as shown in Figure 4.4.

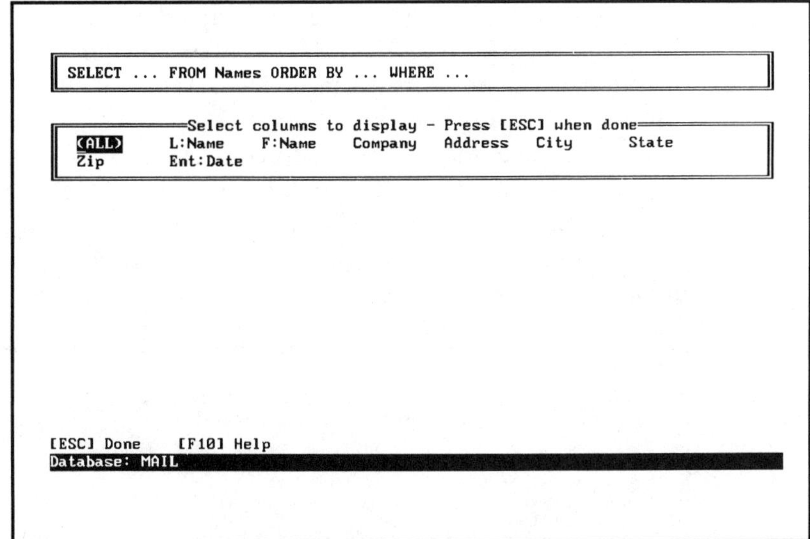

Figure 4.4: The screen to select columns for display

To display the entry date (Ent:Date column) in the leftmost column, move the highlighter to the Ent:Date column and press Enter. To display the L:Name column next, move the highlighter to L:Name and press Enter. To display the F:Name column, move the highlighter to F:Name and press Enter. The names of the columns you selected appear below the menu on the screen as follows:

```
Ent:Date L:Name F:Name
```

Press Esc to indicate that you've finished selecting columns to display.

Next, the screen for selecting sort columns appears (as in Figure 4.2). In this example, select Ent:Date, then select Descending, and then press Esc to finish selecting sort columns.

When the screen for entering search criteria appears, press Esc to bypass it. The command line reads

```
SELECT Ent:Date L:Name F:Name FROM Names ORDER +
+ >BY Ent:Date = D
```

Note the + symbol at the end of the first and the beginning of the second line above. R:BASE uses the + symbol to indicate that a command continues on the next line. Although your screen has enough room to display the entire command on one line, our page doesn't. We've adopted R:BASE's conventions for indicating continuation of a command by using the + and the + > symbols on the starting and ending lines, respectively.

The command that we've constructed tells R:BASE to display the Ent:Date, L:Name, and F:Name columns from the Names table, sorted by Ent:Date in descending (= D) order. Select Execute to execute the command, and the data appear on the screen accordingly, as in Figure 4.5. Press any key when you are finished viewing the data.

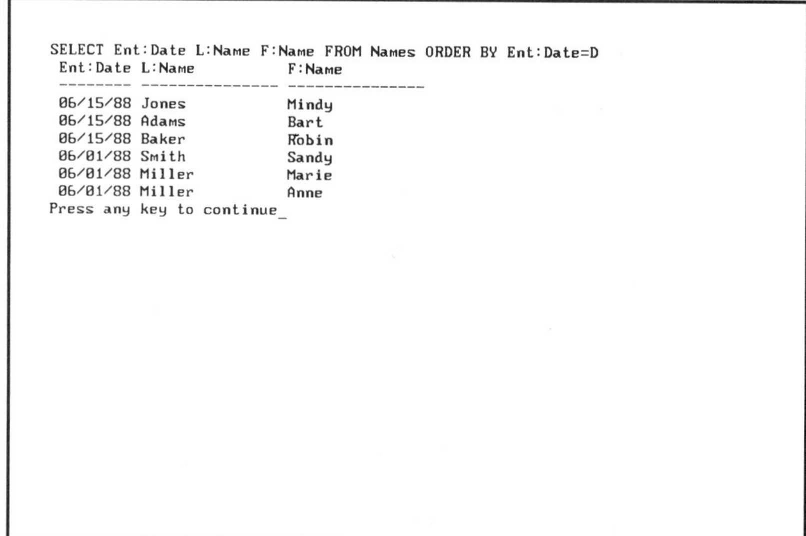

SELECT Ent:Date L:Name F:Name FROM Names ORDER BY Ent:Date=D
Ent:Date L:Name F:Name
-------- --------------- ---------------
06/15/88 Jones Mindy
06/15/88 Adams Bart
06/15/88 Baker Robin
06/01/88 Smith Sandy
06/01/88 Miller Marie
06/01/88 Miller Anne
Press any key to continue_

Figure 4.5: Selected columns from the Names table in descending date order

So far, we've sorted the Names table by a single column only. On a very large table, this type of single-column sort would probably not produce the result that you had in mind. For example, suppose you had a table with 10,000 names on it, and you decided to sort them into alphabetical order by last name. You might find that there were 100 Smiths, listed in totally random order by first name, as follows:

Smith, Norma
Smith, Alan D.
Smith, Jake
Smith, Rudolph
Smith, Sam
Smith, Anne

.

.

.

and so on.

You probably would want the data sorted by last name, and within common last names, sorted by first name, as in the following:

Smith, Alan D.
Smith, Anne
Smith, Jake
Smith, Norma
Smith, Rudolph
Smith, Sam

.

.

.

and so on.

You can easily handle this kind of situation (a sort within a sort or a *secondary* sort) by listing multiple column names in the ORDER BY clause. Where more than one column name is listed, the additional columns act as tie-breakers for the immediately preceding column.

SORTS WITHIN SORTS

To perform sorts within sorts, you merely need to select multiple sorting columns, in order from most important to least important. For example, suppose you want to display the Names database sorted by last name, and within common last names, you want the rows sorted by first name. In this case, you need to select L:Name as the first sort column and F:Name as the second sort column. Let's work through an example.

Choose SELECT, the Names table, and All as before. From the Sort columns menu, select L:Name and Ascending to specify L:Name as the most important sort order. Then select F:Name and Ascending order. The columns you selected for sorting are displayed below the menu, as follows:

```
L:Name F:Name
```

Press Esc to finish selecting sort columns, and press Esc again to bypass the search criteria screen. The command you've built reads

```
SELECT ALL FROM Names ORDER BY L:Name F:Name
```

This command tells R:BASE to display all the columns from the Names table, sorted by last name and by first name within identical last names. When you select Execute from the top menu, R:BASE displays your data as in Figure 4.3. In our case, specifying F:name as a tie-breaker didn't have any effect, but this won't always be the case.

The Names table is too small to demonstrate the full range of sorts within sorts. Suffice it to say that you can sort on up to ten columns, which gives you tremendous flexibility in defining sort orders even in very large tables. (The only restriction on R:BASE sorts is that you can't sort on a column that is NOTE data type.) We'll see more examples of sorts within sorts later in the chapter, but first we'll discuss a shortcut for displaying table data in sorted order.

SORTING FROM THE R> PROMPT

You've probably noticed that the commands that your menu selections have produced have all had a similar format, or *syntax* in computer jargon. That syntax is

```
SELECT column name FROM table name ORDER +
+> BY column list
```

where *column name* is the name of the column or columns to display (or the ALL operator to display all columns); *table name* is the name of the table containing the columns, and *column list* is the name of the column (or columns) to sort by. You can enter commands directly from the R> prompt using this same syntax.

For example, suppose you want to see the Names table sorted into ZIP-code order, and furthermore, you want to see the Zip, City, L:Name, and F:Name columns on the screen. To type in the appropriate command directly at the R> prompt, first press any key and then the Esc key twice to leave PBE, so that the R> prompt appears on the screen. Next, type in the command

```
SELECT Zip City L:Name F:Name FROM Names ORDER BY +
+> Zip
```

and press Enter. Remember, you can type the entire command on one line. However, if you choose to type it in on two lines, as we have, you don't have to type the +> on the second line; R:BASE does it for you. The appropriate columns, in ZIP-code order, appear on the screen as in Figure 4.6.

Suppose you want to display all the columns in alphabetical order by company. To do so, you would type in the command

```
SELECT ALL FROM Names ORDER BY Company
```

and press Enter. R:BASE displays the table in alphabetical order by company name, as in Figure 4.7.

When typing in long commands directly at the R> prompt, you continue a command from one line to the next by ending the first line with a space followed by a plus sign (+). After pressing Enter, you simply continue typing the command on the next line, which will

```
R>SELECT Zip City L:Name F:Name FROM Names ORDER BY Zip
 Zip        City            L:Name          F:Name
 ---------- --------------- --------------- ---------------
 91234      Los Angeles     Miller          Marie
 92111      Malibu          Adams           Bart
 92112      San Diego       Baker           Robin
 92122      San Diego       Jones           Mindy
 94711      Berkeley        Miller          Anne
 94721      Berkeley        Smith           Sandy
R>_
```

Figure 4.6: The Names table sorted into ZIP-code order

begin with a + > prompt. However, you don't need to worry about explicitly typing a space and then a + since R:BASE will do this for you automatically if you just keep typing. Remember that because a computer screen can accommodate more characters per line than a

```
R>SELECT ALL FROM Names ORDER BY Company
 L:Name          F:Name          Company              Address
 --------------- --------------- -------------------- -------------------------
 Jones           Mindy           ABC Co.              123 A St.
 Adams           Bart            DataSpec Inc.        P.O. Box 2890
 Miller          Anne            Golden Gate Co.      2313 Sixth St.
 Smith           Sandy           Hi Tech, Inc.        456 N. Rainbow Dr.
 Baker           Robin           Peach Computers      2311 Coast Hwy.
 Miller          Marie           Zeerox, Inc.         234 C St.
R>_
```

Figure 4.7: The Names table in alphabetical order by Company

page of this book can, you should be careful in entering sample commands. Your plus sign will often fall in a different place than appears here. For example, the single command below tells R:BASE to display the City, L:Name, and F:Name columns from the Names table, sorted by city, by last name within each city, and by first name within each last name (within each city):

```
SELECT City L:Name F:Name FROM Names ORDER BY +
+ > City L:Name F:Name
```

The data are displayed in alphabetical order across all three columns, as shown in Figure 4.8.

```
R>SELECT City L:Name F:Name FROM Names ORDER BY +
+>City L:Name F:Name
 City             L:Name           F:Name
 ---------------- ---------------- ---------------
 Berkeley         Miller           Anne
 Berkeley         Smith            Sandy
 Los Angeles      Miller           Marie
 Malibu           Adams            Bart
 San Diego        Baker            Robin
 San Diego        Jones            Mindy
R>_
```

Figure 4.8: The Names table sorted by city and last and first name

To display the data in chronological order by entry date, with common dates sorted alphabetically by last and first name, use the command

```
SELECT Ent:Date L:Name F:Name FROM Names ORDER BY +
+ > Ent:Date L:Name F:Name
```

This produces the listing shown in Figure 4.9.

```
R>SELECT Ent:Date L:Name F:Name FROM Names ORDER BY +
+>Ent:Date L:Name F:Name
 Ent:Date L:Name          F:Name
 -------- --------------- ---------------
 06/01/88 Miller          Anne
 06/01/88 Miller          Marie
 06/01/88 Smith           Sandy
 06/15/88 Adams           Bart
 06/15/88 Baker           Robin
 06/15/88 Jones           Mindy
R>_
```

Figure 4.9: Data listed chronologically and alphabetically

Any column in a table can be sorted in descending order by using the =D option with the column name. For example, to sort the Names table in descending alphabetical order by last name, enter the command

SELECT ALL FROM Names ORDER BY L:Name = D

This produces the display shown in Figure 4.10.

You can mix and match ascending and descending sorts. For example, the command below displays data in descending chronological order and ascending alphabetical order:

SELECT Ent:Date L:Name FROM Names ORDER BY +
+ > Ent:Date = D L:Name

This display is shown in Figure 4.11.

Again, our sample table is too small to show the full power of R:BASE sorting. But suppose you had a table listing salespersons' last names, first names, sales amounts, and dates of sales. You could display the data in chronological order by date, and within common

```
R>SELECT ALL FROM Names ORDER BY L:Name=D
 L:Name          F:Name          Company              Address
 --------------- --------------- -------------------- -------------------------
 Smith           Sandy           Hi Tech, Inc.        456 N. Rainbow Dr.
 Miller          Marie           Zeerox, Inc.         234 C St.
 Miller          Anne            Golden Gate Co.      2313 Sixth St.
 Jones           Mindy           ABC Co.              123 A St.
 Baker           Robin           Peach Computers      2311 Coast Hwy.
 Adams           Bart            DataSpec Inc.        P.O. Box 2890
R>_
```

Figure 4.10: Names displayed in descending alphabetical order

```
R>SELECT Ent:Date L:Name FROM Names ORDER BY +
+>Ent:Date=D L:Name
 Ent:Date L:Name
 -------- ---------------
 06/15/88 Adams
 06/15/88 Baker
 06/15/88 Jones
 06/01/88 Miller
 06/01/88 Miller
 06/01/88 Smith
R>_
```

Figure 4.11: The Names table sorted in descending date and ascending name order

dates, alphabetical order by name, and within common names, descending order of sales amounts, using the command

```
SELECT ALL FROM Sales ORDER BY S:Date L:Name +
+ > F:Name Amount = D
```

The result might look like this:

06/01/88	Adams	Andy	$999.99
06/01/88	Adams	Andy	$89.90
06/01/88	Adams	Andy	$1.23
06/01/88	Miller	Mike	$1000.00
06/01/88	Miller	Mike	$987.65
06/01/88	Miller	Nancy	$1234.56
06/01/88	Miller	Nancy	$899.00
06/02/88	Adams	Andy	$1200.00
06/02/88	Adams	Andy	$888.99

.

.

.

and so on.

SORTING THE EDIT SCREEN

Recall that in the last chapter when you selected the Modify data and EDIT commands from the PBE menus, R:BASE displayed a screen for selecting sort orders—the same screen, in fact, that the SELECT command displays. You can specify a sort order for the edit screen in the same way that you specify a sort order for the SELECT command.

You can access the edit screen directly from the R> prompt, using the EDIT command and the same syntax as the SELECT command. For example, to put the Names table into alphabetical order by last name on the edit screen, you could enter the command

```
EDIT ALL FROM Names ORDER BY L:Name F:Name
```

The edit screen would display all data in alphabetical order by last name, as shown in Figure 4.12.

```
             Press [ESC] when done, [F2] to delete, [F5] to reset      More→
L:Name          F:Name          Company             Address                C
--------------- --------------- ------------------- ---------------------- -
Adams           Bart            DataSpec Inc.       P.O. Box 2890          M
Baker           Robin           Peach Computers     2311 Coast Hwy         S
Jones           Mindy           ABC Co.             123 A St.              S
Miller          Anne            Golden Gate Co.     2313 Sixth St.         B
Miller          Marie           Zeerox Inc.         234 C St.              L
Smith           Sandy           Hi Tech, Inc.       456 N. Rainbow Dr.     B
```

Figure 4.12: The Edit screen sorted into alphabetical order

Presorting the data in an edit screen can make it easier to find specific items in a large table. You can specify columns with the EDIT command, along with a sort order. The command below presorts the Names table into descending chronological order and displays the L:Name, F:Name, and Ent:Date columns for editing, as shown in Figure 4.13:

```
EDIT Ent:Date L:Name F:Name FROM Names ORDER BY +
+ > Ent:Date = D
```

Needless to say, a SELECT or EDIT command that includes five or ten ORDER BY columns can become awkward to handle. Before you attempt any exceptionally long commands, there are a few things you should know about how to handle them, as well as some common errors that might occur.

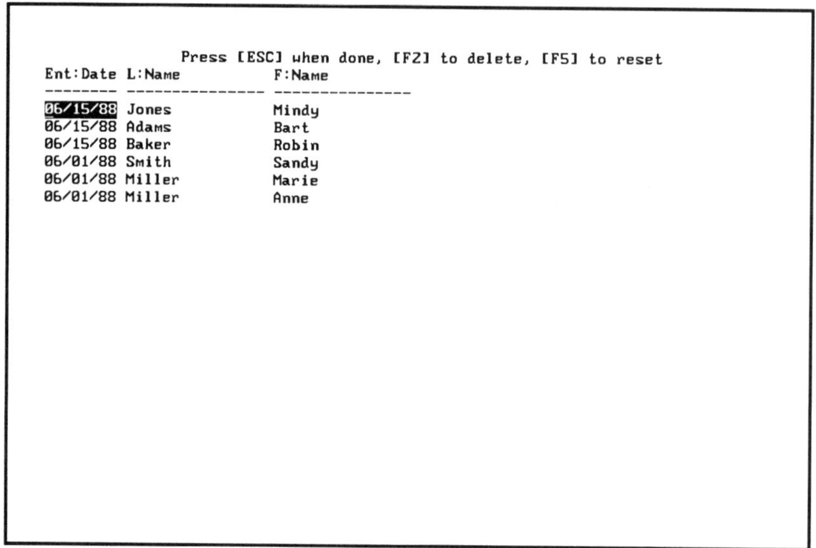

Press [ESC] when done, [F2] to delete, [F5] to reset
Ent:Date L:Name F:Name
06/15/88 Jones Mindy
06/15/88 Adams Bart
06/15/88 Baker Robin
06/01/88 Smith Sandy
06/01/88 Miller Marie
06/01/88 Miller Anne

Figure 4.13: The Edit screen sorted and limited to three columns

MODIFYING PROMPT MODE COMMANDS

When building command lines through the PBE menu selections, you probably will not make errors very often, because PBE "knows" the correct syntax for all the R:BASE commands. However, you may occasionally change your mind about some menu selections you made when you see the final command on your screen, as follows:

```
Execute   Edit   Reset   Help   Quit
SELECT ALL FROM Names ORDER BY F:Name L:Name
```

As you know, the Execute option will send the command to R:BASE to be processed immediately. The other options from the top menu are summarized here:

Edit Displays the command line inside a box, and allows you to make changes to it. You can use the left and right arrow keys to position the cursor anywhere in the command line. You can use the Ins key to insert a blank space and the Del key to delete a character. You can also type new text over existing text.

Reset	Jumps back to the first menu selection you made for the command, and allows you to reselect menu items for the command.
Help	Displays helpful instructions and options for using the command.
Quit	Abandons the command line altogether and returns you to the PBE Menu.

More often than not, you'll probably be able to select Execute to process the command line immediately. When entering your own command lines at the R> prompt, however, you will be more likely to make mistakes. (The advantage of entering commands at the R> prompt is that it is faster; the disadvantage is that doing so requires some familiarity with the syntax of the commands.) The most common errors when entering commands at the R> prompt are discussed in the next section.

CORRECTING COMMANDS MADE AT THE R> PROMPT

Unless you are a truly superb typist, you're likely to get error messages from time to time as you work with R:BASE, particularly with longer commands. No need to worry, you can't do any harm by typing in an invalid command. The worst that will happen is that the computer will beep and display a message. For example, typing in the command

```
SELECT ALL FROM Bananas
```

causes the computer to beep and R:BASE to display the following message:

```
– ERROR – Bananas is an undefined table
```

which means that there is no table named Bananas in the open database. Perhaps you've misspelled the table name, or you've forgotten to open the database containing the table. To review the table names, use the LIST TABLES command to display the names of all the tables in the open database.

Another common error is to enter a command such as

SELECT ALL FROM Names ORDER BY LastName F:Name

R:BASE displays the message

– ERROR – Column LastName is not in the table Names

indicating that there is no LastName column in the table. The actual column name is L:Name.

Some errors are caused by incorrect syntax. For example, if you type in the command

SELECT FROM Names ORDER BY L:Name F:Name City

R:BASE would display the message

– ERROR – Syntax is incorrect for the command

and, as a helping hand, will display a *syntax diagram,* as shown in Figure 4.14.

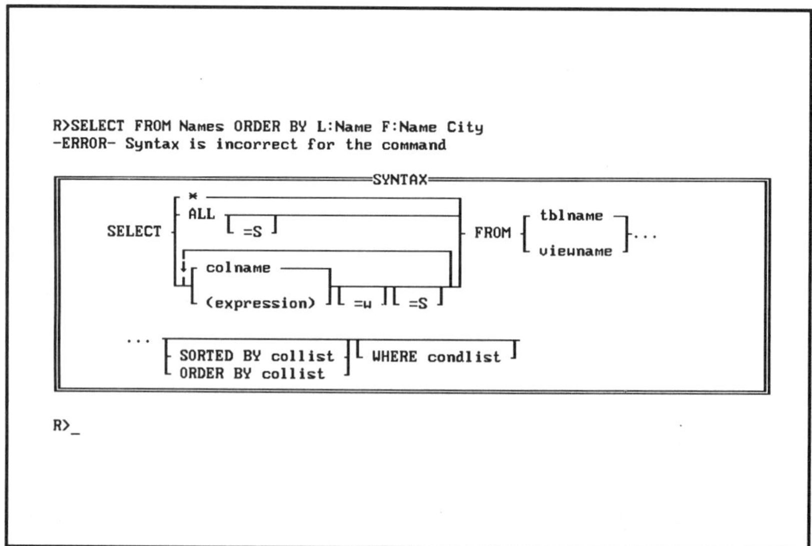

Figure 4.14: The syntax diagram for the SELECT command

The syntax chart in Figure 4.14 shows that the SELECT command can be followed either by the word *ALL* or an asterisk (*), selecting all columns, or by a list of column names (*colname*). You can use the =S (sum) and =w (width) options (which we'll discuss later) in the column list. The next portion of the command is *FROM tblname,* meaning that the word FROM and the name of the table follow. Optionally, the terms ORDER BY or SORTED BY and a list of column names (*collist*) follow. Finally, the *WHERE* clause can follow, using a list of conditions (*condlist*). (The WHERE clause is discussed in the next chapter.) Our syntax error occurred because we forgot to include the ALL option or a list of column names after the SELECT command.

Fortunately, you don't have to type in an entire command from scratch just because of a simple error. R:BASE remembers your command, even after displaying the error message. You can use the following keys to bring back the command line and correct the errors in it:

End or Ctrl-→	Recalls the entire command.
→	Each press brings back one character from the line.
Tab	Recalls the previous command 10 characters at a time.
Ins	Inserts a blank space into the line.
Del	Deletes the character at the cursor.
PgUp	Recalls previous commands, the most recent one first.
PgDn	Recalls subsequent commands when used after PgUp; otherwise recalls the oldest command stored in the command buffer.

For example, suppose you enter the command

```
EDIT ALL FROM Names ORDER BY LName +
+ > F:Name Ent:Date = D
```

R:BASE rejects the line because it can't find the LName column. To correct the error (change LName to L:Name), press the → key repeatedly to bring back all characters up to the error, as below:

```
EDIT ALL FROM Names ORDER BY L_
```

Next, press the Ins key to insert a space, and then type in the missing colon, so that the line looks like this:

```
EDIT ALL FROM Names ORDER BY L:_
```

Now you can recall the rest of the line either by holding down the Ctrl key and pressing the right arrow or by tapping the End key. The entire line appears on the screen, as follows:

```
EDIT ALL FROM Names ORDER BY L:Name F:Name +
+ > Ent:Date = D
```

Press Enter to enter the command.

ABBREVIATING COMMANDS

Another way to deal with long commands is to use abbreviations. Most R:BASE commands can be trimmed down to only the first three letters. For example, the command line

```
SELECT ALL FROM Names ORDER BY L:Name F:Name +
+ > Ent:Date
```

can be abbreviated to

```
SEL ALL FRO Names ORD BY L:Name F:Name Ent:Date
```

Keep in mind that you can't abbreviate your own table names, column names, and so on. However, you can use column numbers rather than their names in column lists, as long as you include a number sign (#). For example, the rather lengthy command

```
SELECT Ent:Date L:Name F:Name Address FROM Names +
+ > ORDER BY Ent:Date = D L:Name F:Name
```

can be abbreviated to

```
SEL #8 #1 #2 #4 FRO Names ORD BY #8 = D #1 #2
```

Since Ent:Date is column number 8 in the Names table, L:Name is column number 1 and so on. From the R> prompt, you can use the LIST command, along with the table name, (for example, LIST Names) to see column numbers, as shown in Figure 4.15.

```
R>LIST Names

   Table: Names            No lock(s)
   Read Password: No
   Modify Password: No

   Column definitions
   # Name      Type      Length          Key    Expression
   1 L:Name    TEXT       15 characters
   2 F:Name    TEXT       15 characters
   3 Company   TEXT       20 characters
   4 Address   TEXT       25 characters
   5 City      TEXT       15 characters
   6 State     TEXT        5 characters
   7 Zip       TEXT       10 characters
   8 Ent:Date  DATE

   Current number of rows:       6

R>_
```

Figure 4.15: Column numbers displayed using the LIST command

For purposes of clarity, we'll continue to use the longer versions of commands throughout this book.

SORTING AND THE PROJECT COMMAND

You may have noticed that the original order of data in the Names table is unaffected by use of the ORDER BY clause. To verify this, type

SELECT ALL FROM Names

and press Enter. You see that the data is still in the order in which you entered it.

One of the characteristics of a relational database is that the order of rows, or records, in your tables is irrelevant. Why, you ask? Because by using commands like SELECT, you can arrange to have the rows displayed (or printed) in any order you need on the spur of the moment.

You may, however, prefer to have your data sorted in a particular order so you don't have to use the ORDER BY clause. The easiest way to do this is to use R:BASE's PROJECT command. At the R> prompt, type

```
HELP PROJECT
```

and press the Enter key. Your screen should look like Figure 4.16.

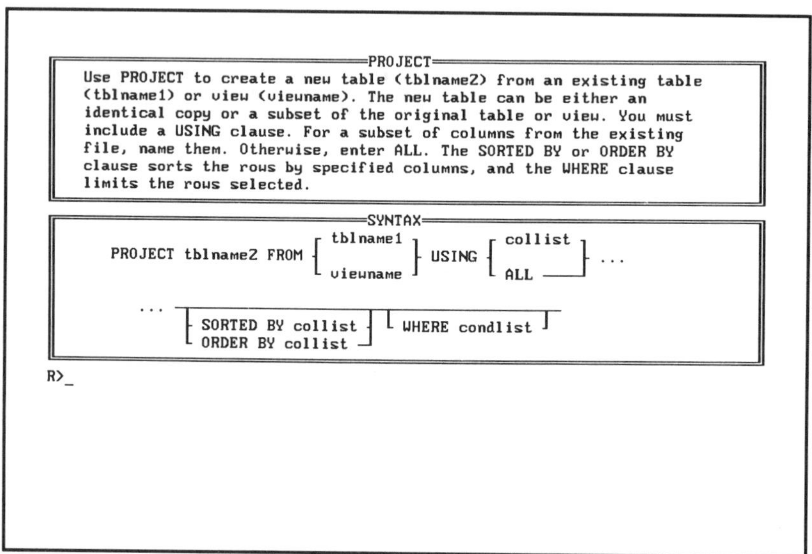

```
PROJECT
Use PROJECT to create a new table (tblname2) from an existing table
(tblname1) or view (viewname). The new table can be either an
identical copy or a subset of the original table or view. You must
include a USING clause. For a subset of columns from the existing
file, name them. Otherwise, enter ALL. The SORTED BY or ORDER BY
clause sorts the rows by specified columns, and the WHERE clause
limits the rows selected.

SYNTAX
                          tblname1            collist
PROJECT tblname2 FROM {             } USING {          } ...
                          viewname            ALL

    ... [ SORTED BY collist ] [ WHERE condlist ]
        [ ORDER BY collist  ]
R>_
```

Figure 4.16: R:BASE's Help screen for the PROJECT command

The PROJECT command is extremely useful for creating table backups and subsets of existing tables, but it can also be used to create a new table that is the same as an existing one, except for the order of the rows.

As an example, type the following at the R> prompt:

```
PROJECT SortName FROM Names USING ALL ORDER BY
L:Name
```

R:BASE should respond with a comforting message that a successful PROJECT was accomplished, and that the new table has six rows in it.

To verify that the new table (called SortName) does indeed contain the same data as the Names table, but in alphabetical order by last name, type

```
SELECT ALL FROM SortName
```

The data should be displayed in the same order as it was in Figure 4.3. At this point, of course, the Mail database has two tables in it with redundant data. Generally, you would want to delete one of the tables by using the REMOVE TABLE command. If you have created the SortName table, go ahead and delete it by typing

```
REMOVE TABLE SortName
```

and pressing Enter. (If you have not already established an owner password for the SortName table, you will need to do so now.) R:BASE will ask you to confirm the command by pressing Enter again. Do this to remove the SortName table.

You've just used one of R:BASE's six *relational* commands, which are generally used to combine data from different tables. You'll learn more about the PROJECT and other relational commands in Chapter 14.

In this chapter we've discussed numerous commands and techniques for displaying data in a table in sorted order. We've also learned more about entering commands at the R> prompt without the aid of the PBE mode.

In the next chapter we'll discuss techniques for searching, or filtering, a table.

Chapter 5

Finding the Data You Need

Fast Track

To search in R:BASE, 88
use the WHERE clause with the SELECT, EDIT, CHANGE, and DELETE ROWS commands.

To perform complex searches, 89
use R:BASE's comparative operators, including equal (= or EQ), not equal (<> or NE), less than (< or LT), greater than (> or GT), less than or equal to (<= or LE), and greater than or equal to (>= or GE). See Table 5.1 for a complete listing of WHERE clause operators.

To search for embedded information 101
in TEXT columns, use the CONTAINS, LIKE, and NOT LIKE operators. Wild-card characters (* and ?) can be used to find matches.

To search based on row position, 103
use the COUNT = *n*, COUNT = LAST, and LIMIT = *n* operators.

To specify multiple search criteria, 104
use the AND and OR operators to broaden or narrow the results of a search.

To search for data that falls within a range 104
of values, use the AND or BETWEEN operators. For example, the clause `WHERE Ent:Date >= 1/1/88 AND Ent:Date <= 3/31/88` or the clause `WHERE Ent:Date BETWEEN 1/1/88 AND 3/31/88` access all rows with dates in the first quarter of 1988.

WHERE clauses containing 108

a number of AND and OR conditions are interpreted from left to right, unless you use parentheses to group the conditions.

To search upper- and lowercase 109

distinctions, enter the SET CASE ON command at the R> prompt. The SET CASE OFF command returns R:BASE to the normal searching technique, which ignores case. The SHOW command shows the current status of such settings.

To compare two columns 110

in a table during a search, add the letter A to the operator (for example, =A or EQA).

To edit or update a table globally, 111

use the CHANGE or UPDATE command with a WHERE clause.

To search 112

for data that contains blank spaces (for example, City = San Diego), use quotation marks to enclose the unit of data (for example, City = "San Diego"), particularly when you are using AND and OR operators.

To delete rows globally 115

from a table, use the DELETE ROWS command with a WHERE clause.

To refine your searches 116

and perform sophisticated data analysis, use the SQL commands SELECT DISTINCT and Group By SELECT.

IN THIS CHAPTER, WE'LL DISCUSS TECHNIQUES FOR searching, or *filtering* or *querying,* a table. When you filter a table, you access only those rows that meet specific search criteria. For example, from the Names table, you might want to list everyone who has an entry date of June 1, 1988, or perhaps everyone who has an entry date in the first quarter of 1988. Alternatively, you might want to list all the individuals who live in a certain city or work for a certain company.

There is no limit to the ways that you can filter a table. Furthermore, you can mix sorting and searching criteria however you wish. For example, suppose you needed to send a form letter to all the individuals listed in a table who work for ABC Company in the state of California. You could easily pull these individuals out of the table, sorted in ZIP-code order, so that you could get the benefits of bulk mailing.

SEARCHING FROM PBE

When you display or edit data using the *Query a database* or *Modify data* options from the PBE Main menu, the last screen to appear before the final command is displayed allows you to specify criteria for filtering the database. We haven't put this screen to use in previous chapters, so let's work through some exercises now to learn how to use this screen.

Suppose there are 1000 or more names in the Names table, and you wish to edit a row for an individual named Miller. If you do not specify a filtering criteria, you'll need to scroll through many rows on the edit screen to locate the appropriate row to edit. However, you can limit the edit screen to displaying only rows with the last name Miller.

First, make sure the Mail database is open. Then, select *Modify data* from the PBE menu and EDIT from the next menu. Select Tabular Edit, and select Names as the table to edit. Select All to have access to all columns. From the next screen, you are given the choice of specifying a sort order or pressing Esc to bypass the option. Press Esc. The screen that follows lets you specify searching criteria, as shown in Figure 5.1.

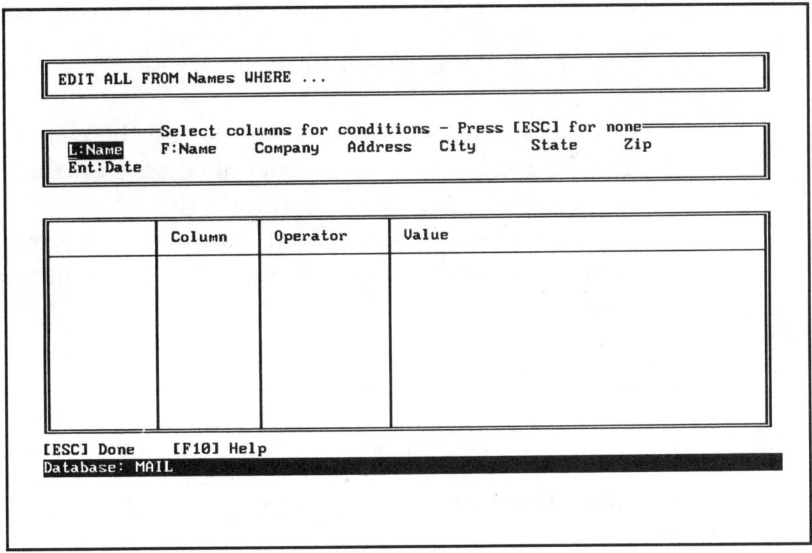

Figure 5.1: A screen for specifying search criteria

In this case we want to limit the display to individuals with the last name Miller. Therefore, select L:Name as the column to search on. The screen displays several operators for performing the search, as follows:

EQ NE GT GE LT LE EXISTS FAILS BETWEEN
NOT BETWEEN IN NOT IN IS NULL IS NOT NULL
CONTAINS LIKE NOT LIKE

We'll discuss these options throughout the chapter, but for now select EQ (which stands for "equals"). The screen then instructs you to

Enter a comparison value:

R:BASE needs to know what L:Name should equal for the search. In this case, we're looking up Miller, so type in **Miller** and press the Enter key.

Next, the screen displays the prompt

Choose an operator to combine conditions
– Choose (Done) when done.
AND OR AND NOT OR NOT (Done)

For now, select Done.

The command you've built appears on the screen, as follows:

EDIT ALL FROM Names WHERE L:Name EQ Miller

This command tells R:BASE to display all the columns from the Names table on the edit screen, but only those rows that have Miller in the L:Name column. When you select Execute to execute the command, the Millers appear on the edit screen as in Figure 5.2. You can make any changes that you wish or press Esc to return to the *Modify data* menu.

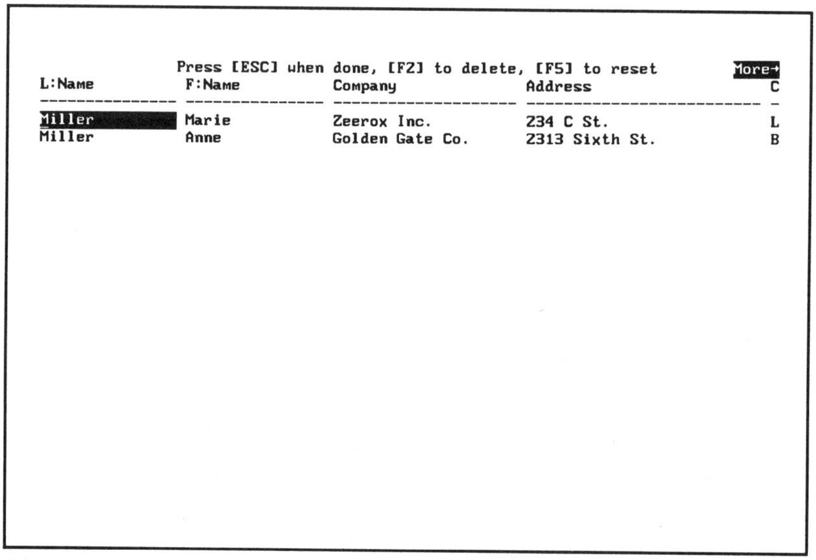

```
                  Press [ESC] when done, [F2] to delete, [F5] to reset      More→
L:Name            F:Name          Company              Address                 C
---------------   --------------- -------------------- ----------------------- -
Miller            Marie           Zeerox Inc.          234 C St.               L
Miller            Anne            Golden Gate Co.      2313 Sixth St.          B
```

Figure 5.2: The Millers ready for editing

Let's look at another example using multiple search criteria. Suppose that this table had 10,000 names on it, and of those about 100 had the last name Miller. If you wanted to look up Anne Miller's address, specifying Miller for the search would still leave you with 100 names to search through. To make this search easier, you could search for rows with the last name Miller and the first name Anne. Let's work though an example.

Press Esc twice to return to the PBE Main menu, and select *Query a database*. Choose *Look at data,* then the SELECT option, the Names table, and All columns. You can specify a sort column or press Esc to bypass the option. When the search criterion screen appears, select L:Name to search on the Last Name column, select EQ for "equals," and type in **Miller** (followed by a press on the Enter key) to specify Miller as the comparison value (the last name to look for).

When the prompt

> Choose an operator to combine conditions
> – Choose (Done) when done.

appears, select the AND option. Then select F:Name as the second column to search on and EQ as the operator, and enter **Anne** as the comparison value (and press Enter). Your screen will look like Figure 5.3.

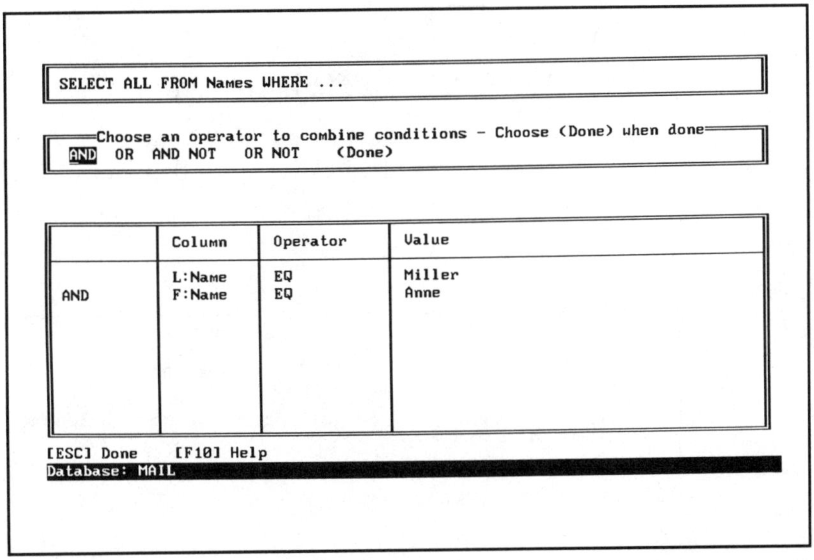

```
SELECT ALL FROM Names WHERE ...

Choose an operator to combine conditions - Choose (Done) when done
AND  OR  AND NOT  OR NOT  (Done)
```

	Column	Operator	Value
	L:Name	EQ	Miller
AND	F:Name	EQ	Anne

```
[ESC] Done   [F10] Help
Database: MAIL
```

Figure 5.3: A search for Anne Miller

Select (Done) to finish entering the search criteria. The new command that you've just created will appear on your screen as follows:

```
SELECT ALL FROM Names WHERE L:Name EQ Miller AND +
+ > F:Name EQ Anne
```

This command tells R:BASE to display all the columns from the Names table that have Miller in the L:Name column and Anne in the

F:Name column. When you select Execute to execute the command, R:BASE displays the one row in the table that meets these search criteria, as in Figure 5.4. Press any key when you are finished viewing the data.

SEARCHING FROM THE R> PROMPT

As we continue our discussion of searching techniques, we'll start presenting commands as they would be entered at the R> prompt. You can type them in as displayed, or use PBE mode to build them. By now, you should be able to build a SELECT or EDIT command using the prompt mode. Press the Esc key three times to leave PBE and get to the R> prompt.

SPECIFYING COLUMN WIDTHS

Before we go any further, let's take advantage of R:BASE's Help function to examine the SELECT command in more detail. If you type

HELP SELECT

```
SELECT ALL FROM Names WHERE L:Name EQ Miller AND F:Name EQ Anne
 L:Name          F:Name          Company              Address
 --------------- --------------- -------------------- -------------------------
 Miller          Anne            Golden Gate Co.      2313 Sixth St.
Press any key to continue_
```

Figure 5.4: Anne Miller displayed on the screen

at the R> prompt, you'll see a screen with a general discussion of the SELECT command. The second screen shows the SELECT command's syntax, as in Figure 5.5.

Although the syntax diagram looks fairly complicated, most uses of SELECT will involve straightforward syntax, in the form

SELECT ALL FROM *table name*

(remember that the asterisk can be used in lieu of the word ALL). Since we're using the Names table, type

SELECT ALL FROM Names

Your output should look similar to Figure 5.4, except that you'll see all six rows.

The problem with this display is that we only see the first four columns. Furthermore, unlike EDIT, SELECT doesn't allow us to scroll back and forth through the columns. In the last section, we built commands that displayed only *some* of the columns; that's one way to deal with the problem of not being able to see the desired data. However, there's another option that can be very useful.

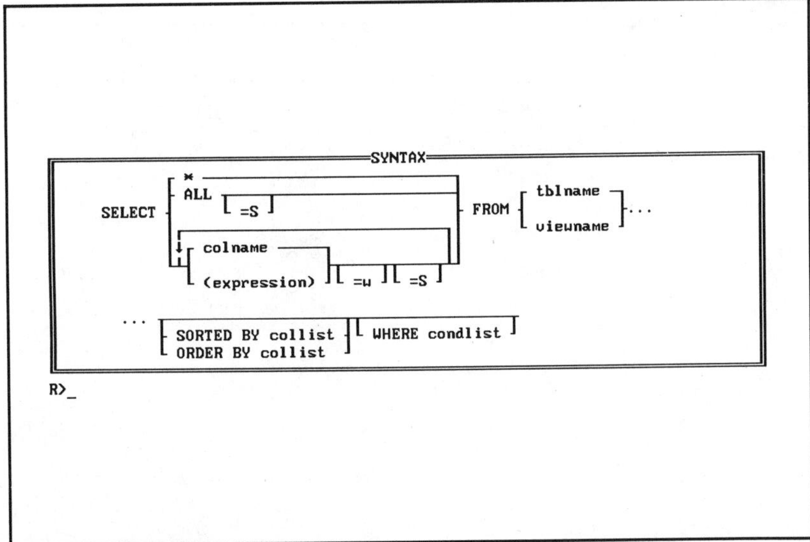

Figure 5.5: R:BASE's Help screen for the SELECT command

Take another look at the syntax diagram in Figure 5.5, and note the =w option to the right of *colname*. If you tell R:BASE which columns to display using *collist*, you can also specify the width of the individual screen fields in which the columns are displayed. For example, you could enter

```
SELECT Ent:Date F:Name=10 L:Name=10 Company=10 +
+> Address=15 City=10 State FROM Names
```

in order to display more data on one screen. Note that R:BASE doesn't simply truncate the data to fit your specifications; any data that runs over the specified width is wrapped around, as in Figure 5.6.

In case you're curious about the =S option, it stands for Sum, and you'll learn more about it in the next chapter!

THE WHERE CLAUSE

You've probably noticed that several searches you've performed included the new keyword WHERE, followed by the search condition; for example:

```
WHERE L:Name EQ Miller AND F:Name EQ Anne
```

```
R>SELECT Ent:Date F:Name=10 L:Name=10 Company=10 Address=15 City=10 State FRO+
+>M Names
 Ent:Date F:Name     L:Name     Company    Address         City       State
 -------- ---------- ---------- ---------- --------------- ---------- --------
 06/01/88 Sandy      Smith      Hi Tech,   456 N. Rainbow  Berkeley   CA
                                Inc.       Dr.
 06/15/88 Mindy      Jones      ABC Co.    123 A St.       San Diego  CA
 06/01/88 Marie      Miller     Zerox,     234 C St.       Los        CA
                                Inc.                       Angeles
 06/15/88 Bart       Adams      DataSpec   P.O. Box 2890   Malibu     CA
                                Inc.
 06/01/88 Anne       Miller     Golden     2313 Sixth St.  Berkeley   CA
                                Gate Co.
 06/15/88 Robin      Baker      Peach      2311 Coast      San Diego  CA
                                Computers  Hwy.
R>_
```

Figure 5.6: Specifying the width of column displays

For the rest of this chapter, we'll discuss numerous searching techniques that you can use with the WHERE clause.

The WHERE clause can be used with both the SELECT and EDIT commands, as well as with several other commands that we'll discuss later. In its simplest form, the WHERE clause contains a column name, the equal sign (=) or EQ symbol, and the search value.

For example, suppose you want to display all the Millers in the Names table. First, be sure that the Mail database is open and that the R> prompt is displayed. From the R> prompt, enter the command

```
SELECT ALL FROM Names WHERE L:Name = Miller
```

Then press the Enter key. This would display all the Millers on the table, as shown in Figure 5.7.

The function of the EQ symbol is identical to that of the equal sign, so the following command would perform exactly the same task:

```
SELECT ALL FROM Names WHERE L:Name EQ Miller
```

The one difference is that when you use the mathematical symbol instead of the alphabetical equivalent, you don't have to put spaces around it.

```
R>SELECT ALL FROM Names WHERE L:Name = Miller
 L:Name          F:Name          Company              Address
 --------------- --------------- -------------------- ------------------------
 Miller          Marie           Zeerox Inc.          234 C St.
 Miller          Anne            Golden Gate Co.      2313 Sixth St.
R>_
```

Figure 5.7: The Millers displayed from the Names table

You can, as usual, specify that only certain columns be displayed. For example, to see the dates and names of people whose entry dates are June 1, 1988, enter the command

```
SELECT Ent:Date L:Name F:Name FROM Names WHERE +
+ > Ent:Date = 6/1/88
```

The display will appear as shown in Figure 5.8.

You can still specify sort orders by using the ORDER BY or SORTED BY clause either before or after the WHERE clause. For example, to display Berkeley residents in alphabetical order by name, you would enter the command either as

```
SELECT City L:Name F:Name Company FROM Names +
+ > ORDER BY L:Name F:Name WHERE City = Berkeley
```

or as

```
SELECT City L:Name F:Name Company FROM Names +
+ > WHERE City = Berkeley ORDER BY L:Name F:Name
```

```
R>SELECT Ent:Date L:Name F:Name FROM Names WHERE +
+>Ent:Date = 6/1/88
 Ent:Date L:Name          F:Name
 -------- --------------- ---------------
 06/01/88 Smith           Sandy
 06/01/88 Miller          Marie
 06/01/88 Miller          Anne
R>_
```

Figure 5.8: Names data displayed for 06/01/88

The screen will display Berkeley residents in alphabetical order by name, as Figure 5.9 shows.

With the addition of some *logical operators,* your searching capabilities are greatly expanded.

USING WHERE CLAUSE OPERATORS

Table 5.1 shows several *operators* that can be used with the WHERE clause. Note that the *operator* and *symbol* can be used interchangeably. For example, LE is equivalent to < = .

Suppose that you wanted a listing of all the individuals whose last names begin with the letters A through M. You could enter the command

```
SELECT ALL FROM Names WHERE L:Name < N
```

This would produce the display shown in Figure 5.10.

To display individuals with names beginning with the letters N through Z, you could use the command

```
SELECT ALL FROM Names WHERE L:Name > M
```

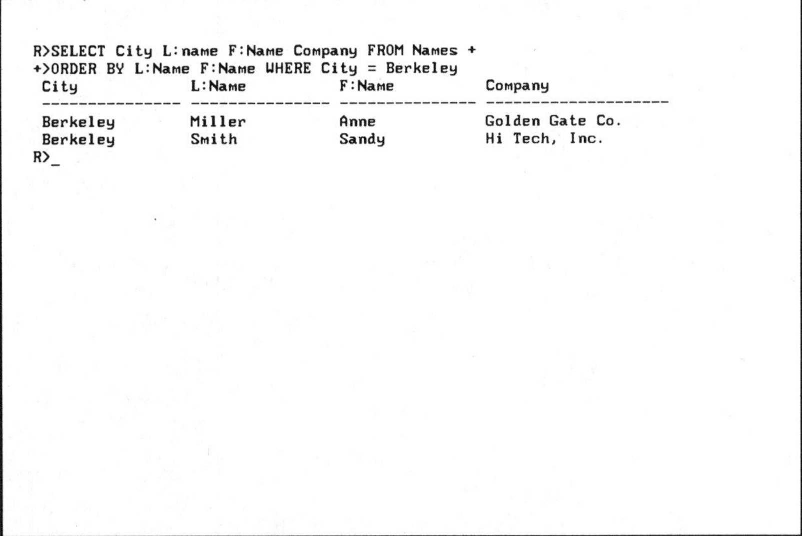

```
R>SELECT City L:name F:Name Company FROM Names +
+>ORDER BY L:Name F:Name WHERE City = Berkeley
 City            L:Name          F:Name          Company
 --------------- --------------- --------------- --------------------
 Berkeley        Miller          Anne            Golden Gate Co.
 Berkeley        Smith           Sandy           Hi Tech, Inc.
R>_
```

Figure 5.9: Berkeley residents displayed in alphabetical order

Table 5.1: WHERE Clause Operators

OPERATOR	SYMBOL	DEFINITION
EQ	=	Equals
NE	<>	Not equal to
GT	>	Greater than
GE	>=	Greater than or equal to
LT	<	Less than
LE	<=	Less than or equal to
CONTAINS "*string*"		Includes a specific string of characters
EXISTS		Column contains data
FAILS		Column doesn't contain data
BETWEEN *value1* AND *value2*		Greater than or equal to *value1* and less than or equal to *value2*
NOT BETWEEN *value1* AND *value2*		Less than *value1* or greater than *value2*
LIKE "*string*"		Column equals "string"
NOT LIKE "*string*"		Column does not equal "string"
IN (*valuelist* or SELECT *clause*)		Value of column exists in selected rows. When used with another SELECT, referred to as a *subselect.*
NOT IN (*valuelist* or SELECT *clause*)		Value of column does not exist in selected rows (like an extended NE)
IS NULL		Value of column is null (doesn't contain data). Same as FAILS.
IS NOT NULL		Value of column contains data. Same as EXISTS.

```
R>SELECT ALL FROM Names WHERE L:Name < N
 L:Name          F:Name          Company              Address
 --------------- --------------- -------------------- -------------------------
 Jones           Mindy           ABC Co.              123 A St.
 Miller          Marie           Zeerox Inc.          234 C St.
 Adams           Bart            DataSpec Inc.        P.O. Box 2890
 Miller          Anne            Golden Gate Co.      2313 Sixth St.
 Baker           Robin           Peach Computers      2311 Coast Hwy
R>_
```

Figure 5.10: Individuals with last names beginning with A through M

Suppose you wanted to display everyone *except* Berkeley residents on your tables. You could use the not-equal operator, as below:

```
SELECT ALL FROM Names WHERE City < > Berkeley
```

To display these same individuals in alphabetical order and show the city on the screen, you could use the command

```
SELECT L:Name F:Name City FROM Names ORDER BY +
+ > L:Name F:Name WHERE City NE Berkeley
```

This would produce the display shown in Figure 5.11.

Most of the WHERE clause operators listed in Table 5.1 work with any type of data. The CONTAINS, LIKE, and NOT LIKE operators are exceptions, working only with TEXT and NOTE fields. For example, to display people whose entry dates are later than June 1, 1988, you could use the command

```
SELECT Ent:Date L:Name F:Name FROM Names WHERE +
+ > Ent:Date > 6/1/88
```

```
R>SELECT L:Name F:Name City FROM Names ORDER BY +
+>L:Name F:Name WHERE City <> Berkeley
 L:Name          F:Name          City
 --------------- --------------- ---------------
 Adams           Bart            Malibu
 Baker           Robin           San Diego
 Jones           Mindy           San Diego
 Miller          Marie           Los Angeles
R>_
```

Figure 5.11: An alphabetical listing excluding Berkeley residents

Suppose you wanted to pull out only those people in the 92111 ZIP-code area. Furthermore, you wanted them displayed alphabetically by last and first names. You could use the command

```
SELECT Zip L:Name F:Name City FROM Names +
+ > WHERE Zip = 92111
```

If you wanted to send something to all the people in the ZIP-code range 92000 to 99999, you could filter out the appropriate data using this command:

```
SELECT ALL FROM Names WHERE Zip BETWEEN 92000 +
+ > AND 99999
```

EMBEDDED SEARCHES

Here's a tricky one for you. Suppose you want to list everyone in the Names table with an address on Rainbow Drive. If you enter the command

```
SELECT ALL FROM Names WHERE Address = Rainbow
```

or

```
SELECT ALL FROM Names WHERE Address LIKE Rainbow
```

R:BASE displays the following message:

```
– WARNING – No rows satisfy the WHERE clause
```

indicating that nobody's address equals "Rainbow." But we know that at least one row contains an address on Rainbow. Even so, R:BASE is correct—the address 456 N. Rainbow Dr. does not *equal* Rainbow. However, that address *contains* the word Rainbow. In this example, we need to use the CONTAINS operator, as follows:

```
SELECT ALL FROM Names WHERE Address +
+ > CONTAINS Rainbow
```

This command displays the data we want, as shown in Figure 5.12.

The CONTAINS operator can only be used with TEXT and NOTE columns, which means that you cannot use a WHERE clause like

```
WHERE Ent:Date CONTAINS 88
```

or

```
WHERE Ent:Date CONTAINS 6/
```

because Ent:Date is a Date data type. However, you can pull out *ranges* of data such as these using the BETWEEN or the AND and OR operators.

Bear in mind, too, that you can use the wild-card operators, * and ?, to narrow down a search that uses CONTAIN, LIKE, or NOT LIKE. For example, a command such as

```
SELECT ALL FROM Names WHERE L:Name LIKE Sm?th
```

will find Smith, Smoth, Smeth, Smyth, and so on, but not Smythe.

CHECKING FOR THE PRESENCE OR ABSENCE OF DATA

Database users frequently need to verify that data exists in a given column. For example, you may want to be sure every person in the

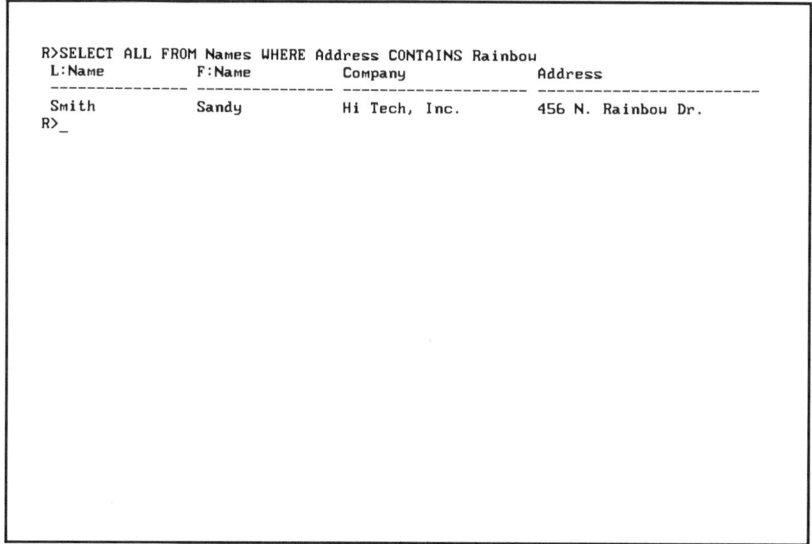

Figure 5.12: Rainbow Drive residents displayed on the screen

Names table has a last name before you use the names for mailing labels. One way of doing this, as you discovered in Chapter 2, is to establish a rule that forces data entry into a given field.

Another approach is to use the SELECT command with the operators EXISTS (or IS NOT NULL) or FAILS (or IS NULL). *Null* is a term used in the database world to indicate an absence of data. In R:BASE, it is usually represented by the -0- symbol. Let's say that you're concerned that some of the records in the Names table don't have ZIP codes. A fast way to check this would be to type

```
SELECT L:Name F:Name Zip FROM Names WHERE Zip FAILS
```

or

```
SELECT L:Name F:Name Zip FROM Names WHERE Zip IS +
+ > NULL
```

R:BASE should respond with a message telling you that none of the rows in the Names table satisfy the WHERE clause. Why? Because all your records have ZIP codes.

The EXISTS or IS NOT NULL operator is often used to locate data with a certain value quickly. For example, imagine that the

Names table has a column called VIP that contained either a Y or nothing. You could quickly find VIPs by giving a command such as

```
SELECT ALL FROM Names WHERE VIP EXISTS
```

LOCATING ROWS BY POSITION

R:BASE provides three additional WHERE clause operators that help you locate data by row position. Although row position is generally insignificant in a relational database, using the COUNT and LIMIT operators can sometimes be handy (see Table 5.2).

For example, if you are interrupted during data entry and want to see where you left off, you can type

```
SELECT ALL FROM Names WHERE COUNT EQ LAST
```

If you only want to see the first three records in the Names table, you can type

```
SELECT ALL FROM Names WHERE LIMIT = 3
```

If you only want to see the last three records, you can enter

```
SELECT ALL FROM Names WHERE COUNT > 3
```

HELP FOR YOUR SPELLING

An undocumented feature of R:BASE is the SOUNDS operator. If you're not sure of the spelling of a data item, you can use this operator.

Table 5.2: WHERE Clause Operators Used to Locate Rows by Position

OPERATOR	EFFECT
COUNT *operator n*	Finds row(s) starting with *n*, where *operator* can be =, <>, <, <=, >, >=, EQ, NE, LT, LE, GT, or GE
COUNT EQ LAST	Finds the last row
LIMIT EQ *n*	Displays the first *n* rows only

For example, suppose you want to find someone whose name you think is Mary, but might be Mari, Marie, or something similar. You can type

```
SELECT ALL FROM Names WHERE F:Name SOUNDS Mary
```

R:BASE would respond with the record for Marie Miller.

Another way to approach the problem would be to use the IN operator. IN can be followed either by another SELECT to find matches within a subset of your table, or by a list of possible matches. For example, if you aren't sure whether someone's first name is Mary, Marie, or Marianne, you could enter

```
SELECT ALL FROM Names WHERE F:Name IN (Mary, Marie,
Marianne)
```

AND *AND* OR *OPERATORS*

You can specify multiple criteria in a WHERE clause by using the AND and OR operators. AND and OR belong to a larger group, sometimes called *logical* or *Boolean* operators, that also includes AND NOT, OR NOT, and some other terms not used in R:BASE. For an example of their operation, suppose you wanted a listing of Berkeley residents whose entry dates are on June 1, 1988. The command below would display them for you:

```
SELECT ALL FROM Names WHERE Ent:Date = 6/1/88 +
+ > AND City = Berkeley
```

You might want a display with these same data listed in alphabetical order by last name, showing only the entry date, name, and address. You could enter the command

```
SELECT Ent:Date L:Name F:Name Address FROM Names +
+ > ORDER BY L:Name F:Name +
+ > WHERE Ent:Date = 6/1/88 AND City = Berkeley
```

Suppose you wanted a listing of everyone whose entry date is in the month of June; in other words, in the range of June 1 to June 30. The command below displays those rows:

```
SELECT ALL FROM Names WHERE Ent:Date > = 6/1/88 +
+ > AND Ent:Date < = 6/30/88
```

or

```
SELECT ALL FROM Names WHERE Ent:Date BETWEEN +
+ > 6/1/88 AND 6/30/88
```

To put that same display in chronological order and show only date, name, and company, you could use the following command:

```
SELECT Ent:Date L:Name F:Name Company FROM Names +
+ > ORDER BY Ent:Date WHERE Ent:Date > = 6/01/88+
+ > AND Ent:Date < = 6/30/88
```

Now, what if you want to send something to everyone who lives on the 2300 block, or higher, of Sixth Street. Piece of cake, right? The command is

```
SELECT ALL FROM Names WHERE Address > = 2300+
+ > AND Address CONTAINS Sixth
```

If you wanted to pull out all the people whose last names begin with the letters J through M, you could use this command:

```
SELECT ALL FROM Names WHERE L:Name > = J AND +
+ > L:Name < N
```

or

```
SELECT ALL FROM Names WHERE L:Name BETWEEN J +
+ > AND M
```

The AND operator is good for locating specific information to edit. For example, suppose you need to change Marie Miller's address. You could enter the command

```
EDIT ALL FROM Names WHERE L:Name = Miller AND +
+ > F:Name = Marie
```

This would display Marie's data on the edit screen, as shown in Figure 5.13.

Suppose you wanted to send something to both San Diego and Los Angeles residents. You could use the OR operator to perform both searches at once, as in the command below:

```
SELECT ALL FROM Names WHERE City = San Diego OR +
+ > City = Los Angeles
```

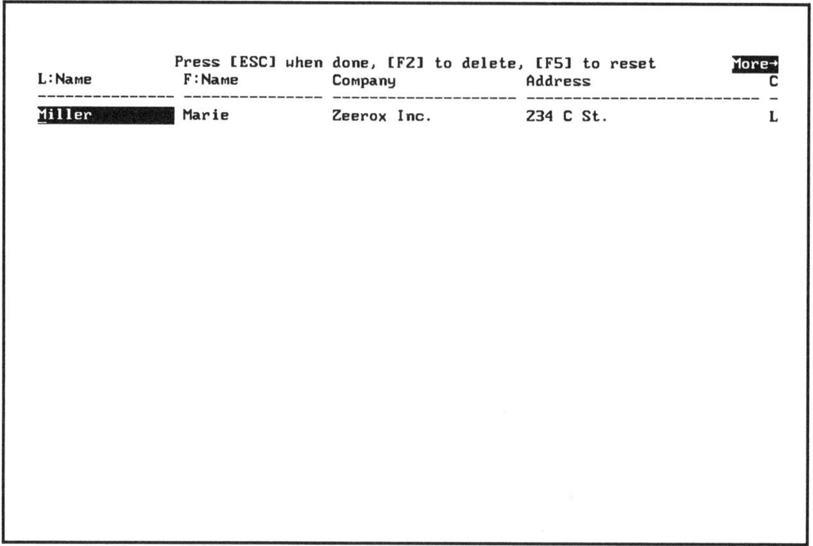

Figure 5.13: The Edit screen limited to Marie Miller

Sometimes you have to think a little before performing a search. For example, had we used the command

```
SELECT ALL FROM Names WHERE City = San Diego +
+> AND City = Los Angeles
```

no rows would have been displayed, because it's impossible for a row to have both San Diego and Los Angeles in the City column at the same time.

Reversing the situation, the command

```
SELECT ALL FROM Names WHERE City = San Diego +
+> AND State = CA
```

will display all San Diego, California, residents. However, the command

```
SELECT ALL FROM Names WHERE City = San Diego OR +
+> State = CA
```

will display *all* California residents, regardless of city, and *all* San Diego residents, regardless of state (which is probably not what you had in mind).

With the OR operator, only one of the searching criteria needs to be true for the command to display the data. Hence, the OR operator generally broadens the result of the search. The AND operator, however, requires that both criteria be met, which generally narrows the result of the search.

A common mistake that people make when performing AND and OR searches is attempting to use English syntax rather than R:BASE syntax. For example, a common mistake is to use a command like

```
SELECT ALL FROM Names WHERE Zip >= 92000 AND +
+> <= 92999
```

Reading that in English, it looks like you're trying to pull out all the ZIP codes between 92000 and 92999. However, that's not what it says to R:BASE. In R:BASE syntax, both criteria must be *complete* expressions. *Zip > = 92000* is a complete expression, but *< = 92999* is not. The computer will wonder what *< = 92999* means, and it will display an error message. To avoid problems, be sure to use complete expressions on both sides of the AND and OR operators.

In the last sentence, "*both* sides of the AND and OR operators" doesn't mean that you can only use a single AND or OR. You can specify as many conditions as you wish, as long as you don't exceed R:BASE's command line limit: 5000 characters, a total of 402 items, or a total of 50 operators and operands! (An *operand* is a column or value acted on by an operator—the items to the left and right of an operator.) For example, the command

```
SELECT ALL FROM Names WHERE City = "San Diego" +
+> AND State = CA AND Ent:Date >= 06/01/88 AND +
+> Ent:Date <= 06/30/88 AND L:Name >= G AND +
+> L:Name <= P
```

is perfectly okay. You'll get San Diego, California, residents with entry dates in June whose last names begin with the letters G through P.

Sometimes, combining AND and OR conditions in a single WHERE clause can produce unexpected results. Generally speaking, R:BASE interprets the conditions in a WHERE clause from left to right. For example, if you give the command

```
SELECT Zip L:Name F:Name FROM Names WHERE +
+ > Zip > 92000 AND L:Name > = M OR F:Name > = M
```

hoping to display all records in which the ZIP code is greater than 92000 *and* either the first or last name starts with the letter M or higher, you'll be disappointed. What you'll get are all instances where both the ZIP is greater than 92000 and the last name starts with M or higher, and then all other records in which the first name starts with M or higher, regardless of what the ZIP code is. In other words, R:BASE has interpreted the WHERE clause as follows:

[Zip > 92000 AND L:Name > = M] OR [F:Name > = M]

[Both of these are true] or [this is true]

Had you entered this command as

```
SELECT Zip L:Name F:Name FROM Names WHERE +
+ > L:Name > = M OR F:Name > = M AND Zip > 92000
```

R:BASE would have displayed all the individuals whose first or last names begin with the letter M or greater, and who furthermore live in areas with ZIP codes greater than 92000. In other words, R:BASE interpreted the WHERE clause as follows:

[L:Name > = M OR F:Name > = M] AND [Zip > 92000]

[either of these is true] and [this is true also]

USING PARENTHESES IN WHERE CLAUSES

Alternatively, you could have grouped your search criteria using parentheses. This feature distinguishes R:BASE for DOS and

R:BASE for OS/2 from earlier versions of R:BASE. For example, you could have entered

```
SELECT Zip L:Name F:Name FROM Names WHERE +
+> Zip > 92000 > AND (L:Name >= M OR +
+> F:Name >= M)
```

R:BASE would then interpret the WHERE clause as follows:

[Zip > 92000] AND [L:Name > = M OR F:Name > = M]

[this must be true] and [either of these is true]

It may take you a few trial-and-error runs to get these more complex searches down. Be sure to check the results of a search visually if you are in doubt about the accuracy of your WHERE clause.

DISTINCTIONS BETWEEN UPPER- AND LOWERCASE LETTERS

R:BASE normally makes no distinction between uppercase and lowercase letters when searching a table. For example, the command

```
SELECT ALL FROM Names WHERE L:Name = miller
```

will produce exactly the same results as the command

```
SELECT ALL FROM Names WHERE L:Name = MILLER
```

If you would rather that R:BASE was *case sensitive* (that is, would take into account uppercase and lowercase distinctions), you can enter the command

```
SET CASE ON
```

at the R> prompt. With the CASE option on, the command

```
SELECT ALL FROM Names WHERE L:Name = MILLER
```

would not display any data from the Names table, because all the last names were entered with only the initial letter capitalized.

To return to "normal" searches, in which R:BASE ignores uppercase and lowercase distinctions, enter the command

```
SET CASE OFF
```

at the R> prompt.

You can check the current status of the CASE option from the R> prompt at any time by entering the command

```
SHOW
```

You'll see the current status of many other settings as well, which we'll discuss throughout the book.

COMPARING COLUMNS IN SEARCHES

You can also compare the contents of two columns to perform a search. For example, suppose you had a table that contained Gross Sales and Salary columns for salespeople. You might want to display all those individuals whose salaries are greater than their gross sales.

When comparing two columns in a search, you need to use the expanded alphabetical form of the operator or follow the mathematical operator symbol with the letter A. Table 5.3 shows the operators used for comparing columns in a table.

Table 5.3: WHERE Clause Operators for Comparing Two Columns

OPERATOR	SYMBOL	DEFINITION
EQA	=A	Equal
NEA	<>A	Not equal
GTA	>A	Greater than
GEA	≥A	Greater than or equal to
LTA	<A	Less than
LEA	≤A	Less than or equal to

In our hypothetical Sales table, you could find all the individuals whose salaries were less than their gross sales using the command

```
SELECT ALL FROM Sales WHERE Salary LEA G:Sales
```

To see how this works, we can compare the contents of the F:Name and L:Name columns in our sample Names table. The command

```
SELECT ALL FROM Names WHERE F:Name GEA L:Name
```

will display all the individuals whose first names are alphabetically greater than or equal to their last names. The command

```
SELECT ALL FROM Names WHERE F:Name LEA L:Name
```

will display those whose first names are alphabetically less than or equal to their last names.

Although these examples aren't particularly useful, comparing columns containing numeric, date, or time data can be very useful.

For example, suppose you had a Credit table which contained the columns Climit and Currbal. You could find out which accounts had exceeded their credit limits by typing

```
SELECT ALL FROM Credit WHERE Climit LTA Currbal
```

Or perhaps you have a Rentals table with columns for Duedate and Retndate. To find those items that were returned after they were due, you could type

```
SELECT ALL FROM Rentals WHERE Rtndate >A Duedate
```

GLOBAL EDITS WITH THE WHERE CLAUSE

We've already learned how to use the WHERE clause to limit the amount of data displayed on the screen during the edits. The WHERE clause can also be used with the CHANGE and DELETE commands to perform *global edits*.

A global edit is one that is performed throughout the entire table (or database) with a single command. For example, suppose you have 5000 entries in the Names table. Eventually, you learn that in some cases the city Los Angeles is stored as L.A. and in other cases it is spelled out. This little inconsistency is causing you problems because you always need to include two options, such as

```
WHERE City = Los Angeles OR City = L.A.
```

in your WHERE clauses. The solution to this problem is to make them consistent.

You could go into the edit mode and change each L.A. to Los Angeles by retyping them. Or you could perform a global edit to change all of them to Los Angeles with a single command. Obviously, the latter is more convenient.

The CHANGE command allows you to perform just this sort of global edit. The general syntax for the CHANGE command can be seen by typing

```
HELP SCREEN
```

at the R> prompt. The resulting syntax is shown in Figure 5.14. To access the CHANGE command from the PBE Main Menu, select Modify data, and then select the CHANGE option from the submenu.

So, in a hypothetical table named MaiList, you might try to change each L.A. to Los Angeles by entering the command

```
CHANGE City TO Los Angeles IN MaiList WHERE City = L.A.
```

You'd probably be surprised when R:BASE displayed an error message informing you that the column *Angeles* wasn't in the Names table.

The problem here is that R:BASE is getting confused by the embedded blank in *Los Angeles*. You have to remember that spaces act as separators in R:BASE. To avoid confusion, it's safe to use quotation marks around strings, not only with the CHANGE command, but also with other R:BASE commands. To remedy the problem with the last command, all you would have to do would be to type

```
CHANGE City TO "Los Angeles" IN MaiList WHERE City = L.A.
```

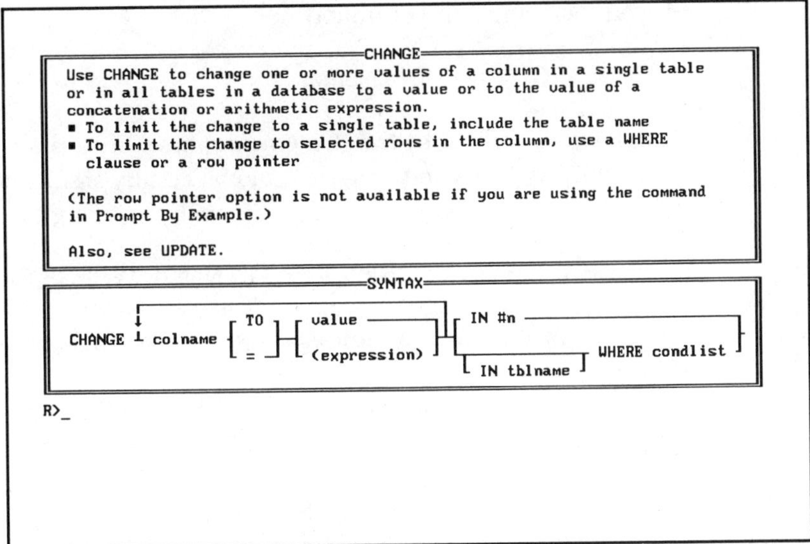

Figure 5.14: The Help screen for the CHANGE command

You must be careful when using this command, though. It has a high "whoops" factor, which means that by the time you finish saying "whoops," the damage is done. For example, suppose you had entered the command

CHANGE City TO "Los Angeles" IN MaiList WHERE CITY > = L

The > = operator in this WHERE clause tells R:BASE to put Los Angeles in the City column of every row in the table that contains a city starting with the letters L through Z. If there were originally 500 cities that met this criterion, there are now 500 Los Angeles cities in their place, whether they were originally Las Vegas, Madrid, or Seattle. The bad news is that you cannot reverse this command. You'd have to reenter all the cities through the edit mode. So be careful!

For practice, you can safely try it out on the Names table. From the R> prompt, enter the command

CHANGE City TO S.D. IN Names WHERE City = "San Diego"

R:BASE will display this message:

The value for City in NAMES has been changed in 2 row(s)

If you then enter the command

```
SELECT City FROM Names
```

you'll see that all of the San Diego cities have been changed to S.D.

In this case, we can reverse the global edit by simply changing all S.D. data back to San Diego. Do so now by entering the command

```
CHANGE City TO "San Diego" IN Names WHERE City = S.D.
```

If you view the City column again, you'll see that the name "San Diego" has returned.

R:BASE includes another command, UPDATE, that can be used in lieu of CHANGE. You could have accomplished the same result by typing

```
UPDATE Names SET City = "San Diego" WHERE City = S.D.
```

Why does R:BASE have two commands that do the same thing? It's because UPDATE is a SQL (Structured Query Language) command. It is included in support of the SQL standard, which will eventually allow you to transfer your applications and databases between many different systems.

You can also change several columns with one CHANGE or UPDATE command if you need to. For example, let's say that the Names table consists mainly of people who live in Los Angeles. To ease the burden of data entry, you have entered LA instead of Los Angeles and have left the State column blank (by pressing Enter when prompted for the State). However, you want to use the data to print mailing labels, and need to have complete data. Although you could use two separate CHANGE or UPDATE commands, a single one will suffice:

```
CHANGE City TO "Los Angeles" State TO CA IN Names +
+> WHERE City = LA AND State FAILS
```

or

```
UPDATE Names SET City = "Los Angeles" State = CA IN +
+> Names WHERE City = LA and State FAILS
```

Also remember that you can use column numbers instead of column names in R:BASE commands, as in

```
CHANGE #5 TO "Los Angeles" #6 TO CA IN Names +
+ > WHERE #5 = > LA AND #6 FAILS
```

R:BASE would change both columns in any row that met the criteria specified by the WHERE clause—no matter which of the three versions of the command you used.

You can also globally delete rows from a table, but we won't try this with the Names table—we need those data for future experiments. The general syntax for global deletions is the following:

```
DELETE ROWS FROM table name WHERE condition(s)
```

(To access the DELETE ROWS command from the PBE menu, select the *Modify data* option, and then select the DELETE and ROWS commands from the submenus.)

Referring back to our hypothetical Sales table, which contains salespersons' salaries and gross sales, you could use the command

```
DELETE Rows FROM Sales WHERE Salary GTA G:Sales
```

which would instantly eliminate all those whose salaries were greater than their gross sales. Assuming that five people met this unfortunate criterion (and fate), R:BASE would display the message

```
5 row(s) have been deleted from SALES
```

If you ever wanted to delete all the rows from the Names table that did not contain either a last name or company value, you could use the command

```
DELETE Rows FROM Names WHERE L:Name FAILS AND +
+ > Company FAILS
```

(Remember! R:BASE actually puts the symbol -0- in empty columns, rather than leaving them blank. The -0- symbol is referred to as the *null value.*)

SQL IMPLEMENTATIONS OF SELECT

R:BASE for DOS and R:BASE for OS/2 include two special SQL implementations of the SELECT command. One allows you to filter out repetitious data; the other is particularly useful in performing statistical calculations for groups of selected columns.

Let's look at the SELECT DISTINCT command first. Its syntax is illustrated in Figure 5.15.

As the Help screen indicates, this command is useful when you do not want to see duplicates. Perhaps, in the sample Sales table referred to earlier, you wanted to see which salespeople had made sales within the last three days. Assuming the Sales table had columns called Emp# (for Employee number), Transamt (for transaction amount), and Trandate (for transaction date), you could type

```
SELECT Emp# FROM Sales ORDER BY Emp# WHERE +
+ > Trandate BETWEEN 6/1/88 AND > 6/3/88
```

using R:BASE's traditional SELECT command. However, you'd have to wade through multiple sales for some of the salespeople, making the visual display less than ideal.

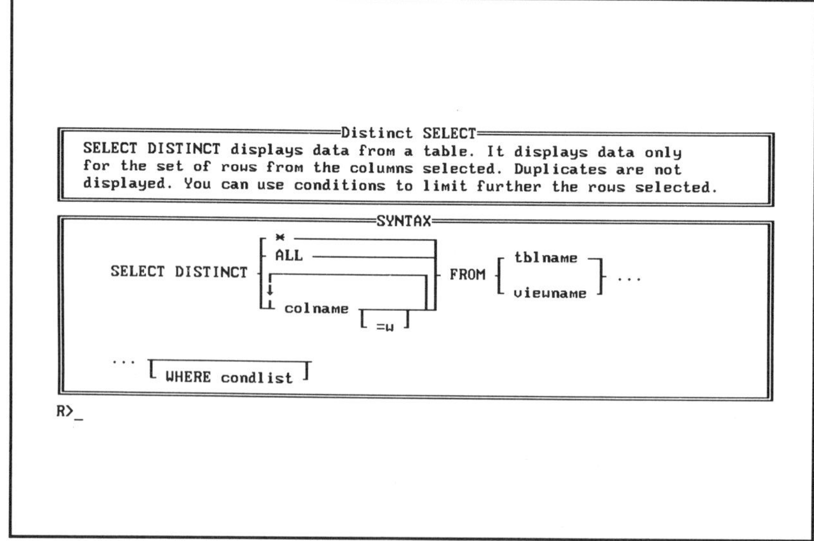

Figure 5.15: The syntax for the SELECT DISTINCT command

By using the SELECT DISTINCT command, you would only have to type

```
SELECT DISTINCT Emp# FROM Sales WHERE Trandate +
+ > BETWEEN 6/1/88 AND 6/3/88
```

You wouldn't have to include the ORDER BY clause, since SELECT DISTINCT automatically sorts for you. The arrow in the syntax diagram means that you can specify more than one column. For example, if you wanted to see if your sales force each had at least one sale per day, you could modify the above command to include Trandate:

```
SELECT DISTINCT Emp# Trandate FROM Sales WHERE +
+ > Trandate BETWEEN 6/1/88 AND 6/3/88
```

In order to see a simple implementation of the command with the Mail database, you could type

```
SELECT DISTINCT L:Name FROM Names
```

and see that Miller is only listed once.

The Group By SELECT command is extremely powerful when you need to perform statistical calculations on your data. Its syntax is displayed in Figure 5.16.

Looking at our hypothetical Sales table, there are some interesting uses of the Group By SELECT command. For example, suppose you wanted to see total sales by salesperson. You could type

```
SELECT Emp# SUM Transamt FROM Sales GROUP BY Emp#
```

The result would be a list of employees followed by their total sales. The Group By SELECT command, like the SELECT DISTINCT command, sorts automatically, but in this case based on the column or columns specified in the GROUP BY clause. The ability to generate ad hoc subtotals is a feature generally associated only with complex reports.

SELECT also comes into play—as a modifier—with SQL's GRANT and REVOKE commands. We'll talk more about GRANT and REVOKE in Chapter 10.

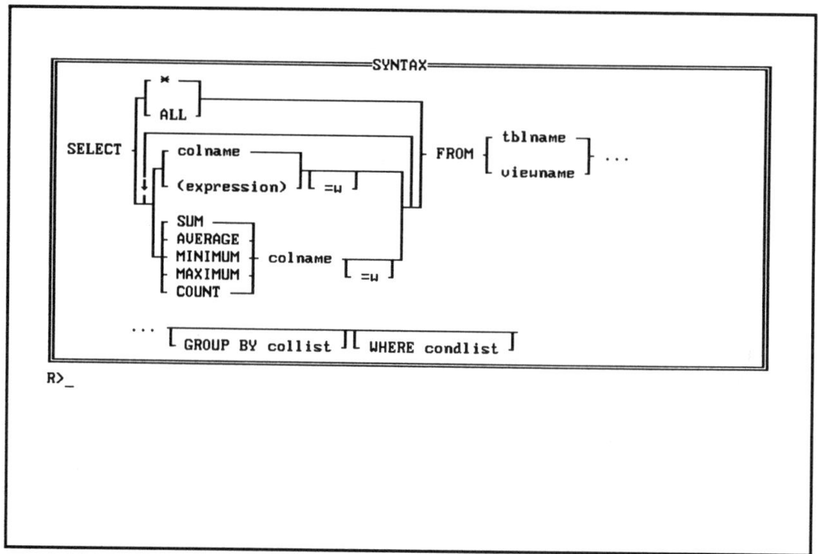

Figure 5.16: The syntax for the Group By SELECT command

In this chapter, we've discussed many techniques for specifying search criteria with the WHERE clause. Because we are working with our small Names table, we could not experiment with the full range of search options. If we had more columns on our sample table, we could do more filtering. For example, had we included a Title column (for Mr., Ms., and so forth), we could have searched for all the doctors by using a

```
WHERE Title = Dr.
```

clause. Or had we included a Job Title (J:Title) column, we could have pulled out all the company presidents and vice presidents by using a

```
WHERE J:title CONTAINS Pres
```

clause. In a Phone column, we could use a

```
WHERE Phone CONTAINS (415)
```

clause to pull out everyone in the 415 area code. There seem to be no limitations to the types of searches that you can perform.

In the next chapter, we'll discuss techniques for displaying information from an R:BASE table.

Chapter 6

Experimenting with Your Database Output

FAST TRACK

To direct output from R:BASE displays 124
to various destinations, use the OUTPUT command. Options are SCREEN, PRINTER, *d:filename.ext*, or any combination using the WITH and BOTH options.

To define various display characteristics 128
of the screen or printer, use the SET WIDTH, SET LINES, SET COLOR, SET DATE, and SET TIME commands. Use SET alone (or the SHOW command) to view your settings.

To define column widths, 130
use the SELECT command with the =w option, as in SELECT L:Name=5 FROM Names.

To clear the screen, 132
enter the CLS (clear screen or NEWPAGE command) at the R> prompt.

To run an external program from within R:BASE, 137
use the ZIP and ZIP ROLLOUT commands. The ZIP command runs an external program that doesn't need more than the currently available memory. ZIP ROLLOUT can be used to run larger programs. Both commands return you to R:BASE where you left off.

To calculate the sum of a specified column or columns, 140
use the SELECT command with the =S option. For example, SELECT ALL=S FROM *table name* will display sums of all numeric data.

To calculate the average, count, maximum, minimum, sum, standard deviation, or variance 140

for a given column, use the COMPUTE command and one of the operations shown in Figure 6.8. For example, COMPUTE COUNT Amount FROM CSales would indicate how many non-null sales entries were in the CSales table.

To find the number of occurrences of data items 142

in a given column, use the TALLY command. For example, TALLY Zip FROM Names would indicate how many records contained the same ZIP code.

To perform sophisticated cross tabulations 143

involving sets of unique pairs from two columns, use the CROSSTAB command.

Commands that work like their operating system counterparts 144

include DIR, CHDIR, MKDIR, RMDIR, COPY, ERASE, RENAME, TYPE, and CLS. A related command, CHDRV, allows you to change active drives. The CHKDSK, BACKUP, and RESTORE commands, while performing much like their operating system counterparts, are customized to work with R:BASE.

To back up your work, 146

use either COPY or BACKUP depending on the size of your database. Use COPY if your database file(s) can fit onto a single floppy disk. If not, use BACKUP.

IN THIS CHAPTER, WE'LL DISCUSS VARIOUS TECHniques for displaying R:BASE data, including printing out information on a printer and storing it in a separate file. You'll also discover how to control various display characteristics, such as column widths, page lengths, colors, and date and time formats. Then we'll change gears. You'll set up another small database that has some numeric information in it, allowing you to experiment with some of R:BASE's commands that help you to analyze that data. Finally, you'll take another look at R:BASE's operating system commands and learn how to back up your database.

To get started with the sample exercises in this chapter, run R:BASE in the usual fashion, and open the Mail database. Then press the Esc key to leave the Prompt menu. The R> prompt should appear on your screen.

DIRECTING THE OUTPUT

So far, we've displayed the results of all SELECT commands on the screen. The OUTPUT command allows you to print out these data on a printer or to save them in a separate file that you can print out later. Options for the OUTPUT command are the following:

OUTPUT SCREEN	Data are displayed on the screen.
OUTPUT PRINTER	Data are displayed on the printer.
OUTPUT *d:filename.ext*	Data are stored on a file. (*d:filename.ext* stands for any file name. The *d:* stands for a letter specifying a disk drive.)

The WITH clause allows you to combine OUTPUT options. For example, the OUTPUT SCREEN WITH PRINTER command displays data on both the screen and printer. The command

```
OUTPUT C:MyReport.txt WITH BOTH
```

stores a copy of the output on a file named MyReport.txt on drive C, and also displays the data on both the screen and printer.

OUTPUT TO THE PRINTER

If you have a printer handy, you can try the OUTPUT command from the R> prompt. To direct the display to both the screen and the printer, enter the command

```
OUTPUT SCREEN WITH PRINTER
```

Next, enter the command

```
SELECT ALL FROM Names ORDER BY L:Name F:Name
```

A copy of the first four columns (all that will fit) will appear on the screen and printed page. Later on, we'll describe how to format the columns so that they will all fit. For now, display the rest of the columns by entering the command

```
SELECT City State Zip Ent:Date FROM Names ORDER BY +
+> L:Name F:Name
```

The City, State, Zip, and Ent:Date columns are displayed on the screen and printer. To eject the printed page (and clear the screen), enter the command

```
NEWPAGE
```

The printed report is displayed on the printer, as shown in Figure 6.1.

To disconnect from the printer and return to the normal screen display, enter this command:

```
OUTPUT SCREEN
```

OUTPUT TO A FILE

You can direct displays to disk files rather than to the screen. This allows you to integrate the R:BASE display into an external word processor (such as WordStar) or to use a print spooler (such as the DOS PRINT.COM program), which is a program that allows you to use your computer at the same time a file is being printed. In this

L:Name	F:Name	Company	Address
Adams	Bart	DataSpec, Inc.	P.O. Box 2890
Baker	Robin	Peach Computers	2311 Coast Highway
Jones	Mindy	ABC Co.	123 A St.
Miller	Anne	Golden Gate Co.	2313 Sixth St.
Miller	Marie	Zeerox, Inc.	234 C St.
Smith	Sandy	Hi Tech, Inc.	456 Rainbow Dr.

City	State	Zip	Ent:Date
Malibu	CA	92111	06/15/88
San Diego	CA	92112	06/15/88
San Diego	CA	92122	06/15/88
Berkeley	CA	94711	06/01/88
Los Angeles	CA	91234	06/01/88
Berkeley	CA	94721	06/01/88

Figure 6.1: The Names table on the printed page

example, we'll store the display on a file named MyReport.txt. If you are using a hard-disk system, enter the command

```
OUTPUT MyReport.txt WITH SCREEN
```

Next, enter the command

```
SELECT ALL FROM Names
```

When the R> prompt reappears, return to the normal screen display by using the command

```
OUTPUT SCREEN
```

You can verify that the file exists by using the TYPE command at the R> prompt. Enter the command

```
TYPE MyReport.txt
```

You'll see the contents of the MyReport.txt file on the screen, as shown in Figure 6.2.

When naming these text files with the OUTPUT command, you can specify a directory and path name as well. For example, the command

```
OUTPUT C:\WP\MyReport.txt
```

stores the MyReport.txt file in the WP directory on drive C.

To access the OUTPUT command from PBE, select *Query a database* and then the Print data option. When asked to specify an output device, select Screen or Printer, or press Esc to enter a file name for the output. The prompts will also allow you to enter a second output device, or you can press Esc to use a single output device. However, if you use PBE to build a command now, R:BASE will warn you that no reports are available from which to choose. Use PBE to print only stored reports, and not just to redirect the OUTPUT for other commands.

```
R>TYPE MyReport.txt
 L:Name           F:Name           Company              Address
 ---------------  ---------------  -------------------- -------------------------
 Smith            Sandy            Hi Tech, Inc.        456 N. Rainbow Dr.
 Jones            Mindy            ABC Co.              123 A St.
 Miller           Marie            Zeerox, Inc.         234 C St.
 Adams            Bart             DataSpec Inc.        P.O. Box 2890
 Miller           Anne             Golden Gate Co.      2313 Sixth St.
 Baker            Robin            Peach Computers      2311 Coast Hwy.
R>_
```

Figure 6.2: The contents of the MyReport.txt file

CONTROLLING DISPLAY CHARACTERISTICS

You can control the length and width of screen displays, printed reports, and files using the SET WIDTH and SET LINES commands. You can also control the width of individual columns with the SELECT command by specifying widths with column names.

CONTROLLING PAGE LENGTH

When displaying large tables, R:BASE will pause after printing 20 lines of text in order to accommodate a typical screen display. If you are sending a SELECT command to the printer, you'll see a new *header line* (defining the columns being displayed) printed every 20 lines. You can change this setting using the SET LINES command. For example, the standard 8½-by-11-inch sheet of paper can hold 66 lines of text per page. The command

```
SET LINES 66
```

will change the page length to 66 lines. To return to the normal page length, enter the command

```
SET LINES 20
```

To set the page length from the PBE menu, select option 8, *R:BASE and operating system utilities,* and then the Environment option from the next menu. Then select the SET option and the *Keywords and characters* option from the subsequent menus. Press any key when so prompted, select Execute, and press the ↓ key eleven times to highlight the LINES per page option. Type in the new page length, and press the Enter and Esc keys when you are finished. To return to the PBE Main menu, press any key and then Esc.

CONTROLLING WIDTH

R:BASE normally displays as much data as will fit across 79 characters. You can change this to a maximum of 256 or a minimum of 40 characters using the SET WIDTH command. For example, if your printer uses wide paper, the command (entered at the R> prompt)

```
SET WIDTH 132
```

will take advantage of the full paper width. This command will also cause screen displays to wrap around the screen, as in Figure 6.3.

If you print data with compressed print (an option available on most dot matrix printers), the SET WIDTH command will allow you to use more columns on the printed page. In fact, you would have to put your printer into compressed print mode in order to take advantage of a command such as SET WIDTH 132 or SET WIDTH 240.

The SET WIDTH command will also affect displays stored on files. When you use the TYPE command, however, you may not see the columns that extend beyond the right edge of the screen. However, proceed as you did earlier by selecting R:BASE and operating system utilities from the PBE Main menu, then if you load the file into a word processor, the columns will be there.

```
R>SET WIDTH 132
R>SELECT ALL FROM Names
 L:Name          F:Name             Company               Address
City             State    Zip          Ent:Date
 --------------- ---------------   --------------------  -------------------------
--------------- -------- ---------- --------
 Smith            Sandy             Hi Tech, Inc.         456 N. Rainbow Dr.
Berkeley         CA       94721        06/01/88
 Jones            Mindy             ABC Co.               123 A St.
San Diego        CA       92122        06/15/88
 Miller           Marie             Zeerox, Inc.          234 C St.
Los Angeles      CA       91234        06/01/88
 Adams            Bart              DataSpec Inc.         P.O. Box 2890
Malibu           CA       92111        06/15/88
 Miller           Anne              Golden Gate Co.       2313 Sixth St.
Berkeley         CA       94711        06/01/88
 Baker            Robin             Peach Computers       2311 Coast Hwy.
San Diego        CA       92112        06/15/88
R>_
```

Figure 6.3: A screen display of the Names table with 132-character width

To set the page width from the PBE menu, Environment; then select the SET option and the Keywords and characters option from the submenus. Press any key, select Execute, and press the down arrow key 12 times to highlight the WIDTH per line option. Type in the new page width, and press the Enter and Esc keys when you are finished.

Some of you may be enamored with the screen you saw in the last paragraph, because it makes it easy to view and change all sorts of R:BASE default settings. Although you've discovered how to get at the settings screen via PBE, there's a shortcut. If you just type SET at the R> prompt, you'll see the same thing, as shown in Figure 6.4.

CONTROLLING COLUMN WIDTHS

To specify the widths of individual columns, use the SELECT command, followed by the column name, an equal sign (=), and the number of spaces that you want in the column. You may want to review the syntax diagram for the SELECT command by typing HELP SELECT at the R> prompt or by looking back at Figure 4.14. Note that =w and =S are optional qualifiers you can add to column names. The w stands

```
Type in the new character or value, press [ESC] when done

Characters      | User set values                       | Currency
                |                                       |
BLANK     █     | DATE format       MM/DD/YY            | SYMBOL      $
DELIMIT   ,     | DATE sequence     MMDDYY              | LOCATION    PREF
SEMI      ;     | TIME format       HH:MM:SS            | DIGITS         2
QUOTES    "     | TIME sequence     HHMMSS              | CONVENTION B
PLUS      +     | LINES per page      20                |
SINGLE    ?     | WIDTH per line      79                |
MANY      *     | TOLERANCE                    0.       |
                | NULL symbol       -0-                 |
                | Lock WAIT time        4               |

Toggle switches for the environment

<AUTOSKIP > OFF AUTOmatically SKIP to the next field when editing
<BELL     > ON  Sound the BELL on an error
<CASE     > OFF Distinguish between UPPER and lower CASE
<CLEAR    > ON  CLEAR data buffers after modifications
<ECHO     > OFF ECHO input from command files
<ERROR    > ON  Display ERROR messages during processing
<ESCAPE   > ON  ESCAPE allowed to abort processing
<HEADINGS > ON  Display column HEADINGS on SELECT and TALLY commands
```

Figure 6.4: Displaying and changing R:BASE's environment settings

for width, while the S stands for Sum (we'll discuss the =S qualifier in more detail later in this chapter). To see how adding the =w qualifier works, enter the following command:

```
SELECT L:Name = 9 F:Name = 9 Company = 10 Address = 12 +
+ > City = 12 State = 2 Zip = 5 Ent:Date = 8 FROM Names +
+ > SORTED BY L:Name F:Name
```

Note that R:BASE can fit all the columns onto an 80-column screen by using more vertical space, as shown in Figure 6.5.

COLOR DISPLAYS

If you have a color monitor, you can use any combination of colors on the screen that you wish. Just enter the command

```
SET COLOR
```

at the R> prompt. The screen will display a table of options for both foreground and background colors. Use the arrow keys to move the cursor to the color that you want for the foreground, and then press

```
R>SELECT L:Name=9 F:Name=9 Company=10 Address=12 +
+>City=12 State=2 Zip=5 Ent:Date=8 FROM Names +
+>ORDER BY L:Name F:Name
 L:Name    F:Name    Company    Address      City         st Zip   Ent:Date
 --------- --------- ---------- ------------ ------------ -- ----- --------
 Adams     Bart      DataSpec   P.O. Box     Malibu       CA 92111 06/15/88
                     Inc.       2890
 Baker     Robin     Peach      2311 Coast   San Diego    CA 92112 06/15/88
                     Computers  Hwy.
 Jones     Mindy     ABC Co.    123 A St.    San Diego    CA 92122 06/15/88
 Miller    Anne      Golden     2313 Sixth   Berkeley     CA 94711 06/01/88
                     Gate Co.   St.
 Miller    Marie     Zeerox,    234 C St.    Los Angeles  CA 91234 06/01/88
                     Inc.
 Smith     Sandy     Hi Tech,   456 N.       Berkeley     CA 94721 06/01/88
                     Inc.       Rainbow Dr.
R>_
```

Figure 6.5: The Names table displayed with column widths specified

the Enter key to choose the color. Press the → key to move to the background color options, move the cursor to the color that you want, and press Enter again. Press the Esc key when you're finished making your selections. You'll return to the R> prompt, with the colors that you selected in effect for the duration of the session. (See Appendix A for more on color display.)

To set the screen colors from the Prompt menu, select *R:BASE and operating system command,* the Environment option from the menu, and then select the Set and Color options from the submenus. Press any key, select Execute, and choose your screen colors as discussed above.

CLEARING THE SCREEN

To clear any existing data from the screen, type in the command

```
CLS
```

or optionally, type the command

```
NEWPAGE
```

after the R> prompt, and press Enter. Note that this only erases the screen display and has no effect on information in the database.

DATE DISPLAYS

R:BASE typically displays the date in MM/DD/YY format. You can alter the format of date displays using the SET DATE command and any of the options below:

MM	Displays the month as a number, 01 through 12
MMM	Displays the month as a three-letter abbreviation, Jan through Dec
MMM +	Displays the month spelled out, January through December
DD	Displays the day as a number, 01 through 31
WWW	Displays the day of the week as a three-letter abbreviation, Sun through Sat

WWW +	Displays the day of the week spelled out, Sunday through Saturday
YY	Displays the year as a two-digit number, 88
YYYY	Displays the year as a four-digit number, 1988
CC	Allows dates for the B.C. range to be entered

You can also use other characters such as commas and colons in dates. When setting a date format, enter the command SET DATE followed by the appropriate format in quotation marks. For example, to display dates in "January 30, 1988" format, enter the command

```
SET DATE "MMM + DD, YYYY"
```

If you prefer to use the SET screen to do this, you don't have to use the quotation marks. Just type **MMM + DD, YYYY** next to the DATE format prompt, just below "User set values." To see the dates in this format, enter the command

```
SELECT Ent:Date FROM Names
```

Figure 6.6 shows an example of dates listed in the "MMM + DD, YYYY" format. Examples of other formats are listed below:

FORMAT	*EXAMPLE*
WWW: MMM DD, YYYY	Wed: Jun 01, 1988
MMM + DD YYYY (WWW +)	June 01 1988 (Wednesday)
MM/YY	06/88
YY-MMM-DD	88-Jun-01
MMM + DD	June 01

When entering dates into a database, R:BASE assumes that you mean this century whenever you enter two digits for the year (for example, if you use YY for the year in the SET DATE format, and enter 88 as the year, R:BASE assumes that you mean 1988). To enter

```
R>SET DATE "MMM+ DD, YYYY"
R>SELECT Ent:Date L:Name F:Name Company FROM Names ORDER BY Ent:Date
 Ent:Date           L:Name          F:Name          Company
 ------------------ --------------- --------------- --------------------
 June 01, 1988      Smith           Sandy           Hi Tech, Inc.
 June 01, 1988      Miller          Marie           Zeerox, Inc.
 June 01, 1988      Miller          Anne            Golden Gate Co.
 June 15, 1988      Jones           Mindy           ABC Co.
 June 15, 1988      Adams           Bart            DataSpec Inc.
 June 15, 1988      Baker           Robin           Peach Computers
R>_
```

Figure 6.6: Dates displayed in MMM + DD, YYYY format

dates in other centuries, use a four-digit format (YYYY) in the SET DATE command and in the entered date as well: for example,

SET DATE "MM/DD/YYYY"

and

6/1/1842

If you need to use B.C. dates, use CC in the format, as in the following command:

SET DATE "MM/DD/YYYY CC"

To enter a B.C. date, add the letters BC to your entry; for example,

6/1/3000 BC

To enter an A.D. date into a database field, just enter the date without any letters, as follows:

6/1/1988

Note that regardless of the date format that you set to display dates, you can *enter* the date in any format you wish as long as the sequence of month, day, and year matches the sequence of the date format. For example, in the command

```
SET DATE "WWW+: MMM+ DD, YYYY"
```

the sequence is weekday, month, day, and year. (Weekday is always calculated automatically from the date, so you never need to type it in yourself.) You can enter dates into a date field using any of the formats below, since each follows the same sequence of month, day, and year.

```
Jun 1 1988
6/1/1988
6-1-1988
June 01, 1988
```

You can specify a sequence for entering dates that is separate from the sequence in which dates are displayed. To do so, use the command SET DATE SEQUENCE to define the sequence for entering dates. Use the command SET DATE FORMAT to define the display format. For example, entering the commands

```
SET DATE SEQUENCE MMDDYY
SET DATE FORMAT "YY-MMM-DD"
```

allows you to enter dates in MM/DD/YY sequence, but displays them in "88-Jun-01" format.

TIME FORMATS

Even though we did not include a column with the TIME data type in this database, now is a good time to discuss R:BASE time formats, since they follow the same basic style as date formats. The command to define the sequence of hours, minutes, and seconds for entering times into a database is SET TIME SEQUENCE followed by the sequence of characters. The command for displaying times is SET TIME FORMAT followed by the time format. The commands below allow you to enter and display times in HH:MM:SS AM/PM format:

```
SET TIME SEQUENCE HHMMSS AP
SET TIME FORMAT "HH:MM:SS AP"
```

The symbols you can use in time formats are listed below:

HH	Hours as a two-digit number, 01 through 24
MM	Minutes as a two-digit number, 00 though 60
SS	Seconds as a two-digit number, 00 through 60
AP	A.M. or P.M. displayed

If you do not set your own time format, R:BASE uses the format HH:MM:SS, wherein the time is displayed on a 24-hour clock in the format HH:MM:SS. For example, 2:30 in the afternoon is displayed as 14:30:00. Examples of the time 2:30:15 P.M. displayed in several different formats are listed below:

FORMAT	*EXAMPLE*
HH:MM:SS	14:30:15
HH:MM:SS AP	2:30:15 PM
HH:MM AP	2:30 PM
SS Seconds	15 Seconds

To set the date or time format from the PBE menu, select *R:BASE and operating system utilities,* the Environment option, and then the Set option and the Keywords and characters option from the submenus. Press any key and select Execute and any one of the following options: DATE sequence, DATE format, TIME sequence, or TIME format. Type in the new sequence or format, and press the Enter and Esc keys when you are finished.

VIEWING SETTINGS

For a quick review of the various settings we've discussed in this chapter (and additional settings we'll discuss later), type in either the command

```
SHOW
```

or the command

```
SET
```

at the R> prompt, and press Enter.

ZIPPING IN AND OUT OF R:BASE

Changing the R:BASE environment settings gives you a great deal of flexibility in working with your database, as you have just seen. The ZIP command provides you with yet another tool, allowing you to run external programs without really leaving R:BASE.

For example, let's assume that you have just completed some major data entry and want to back up your database onto a floppy disk. However, you don't have any formatted disks ready to receive the three .RBF files. What can you do? One approach would be to leave R:BASE, enter the operating system subdirectory that you probably have on your hard disk, and format a floppy disk. Then you could use another operating system command to copy the database files from the \DBFILES subdirectory on the floppy. If you wanted to continue working in R:BASE, you'd have to start it all over again.

Another possibility would be to use R:BASE's ZIP command. By typing

ZIP *directory name*\FORMAT A:

where *directory name* is the name of the subdirectory that contains your operating system programs, you could execute the FORMAT command and return automatically to the R> prompt where you left off. Of course, if you are using R:BASE for OS/2, you may prefer to use OS/2's multitasking functions via the Program Selector.

There are some limitations to the use of this command. Your system has to have enough available memory to run the external program you name. (R:BASE for DOS users can find out how much memory is available at any given time by typing CHKDSK at the R> prompt.) Similarly, you shouldn't run memory-resident programs using the ZIP command, because they may overwrite part of the R:BASE program in your system's RAM. You can, however, use most memory-resident programs with R:BASE simply by running them before you start R:BASE.

What if you want to run a longer program from within R:BASE? You can do that, too, by using an alternative form of the ZIP command: ZIP ROLLOUT. Assume you have the program 1-2-3 in your root directory as an .EXE file. If you type

ZIP 123

R:BASE will probably tell you the program is too big to fit in memory. However, if you type

```
ZIP ROLLOUT 123
```

1-2-3 will run. When you exit 1-2-3, you'll be returned to R:BASE. If you need to run a program via its batch file, you'll have to modify the ZIP command by adding COMMAND.COM/C and then change directories before you can do so. For example, to run WP.BAT to start your word processing program, you would type

```
CHDIR \
ZIP ROLLOUT COMMAND.COM /C WP
```

Don't forget to change back to the DBFILES subdirectory when you return to R:BASE.

LETTING R:BASE DO YOUR MATH FOR YOU

In order to begin exploring some of R:BASE's mathematical capabilities, we need to create a new database that has some numeric data in it. Imagine that you're the sales manager for a car dealership. Naturally, you want to keep track of sales, not only for given time periods, but also by salesperson. You decide to set up a simple database called Sales containing a table called CSales. CSales (for car sales) contains the following columns:

```
SName   TEXT       10
SDate   DATE
Amount  CURRENCY
```

See if you can remember how to create a new database. From the PBE Main menu, you should select *Define or modify a database*. Then follow the prompts using these steps:

1. Select RBDEFINE and press any key.
2. Press Enter to select Execute.

3. Select the *Define a new database* option.
4. When prompted for the database name, type in **Sales,** and press Enter.

Now fill in the table and column names and data types as you did in Chapter 2. Your screen should look like Figure 6.7.

Once you've defined the CSales table, press Esc four times to return to the PBE Main menu. Now you need to enter some data into the CSales table. You can either use PBE as you did in Chapter 2 or type a LOAD command directly from the R> prompt. If you prefer to do the latter, press Esc again, and type

```
LOAD CSales WITH PROMPTS
```

Then, enter the following data:

```
Smith 6/4/88 14350
Jones 6/4/88 6349
Smith 6/4/88 8999
Smith 6/5/88 21000
Jones 6/5/88 24999
```

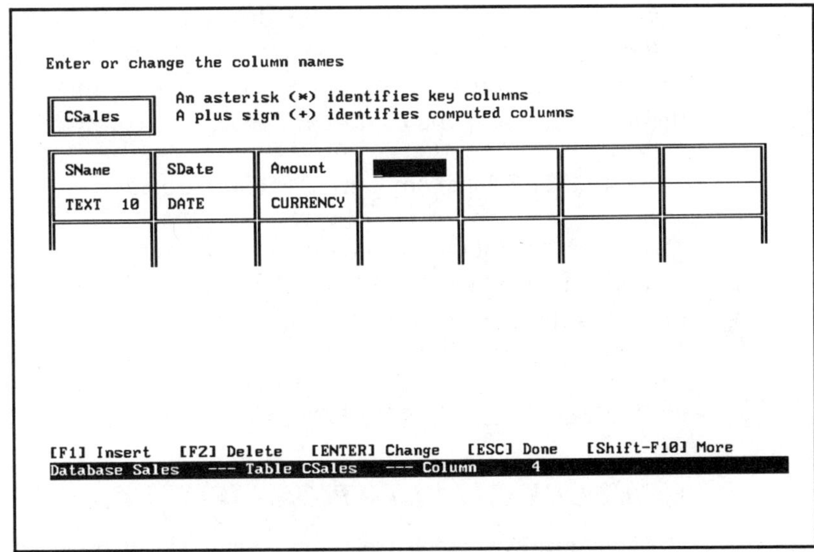

Figure 6.7: Defining the Sales database

Press Esc after entering all the data. From the R> prompt, enter the command

```
SELECT ALL FROM CSales
```

and press Enter. Keep in mind that you never need to enter dollar signs or commas for the Amount data. Since the Amount column is defined for the CURRENCY data type, the amounts will be displayed in dollar and cents format, with commas as appropriate.

CALCULATING SUMS WITH THE SELECT COMMAND

Let's say you want to know what total sales are. To do this, you'll need to enter a command from the R> prompt, so if you're in PBE, press Esc until you see the R> prompt. Then type

```
SELECT ALL = S FROM CSales
```

and press Enter. R:BASE displays the same data as before, but this time with the total sales ($75,697.00) displayed at the bottom of the list under the Amount column data. The =S tells R:BASE to calculate the sum of the data for you. If CSales had additional numeric columns, their sums would also be displayed.

There are situations where your table has several numeric columns, but you are only interested in seeing totals for some of them. In that case, you can use the SELECT command in the form

```
SELECT SName Amount = S FROM CSales
```

specifying =S only for the columns where sums are desired.

You can, of course, use ORDER BY and WHERE clauses to ask more specific questions. If you only wanted to know total sales for June 4th, you could type

```
SELECT ALL = S FROM CSales WHERE SDate = 6/4/88
```

COMPLEX CALCULATIONS WITH R:BASE

Totals are extremely useful, but what about other calculations? Maybe you want to find an average or the largest sale in a given period.

For cases like these, R:BASE provides the COMPUTE command. Let's return to PBE mode by pressing Esc.

From PBE, select *Query a database* and then *Look at data*. You want to experiment with the COMPUTE command, so select it and then the CSales table. When prompted for the column to compute on, select Amount, since it's the only column with Numeric data. Finally, when asked for the type of calculations you want, choose the default ALL, skip the section on setting up conditions by pressing Esc, and have R:BASE execute the command. Your screen should look like Figure 6.8.

You may wonder about some of the items on your screen. Why does R:BASE bother to distinguish between COUNT and ROWS, for example? If you had null entries for the Amount column in some of your rows, ROWS would be a larger number than COUNT, since COUNT only reports the number of entries that are not null. R:BASE's calculations of average, maximum, and minimum sales amounts are straightforward, and notice that a sum is provided here as well. Furthermore, if you need to know about standard deviations and variances, R:BASE provides them quickly and painlessly as well.

If you aren't interested in all the calculations, you can alter the command by selecting just the type of calculation you want. For

```
COMPUTE ALL Amount FROM CSales
Amount    Count =              6
          Rows =               6
          Minimum =                     $6,349.00
          Maximum =                    $24,999.00
          Sum =                        $82,197.00
          Average =                    $13,699.50
          Std Dev =                     $7,180.49
          Variance =               $51,559,416.92

Press any key to continue_
```

Figure 6.8: Operations available with the COMPUTE command

example, to find Smith's average sales, you would proceed as you did above, except that, instead of choosing ALL, you would select AVERAGE. Then, rather than skipping the question about the column for specifying conditions, you'd select SName, EQ, and enter **Smith** to execute the command.

Some of you may want to experiment with the COMPUTE command from the R> prompt. If you do, remember that you can use R:BASE's Help screen to be reminded of the syntax.

USING THE TALLY COMMAND

Let's say you want to know how many sales each of your salespeople has made. One way to do that would be to use the SELECT command many times, each time limiting it to an individual salesperson, and then physically count the number of rows on the screen (or screens). Clearly, this would not be feasible if you had a large database. Another way would be to use R:BASE's COMPUTE command, as in

```
COMPUTE COUNT SName FROM CSales WHERE +
+> SName = Smith
```

This would save you the chore of manually counting the rows on the screen, but you would still have to enter the command for each salesperson.

Now enter the TALLY command. As usual, TALLY is accessible either from PBE, using the *Query a database*, *Look at data*, and TALLY option, or directly from the R> prompt. We'll continue to use the R> prompt in our examples. Enter the command

```
TALLY SName FROM CSales
```

R:BASE responds with the information you wanted: Smith has made three sales, while Jones has made only two. If you substitute SDate for SName, you'll see how many sales were made on each day.

The TALLY command counts the occurrences of identical data for the column you specify. For example, if you tally CSales by Amount, you'll see that there's only one occurrence of each amount—in other words, no two sales were for the exact same amount. TALLY is extremely useful when you have a table containing items that should all have unique identification codes of some type. If you have a table with invoices, for example, no two rows should have the same invoice number. Using the TALLY command, you can quickly verify that each invoice number is unique.

USING CROSSTAB FOR COMPLEX SEARCHES AND CALCULATIONS

CROSSTAB is another R:BASE command that lets you do sophisticated data analysis. CROSSTAB is used primarily to find unique pairs of values from two columns, but you can also have calculations done on the columns you specify. Let's experiment. Let's say you want to cross-tabulate salespeople with sales dates. You can type either

```
CROSSTAB SName BY SDate FROM CSales
```

or

```
CROSSTAB SDate BY SName FROM CSales
```

depending on how you wanted the results displayed. The values from the first column you list will be displayed horizontally along the top of the screen. Note that CROSSTAB automatically sorts your data in ascending order.

If you're less interested in tabulations than in sums or averages, you can modify the command using a variation of the command's syntax. For example, if you type

```
CROSSTAB SUM Amount BY SName FROM CSales
```

you'll see a table that displays total sales by salesperson.

One further variation on the above command would be to ask R:BASE to display the sum of the daily sales for each salesperson. You could do that by entering

```
CROSSTAB SUM Amount FOR SName BY SDate FROM CSales
```

The results, shown in Figure 6.9, give a clear picture of daily sales activity.

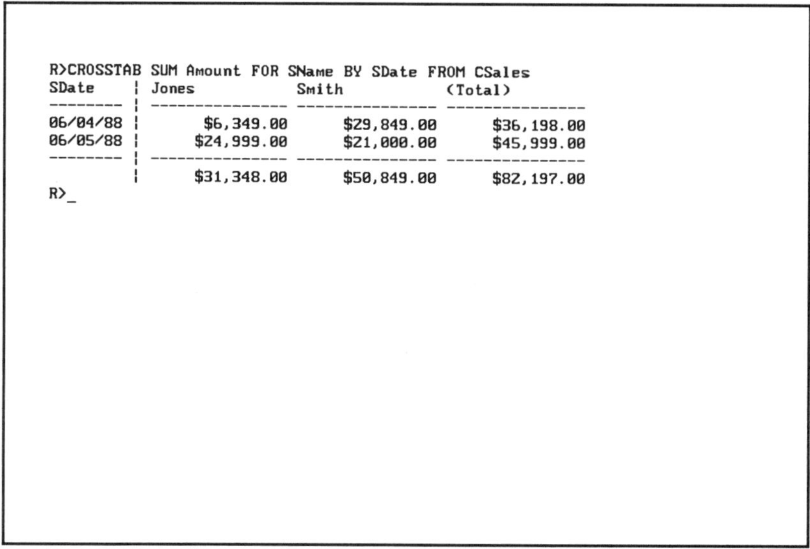

```
R>CROSSTAB SUM Amount FOR SName BY SDate FROM CSales
SDate    | Jones           Smith           (Total)
-------- | --------------- --------------- ---------------
06/04/88 |       $6,349.00      $29,849.00      $36,198.00
06/05/88 |      $24,999.00      $21,000.00      $45,999.00
-------- | --------------- --------------- ---------------
         |      $31,348.00      $50,849.00      $82,197.00
R>_
```

Figure 6.9: Total daily sales by salesperson, displayed with CROSSTAB

Before we leave the subject of data analysis, you may want to experiment with the SQL Group By SELECT command discussed in Chapter 5. The small database presented here gives you a better base for exploration than the Mail database did.

OPERATING SYSTEM COMMANDS

R:BASE includes about a dozen operating system commands that you can execute directly from R:BASE either in command mode or from PBE. We'll take a look at these commands in this section.

DIR displays the contents of the current directory. You can display the contents of other directories or other drives by providing the appropriate pathname, as in DIR A: or DIR \RBFILES; if you have a particularly large number of directories, you can have R:BASE pause the display automatically after each screenful by typing DIR/P.

You can use CHDIR or CD to change the current directory. If you need to create a directory, or want to remove one, you can use MKDIR (MD) or RMDIR (RD), respectively. (You can also change the active drive by using CHDRV followed by the drive name.)

R:BASE's COPY command works much like the operating system COPY command, too, even to the point of letting you use wildcard characters to designate files to be copied. Be careful, however, to make a backup of your database when using COPY, if you want the backup database to have a different name. For example, if you type

```
COPY SALES?.RBF S?.RBF
```

you'll only end up with one file for the S database. When file names for the original and backup database files are different lengths, copy each file separately. Similar care should be taken when renaming files with the RENAME command.

You can use ERASE to delete entire files. R:BASE will not, however, let you delete the database files of the currently open database. If you want to erase all traces of the currently active database, close it first (you can do that by typing CLOSE at the R> prompt), and then type something like

ERASE *dbname*?.RBF

where *dbname* is the name of the database to be erased. You can also include paths in the ERASE command.

CLS, an alternative to R:BASE's own NEWPAGE, can be used either to clear the screen or to produce a form feed on your printer.

TYPE, like its operating system counterpart, can be used to display the contents of an ASCII file.

Several other R:BASE commands work much like, but not exactly like, their operating-system counterparts. You can use CHKDSK in R:BASE for DOS to find out not only the total number of bytes of memory and disk space on your active drive, but also the percentage of that memory and disk space that is currently available. If you want to find out about disk utilization on a drive that isn't the active drive, you can use CHKDSK in the form

CHKDSK *d:*

where *d:* is the drive in question. R:BASE's CHKDSK does not, however, support the optional parameters /F and /V, available from your operating system.

BACKING UP YOUR DATABASE

R:BASE's BACKUP and RESTORE commands are also similar to the operating system commands of the same name. However, they are optimized for use with R:BASE databases, and allow you to back up an entire database or just parts of it. The easiest way to back up a database, of course, is to copy all three .RBF files onto a floppy disk. But if your database is too large to fit onto a floppy disk, you'll be glad to know that BACKUP and RESTORE can span multiple floppy disks. (Users of dual 3½-inch disk systems, however, should not use these commands.)

How can you use the BACKUP command? Let's say you have the Sales database on your hard disk and want to back it up onto a floppy disk in drive A. The floppy should be formatted, but otherwise empty. Then, assuming you were in R:BASE and had opened the Sales database, you could type the following commands in sequence:

1. **OUTPUT A:SALES.BAK**
2. **BACKUP ALL**
3. **OUTPUT SCREEN**

The first command redirects R:BASE's output to the file called SALES.BAK on drive A. You could have chosen any legal operating system file name in lieu of SALES.BAK. The second command tells R:BASE to back up the entire database into the SALES.BAK file. If more than one floppy disk is required, R:BASE will prompt you to supply additional ones. When the backup is completed, the last OUTPUT command redirects R:BASE's output back to the screen.

When you use the BACKUP command, you should remember three things. First, be sure to have enough blank, formatted floppy disks to accommodate your database. Second, don't be worried if the backed-up database seems very small. The total byte size of your backup may be one fifth the size of the original database. Third, be sure the R:BASE environment setting NULL is set to its default -0- when you use BACKUP.

If you later need to restore a database, how do you do it? If you have backed up the entire database, and need to restore it, make sure you have removed or renamed any database with the same name from the current directory. Then, from the R> prompt, type

```
RESTORE d:filename.ext
```

To restore the Sales database, you would type

```
RESTORE A:SALES.BAK
```

If the backup spans more than one disk, you'll be prompted to replace one floppy disk with the next.

BACKUP and RESTORE can also be used to move a database from one machine onto another one.

Remember, BACKUP and RESTORE are used primarily to back up a large database that can't fit onto a single floppy disk. COPY will be faster if your database files can fit onto a single floppy disk. Only hard disk users should use BACKUP and RESTORE.

In this chapter we've discussed techniques for managing R:BASE displays using the SET command. In later chapters, we'll discuss more of R:BASE's environment settings. You've discovered how to ZIP in and out of R:BASE if you need to. We've also explored some of the ways to harness R:BASE's power to perform calculations and help you analyze data. We'll continue this discussion in Chapter 11 when we talk about SuperMath functions. Finally, we've talked about R:BASE's operating system commands and shown you several ways you can back up an R:BASE database.

In the next chapter, we'll learn how to use R:BASE's powerful report generator.

Chapter 7

Creating Custom Reports

FAST TRACK

To design report formats, 152

use the REPORTS command. The general steps for developing a report format are as follows:

1. Design the report on paper.
2. Determine the variables to be used in the report.
3. Name the report and associated table using REPORTS EXPRESS.
4. Define the report variables on-line with the Expression and Define options.
5. Type in headings, footings, and any other text in the report with the Edit option.
6. Locate column and variable positions on the report with the F6 key.
7. Save the report by quitting the menu and selecting *Save Changes*.
8. Print the report and make changes as necessary.

To print reports, 167

use the PRINT <*report name*> command. Optionally, use the ORDER BY and WHERE clauses to sort and filter reports.

To use R:BASE's special print attributes, 169

enter printer attribute codes (see Table 7.2) as report variables and locate those codes in the report as you would any other variable or column name.

To edit report formats, **170**

enter the REPORTS command and the name of the report; then select options similar to those used when creating the report format.

To print multiple column mailing labels, **175**

type **RUN 3LABELS IN 3LABELS PRO** at the R> prompt.

To view the report formats **180**

associated with a database, use the LIST REPORTS command.

IN THIS CHAPTER, WE'LL DISCUSS TECHNIQUES FOR generating reports based on your R:BASE database. You'll learn how to set up and modify a formatted report, print mailing labels, and even print form letters.

To follow along with the examples in this chapter, start R:BASE so that you see the PBE Main menu.

CREATING CUSTOMIZED REPORTS

R:BASE includes a report generator that allows you to create customized reports with headings, footings, totals, subtotals, and modified column displays. In this section, we'll experiment with reports and develop a mailing-list report for the Names table, similar to the one shown in Figure 7.1.

Developing a report can be broken down into eight steps:

1. Design the report on paper, marking headings, footings, and detail (the body of the report).
2. Determine variables for the report on paper (information that is to be included in the report but does not come directly from the table).
3. Start the report generator, name the report, and identify the associated table.
4. Define report variables on-line.
5. Enter the report headings, footings and any other text.
6. Locate the report columns and variables.
7. Modify the output characteristics if necessary and save the report.
8. Print the report and make changes as needed.

Each of these steps is discussed in detail below.

MAILING LIST DIRECTORY		
July 31, 1988		Page: 1
Adams, Bart P.O. Box 2890	DataSpec Inc. Malibu, CA 92111	Jun 15,1988
Baker, Robin 2311 Coast Hwy.	Peach Computers San Diego, CA 92112	Jun 15,1988
Jones, Mindy 123 A St.	ABC Co. San Diego, CA 92122	Jun 15,1988
Miller, Anne 2313 Sixth St.	Golden Gate Co. Berkeley, CA 94711	Jun 1,1988
Miller, Marie 234 C St.	Zeerox Inc. Los Angeles, CA 91234	Jun 1,1988
Smith, Sandy 456 N. Rainbow Dr.	Hi Tech, Inc. Berkeley, CA 94721	Jun 1,1988

Figure 7.1: A mailing list report for the Names table

STEP 1: DESIGN THE REPORT

The first step in developing a report is to jot down on paper a rough draft of how you want each printed page to look. Note the headings that appear at the top of each page, footings that appear at the bottom of each page, and the detail lines (the main body of the report where rows from the table are displayed). Figure 7.2 shows a sample rough draft.

STEP 2: PLAN THE REPORT VARIABLES

Report variables are any type of information that does not come directly from a database table (excluding headings and footings). Page numbers, dates, totals, and subtotals are all variables. Special characters that you want to insert into a column, such as commas, can be defined as variables as well.

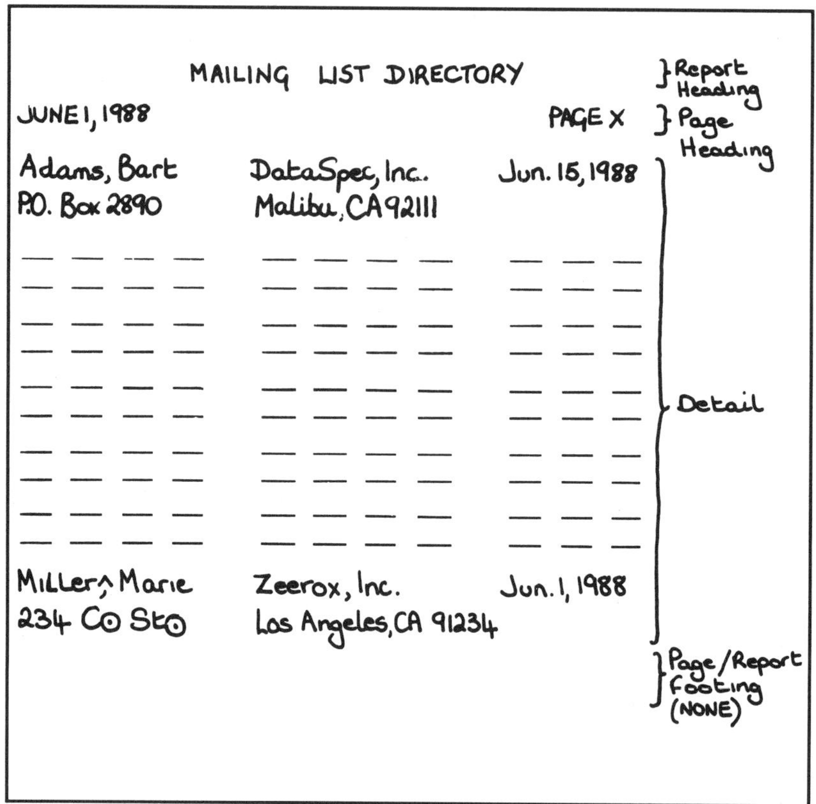

Figure 7.2: A rough draft of a report on paper

Therefore, in our mailing-list report, the name is a variable because it is modified to include a comma and has extraneous blanks removed, as in *Miller, Marie.* The City, State, and Zip columns are also modified, as in *San Diego, CA 92122.* Jot down brief names for each of the following variables (but do not use spaces in the variable names):

PgNo = Page number

RepDate = Report date

Comma = ","

FullName = Last and first names, separated by a comma

FullCSZ = City, state, and ZIP code with a comma inserted

Once you've jotted down this information, you can go on-line and develop the report format.

STEP 3: START REPORTS EXPRESS

There are two different methods that you can use to enter the R:BASE report generator (also called *Reports EXPRESS*). From the PBE Main menu, select *Define or Modify a database,* and then Reports. Press any key when prompted, and execute the command. Alternatively, from the R:BASE R> prompt you can type the command

```
REPORTS
```

and press Enter.

Highlight the appropriate database name and press Enter. R:BASE should now ask you to enter the database owner password. Why? Because when we created the Mail database in Chapter 2, we established an owner password. When a database has an owner password, only people who know that password can change the basic database structure. What we're going to do—create a report—affects the basic database structure, in the sense that it adds something to the database structure. Enter the password you set in Chapter 2 (we recommended that you use your name) and press Enter.

Once the database is open, you'll see the Report Options menu, as shown in Figure 7.3. (Notice that the name of the currently open database also appears in the highlighted *status bar* near the bottom of the screen.)

We'll discuss options 2 through 6 later. For now, you want to create a new report format, so select option 1, *Edit/Create a report.* If there were any reports associated with the Mail database, R:BASE would list them, along with the option (New) to create a new report, as follows:

```
──────────────── Choose a report ────────────────
Standard (New)
─────────────────────────────────────────────────
```

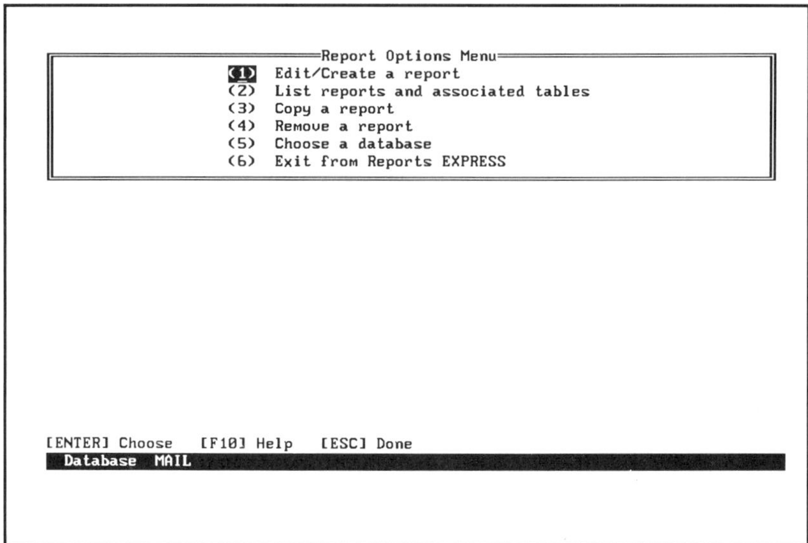

Figure 7.3: The Report Options menu

Since the Mail database doesn't have any reports, R:BASE asks that you enter a name for the new report, up to eight characters long, as shown below:

Enter your report name (1–8 characters)

For this example, enter the name **Director** (short for Directory), and press Enter.

Next, R:BASE asks for the name of the table containing the data to be printed, as follows:

Select a table or view

Names

The Mail database contains only the table named Names, so select Names.

Next, R:BASE displays the *Report Definition menu* and screen. This is your clean slate for creating your report format. Now you can begin to design the actual report format.

STEP 4: DEFINE VARIABLES ON-LINE

To define variables to use in a report, select the Expression option from the Report Definition menu. From the Expression menu, select Define. Next, R:BASE will ask you to enter an expression. You define an expression by typing in a variable name (from one to eight characters in length with no spaces), followed by a space, an equal sign (=), another space, and an expression or code to define the contents of the variable.

First, define the PgNo (page number) variable by typing in the following:

```
PgNo = .#PAGE
```

.#PAGE is a code that is always used to display page numbers in reports. After you press the Enter key, you'll see the expression on the screen, as shown in Figure 7.4, and R:BASE will ask for the next expression.

Next, define the RepDate (report date) variable. The code for the system date is .#DATE. Type in the expression

```
RepDate = .#DATE
```

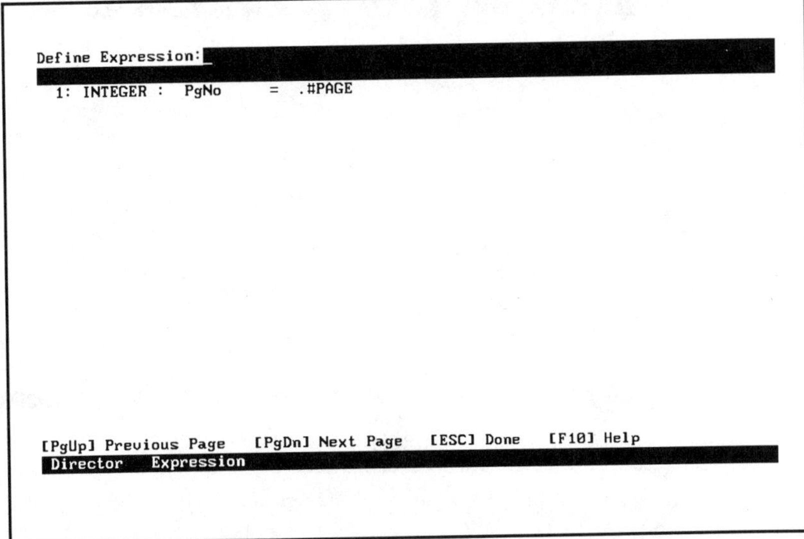

Figure 7.4: The PgNo variable defined on the screen

and press Enter. .#DATE uses the system date that you entered when you started your computer. The new expression appears on the screen, as shown in Figure 7.5.

Note that you can also include the time of day on a report using the code .#TIME (but we won't do so in this example). Like .#DATE, .#TIME uses the system time.

Define the Comma variable next. When you are defining literal characters for use in a report, surround them with quotation marks. Type in the expression for the Comma variable as

```
Comma = ","
```

and press Enter.

Next we'll define the FullName variable, which contains the last name, a comma, and the first name. To join Text data, you can use either of the following two operators:

- & Joins two items of text, placing a blank space between them.
- \+ Joins two items of text without a blank space.

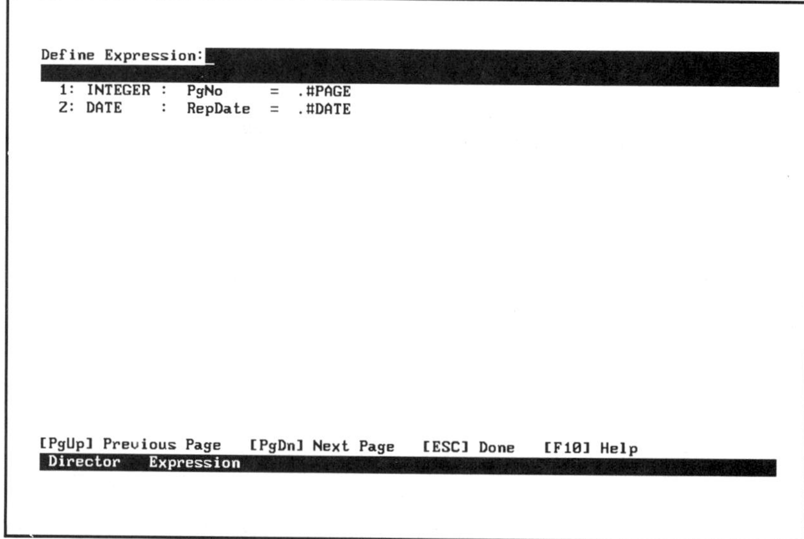

Figure 7.5: The RepDate variable defined on the screen

Since we want to place the comma right next to the last name, with a space after the comma and then the first name, enter the expression

FullName = L:Name + Comma & F:Name

This expression will print all the names in the following format:

Miller, Anne

Without using the variable to join the two parts of the name, Anne Miller would have been printed like this:

Miller Anne

When you press the Enter key, you'll see that the FullName variable and its expression are listed with the others. You've also noticed by now that R:BASE automatically places the type of data that the variable contains to the left of each variable name (for example, DATE, INTEGER, and TEXT). You need not concern yourself with these data types yet.

We want to display the city, state, and ZIP code in the format

San Diego, CA 92345

We'll use the variable FullCSZ for this format. Type in the expression

FullCSZ = City + Comma & State & Zip

Press Enter after typing in the expression. Then press the Esc key to indicate that you've finished entering expressions. You'll see all the variable names and their expressions listed on the screen as in Figure 7.6.

MAKING CORRECTIONS

If you find that you've made an error in an expression and you wish to change it, select the Define option from the menu. Type in the entire corrected expression, including the variable name, and press Enter. R:BASE will inform you that the variable name already exists and ask if you want to replace the original expression with the new one. Select Yes to do so.

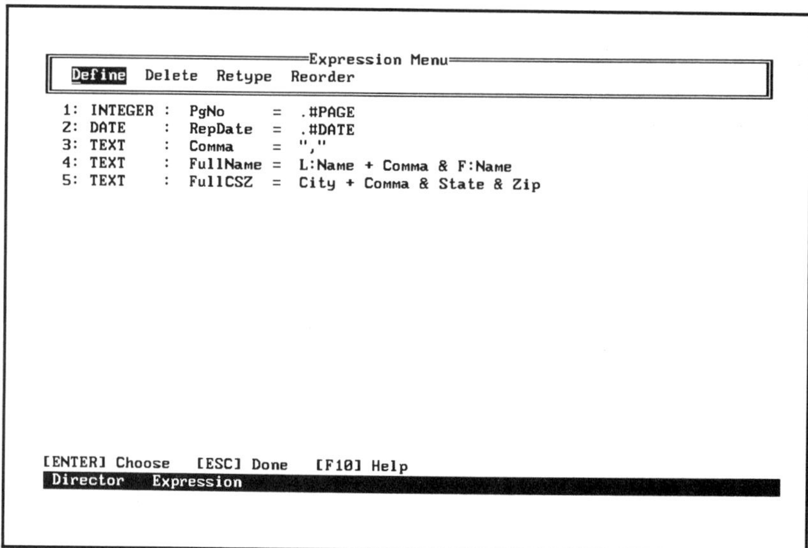

Figure 7.6: The report variables and expressions defined

By the way, if you are feeling uncomfortable with this discussion of variables and expressions, don't worry about it. Chapter 10 goes into these topics in greater detail.

Now you are ready to design the layout of the report. Press Esc to return to the Report Definition Menu.

STEP 5: ENTER THE REPORT TEXT

A report can have three types of headers and three types of footers, as summarized below:

SYMBOL	*NAME*	*TYPE*
RH	Report header	Displayed once at the top of the report
PH	Page header	Displayed at the top of each page
H1...H10	Break header	Appears at the top of each group in a report (used for reports containing subtotals)

F1...F10	Break footer	Appears at the bottom of each group in a report (used for reports containing subtotals)
PF	Page footer	Displayed at the bottom of each page
RF	Report footer	Displayed once at the bottom of the report

The symbol for each type of header and footer will appear highlighted in the far-left margin of the screen. Learning to specify, insert, and delete header and footer types can be tricky (although it's easy once you get used to it). Take a moment to review the keys that you can use while designing a report format, as shown in Table 7.1, before developing the mailing list report.

Let's add a report header to the Mail list report that consists of the words "Mailing List Directory" with a blank line beneath. We'll also add a page header that shows the date the report was printed and the page number. (We'll deal with break headers and footers in Chapter 12.)

To move the cursor onto the screen and begin laying out the report format, select Edit from the top menu. Notice that the cursor moves to the right of the RH (report header) symbol. The bottom-right corner of the screen displays the indicator <1: 1, 1>. This shows the current row position of the cursor, the number of rows in the report format, and the current column position of the cursor.

To fill in the heading "Mailing List Directory" centered as the report header, hold down the right arrow key until the cursor reaches column 25 (the indicator will read <1:1, 25>) and type in

```
Mailing List Directory
```

Now we want to add another RH (report header) line so that there will be a blank line beneath this heading. To do so, make sure the expand mode is on. (Look for the word *Expand* in the highlight near the bottom of the screen. If you do not see it, press the F9 key.) When the expand mode is on, press the Enter key. Notice that this creates a new line with the symbol RH.

On the next line we'll begin the page heading. To create the next section, press the F8 key. Another new line appears, this one with the

Table 7.1: Keys Used When Creating Reports

KEY	FUNCTION
F1	Inserts a blank line above the current line.
F2	Deletes the current line.
F3	Displays variables and columns associated with the current report.
F9	Turns the expand mode on and off. The word "Expand" appears near the bottom of the screen when expand mode is on.
F7	With the expand mode on, moves the cursor to the previous section, or creates a new section if one does not exist. With the expand mode off, moves the cursor to the previous section.
F8	With the expand mode on, moves the cursor to the next section, or creates a new section if one does not exist. With the expand mode off, moves the cursor to the next section.
↑	Moves the cursor up one line. If the expand mode is on, creates a new line in the current section.
↓	Moves the cursor down one line. If the expand mode is on, creates a new line in the current section.
→	Moves the cursor to the right one character.
←	Moves the cursor to the left one character.
Ctrl-→	Moves the cursor to screen column number 255.
Ctrl-←	Moves the cursor to screen column number 1.
Ins	Inserts a space at the cursor position.
Del	Deletes the character at the cursor position.
Tab	Moves the cursor to the next tab setting (10 spaces).
Shift-Tab	Moves the cursor to the previous tab setting (10 spaces).
Home	With the expand mode on, moves to the upper-left corner of the current section. With the expand mode off, moves to the upper-left corner of the report format.
End	With the expand mode on, moves to the bottom-right corner of the current section. With the expand mode off, moves to the bottom-right corner of the report format.
F10	Displays a help screen.
Esc	Exits from editing and redisplays the menu.

symbol PH (page header) in it. On this line, press the space bar once and type the word

Date:

Hold down the right arrow key until the cursor reaches column 58 (the indicator will read <3:3, 58>). Type in the word

Page:

Press the Enter key to create another blank line. This one will also be a PH line and will serve as a blank line in the page header.

Now there are two sections on the screen: RH (report header) and PH (page header), as shown in Figure 7.7. Next we'll begin placing *variable* data (items from the Names table and report variables) on the report.

STEP 6: LOCATE COLUMN AND VARIABLE POSITIONS

To *locate* (or place) a table column name or report variable on the report format, you press the F6 key. Generally, it's easier to place the

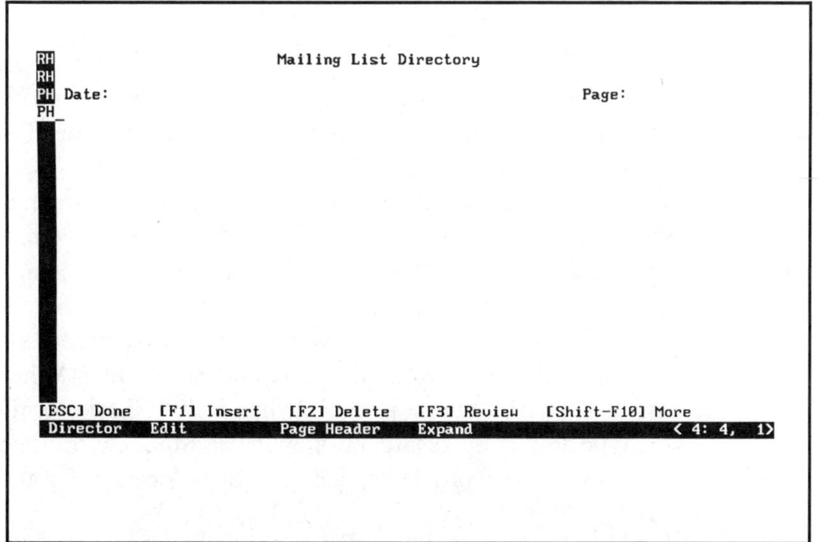

***Figure** 7.7:* A report header and page header on the screen

cursor to the far left of the location of the column data or variable first, and then press the F6 key. Let's get started.

To locate the report date (RepDate) variable in the page heading, first use the arrow keys to move the cursor to the right of the *Date:text* (<3: 4, 8> on the position indicator). Next, press F6 to locate the variable. R:BASE displays the prompt

```
Column or variable name:
```

In this case we want to locate the RepDate variable, so type in the name

```
RepDate
```

and press Enter. R:BASE asks that you

```
Move cursor to start location and press [S]
```

Since the cursor is already in the start location, just press the letter S. An S appears on the screen, and R:BASE asks that you

```
Move cursor to end and press [E]
```

The cursor automatically moved about 30 spaces to the right (which is the maximum width for DATE data). This is a good location for the end of the date, so just type the letter **E**. The E appears on the screen. Now you can see the starting and ending location where the date will appear in the printed report (between the S and the E, aligned to the left).

Next you can locate the PgNo variable. Move the cursor to column 64 (the indicator will read <3:4, 64>), and press F6. Now suppose you've forgotten the names of the variables and columns available to this report. To quickly review them, press the F3 key. Press Esc after viewing the variable and column names.

Enter PgNo as the variable name, and press Enter. When R:BASE asks for the start location, press S. When R:BASE asks for the end location, type an **E** at the default position in column 73. Now the page heading includes the word Date: followed by a location for the RepDate variable and the word Page: followed by the location of the PgNo variable, as shown below:

```
Date: S                    E                    Page: S   E
```

Now we need to fill in locations for table data to appear on the screen. But these do not belong in a heading or footing, because headings and footings only appear once on each page or once in the entire report. Instead, we'll locate the table column names in a *detail* section of the report.

THE DETAIL SECTION OF THE REPORT

The detail section displays data repeatedly on a page. In fact, it is generally repeated once for each row in the table. We need to create a detail section for this report now. First, press the down arrow key to move the cursor to the next row down (row 4). Next, make sure that the expand mode is on (press F9 if the word "Expand" does not appear in the status bar at the bottom of the screen). Then press F8 to create the next section. The letter D (for Detail) appears at the far-left edge of the new line.

First let's locate the FullName variable (which, as you'll recall, displays the L:Name and F:Name from the database table). Move the cursor to <5,2> and press F6. This time, instead of typing the variable name yourself, press Enter. You should see the Locate menu. Select Variables, since Fullname is a variable. When your list of variables appears, select Fullname. Type S to mark the start location. Move the cursor to 5,30, and press E to mark the end location. When R:BASE asks you to move the cursor to the end location and press either [E] or [W], it is giving you the option of specifying wraparound.

Use the right arrow key to move the cursor to <5,35>, press F6, and enter Company as the column name to display. Press S to start the location; then move the cursor to <5,54> and press E.

To locate the Ent:Date column, move the cursor to <5,58> and press F6. Type Ent:Date as the column name and press Enter. Type S to mark the start location. Move the cursor back to <5,73> and press E. Since most of your report seems to disappear from the screen, press Ctrl-left arrow (hold down the Ctrl key and press the ← key) to move the cursor back to column 1.

Assuming that the expand mode is still on, you can just press the down arrow key to create another detail line. To locate the Address column, move the cursor to <6, 5> and press F6. Enter Address as the column name, press S, move the cursor to <6, 29>, and press E. Move the cursor to <6, 35> and use the F6 key to locate FullCSZ from <6, 35> to <6, 73>.

To insert a blank line between names printed in the directory, press the down arrow key to create another detail line. (You can press Ctrl-left arrow to move the cursor back over to column 1.) You'll see the start and end locations of all the column names and variables on the screen as in Figure 7.8.

Now that the report format is laid out, you only need to save it.

STEP 7: SAVE THE REPORT FORMAT

To save the report format, press the Esc key to bring back the Report Definition menu. Press the Esc key again to call up the Report Exit

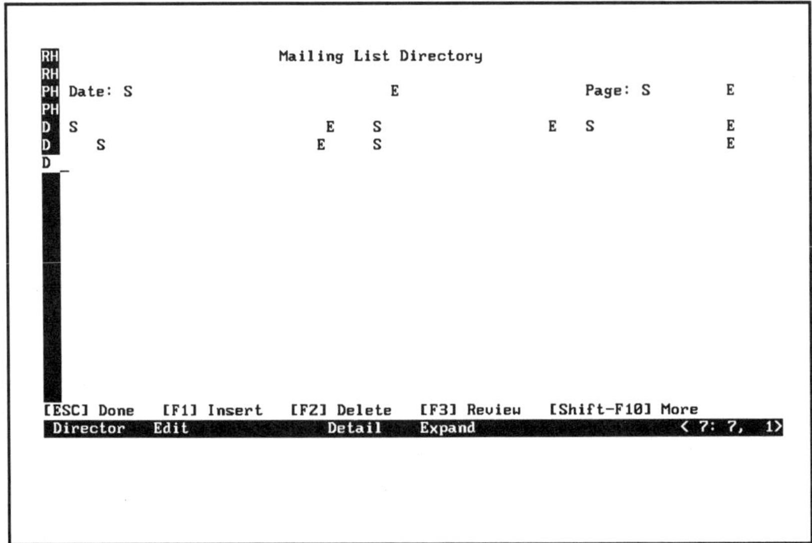

Figure 7.8: All column names and variables located on the screen

Options menu. This menu offers the following options:

Save changes   Discard changes   Return

Select *Save Changes* to save the report format. (Selecting *Discard Changes* "abandons" any new or changed information in the report, while selecting Return returns you to the Report Definition menu.) You'll see the message "Storing Report" and "End REPORTS Definition" appear on the screen briefly. From the next menu to appear, select option 6, *Exit from Reports EXPRESS.* You'll be returned to the place from which you entered Reports EXPRESS (either the R> prompt or the PBE *Define or modify a database* menu).

Now let's try out the report. If you are not at the R> prompt now, work your way to it before trying the rest of the examples in this chapter.

STEP 8: PRINT THE REPORT

To display the Mail List report in sorted order, use the PRINT command, followed by the name of the report and the ORDER BY clause. In this example, enter the command

```
PRINT Director ORDER BY L:Name F:Name
```

The report will appear on the screen, as shown in Figure 7.9.

To print out the report on a printer, enter the following commands:

```
OUTPUT PRINTER
PRINT Director ORDER BY L:Name F:Name
```

After the report is printed, you can enter the command

```
NEWPAGE
```

to eject the report from the printer. Then enter the command

```
OUTPUT SCREEN
```

to disconnect from the printer.

You can also send a copy of the report to a disk file using the Output *d:filename.ext* command.

```
R>PRINT Director ORDER BY L:Name F:Name
                       Mail List Directory

Date: 01/30/88                                            Page:        1

Adams, Bart                     DataSpec Inc.             06/15/88
   P.O. Box 2890                Malibu, CA 92111

Baker, Robin                    Peach Computers           06/15/88
   2311 Coast Hwy.              San Diego, CA 92112

Jones, Mindy                    ABC Co.                   06/15/88
   123 A St.                    San Diego, CA 92122

Miller, Anne                    Golden Gate Co.           06/01/88
   2313 Sixth St.               Berkeley, CA 94711

Miller, Marie                   Zeerox, Inc.              06/01/88
   234 C St.                    Los Angeles, CA 91234

Smith, Sandy                    Hi Tech, Inc.             06/01/88
   456 N. Rainbow Dr.           Berkeley, CA 94721

R>_
```

Figure 7.9: The Director report displayed on the screen

To display the dates in the report in Jan 1, 1988 format, enter the command

```
SET DATE "MMM DD, YYYY"
```

and print the report.

To print the report using only certain rows from the Names table, use the WHERE clause after the ORDER BY clause, as below:

```
PRINT Director ORDER BY L:Name F:Name WHERE +
+> City = "San Diego"
```

PRINTING ON SINGLE SHEETS

When displaying lengthy reports on the printer, you can use either continuous-form (tractor-fed) paper or single sheets. For continuous form, use the OUTPUT PRINTER option before entering the PRINT command. For single sheets, use the command

```
OUTPUT PRINTER WITH SCREEN
```

before entering the PRINT command. R:BASE will print one page at a time and wait for you to tell it to print the next page.

USING YOUR PRINTER'S ENHANCEMENTS

Most dot-matrix printers allow you to use special printer attributes such as compressed or expanded print. Some printers even allow you to change type sizes and fonts. You can use these settings in your reports if you know the appropriate codes for your printer. For example, the Okidata MicroLine 83A printer uses ASCII code 29 for compressed print, code 31 for expanded print, and code 30 for regular print. To use the settings in a report, you would need to define three variables (in the same way we defined the PgNo and RepDate variables in the Director report), as below:

```
ComPrint = <29>
ExpPrint = <31>
RegPrint = <30>
```

Next, you would locate these variables in the report, just as you would locate any other variable. For example, to print the heading in expanded print, locate the ExpPrint variable either above or to the left of the heading. To return to normal print for the body of the report, locate the RegPrint variable beneath or to the right of the heading. Be sure to put the variable for normal printing below the last line of the report so that the printer returns to normal printing after printing the reports.

Some printers use multicode sequences to activate special attributes. For example, the Epson printer uses Esc – to start and stop underlining. The ASCII code for the Esc key is always 27. The ASCII code for the minus (–) sign is 45. Therefore, you could define a variable to start and stop underlining, as below:

```
PrUnder = <27 45>
```

Locate the PrUnder variable before and after the text that you want underlined in the report.

Different printers use different codes for special print attributes. Table 7.2 shows codes for some popular printers. See your printer manual for the codes that your printer uses.

Table 7.2: Attribute Codes for Various Printers

MANUFACTURER/ MODEL		COMPRESSED PRINT ON	COMPRESSED PRINT OFF	EXPANDED PRINT ON	EXPANDED PRINT OFF
Epson	FX or RX	<15>	<18>	<27 87 49>	<27 87 50>
	MX 80 or 100	<15>	<18>	<27 83>	<27 84>
IBM	PC Printer	<15>	<18>	<14>*	<20>
Okidata	82A, 83A, 84	<29>	<30>	<31>	<30>
	92, 93	<29>	<30>	<31>	<30>
Hewlett-Packard	LaserJet**				

* Automatically returns to normal print after each printed line.

** The codes for the Hewlett-Packard LaserJet follow a slightly different system, as shown below:

MODE	CODE
Portrait	<27 69 27 38 108 48 79>
Compressed Portrait	<27 69 27 38 108 48 79 27 38 107 50 83>
Landscape	<27 69 27 38 108 49 79>
Compressed Landscape	<27 69 27 38 108 49 79 27 38 107 50 83>

MAKING CHANGES TO YOUR REPORT

Quite often, you'll find that you want (or need) to make changes to a report format after viewing the report. To do so, just reenter Reports EXPRESS using either of the techniques discussed earlier in this chapter. Select the name of the report that you want to edit from the menu that appears.

Your original report format will appear on the screen. You can use the Edit and Expression options from the menu to add, change, or delete text, variables, and column names on the report format. Use the function keys (F1, F2, F6, F7, F8, and F9) to insert and delete lines and sections.

RELOCATING VARIABLES AND COLUMN NAMES

To change the location of a column name or variable on the report format, move the cursor inside the existing S and E symbols for the column or variable. Press the F6 key, and R:BASE will allow you to assign new start and end locations for the column or variable.

DELETING VARIABLES AND COLUMN POSITIONS

To remove a located column name or variable from the report format, move the cursor inside the S and E of the appropriate column or variable, hold down the Shift key, and press F2.

REORDERING VARIABLES

Variables must be defined in the order that they are created. For example, the two expressions below are out of order because the Comma variable is defined *after* it is used in the FullCSZ variable:

```
1. FullCSZ = City + Comma & State & Zip
2. Comma = ","
```

To reorder the variables and expressions, select Expressions and Reorder from the report menus. R:BASE will display the prompt

```
Enter expression name: New position:
```

In this example, you could enter FullCSZ as the expression name and 2 as its new position, to place the Comma variable above the FullCSZ variable.

DELETING VARIABLES

To delete a variable, select Expression and Delete from the report menus. You will have to type the variable name and press Enter. The variable will be deleted from the list of expressions. Furthermore, the variable (along with its S and E) will be deleted from the report format if it was already in use there.

CHANGING VARIABLES

To change a variable (expression), select Define from the Expressions menu. Type in the variable name and new expression exactly as you want it to appear in the expressions list. R:BASE will double-check for permission. Select Yes to replace the original variable and expression with the new one.

SAVING CHANGES

Press the Esc key when you are finished editing, and use the same techniques discussed earlier to save the modified report format.

PRINTING MAILING LABELS

Mailing labels are simple to produce with the R:BASE report generator. From the R> prompt enter the command

```
REPORTS
```

and choose the Mail database. Enter your password if prompted. (R:BASE only "remembers" that a password has been entered for the duration of a session.) Select option 1 to Edit/Create a report, select New, and enter the report name **Labels.** Next, enter **Names** as the associated table.

Select the Expression and Define options from the menus, and enter the following expressions:

```
Comma = ","
FullName = F:Name & L:Name
FullCSZ = City + Comma & State & Zip
```

After entering all the variables, the screen will look like Figure 7.10. Press Esc after you've defined the variables.

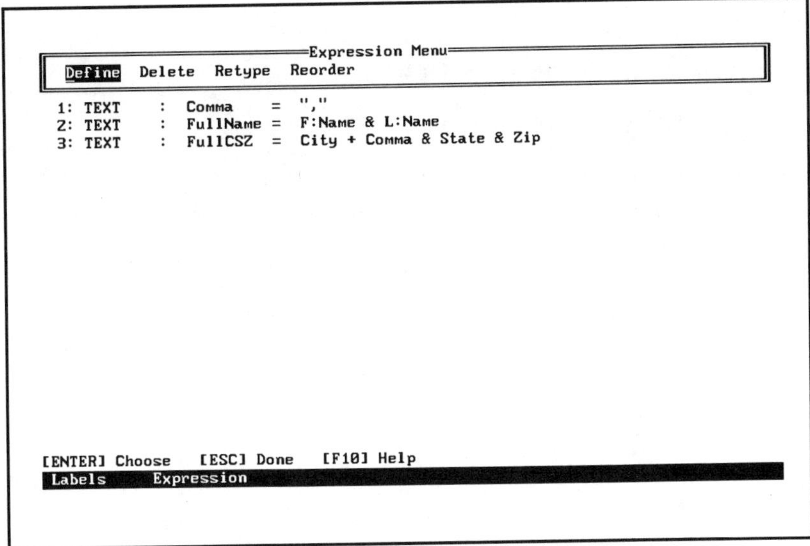

Figure 7.10: Variables defined for mailing labels

To lay out the report format, select the Edit option from the menu. Turn on the expand mode (press F9 until "Expand" appears on the status line); then press F8 twice to skip the header sections. (Mailing labels consist only of detail lines.)

On the first line, press F6 and enter FullName as the variable to locate. Start the variable at <1,1> and end it at about <1,35>.

Press the down arrow to create another detail line. Press F6 and enter Company as the column name. Start the location at <2,1> and end it at about <2,20>. Press the down arrow to create a third detail line, and press F6 to locate the Address variable. Start the location at <3,1> and end it at about <3, 25>. Press the down arrow to create a fourth detail line, and press F6 to locate the FullCSZ variable. Start the location at <4,1> and end it at about <4,35>.

Since most mailing labels are one inch tall and most printers print six lines to the inch, you'll want to be sure that R:BASE prints six lines for each label. Press the down arrow two more times to make a total of six detail lines. Your screen should look like Figure 7.11.

Press Esc after laying out the format. To ensure that R:BASE does not attempt to skip pages while printing labels, select the Configure

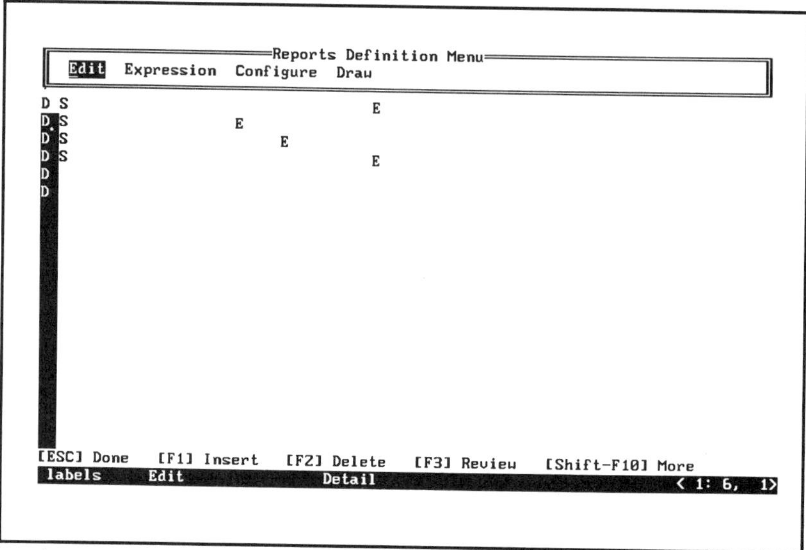

Figure 7.11: The mailing-label format laid out on the screen

option from the top menu. Set the number of lines per page to zero by typing the number 0 and pressing Enter. (We'll discuss these configuration settings in more detail later.) Press Esc twice to call up the Exit Options menu.

Select Save Changes to save the report format. Select option 6 to return to the R> prompt.

Before printing labels, you can check the alignment of the labels in the printer. To do so, enter the command

```
OUTPUT PRINTER
```

at the R> prompt. Then, to print two mailing labels, enter the command

```
PRINT Labels WHERE LIMIT = 2
```

If the mailing-label alignment is not correct, adjust the labels in the printer, then press the End key to repeat the PRINT command. Press Enter. Repeat this process until the labels are properly aligned in the printer.

To print the labels in ZIP-code order (for bulk mailing) use the command

```
PRINT Labels ORDER BY Zip
```

The labels will appear on the screen. The label format designed here is for single-column, 3½-by-15/16-inch (or 1-inch) continuous-form mailing labels.

When printing labels, you can use the WHERE clause to specify search criteria, as follows:

```
PRINT Labels ORDER BY Zip WHERE Ent:Date = 06/01/88
```

After the labels are printed, enter the command OUTPUT SCREEN to detach from the printer.

USING R:BASE'S 3LABELS PROGRAM

Many of you will want to explore the mailing-label program that comes with R:BASE. In order to do that, you must have already told R:BASE to install the utilities. If you did, the two programs 3LABELS.PRO and 3LABELS.ASC should be in the \RBFILES subdirectory. Copy them into your active directory by typing

```
COPY \RBFILES\3LABELS.*
```

You can run 3LABELS either from the R> prompt by typing

```
RUN 3LABELS IN 3LABELS.PRO
```

and pressing Enter or from the PBE Main menu. If you prefer the latter, select option 8, *R:BASE and operating system utilities*, and then 3Labels. After reading the program description, press any key and then Enter to execute the program.

You should see a menu entitled *R:BASE Mailing Label Application*. If you select the first option, you'll be able to read a short screen with instructions on how to proceed. Select item 2 to print the labels. The next screens are fairly self-explanatory. You're asked to pick a database, so select Mail. When prompted for a table, choose Names. When asked how many lines you want to print, select 4.

The next questions ask you which columns should be printed on each line. Select F:Name and L:Name for the first line, and then press the Esc key. Select Company for the second line, and press Esc to tell R:BASE that's all for that line. Select Address for the third line, and City, State, and Zip for the last one.

If you want the mailing labels sorted, or want only some of them printed, respond appropriately when prompted for sort columns and/or row selection conditions.

Finally, 3LABELS asks you the label format for the mailing labels. Notice that you can print not only simple mailing labels as your own Labels report did, but also two-, three-, and even four-across mailing labels! Select option 2, *3½ × 15/16 × 2-up*, route the labels to the screen or the printer as you see fit, and give 3LABELS the command to print the labels by selecting option 3, *Print labels*, from the Select Option menu. Your output should look like Figure 7.12.

Those of you who are detail-oriented may notice that 3LABELS' output isn't as nice as yours, since it doesn't have a comma between the city and state. In Chapter 16 you'll learn techniques that will enable you to modify 3LABELS so that commas are included.

For now, press any key and select option 3 to exit 3LABELS—unless you want to experiment with other label formats. Once you decide to quit 3LABELS, though, you'll see a message telling you that R:BASE is "terminating all WHILE and IF blocks," followed by the R> prompt. (This message is a result of the 3LABELS program instructions containing several WHILE and IF blocks, which you'll learn more about in Chapter 16.) The message simply informs you that the 3LABELS program has ended normally.

You should now be ready to try your hand at generating form letters.

FORM LETTERS

The R:BASE Reports command also provides a quick and easy way to create form letters from a table. To try one out, make sure that the R> prompt appears on the screen. Then, enter the command

```
REPORTS
```

If Mail isn't open, select it as your database. Enter your password if necessary. Select option 1 to Edit/Create a report, and select (New).

```
Sandy Smith                     Mindy Jones
Hi Tech, Inc.                   ABC Co.
456 N. Rainbow Dr.              123 A St.
Berkeley CA 94721               San Diego CA 92122

Marie Miller                    Bart Adams
Zeerox, Inc.                    DataSpec Inc.
234 C St.                       P.O. Box 2890
Los Angeles CA 91234            Malibu CA 92111

Anne Miller                     Robin Baker
Golden Gate Co.                 Peach Computers
2313 Sixth St.                  2311 Coast Hwy.
Berkeley CA 94711               San Diego CA 92112


Press any key to continue
_
```

Figure 7.12: Screen output from the 3LABELS program

Name the form letter **Letter1**. Select **Names** as the table to use with the report.

Next, select the Expression and Define options to define the following variables:

```
LetDate = .#DATE
Comma = ","
FullName = F:Name & L:Name
FullCSZ = City + Comma & State & Zip
Salut = F:Name + ":"
```

The Salut variable will be used as part of the salutation for the letter. It consists of the first name, with a colon attached. Hence, with the addition of the word **Dear**, the report will print the salutation as **Dear Marie:**.

After entering the variables, the screen should look like Figure 7.13. Press Esc twice after you've defined the variables.

Next you'll want to lay out the form letter. To begin, select Edit from the top menu. Make sure the expand mode is on (press F9 if it isn't); then press F8 to change the RH (report header) symbol to the PH (page header) symbol.

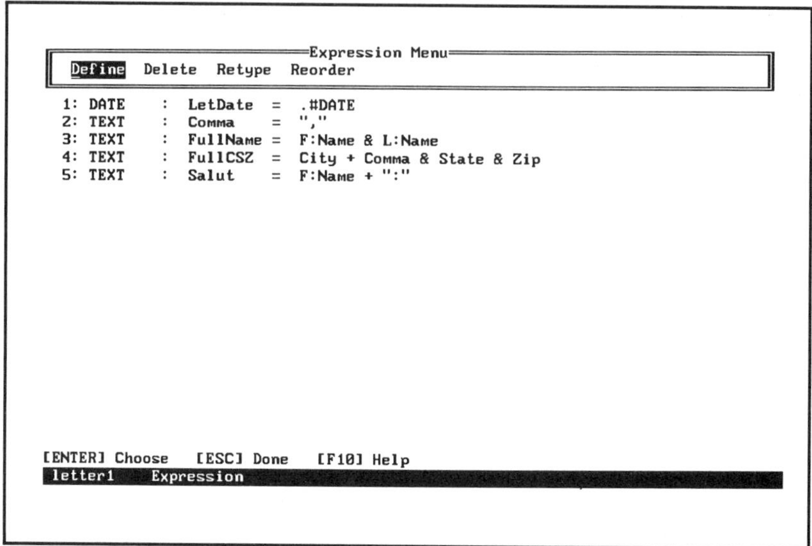

Figure 7.13: Variables for the form letter defined

With the cursor in <1,1>, press F6 and enter LetDate as the name of the variable to locate. Make <1,1> the start location and <1,30> the end location. Use the arrow keys and the F6 key to locate the rest of the column names and variables as listed below:

COLUMN/VARIABLE NAME	*START*	*END*
FullName	<3,1>	<3,30>
Company	<4,1>	<4,20>
Address	<5,1>	<5,25>
FullCSZ	<6,1>	<6,40>

Move the cursor to row 8, column 1 <8,1> and type in the word **Dear**. Press the space bar, press F6, and enter Salut as the variable name. Start the location at <8,6> and end it at <8,25>. Then move the cursor to line 10 and type in the letter. Be sure to press the Enter key before you get to the right edge of the screen when you're typing the letter. (R:BASE does not automatically wrap the text down to the next line.) Figure 7.14 shows a sample letter typed onto the screen, with start and end locations for column names and variables. You can use the arrow keys to move the cursor around, and you can use the Ins and Del keys to insert spaces and delete characters as necessary. Use the F1 (or Enter) key to insert new lines and the F2 key to delete lines as necessary.

You may have noticed that every line in this report is defined as a page header (PH) in the left column. We do not need any other type of line in this report, because each letter is to be printed on a separate page, and page headings always print once on each page. (In a sense, we've tricked the report generator into printing form letters by giving it only page headers to print.)

When your letter looks the way you want it to, press the Esc key twice to work your way to the exit options. Select Save Changes, and then select option 6 from the next menu to work your way back to the R> prompt.

PRINTING THE FORM LETTERS

To print the form letters, align the paper in the printer so that there is a page perforation (or the start of a new page) just above the print head. (To do so, it's best to turn the printer off, line up the paper, and

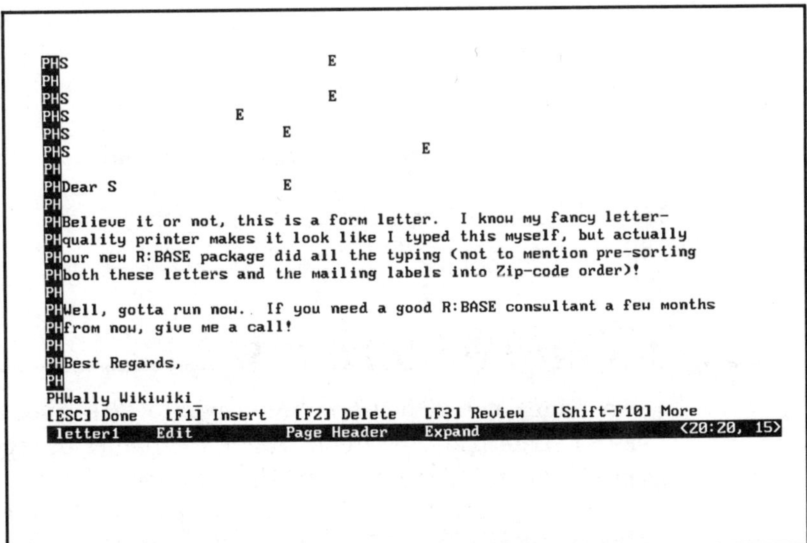

Figure 7.14: A form letter typed on the screen

then turn the printer back on so that R:BASE "knows" where the top of the page is.)

Before printing the letters, you can specify a date format for the date at the top of the letter. For letters, you might want to enter the command

```
SET DATE "MMM + DD, YYYY"
```

for a more formal date format.

To print letters on continuous-form paper, enter the command

```
OUTPUT PRINTER
```

at the R> prompt. To print letters one page at a time (on letterhead, for instance) enter the command

```
OUTPUT PRINTER WITH SCREEN
```

at the R> prompt, and then enter the command

```
PRINT Letter1 ORDER BY Zip
```

to print letters in ZIP-code order. (Might as well print the letters in the same order as the mailing labels, no?)

As with other types of printing, you can use the WHERE clause to specify search criteria for printing letters. For example, to print letters for everyone with entry dates of June 1, 1988, enter the command

```
PRINT Letter1 ORDER BY Zip WHERE Ent:Date = 06/01/88
```

Figure 7.15 shows a form letter created by the Letter1 report format, with the date set to "MMM + DD, YYYY".

MANAGING REPORTS

The Mail database now has three report formats associated with it: Director, Labels, and Letter1. To see the names of report formats associated with a database, enter the command

```
LIST REPORTS
```

at the R> prompt. The screen will display all report formats, as shown in Figure 7.16.

```
R>SET DATE "MMM+ DD, YYYY"
R>PRINT Letter1 ORDER BY Zip
January 30, 1988

Marie Miller
Zeerox, Inc.
234 C St.
Los Angeles, CA 91234

Dear Marie:

Believe it or not, this is a form letter.  I know my fancy letter-
quality printer makes it look like I typed this myself, but actually
our new R:BASE package did all the typing (not to mention pre-sorting
both these letters and the mailing labels into Zip-code order)!

Well, gotta run now.  If you need a good R:BASE consultant a few months
from now, give me a call!

Best Regards,

Wally Wikiwiki
More output follows - press [ESC] to quit, any key to continue_
```

Figure 7.15: A form letter created by the Letter1 report format

```
R>LIST REPORTS

     Report    Table / View
     --------  ------------
     director  Names
     labels    Names
     letter1   Names

R>_
```

Figure 7.16: Reports in the Mail database

The Report Options menu offers additional techniques for managing reports.

(1) Edit/Create a report
(2) List reports and associated tables
(3) Copy a report
(4) Remove a report
(5) Choose a database
(6) Exit from Reports EXPRESS

We've used the *Edit/Create a report* and *Exit from Reports EXPRESS* options with all the reports in this chapter already. The other options from this menu are summarized below:

List reports and associated tables	Displays a list of reports associated with the currently open database, and displays the names of their associated tables or views. (Same as entering the command LIST REPORTS at the R> prompt.)
Copy a report	Copies an existing report in the database to another report in the same database. R:BASE will prompt you for the name of the report to copy and a name for the new, copied report. Useful for creating new reports that resemble existing reports or that use the same expressions.
Remove a report	Prompts you for the name of the report to remove, and deletes the report format from the database.
Choose a database	Allows you to change the active database.

In this chapter, we've discussed many techniques used to design and create reports. In later chapters, we'll discuss more advanced techniques for formatting reports, including printing totals and subtotals. In the next chapter, we'll learn techniques for creating custom data entry forms.

Chapter 8

Creating Custom Data-Entry Forms

FAST TRACK

To simplify data entry in your forms, **210**

use default values or suggested responses to suggest a likely entry into a field. Use Field Customization when locating or relocating a field to establish default values for the field.

To examine further options for managing forms, **213**

call up the Forms EXPRESS Main menu and the Form Options menu by typing **FORMS** at the R> prompt and opening a database.

IN THIS CHAPTER, WE'LL DISCUSS TECHNIQUES FOR creating custom forms for entering and editing table rows. The techniques used to create custom forms are similar to those that we used to create custom reports.

If you are following along on-line, make sure that the Mail database is open and that the R> prompt is displayed. If you have just started R:BASE, type

USER ***password***

and press Enter (substituting your own password in place of *password*). This establishes you as the database owner—someone who can change the database structure. You'll be changing the Mail database structure when you create forms for it.

CREATING CUSTOM FORMS

There are two primary reasons for creating custom forms: they generally look better than the standard displays, and you can add helpful advice to your screens to simplify the process of entering and editing data.

Let's look at an example. Figure 8.1 shows the standard display used for entering rows with the LOAD WITH PROMPTS command. Figure 8.2, on the other hand, shows a custom form. Notice how the column names are spelled out (for example, Entry Date rather than Ent:Date) and that the instructions for managing the highlighting and cursor appear at the bottom of the screen.

To create custom forms in R:BASE, use Forms EXPRESS to "draw" a facsimile of the form on the screen, in much the same way that you used Reports EXPRESS to draw a facsimile of printed reports in the last chapter. As with Reports EXPRESS, you can enter Forms EXPRESS either from PBE or the R> prompt. From the PBE Main menu, select *Define or modify a database, FORMS,* and then execute the command. From the R> prompt, type in the command

FORMS

and press Enter.

```
R>LOAD Names WITH PROMPTS
 Begin R:BASE Data Loading

 Press [ESC] to end, [ENTER] to continue
 L:Name   (TEXT     ):Janda
 F:Name   (TEXT     ):Chrissie
 Company  (TEXT     ):UCLA Medical Center
 Address  (TEXT     ):345 Westwood Blvd.
 City     (TEXT     ):Los Angeles
 state    (TEXT     ):CA
 Zip      (TEXT     ):92122
 Ent:Date (DATE     ):6/27/88_
```

Figure 8.1: The LOAD WITH PROMPTS display

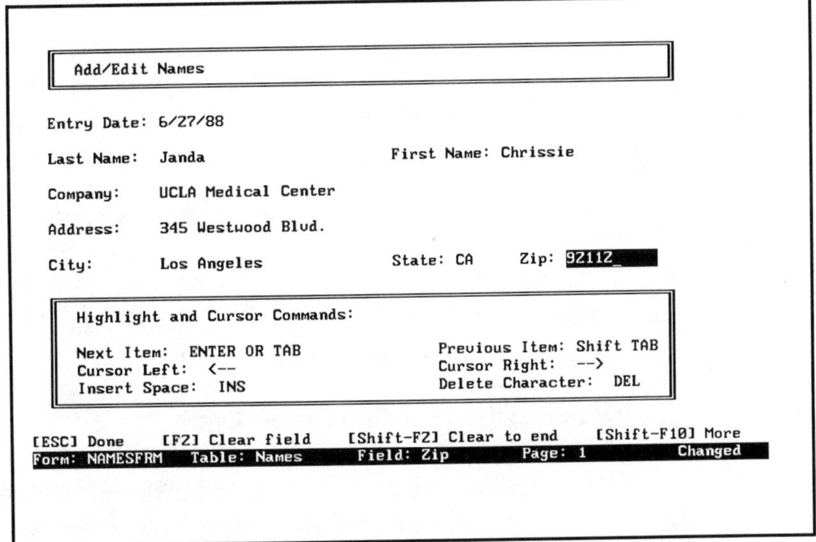

Figure 8.2: A custom form for entering and editing data

If no database is open, you'll be given the opportunity to *Choose a database.* Select Mail and enter your password. Once a database is open,

Forms EXPRESS displays the Form Options menu shown below:

(1) Edit/Create a form
(2) List forms
(3) Copy a form
(4) Remove a form
(5) Choose a database
(6) Exit from Forms EXPRESS

To create a new form or change an existing one, select option 1. R:BASE asks that you choose a form or select New to create a new form. For this exercise, select New. R:BASE asks that you

Enter the form name:

For our first sample form, type in NamesFrm and press Enter. Next, the screen will ask

Do you want to customize the form characteristics? Yes No

You can customize the form later, so just select No for now. The screen then displays the names of tables in the open database and asks that you select a table for the form. For this example, select Names.

Next the screen asks

Do you want to customize the table characteristics? Yes No

There is no need for this yet, so select No for the time being. Next the Form Definition menu appears (which resembles the Report Definition menu), presenting the following options:

Edit   Expression   Customize   Draw

The Edit option allows you to "draw" your form on the screen and locate column names in much the same way that you would on a report format screen. The keys used for creating forms are listed in Table 8.1. (Additional keys can be used when creating more complicated forms, which we'll discuss in Chapter 13.)

Table 8.1: Keys Used to Create and Edit Forms

KEY	PURPOSE
F1	Insert a blank line above the cursor
F2	Delete the current line
Shift-F2	Delete a field
F3	Display column and variable names
F4	Repeat a character
F6	Locate or relocate a column name or variable
F10	Display a help screen
Shift-F10	Display more function keys at the bottom of the screen
Ins	Insert a space at the cursor
Del	Delete the character at the cursor
↑	Move the cursor up one line
↓	Move the cursor down one line
→	Move the cursor right one character
←	Move the cursor left one character
Ctrl-→	Move the cursor to the right of the screen
Ctrl-←	Move the cursor to the left of the screen
Tab	Move the cursor ten spaces to the right
Shift-Tab	Move the cursor ten spaces to the left
Home	Move the cursor to the top left of the screen (or page)
End	Move the cursor to the bottom right of the screen (or page)
Enter ↵	Move the cursor down a line
Esc	Finish the current task and bring back the previous menu

Select Edit from the menu so that the menu disappears and the cursor is on the screen ready to lay out the form format.

PLACING PROMPTS

To begin creating the form we displayed earlier, you must place all of the necessary prompts in the form. Use the arrow keys to move the cursor to row 2, column 6 (as indicated by the symbol <2,6> at the bottom-right corner of the screen), and type in the title

Add/Edit Names

Given your experience in drawing report formats in the last chapter, you should be able to move the cursor easily to any location you wish using the arrow keys. (In fact, forms are much easier to draw because there is no need for headings, detail lines, footings, and so forth.) The starting locations for the various prompts on the NamesFrm form are listed below. Position the cursor to the coordinates listed in the left column, and type in the prompts listed in the right column. Figure 8.3 shows how your screen should look after typing in all the prompts.

LOCATION	*PROMPT*
<2,6>	Add/Edit Names
<5,3>	Entry Date:
<7,3>	Last Name:
<7,40>	First Name:
<9,3>	Company:
<11,3>	Address:
<13,3>	City:
<13,40>	State:
<13,54>	Zip:
<16,6>	Highlight and Cursor Commands:
<18,6>	Next Item: ENTER or TAB
<18,45>	Previous Item: SHIFT-TAB
<19,6>	Cursor Left: ←

```
   Add/Edit Names

Entry Date:

Last Name:                          First Name:

Company:

Address:

City:                               State:        Zip:

   Highlight and Cursor Commands:

   Next Item:  ENTER OR TAB                 Previous Item: Shift TAB
   Cursor Left:  <--                        Cursor Right:  -->
   Insert Space:  INS                       Delete Character:  DEL_

[ESC] Return  [F1] Insert  [F2] Delete  [F3] Review  [Shift-F10] More
Form: namesfrm   Edit            Table: Names              Page 1  <20,67>
```

Figure 8.3: Prompts typed into the form

<19,45> Cursor Right: →

<20,6> Insert Space: INS

<20,45> Delete Character: DEL

PLACING COLUMN NAMES

After all the prompts are on the screen, locate the column names on the screen using the same techniques we used to locate columns and variables on the report format. For example, to locate the Ent:Date field next to the Entry Date prompt, move the cursor to row 5, column 15 <5,15>, and press the F6 key. R:BASE will ask that you

Enter column or variable name:
(Press [ENTER] for menu selection)

(If at some point you cannot remember the name of a column or variable, you can press the Enter key to select the appropriate column name from a menu.) For this example, type in **Ent:Date** and press Enter.

R:BASE asks the following:

Do you want to define an expression for Ent:Date? Yes No

Since Ent:Date is a column name, we don't need to define an expression for it, so select No. R:BASE then asks

> Do you want to customize field characteristics? Yes No

We can customize the form later for a fancier display, so for now just select No.

Next R:BASE asks that you

> Move cursor to start location and press [S]

With the cursor on <5,15>, press the letter S on your keyboard. The S appears on the screen and the cursor jumps to <5,44>. The screen displays

> Move cursor to end and press [E]

With the cursor on <5,44>, type the letter E. That completes the job of locating the Ent:Date column name on the form. You'll see the S and the E for the Ent:Date column name next to the Entry Date prompt, as in Figure 8.4.

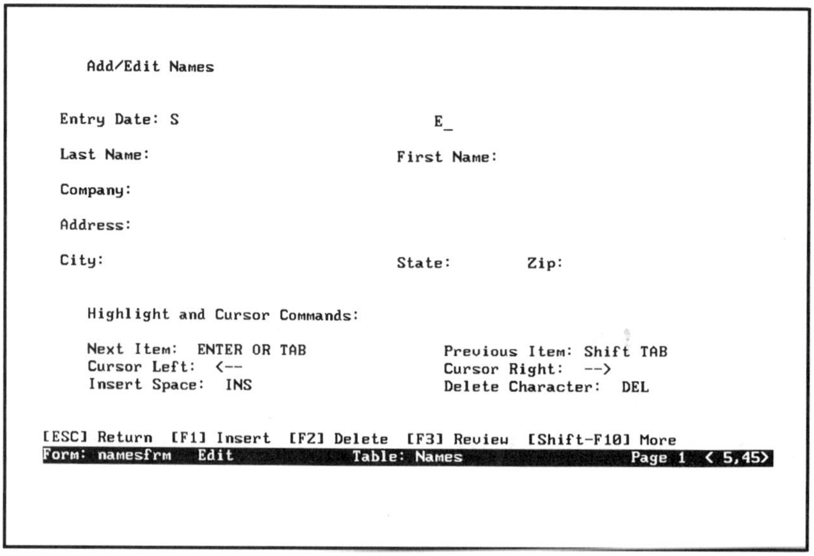

```
   Add/Edit Names

 Entry Date: S                          E_

 Last Name:                           First Name:

 Company:

 Address:

 City:                                State:       Zip:

   Highlight and Cursor Commands:

   Next Item:  ENTER OR TAB              Previous Item: Shift TAB
   Cursor Left:  <--                     Cursor Right:  -->
   Insert Space:  INS                    Delete Character:  DEL

[ESC] Return  [F1] Insert  [F2] Delete  [F3] Review  [Shift-F10] More
Form: namesfrm   Edit            Table: Names               Page 1  < 5,45>
```

Figure 8.4: Start and end locations for the Ent:Date column

Use the same technique of positioning the cursor—pressing F6 and typing S and E—to place the rest of the column names on the form. You can answer No to the two "Yes No" questions that appear on the screen for each of these column names. The column names, start locations, and end locations to use on this form are listed below:

COLUMN NAME	*START*	*END*
L:Name	<7,15>	<7,29>
F:Name	<7,52>	<7,66>
Company	<9,15>	<9,34>
Address	<11,15>	<11,39>
City	<13,15>	<13,29>
State	<13,47>	<13,48>
Zip	<13,59>	<13,68>

After you're finished locating all of the column names, press Esc. Your screen should look like Figure 8.5.

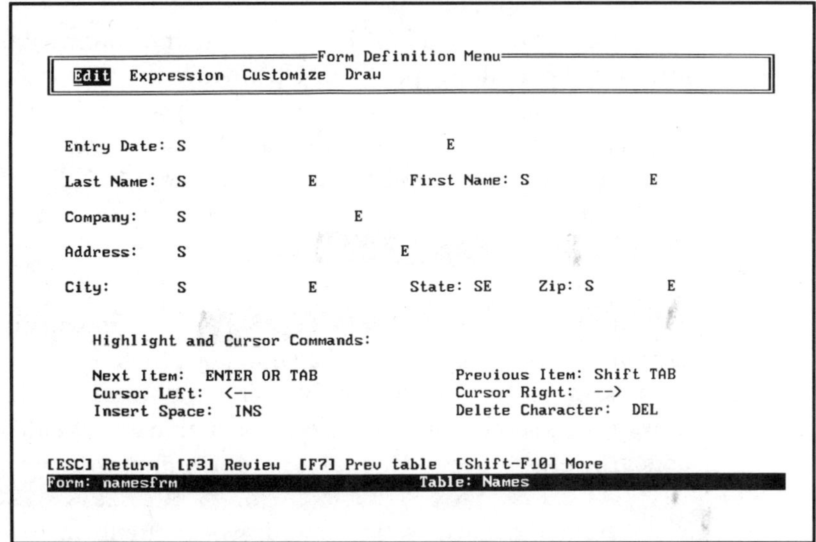

Figure 8.5: Column names located on the screen

DRAWING BOXES ON THE FORM

For a fancier display, you can add double- or single-bar boxes. To do so, select Draw from the top menu. The submenu displays the options

Single line   Double line   Erase

Select Double line to draw a double-line box.

Notice that in the upper-right corner the screen displays Pen Up. This indicates that you can freely move the cursor without drawing anything on the screen. Let's draw a box around the screen title at the top of the screen.

With the Pen Up indicator still on, move the cursor to <1,3>. To put the pen down, press the F4 key (the upper-right corner now reads Pen Down). Hold down or repeatedly press the → key until the cursor gets to <1,70>. You'll notice that with Pen Down, the cursor draws the double line as it moves. Press the ↓ key twice to move the cursor to <3,70>. Hold down the ← key until the cursor reaches <3,3>. Press the ↑ key twice to move the cursor to <1,3>. Now press the → key to move the cursor to <1,4>. That completes the box drawn around the title.

To draw a box around the instructions at the bottom of the screen, first press F4 to lift the pen (Pen Up). Move the cursor to <15,3>. Press F4 to put the pen back down; then press → until the cursor reaches <15,70>. Press ↓ repeatedly to move the cursor to <21,70>. Press ← until the cursor reaches <21,3>. Press ↑ to move the cursor to <15,3>; then press → to move the cursor to <15,4>. Press F4 to lift the pen. Figure 8.6 shows the form with the boxes added.

When you are finished, press the Esc key. The top menu for drawing boxes appears on the screen again. The Single Line option works in the same fashion as the Double Line option we just used, but it draws only a single thin line. The Erase option erases either single or double lines as you move the cursor over the lines with the pen down.

Press Esc to leave the Draw menu and return to the Form Definition menu. For now, we're done drawing our form, so press Esc again to view the exit options, as listed below:

Save Changes   Discard Changes   Return

```
                                                              Pen Up
 ┌──────────────────────────────────────────────────────────────────┐
 │  Add/Edit Names                                                  │
 └──────────────────────────────────────────────────────────────────┘
 Entry Date: S                          E
 Last Name:  S            E          First Name: S             E
 Company:    S                 E
 Address:    S                      E
 City:       S            E          State: SE      Zip: S       E

 ┌──────────────────────────────────────────────────────────────────┐
 │ Highlight and Cursor Commands:                                   │
 │                                                                  │
 │ Next Item:  ENTER OR TAB              Previous Item: Shift TAB   │
 │ Cursor Left:  <--                     Cursor Right:  -->         │
 │ Insert Space:  INS                    Delete Character:  DEL     │
 └──────────────────────────────────────────────────────────────────┘

[ESC] Return  [F4] Pen Up/Dn  [F10] Help  [↑] Up  [Shift-F10] More
Form: namesfrm   Draw borders     Table: Names           Page 1  <15, 4>
```

Figure 8.6: Boxes drawn on the custom form

Select *Save Changes.* As with Reports EXPRESS, selecting this option saves your work and brings you to a higher-level menu. Select option 6 from the next menu to return to PBE or the R> prompt, depending on where you started.

Although the form we created fits onto a single screen, you are not limited to that. R:BASE lets you create forms that are up to five screens long.

USING A FORM FOR DATA ENTRY

To enter new data using the new form, type in the ENTER command, followed by the name of the form. For this example, make sure you are at the R> prompt, type in the command

```
ENTER NamesFrm
```

and press the Enter key. The form appears on the screen, as shown in Figure 8.7.

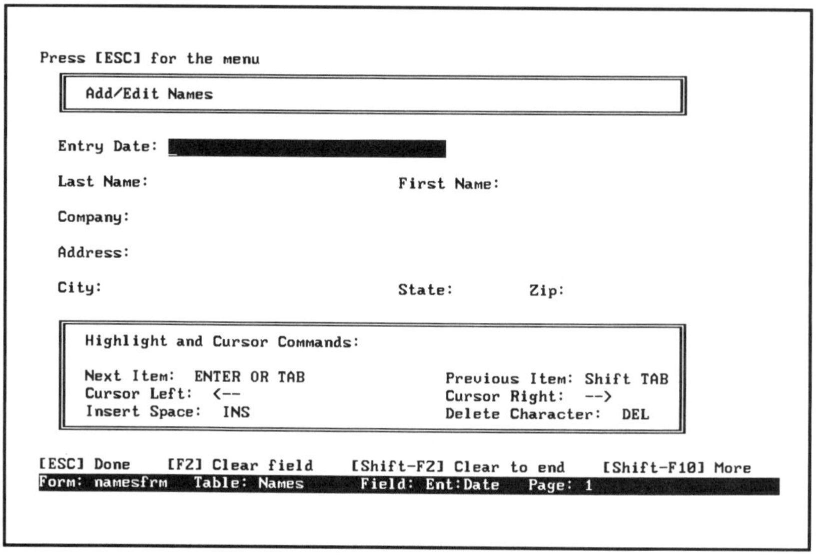

```
Press [ESC] for the menu

  Add/Edit Names

 Entry Date:

 Last Name:                        First Name:

 Company:

 Address:

 City:                             State:        Zip:

  Highlight and Cursor Commands:

  Next Item:  ENTER OR TAB                Previous Item: Shift TAB
  Cursor Left:  <--                       Cursor Right:  -->
  Insert Space:  INS                      Delete Character:  DEL

[ESC] Done    [F2] Clear field    [Shift-F2] Clear to end    [Shift-F10] More
Form: namesfrm   Table: Names      Field: Ent:Date    Page: 1
```

Figure 8.7: The NamesFrm form on the screen

Type data into the highlighted area, and then press Enter to move the highlighting to the next prompt. You can move from item to item using the Tab key. You can move the cursor within the highlighted area by using the arrow keys. Use the Ins and Del keys to insert and delete characters inside the highlighted area. Figure 8.8 shows the NamesFrm screen with data for a new row. If you're following along on-line, type these data into the screen.

After you've entered all the data on the screen, a menu will appear at the top of the screen, as follows:

Add   Duplicate   Edit again   Discard   Quit

These options are summarized below:

Add	Adds the data on the screen to the table in the database, thereby saving it. The screen is then cleared so that you can enter another record (row).
Duplicate	Adds the data on the screen to the database, but does not clear the entry from the screen. Useful for entering records that are similar; for

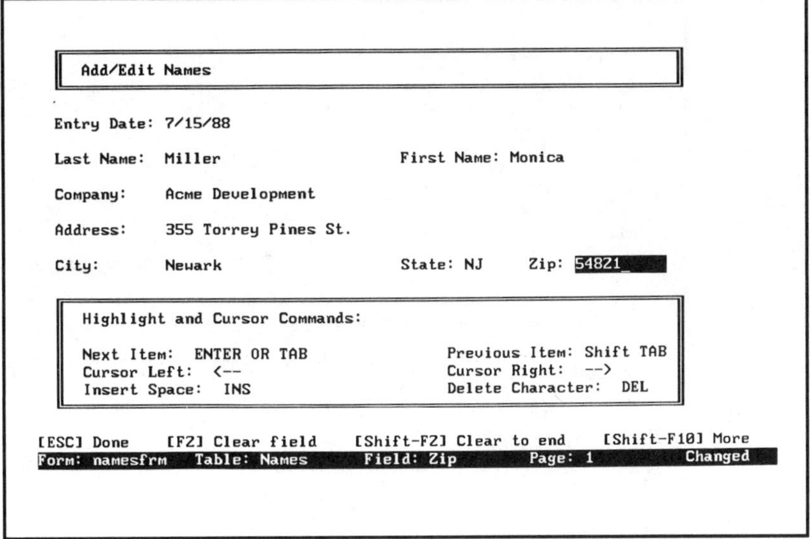

Figure 8.8: Data for one new row typed in the NamesFrm screen

example, many individuals who work for the same company and therefore have the same company name and address.

Edit Again — Does not save the information on the screen, but instead lets you make further changes before saving the data.

Discard — Removes the data from the screen and from the database as well if already saved. (Asks for permission first.)

Quit — Leaves the data-entry mode after saving the current data, and returns to the R> prompt or the Prompt menu.

This menu appears each time you fill in all the prompts on the form. You can also call this menu up at any time while using the form by pressing the Esc key. Now select the Add option to add the data to the Names table.

The form remains on the screen, but the data are erased. Go ahead and fill out the screen once again, so that it looks like Figure 8.9.

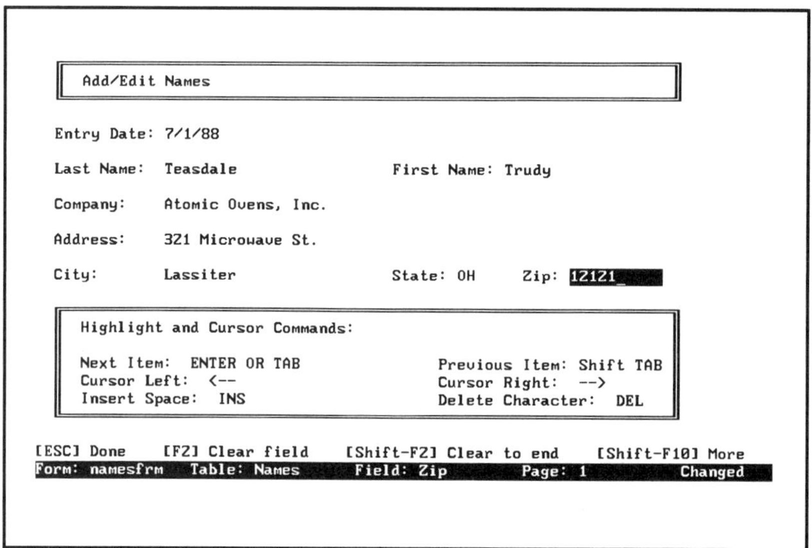

Figure 8.9: The entry form with another row typed in

Suppose that you were about to add another row of data for a person who works at this same company. You could save yourself some typing by selecting the Duplicate option rather than the Add option. The Duplicate option will store these data in the Names table and also keep them on the screen for the next row. Now, just change the Last Name field to **Martin** and the First Name field to **Mary,** so the screen looks like Figure 8.10.

To save these data, press the Esc key and select the Add option. When you're finished entering data, press Esc and select the Quit option.

From the R> prompt, you can verify that the new data have been added to the table by entering the command

```
SELECT ALL FROM Names
```

You'll see the new rows at the bottom of the table, as shown in Figure 8.11.

The same form that you created to enter data can also be used to edit data, as we'll discuss next.

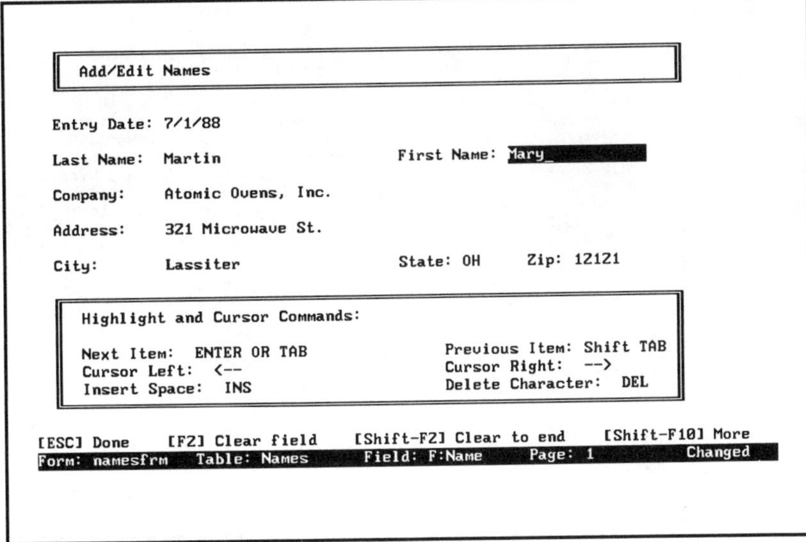

Figure 8.10: A third row added to the Names table

EDITING YOUR DATA WITH CUSTOM FORMS

To edit data using a custom form, use the EDIT USING command, followed by the name of the form. For this example, at the R> prompt, enter the command

```
EDIT USING NamesFrm
```

The first row from the table appears on the screen, along with a menu of editing options, as shown in Figure 8.12.

Once you select Edit, you can move the highlighting with the Tab and Shift-Tab keys, and you can make changes within the highlighted area using the arrow, Ins, and Del keys. After making the necessary changes, press the Esc key and bring back the menu. You can then select any of the options from the menu, as listed below:

OPTION	*FUNCTION*
Edit	Moves the cursor into the form to make changes
Save	Saves current changes on the screen

```
R>SELECT ALL FROM Names
 L:Name          F:Name          Company              Address
 --------------- --------------- -------------------- -------------------------
 Smith           Sandy           Hi Tech, Inc.        456 N. Rainbow Dr.
 Jones           Mindy           ABC Co.              123 A St.
 Miller          Marie           Zeerox, Inc.         234 C St.
 Adams           Bart            DataSpec Inc.        P.O. Box 2890
 Miller          Anne            Golden Gate Co.      2313 Sixth St.
 Baker           Robin           Peach Computers      2311 Coast Hwy.
 Miller          Monica          Acme Development     355 Torrey Pines St.
 Teasdale        Trudy           Atomic Ovens, Inc.   321 Microwave St.
 Martin          Mary            Atomic Ovens, Inc.   321 Microwave St.
R>_
```

Figure 8.11: Verification that new rows have been added

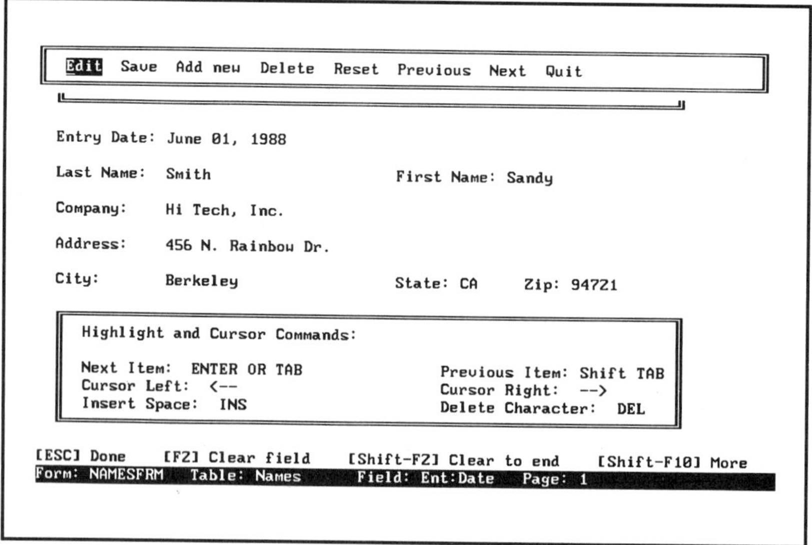

Figure 8.12: Data from the first row of the Names table with editing options displayed

OPTION	*FUNCTION*
Edit	Moves the cursor into the form to make changes
Save	Saves current changes on the screen
Add New	Enters modified data into the database as a new row, and leaves the original row in the database unchanged
Delete	Deletes the row from the table
Reset	Undoes the latest edits (assuming they have not already been saved on the database)
Previous	Saves any changes made to the current row; then skips to the previous row in the table if one exists (when only one table is being edited)
Next	Saves any changes in the current row; then skips to the next row in the table if one exists (when only one table is being edited)
Quit	Returns to the R> prompt or the PBE menu

The general procedure for editing records in a table is to pinpoint the row to edit either by specifying a WHERE clause in the initial EDIT USING command or by using the Next and Previous options from edit mode. Once the row to edit is on the screen, select the Edit option and make the necessary changes using the arrow, Tab, Ins, Del, and other keys to move the highlight and the cursor. While the cursor is inside the form for editing, you can also use the following keys (as indicated at the bottom of the screen):

F2	Empties the entire currently highlighted field
Shift-F2	Deletes the contents of the currently highlighted field to the right of the cursor
F5	Brings back the unedited contents of the currently highlighted field
F7	Skips back to the previous row in the table (same as Esc, Previous)
F8	Skips to the next row in the table (Same as Esc, Next)

F10	Displays help
Shift-F10	Shows more function keys at the bottom of the screen
Esc	Returns to the top menu

When you've finished editing the row, press Esc to bring back the top menu. Selecting Save, Add New, Previous, Next, or Quit will save all the changes you've made. Selecting Reset (before selecting any of the other commands) will undo all the changes you've just made. You may want to practice on your own to get used to editing with the form.

The process of looking for the rows that you want to edit can be sped up considerably by using the ORDER BY and WHERE clauses. For example, if you want to edit the data for somebody with the last name of Miller, from the R> prompt you can enter the command

```
EDIT USING NamesFrm WHERE L:Name = Miller
```

Each time you select the Next option from the top menu, another Miller will be displayed. After the last Miller is displayed, R:BASE will beep to indicate that there are no more Millers left.

To skip through the Millers in alphabetical order by first name while editing, you can enter the command

```
EDIT USING NamesFrm ORDER BY F:Name WHERE +
+> L:Name = Miller
```

If you specifically want to edit data for Marie Miller, you can enter the command

```
EDIT USING NamesFrm WHERE L:Name = Miller AND +
+> F:Name = Marie
```

This single row will be displayed for editing. Select the Edit option and make your changes.

You can also use the edit mode to add new data. Suppose you want to add the name of someone who works at a company already listed in the table (ABC Co., for example). Enter the command

```
EDIT USING NamesFrm WHERE Company = "ABC Co."
```

The form will appear containing all the data for the first row that contains ABC Co. Select the Edit option, and change whatever is necessary for the new row—probably the L:Name, F:Name, and Ent:Date columns. Then, press Esc and select Add New. The new row will be added to the table, and the original row will be left unchanged.

EDITING EXISTING FORMS

To modify an existing form, enter Forms EXPRESS again (by entering the command **FORMS** at the R> prompt). From the Form Options menu, select option 1, *Edit/Create a Form,* and then select the name of the form to edit when R:BASE displays the next menu.

You can use the Edit option from the top menu to change and enter prompts. You can use the Draw option to enter and change boxes. Use the Ins, Del, F1, and F2 keys on the screen to make changes.

To change a location of a field on the form, move the cursor anywhere between the S and E for the field. Press the F6 key as though entering the field for the first time. The screen will ask if you want to customize the characteristics for the field. Select No (we'll discuss *field characteristics* later). R:BASE will ask if you want to relocate the field. Select Yes. R:BASE will eliminate the current location for the field and allow you to reenter the start and end locations for the field.

To delete a field from the screen, move the cursor to any position between the S and the E, and type Shift-F2.

Other ways in which you can customize forms are discussed in the following sections.

CUSTOMIZING FEATURES OF YOUR FORM

You can customize several overall features of a form, such as its color and top-menu display. To do so, select Customize from the Form Definition menu and Form from the customize submenu. You'll see a screen, as in Figure 8.13, displaying all your options for customizing the overall form. (This same form will appear if you answer Yes to the opening question about customizing form characteristics when you are creating a new form.)

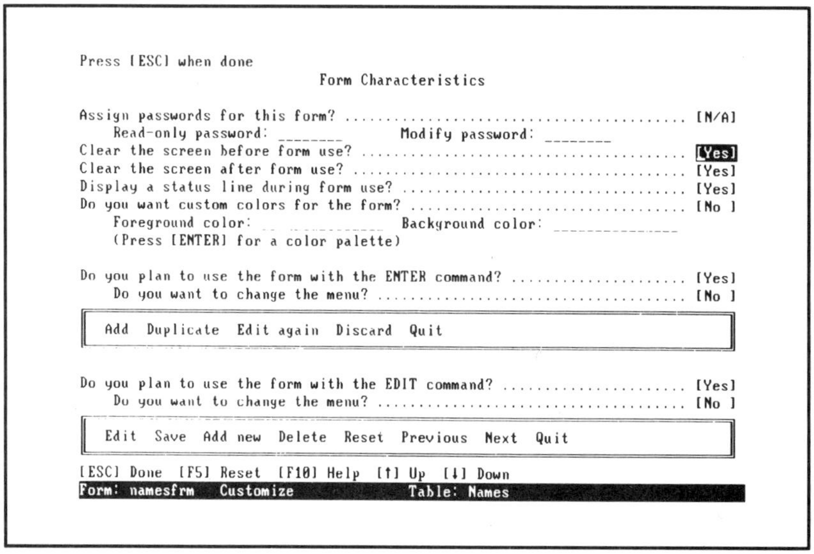

```
Press [ESC] when done
                                Form Characteristics

Assign passwords for this form? ........................................ [N/A]
    Read-only password: ________        Modify password: ________
Clear the screen before form use? ...................................... [Yes]
Clear the screen after form use? ....................................... [Yes]
Display a status line during form use? ................................. [Yes]
Do you want custom colors for the form? ................................ [No ]
    Foreground color: ______________    Background color: ______________
    (Press [ENTER] for a color palette)

Do you plan to use the form with the ENTER command? .................... [Yes]
    Do you want to change the menu? .................................... [No ]
 | Add  Duplicate  Edit again  Discard  Quit                               |

Do you plan to use the form with the EDIT command? ..................... [Yes]
    Do you want to change the menu? .................................... [No ]
 | Edit  Save  Add new  Delete  Reset  Previous  Next  Quit                |
[ESC] Done  [F5] Reset  [F10] Help  [↑] Up  [↓] Down
Form: namesfrm   Customize            Table: Names
```

Figure 8.13: The form customization menu

You can use the ↑ and ↓ keys to move the highlight from question to question. Typing Y changes a No answer to Yes, and vice versa. Questions followed by an N/A are not applicable to the form being customized.

The first question on the form reads

Assign passwords for this form? .... [N/A]
Read-only password: __________ Modify password: __________

On tables that use password protection, you can change this option to Yes, and then assign passwords for Read-only access and Modify access. If you assign a password for Read-only access, only users who know the password will be able to view data through this form. If you assign a Modify password, any user will be able to view data on the form, but only those who know the password will be able to change data on the form.

The second two questions on the screen are

Clear the screen before form use? .... [Yes]
Clear the screen after form use? .... [Yes]

Usually you'll want to leave these as Yes so that the form appears on a clear screen and erases itself from the screen when no longer in use.

The next question on the form,

```
Display a status line during form use? ................................ [Yes]
```

lets you decide whether to leave the status bar on the bottom of the screen while the form is in use [Yes] or to hide it while the form is in use [No].

The next question, shown below, refers to color monitors:

```
Do you want custom colors for the form? ............................ [No ]
Foreground color: ___________ Background color: ___________
(Press [ENTER] for a color palette)
```

If you change this answer to Yes, you can then press the Enter key twice for a palette of colors to select from. Select the colors for the form in the same fashion as you would using the SET COLOR command, and then press Esc.

The next question asks whether the form will be used with the ENTER command (for entering new data into the table). Usually, you will want to leave this as a Yes answer:

```
Do you plan to use the form with the ENTER command? ...... [Yes]
```

If you do want to use the ENTER command, you can change the menu that automatically appears at the top of the form when you use the ENTER command, as the next question in the form indicates:

```
Do you want to change the menu? ..................................... [No ]
Add   Duplicate   Edit again   Discard   Quit
```

If you select Yes (by typing Y and pressing Enter), R:BASE will ask if you wish to enter a title, which will appear above the menu. Type in the title and press Enter.

Next R:BASE will display all the menu options that the menu can contain. You can select all the options or just the ones that you want to appear in the menu. You can also determine the order of the options in the menu by selecting them in the order in which you want them to appear (left to right).

The next question is

Do you plan to use the form with the EDIT command? .... [Yes]
Do you want to change the menu? .... [No]
Edit Save Add new Delete Reset Previous Next Quit

As in the previous question, this one allows you to determine whether the form can be used with the EDIT command, and it allows you to add a title and modify the default edit menu.

When you've finished selecting form characteristics, press the Esc key.

CUSTOMIZING THE CHARACTERISTICS OF YOUR TABLE

You can also customize several characteristics of the table associated with the form. Select Customize from the Form Definition menu, and then select Table and Characteristics from the submenus to do so. This brings up the Table Characteristics menu. (Also, when you create a new form, the Table Characteristics menu will appear if you select Yes to the opening prompt about customizing table characteristics.) Figure 8.14 shows the Table Characteristics menu on the screen.

The questions on the form are summarized below:

Do you want to add new rows to the table? .... [Yes]

Unless you do not ever want to add new rows to a table, this answer should be left as Yes. Similarly, the following three answers should be left as Yes unless the data on the table are never to be edited or deleted:

Do you want to replace existing rows in the table? .... [Yes]
Is the replace automatic when the user leaves the row? ....[Yes]
Do you want to delete rows from the table? .... [Yes]
Restrict the delete to the current table? .... [Yes]

```
Press [ESC] when done
                            Table Characteristics

Do you want to add new rows to the table? ............................. [Yes]

Do you want to replace existing rows in the table? .................... [Yes]
    Is the replace automatic when the user leaves the row? ............ [Yes]

Do you want to delete rows from the table? ............................ [Yes]
    Restrict the delete to the current table? ......................... [Yes]

Is this table on the MANY side of a ONE-to-MANY relationship? ......... [N/A]

Do you want to define a region? ....................................... [No ]
    Do you want a border around the region? ........................... [N/A]
    How many lines in the border - enter 1 or 2: _
    Do you want custom colors for the region? ......................... [N/A]
    Foreground color: ______________   Background color: ______________
    (Press [ENTER] for a color palette)


[ESC] Done  [F5] Reset  [F10] Help  [↑] Up  [↓] Down
Form: namesfrm   Customize table          Table: Names
```

Figure 8.14: Customizing table characteristics

The remaining questions on the menu are for more advanced applications. We'll discuss these in Chapter 11.

CUSTOMIZING FIELD CHARACTERISTICS

Whenever you locate, or relocate, a field on the form using the F6 key, the screen will ask if you want to customize the field characteristics. For example, place yourself in Edit mode, and press F6 when the cursor is between the S and E for Ent:Date. When asked about customizing field characteristics, answer Yes. The Field Characteristics menu appears on the screen, as in Figure 8.15.

Options on this menu affect only the individual field being located or relocated, not the overall form or table. The first questions asked—

```
Will new data be entered in the field? ........................ [Yes]
Can the user change the data displayed in the field? ........... [Yes]
Restrict changes to the current table? ......................... [Yes]
```

```
Press [ESC] when done
                          Field Characteristics

Will new data be entered in the field? ................................ [Yes]

Can the user change the data displayed in the field? .................. [Yes]
    Restrict changes to the current table? ............................ [Yes]

Do you want to display a default value in the field? .................. [No ]
    Enter the default value OR #DUP to use the previous row value
_____________________________

Do you want custom colors for the field? .............................. [No ]
    Foreground color: ____________ Background color: ______________
    (Press [ENTER] for a color palette)




[ESC] Done  [F5] Reset  [F10] Help  [↑] Up  [↓] Down
Form: namesfrm   Column     Field: Ent:Date   Type: DATE        Table: Names
```

Figure 8.15: Customizing field characteristics

—should all be left with Yes answers, except in more advanced applications involving multiple tables. (Again, this is a topic we'll discuss in Chapter 13.)

The next question about default values will be discussed in detail in the next section.

The last question on the menu, shown below, lets you select color for the single field:

```
Do you want custom colors for the field? ............................. [No ]
Foreground color: ___________ Background color: ___________
(Press [ENTER] for a color palette)
```

Changing the answer to Yes and pressing the Enter key twice will allow you to define colors for the individual field from the color palette. (Answer No for now.)

When you finish defining the field characteristics, press the Esc key. Then answer N when asked if you want to relocate your Ent:Date field.

DEFINING DEFAULT VALUES

Default values (also called *suggested responses*) are a valuable asset to forms, particularly in forms where information might otherwise have to be typed in repeatedly. For example, NamesFrm contains the column Ent:Date, which is the date that the row was entered into the database. On any given day, this is likely to be the same for every row entered into the database. Therefore, you could make the current date the *default value* for the field. When entering new rows into the database, the current date will automatically appear in the Ent:Date field. You (or whoever is entering the data) can just press the Enter key to accept the default date, or you can type in a new date.

Another example is the State column in the Names table. If 90 percent of the individuals in the table were from the state of California, you could make CA the default value for the field. That way, when entering data, you need only press Enter to skip over the State field and use the "suggested" value, CA. If the state weren't CA, you could type a different state into the field.

To establish these default values into NamesFrm, select Edit to move the cursor to the screen, and place the cursor between the S and the E for the Ent:Date column name. Press F6, and the screen asks if you want to customize the field characteristic. Select Yes, and then change the answer to the question about default values to Yes and press Enter. Type in **#DATE** (which stands for the current date) as the default value. Press Esc and answer No to the prompt about relocating the field.

To make CA (or another state) the default value for the State field, move the cursor between the S and the E for the State field, and press F6. Select Yes to change the field characteristics and Yes to enter the default field. Type in **CA** (or whatever abbreviation you wish) as the default value, and press Enter. Answer No to the prompt about relocating the field.

The #DUP function is a special type of default value that repeats whatever was entered into the last row as the default value. An example where this would be useful would be when you are entering data for individuals from several states, but entering them grouped by states. If you entered AK residents first, AK would be the default value fcr all the records, until you typed in a new state on the form. The new state would be the default value in later records, until you typed in another new state.

When you are finished entering the default values for the fields, use the Esc key to work your way back to the exit options, and select

Save Changes. From the R> prompt, enter the command

```
ENTER NamesFrm
```

to call up the form and enter new data. The form will appear with the default values already in their fields, as shown in Figure 8.16. Notice how the date is being displayed in "long " form. This is because, in the last chapter, we set the date to "MMM + DD, YYYY" format prior to printing a report. The date format setting has been saved with the database. Pressing Enter while the default value is highlighted accepts the suggested value as the entered data. Optionally, you can type over the suggested value (or use F2 to delete it) to enter a different value into the column.

CHANGING THE ORDER OF ENTRY FOR FIELDS

When you create a form, the order in which you locate column names on the form determines the order in which R:BASE cycles through them when entering or editing data through the form. You

```
Press [ESC] for the menu

  Add/Edit Names

 Entry Date: January 31, 1988

 Last Name:                          First Name:

 Company:

 Address:

 City:                               State: CA     Zip:

  Highlight and Cursor Commands:

  Next Item:  ENTER OR TAB                Previous Item: Shift TAB
  Cursor Left:  <--                       Cursor Right:  -->
  Insert Space:  INS                      Delete Character:  DEL

[ESC] Done   [F2] Clear field   [Shift-F2] Clear to end   [Shift-F10] More
Form: namesfrm   Table: Names    Field: Ent:Date   Page: 1
```

Figure 8.16: Default values in the Ent:Date and State fields

can change the order in which R:BASE cycles the highlighter through the prompts by selecting Customize and Field Order from the top menu in Forms EXPRESS. When you select Field Order, you'll be given the following options:

```
Reorder   Cycle
```

To change the order, select Reorder. R:BASE displays the current order in which it moves the highlighter through the form and allows you to define a new order. Simply type in the number of the item to reorder and its new position, as instructed on the screen. Press Esc when you are finished.

To test the new order, select the Cycle option from the menu. Press the Enter key repeatedly to see the order in which R:BASE will move the highlighter through the prompts. Press Esc when you are finished.

When you've determined the appropriate order for your form, press the Esc key a few times to get back to the Exit Options menu, and select Save Changes to save the new order.

MANAGING FORMS

You can manage forms in the same way that you manage reports. The Forms EXPRESS Main menu lets you manage and view your forms, as does the Reports EXPRESS Main menu.

The Form Options menu, shown below, allows you to edit, create, list the names of, copy, and remove forms.

```
(1) Edit/Create a form
(2) List forms
(3) Copy a form
(4) Remove a form
(5) Choose a database
(6) Exit from Forms EXPRESS
```

These options work the same as they do under Reports EXPRESS.

In this chapter we've discussed Forms EXPRESS and various techniques for creating and using custom forms. In the next chapter we'll look at ways in which you can alter the structure of your tables.

Chapter 9

Improving the Structure of Your Database

Fast Track

To change a column's name, **218**
use the RENAME COLUMN command.

To change the definition of a column, **219**
use the REDEFINE command with the syntax REDEFINE *column name* IN *table name* TO <*data type*> <*width*>.

To add columns to and delete columns from a table, **221**
use the F1 and F2 keys in Definition EXPRESS.

To add columns to the end of a table, **224**
use the EXPAND or ALTER TABLE command.

To modify existing reports and forms **226**
to match the new table structure after changing a table structure, use Reports EXPRESS and Forms EXPRESS.

To change the names **232**
of your reports, forms, views, and passwords, use the RENAME command.

To delete entire columns from a table, **234**
or even entire tables, reports, forms, or views from a database, use the REMOVE command. Although R:BASE will ask you to verify this sort of deletion, use this command with care. When you need to delete a table, an index (key), or a view, use the SQL DROP command instead if you wish.

To establish a given column as a table's key column, 235
use the BUILD KEY or CREATE INDEX commands. Keys, which serve to identify the unique contents of a record, can enhance R:BASE's performance during searches and sorts.

To remove a column's key status, 236
use the DELETE KEY or DROP INDEX command.

To review the rules you've established 236
for your database, use the LIST RULES command. If you need to delete one, find out its rule number (using LIST RULES), and use the REMOVE RULE command.

MURPHY'S LAW DICTATES THAT AFTER CAREFULLY planning a database structure and adding some data to it, you'll want to make some changes. For example, you might find that the assigned width of 20 characters is not enough for the Company column in the Names table. You might also decide that you want to add columns to the Names table for telephone numbers and customer numbers.

Once you've made the appropriate modifications to the basic structure of the table, you'll probably want to modify reports and forms accordingly. This chapter explains how to make these modifications.

If you are following along on-line, start R:BASE in the normal fashion so that you are at the PBE Main menu.

CHANGING COLUMN NAMES

Probably the simplest type of table modification involves changing a column's name. Let's say you've decided you'd like to call the last name column Lastname instead of L:Name. The command you need is called RENAME, and its syntax is straightforward:

```
RENAME COLUMN column name 1 TO column name 2 IN table +
+> name
```

The IN *table name* clause is optional.

Let's try the command using PBE. Since what we want to do is going to change the database, select option 1, *Define or modify a database*. The *Define or modify a database* menu lists options that are by now familiar: RBDEFINE, FORMS, and REPORTS. One way to change a column's name would be to select RBDEFINE and simply rename the column in question. However, let's explore the *R:BASE commands* option. When you select it, you'll see a fairly large menu, indicating the variety of commands available to you for changing a database's structure.

Select RENAME. When you are asked to choose the item to rename, select COLUMN. PBE will prompt you to open a database if you haven't already; in that case go ahead and open Mail. Next you'll be asked to choose a table. Select Names. When asked for the column to rename, select L:Name, and when prompted for the new name, type **Lastname** and press Enter. Examine the command you have built—

```
RENAME COLUMN L:Name TO Lastname IN Names
```

—and execute it.

Now press Esc a few times to leave PBE and return to the R> prompt. Return the column to its original name from the R> prompt by typing

```
RENAME COLUMN Lastname TO L:Name IN Names
```

and pressing the Enter key.

CHANGING COLUMN DEFINITIONS

Another simple form of table modification is changing the definition of a column. For example, let's change the width of the Company column from 20 to 25 characters. You use the REDEFINE command with the following syntax:

REDEFINE *column name* IN *table name* TO *<data type>* *<width>*

For our example, at the R> prompt enter the command

```
REDEFINE Company IN Names TO TEXT 25
```

The TEXT part of the command assigns the TEXT data type, and the 25 specifies the new width. (Note: Only the TEXT data type requires that you enter a width.)

That's all there is to it. If you give the command

```
SELECT ALL FROM Names
```

you'll notice that the column is, indeed, five characters wider. Later in the chapter, we'll change the reports and forms associated with the Names table to take advantage of the new width.

You can also use the REDEFINE command to change a column's data type—within reason. You can't, however, change an INTEGER column to TIME, because the two formats simply aren't compatible. R:BASE has no idea how to convert something like 10:32:43 into an integer, or a value such as 500 into a time. You *can* change an INTEGER column to TEXT, or vice versa, although in the latter case you would lose any data that wasn't numeric. R:BASE would simply change any nonnumeric data to nulls.

SIDE EFFECTS

You've seen how easy it is to change column names and/or definitions, but you should also realize that doing so can be a risky proposition.

Consider all that would have happened had we permanently changed the L:Name column's name to Lastname:

- The rule we had set up forcing an entry in the L:name field—

  ```
  L:Name IN Names EXISTS
  ```

  —would no longer work, since the L:Name field wouldn't exist.
- None of the reports would work properly. All three of the reports associated with Names rely on FullName variables, which join L:Name and F:Name. But L:Name wouldn't exist.
- The NamesFrm form wouldn't work until the new Lastname column was placed where L:Name had been. L:Name's S and E would have disappeared, since L:Name would no longer be part of the Names table. It would thus be up to us to place the new column, Lastname, in the appropriate location.

These and other results are referred to as *side effects*, which occur because R:BASE doesn't automatically change all references to a given column when you change its name or definition. If you make such a change in your table, you need to change all references yourself.

ADDING COLUMNS TO YOUR TABLE

There are several ways to add new columns to a table. One way would be to return to Definition EXPRESS (which we used to create the Mail database) and to insert the new columns directly into the table.

Like Forms and Reports EXPRESS, you can enter Definition EXPRESS either from PBE or from the R> prompt. From the R> prompt, simply type in the command

```
RBDEFINE
```

and press Enter. From the PBE Main menu, select *Define or modify a database,* and RBDEFINE from the submenu.

The Definition EXPRESS Main menu, which appears when you first enter Definition EXPRESS, displays the following options:

```
(1) Define a new database
(2) Modify an existing database definition
(3) Exit from Definition EXPRESS
```

To modify an existing database, select option 2. When you do so, you'll be asked to choose a database if one isn't open. Choose Mail and supply the owner password if so prompted. The Database Definition menu will appear and present the options below:

```
(1) Tables
(2) Views
(3) Passwords
(4) Rules
(5) Return to Definition EXPRESS Main Menu
```

In this case, we want to add some columns to the Names table, so select option 1. The Tables menu displays the following options:

```
(1) Add a new table to the database
(2) Change an existing table
(3) Remove a table from the database
(4) Return to the Database Definition Menu
```

You want to change an existing table structure, so select option 2. The screen will ask for the name of the table to change. Select Names. The table structure appears on the screen as in Figure 9.1.

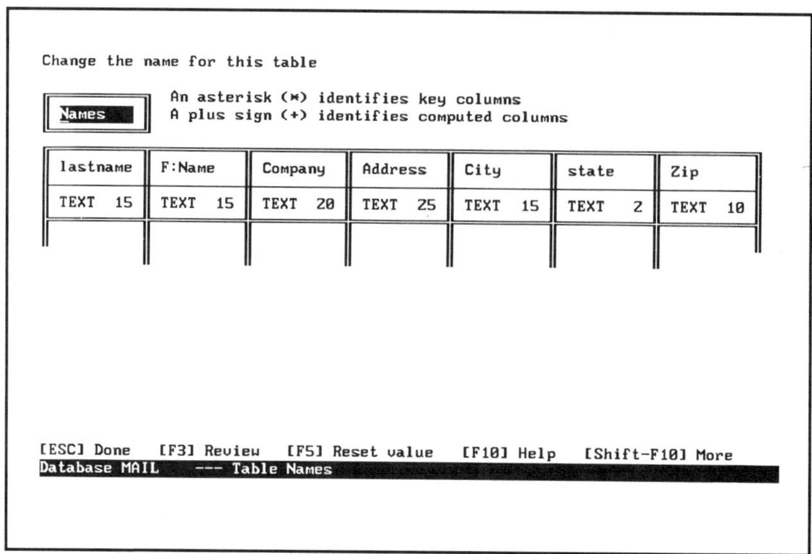

Figure 9.1: The Names table structure on the screen

You can change the table name or any of the column names simply by positioning the cursor with the arrow keys or the Tab key and typing in the new name. You can use the F1 key to insert a column and the F2 key to delete a column. Let's try it out.

First, press the ↓ key to move the highlight to the L:Name column name. Press F1 to insert a new column. All other column names shift one space to the right. Type in the new column name

CustNo

and press Enter. Select INTEGER as the column type. When the screen asks

Do you want this to be a key column?

select No.

Figure 9.2 shows how the screen looks after adding the CustNo (Customer Number) column, as the INTEGER data type, into the Names table.

Now suppose you also want to add a column for storing phone numbers. First, what data type should a phone number be? Granted, a phone number consists mostly of numbers, but of course it also consists

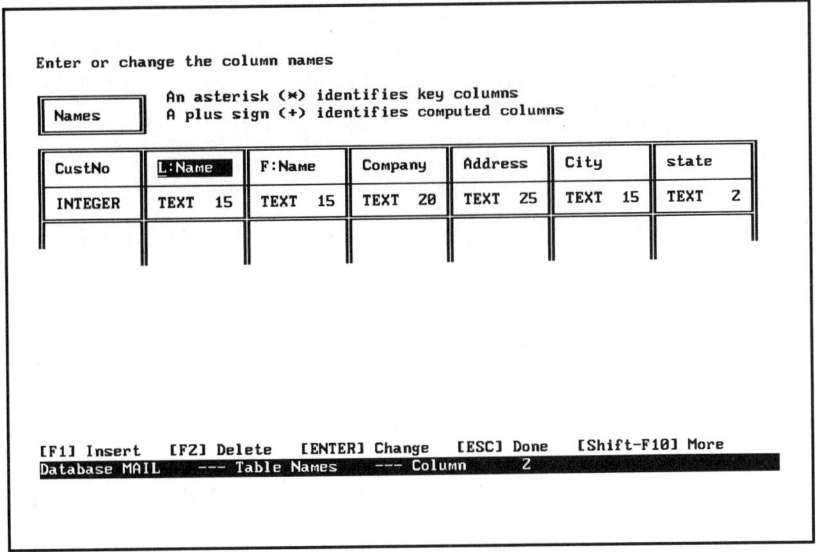

Figure 9.2: The CustNo column added to the Names table

of some nonnumeric characters such as parentheses and a hyphen (for example, (818)555-1212). Therefore, since phone numbers are not truly numbers, they should be treated as Text data. A length of 13 characters should be adequate for storing phone numbers.

To add a column named Phone to the Names table, first press the End key to move the highlight to the right side of the column names. Type in the column name

```
Phone
```

and press the Enter key. Select TEXT as the column type, and enter 13 as the column width when requested. When the screen asks if this should be a key column, select No. Figure 9.3 shows the Names column with the new Phone column added.

When you have finished making changes to the table structure, press the Esc key. R:BASE will display a message indicating it is adjusting data in the table. You can exit Definition EXPRESS by working your way back through the menus (select options 4, 5, and 3).

To fill in data for the new columns, make sure you are at the R> prompt and the Mail database is open. Then enter the command

```
EDIT CustNo L:Name F:Name Phone FROM Names
```

The screen should look like Figure 9.4.

Notice that the new columns contain null characters (-0-), since there are no data in them. Go ahead and type the data shown in Figure 9.5 in these columns. Press the Esc key after you've filled in the new data.

THE ALTER TABLE AND EXPAND COMMANDS

The benefit of using Definition EXPRESS to add columns is that by using the F1 key, you can insert the new column in any position you choose within the database. Although the relative column positions are really irrelevant in a relational database, most of us like to have columns listed in a logical fashion. R:BASE's other methods for adding columns to a table don't allow you to specify the position of the new column; the new column is added automatically to the end of the table.

You can access either the ALTER TABLE or EXPAND commands via PBE by selecting *Define or modify a database* and then *R:BASE commands*. Alternatively, you can enter either command at the R> prompt. The syntax for the EXPAND command is

EXPAND *table name* WITH *column name* <*data type*> <*length*>

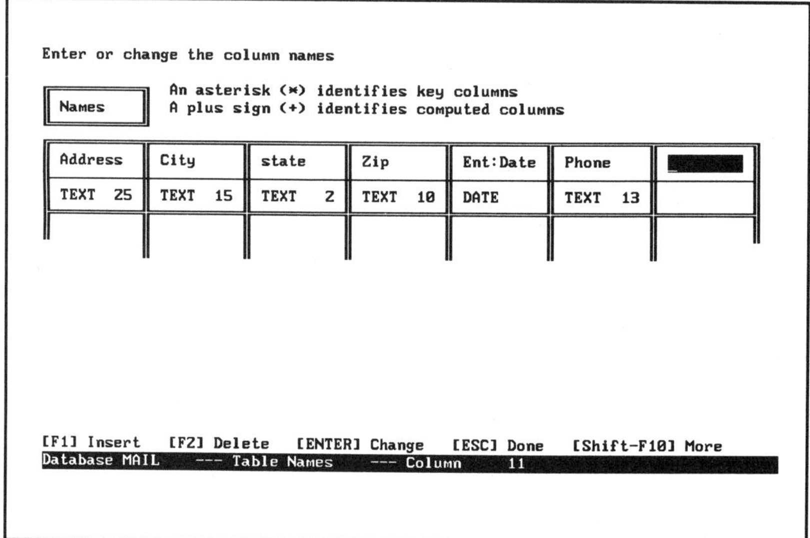

Figure 9.3: The Phone column added to the Names table

```
            Press [ESC] when done, [F2] to delete, [F5] to reset
CustNo     L:Name          F:Name          Phone
---------- --------------- --------------- -------------
-0-        Smith           Sandy           -0-
-0-        Jones           Andy            -0-
-0-        Miller          Marie           -0-
-0-        Adams           Bart            -0-
-0-        Miller          Anne            -0-
-0-        Baker           Robin           -0-
-0-        Miller          Monica          -0-
-0-        Teasdale        Trudy           -0-
-0-        Martin          Mary            -0-
```

Figure 9.4: The Names table with new columns displayed

```
      Update  Press [ESC] when done, [F2] to delete, [F5] to reset
CustNo     L:Name          F:Name          Phone
---------- --------------- --------------- -------------
      1001 Smith           Sandy           (123)555-1212
      1002 Jones           Mindy           (123)555-1010
      1003 Miller          Marie           (123)555-2222
      1004 Adams           Bart            (213(123-4567
      1005 Miller          Anne            (213)234-5678
      1006 Baker           Robin           (345)678-9012
      1007 Miller          Monica          (345)678-1111
      1008 Teasdale        Trudy           (619)455-7442
      1009 Martin          Mary            (619)555-1810
```

Figure 9.5: The Names table with data entered in the new columns

Length need only be specified for TEXT fields that are to be a length other than the default eight characters.

The SQL equivalent of EXPAND is ALTER TABLE. The syntax for this command is

ALTER TABLE *table name* ADD *column name* <*data type*> <*length*>

If you look at the Help screens for these commands, you'll notice that R:BASE lets you add a column as an expression. When you add such a column, it's called a *computed column* and is generally based on data in some other column. For example, if you had an Invoice table with a purchase date (PDate) column and wanted to add a due date (DDate) column, where the due date was to be 30 days after the purchase date, you could enter

```
EXPAND Invoice WITH DDate = (PDate + 30) DATE
```

or

```
ALTER TABLE Invoice ADD DDate = (Pdate + 30) DATE
```

to create a computed DDate column.

MODIFYING REPORTS

The addition of the CustNo and Phone columns will not affect the Labels or Letter1 reports we developed earlier, but the Director report should be modified to display these new columns. (Alternatively, you could create a fourth report format to display these new data.) In this section, we'll revise the Director report so that it appears as shown in Figure 9.6.

The first step in modifying the report is to enter the Reports EXPRESS by typing

```
REPORTS
```

at the R> prompt. Select option 1 from the first menu, and select the report name, Director, when requested. From the Report Definition menu option, select the Edit option.

For our modified report, we'll indent the FullName and Address columns a bit and add the CustNo to the left column next to

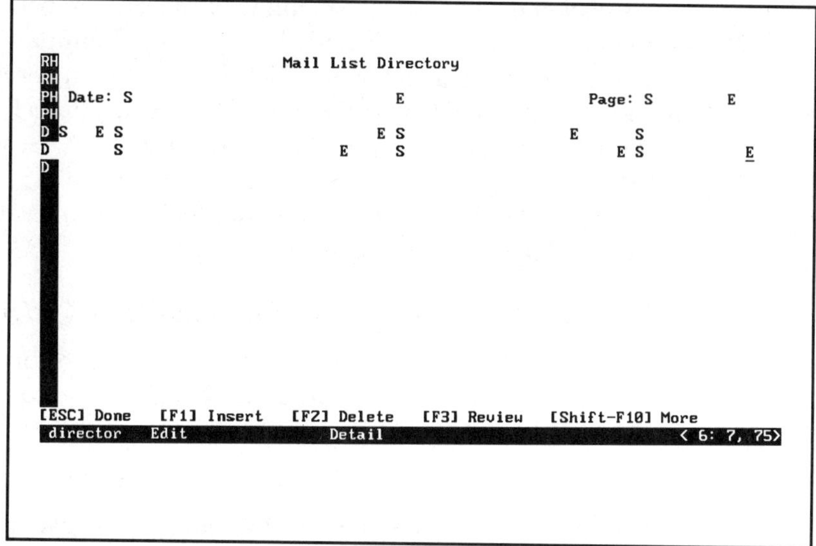

Figure 9.6: The Director report format with CustNo and Phone added

FullName. Then, we'll put the Phone column data under the Ent:Date column.

One way to reposition a column name or variable on the report format is to move the cursor between the S and the E for the appropriate column name or variable and then press F6. (If you are not sure which S and E the cursor is positioned on at a particular moment, press the F3 key. The column or variable name appears at the top of the screen.)

You can also move column or variable names by inserting spaces with the Ins key. For this report, try doing so now by following these steps:

1. Move the cursor to row 5, column 1 (so that the indicator reads <5:7,1>.
2. Press the Ins key five times to shift everything to the right five spaces.
3. Place the CustNo field name in this new space by pressing F6 and typing in the column name **CustNo**. Press Enter.
4. Make <5:7,1> the start location.
5. Move the cursor to <5:7,5> and type **E** to mark the end location.

To realign the Company column with the column beneath, move the cursor between the S and the E for the Company column. (Remember, if you are not sure which S and E the cursor is between, press the F3 key and look at the top of the screen.) Press F6 and relocate the Company column so that it starts at <5:7,37> and ends at <5:7,56>.

To realign the Address column under the FullName variable, and place the phone number, follow these steps:

1. Press ↓ and Ctrl-← so the cursor moves to <6:7,1>.
2. Press the Ins key twice to insert a couple of blank spaces. You'll now need to shorten the FullCSZ field to make room for the phone number.
3. Move the cursor to <6:7,37> and press F6.
4. Make <6:7,37> the start location, then move the cursor to <6:7,61> and mark that as the end location.
5. To place the phone number, move the cursor to <6:7,63>.
6. Press F6 and type in the column name **Phone** (and press Enter).
7. Start the Phone column at <6:7,63> and end it at <6:7,75>.

Figure 9.6 shows the modified Director report format on the screen.

Press Esc twice after making the changes, and select Save Changes from the menu. Select option 6 from the next menu to return to the R> prompt.

Since the Ent:Date is a bit narrow on this report format, you may want to type in the command

```
SET DATE MM/DD/YY
```

at the R> prompt. (If a report column is too narrow to display data, the report displays a series of asterisks instead.)

To see the modified report, enter the command

```
PRINT Director
```

Figure 9.7 shows a portion of the modified Director report. To see only certain rows in this report, you can use the ORDER BY and WHERE clauses. For example,

```
PRINT Director ORDER BY CustNo WHERE Phone +
+ > CONTAINS "(123)"
```

displays rows in customer-number order, showing only individuals whose telephone numbers have a 123 area code.

MODIFYING FORMS

Now that the Names table has two new columns, the NamesFrm form screen needs to be modified so that you can use it for entering

MAIL LIST DIRECTORY

Date: 01/31/88		**Page: 1**
1001 Smith, Sandy 456 N. Rainbow Dr.	Hi Tech, Inc. Berkeley, CA 94721	06/01/88 (123)555-1212
1002 Jones, Mindy 123 A St.	ABC Co. San Diego, CA 92122	06/15/88 (123)555-1010
1003 Miller, Marie 234 C St.	Zeerox, Inc. Los Angeles, CA 91234	06/01/88 (123)555-2222
1004 Adams, Bart P.O. Box 2890	DataSpec Inc. Malibu, CA 92111	06/15/88 (213)123-4567
1005 Miller, Anne 2313 Sixth St.	Golden Gate Co. Berkeley, CA 94711	06/01/88 (213)234-5678
1006 Baker, Robin 2311 Coast Hwy.	Peach Computers San Diego, CA 92112	06/15/88 (345)678-9012
1007 Miller, Monica 355 Torrey Pines St.	Acme Development Newark, NJ 54821	07/15/88 (345)678-1111
1008 Teasdale, Trudy 321 Microwave St.	Atomic Ovens, Inc. Lassiter, OH 12121	07/01/88 (619)455-7442
1009 Martin, Mary 321 Microwave St.	Atomic Ovens, Inc. Lassiter, OH 12121	07/01/88 (619)555-1810

Figure 9.7: The modified Director report

and editing rows. We'll modify the basic appearance of the screen and add the CustNo and Phone columns so that the screen looks like Figure 9.8.

First, you need to specify that you want to modify a form by entering the command

FORMS NamesFrm

at the R> prompt. (Using the form name next to the Forms command is a shortcut method to Forms EXPRESS, if your database is open.) The form will appear on the screen along with the top menu.

To begin modifying the form, select the Edit option from the top menu. To make room for the CustNo column, move the cursor to <5,3>. Then, press the Ins key about 25 times to move the Entry Date prompt to the right. With the cursor on <5,3> type in the prompt

Customer Number:

and press the space bar. Press F6 and enter the column name

CustNo

```
 Add/Edit Names

Customer Number:              Entry Date: 02/01/88

Last Name:                        First Name:

Company:

Address:

City:                             State: CA      Zip:

Phone Number:

 Highlight and Cursor Commands:

 Next Item:   ENTER OR TAB                 Previous Item: Shift TAB
 Cursor Left:   <--                        Cursor Right:   -->
 Insert Space:   INS                       Delete Character:   DEL

[ESC] Done    [F2] Clear field    [Shift-F2] Clear to end    [Shift-F10] More
Form: namesfrm   Table: Names      Field: CustNo      Page: 1
```

Figure 9.8: The modified NamesFrm screen in data entry mode

and press Enter. Answer No to both of the questions about customization. Start the field at <5,20> and end it at <5,23>, so that it's just large enough for four-digit customer numbers.

To make room for the phone number, move the cursor to <14,3> and press F1 to insert a new line. Press ↓ to move the cursor to <15,3>. Type in the prompt

Phone Number:

and press the space bar. Press F6 and enter the column name

Phone

and press Enter. Answer No to the customization prompts. Start the phone number at <15,17> and end it at <15,29>. Figure 9.9 shows the new prompts and column name locations on the screen.

To ensure that the Customer Number field is the first to be highlighted when entering or editing data, press the Esc key and select Customize from the top menu. Select Field Order and Reorder from the submenus. Enter 9 as the number of the field to move and 1 as the new position.

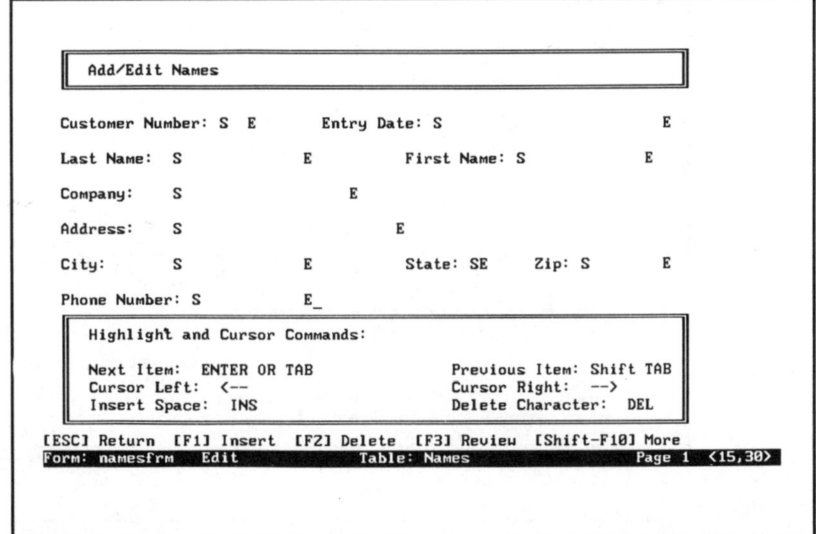

Figure 9.9: The customer number and phone on the modified form

Press Esc several times, select Save changes, and finally option 6 to return to the R> prompt.

To see how the modified form looks, use either the ENTER or EDIT command. Figure 9.10 shows the modified NamesFrm screen in the Edit mode, brought up by entering the command

```
EDIT USING NamesFrm
```

After you select the Edit option, pressing the Tab key moves the highlighting through the items in an orderly way. Had we not reordered the fields, the highlighting would move in an awkward fashion, starting with Entry # Date and ending with Customer Number.

Select the Quit option from the Edit menu to return to the R> prompt.

RENAMING AND DELETING

R:BASE's RENAME and REMOVE commands are extremely useful general tools for modifying the structure of a table. Study their syntax diagrams, shown in Figure 9.11.

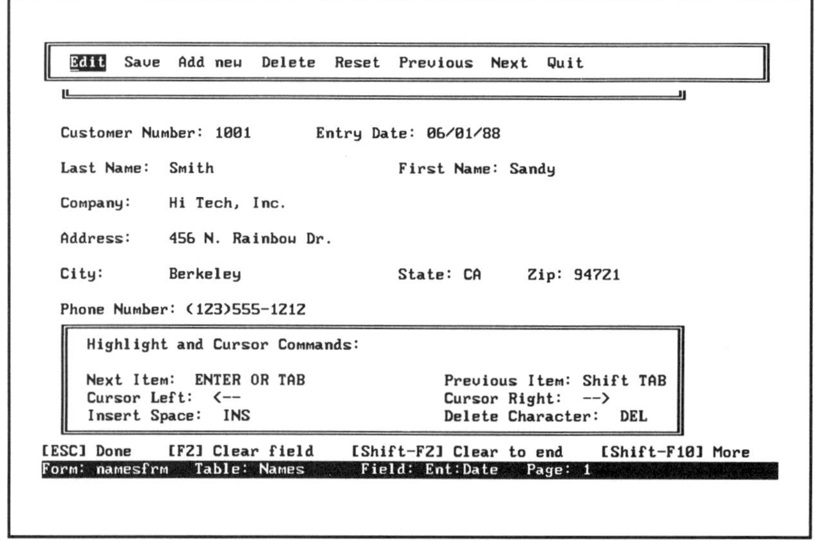

Figure 9.10: The modified NamesFrm screen in edit mode

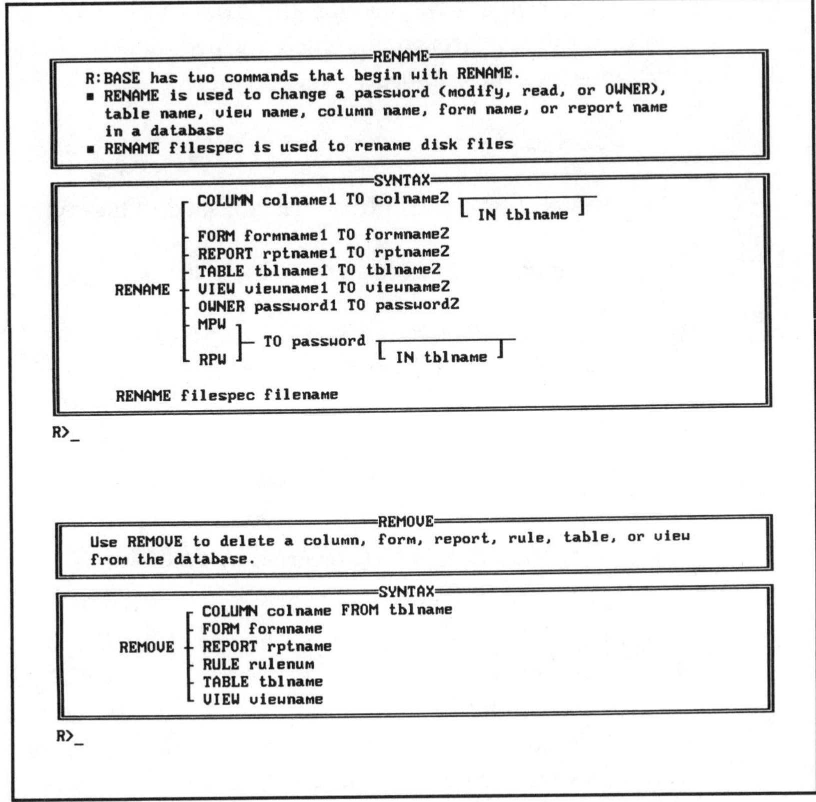

RENAME
R:BASE has two commands that begin with RENAME.
■ RENAME is used to change a password (modify, read, or OWNER), table name, view name, column name, form name, or report name in a database
■ RENAME filespec is used to rename disk files
SYNTAX
RENAME
COLUMN colname1 TO colname2
IN tblname
FORM formname1 TO formname2
REPORT rptname1 TO rptname2
TABLE tblname1 TO tblname2
VIEW viewname1 TO viewname2
OWNER password1 TO password2
MPW
RPW
TO password
IN tblname
RENAME filespec filename
R>_
REMOVE
Use REMOVE to delete a column, form, report, rule, table, or view from the database.
SYNTAX
REMOVE
COLUMN colname FROM tblname
FORM formname
REPORT rptname
RULE rulenum
TABLE tblname
VIEW viewname
R>_

Figure 9.11: Syntax diagrams for the RENAME and REMOVE commands

THE RENAME COMMAND REVISITED

Let's look at the RENAME command first. You've already used this command earlier in the chapter to change the name of the L:Name column to Lastname, and then to change it back. You read then about possible unwanted side effects of using RENAME. In Chapter 6, you saw how the RENAME command can also be used to change file names. Now we'll look at how RENAME can be used in a host of other situations. You can use it to change the name of a table, a form, or a report. You can also change the name of a *view*, the pseudo-tables we'll be talking about in the next chapter. The database owner can also change any passwords using RENAME.

Let's experiment by deleting the database's owner password. If you're at the R> prompt and have opened the Mail database, identify yourself as the database owner by typing

USER *password*

where *password* is the one already established. Then type

RENAME OWNER *password* TO NONE

By changing your original password to NONE, you delete it. To make sure the change is in effect, you'll have to exit R:BASE and start it again, since, once you've entered the correct password, R:BASE remembers that the owner password has been entered for the duration of your R:BASE session.

THE REMOVE AND DROP COMMANDS

The REMOVE command is also easy to use. With it, you can remove an individual column from a given table, remove a report or form from their respective tables, or even delete an entire table or view. The important thing to remember with both the RENAME and REMOVE commands is that you must include the name of the item you want to change in the command syntax. For example, to delete a table called Temp from its database, you would have to type

REMOVE TABLE Temp

not just

REMOVE Temp

Since we don't want to delete any major components from the Mail database, let's not experiment with the REMOVE command now.

SQL also provides a command that lets you delete an entire table. The DROP command can be used to delete tables, indexes (which we'll talk about next), and views. To remove a table called Temp using the DROP command, you'd type

DROP TABLE Temp

at the R> prompt.

USING KEYS TO SPEED DATABASE OPERATIONS

You may remember that when you used Definition EXPRESS to define—and later modify—the Mail database, you were asked with each column whether it was to serve as a key. We'll take a look at keys now, and see how they can help make your database operations more efficient.

Keys (sometimes called *indexes*) are often established to speed up searches and sorts. You should consider establishing keys for columns that you use often to look up data that is unique to each row. In the case of the Names table, CustNo is the best candidate for key column status, since each customer will have a unique customer number. If Names were a large table, having a key column for CustNo would significantly enhance performance. Assuming Mary Jones's customer number was 10443, for example, the command

```
SELECT ALL FROM Names WHERE CustNo = 10443
```

would work faster than

```
SELECT ALL FROM Names WHERE L:Name EQ JONES AND +
+> F:Name = Mary
```

You can establish a column as a key column in any of several ways. When you are first defining a table, you can answer yes to the question "Do you want this column to be a key?" If you don't decide until later that you want a given column to be a key, you can either modify the table's structure in Definition EXPRESS and redefine any column you wish as a key or use the BUILD KEY or CREATE INDEX commands from either PBE or from the R> prompt.

Let's say we want to make CustNo a key column. Assuming the Mail database is open, and you're at the R> prompt, enter the following:

```
BUILD KEY FOR CustNo IN Names
```

or

```
CREATE INDEX ON Names CustNo
```

Nothing much seems to happen. However, if you type

```
LIST Names
```

now, you'll see a yes to the right of CustNo underneath the word Key, as shown in Figure 9.12.

Other, more subtle changes have also taken place. Part of the Mail3.RBF file will now be used to keep a fast "lookup" table that R:BASE can use to locate data quickly from the Names table when the CustNo is supplied. You may notice a slight decrease in speed when you are adding data to or editing data in the Names table, because R:BASE must now change both the column and the index file to keep the database up-to-date.

Deleting a column's key status is as easy as establishing it. The easiest way is to do this is from the R> prompt, using the command

```
DELETE KEY FOR CustNo IN Names
```

or

```
DROP INDEX CustNo IN Names
```

Go ahead and delete the key. Keys are generally inefficient in small tables; R:BASE's overhead in maintaining them simply isn't worth the minor increase in search and sort performance.

Why are there two different commands for both creating and deleting keys? The CREATE and DROP INDEX commands are SQL commands; the BUILD and DELETE KEY commands are original R:BASE commands. As we have already seen, SQL commands are being implemented in hopes of eventually standardizing operations for all database software. For those of you who are already experienced with R:BASE, however, the familiar R:BASE commands may be easier to remember.

CHANGING RULES

Occasionally you'll set up a rule that doesn't work, and you'll want to delete it. As your database grows, you may even decide that using rule-checking slows things down too much, and that you value

```
R>LIST Names

   Table: Names           No lock(s)
   Read Password: No
   Modify Password: No

   Column definitions
   # Name      Type     Length         Key   Expression
   1 CustNo    INTEGER                 yes
   2 L:Name    TEXT      15 characters
   3 F:Name    TEXT      15 characters
   4 Company   TEXT      20 characters
   5 Address   TEXT      25 characters
   6 City      TEXT      15 characters
   7 state     TEXT       2 characters
   8 Zip       TEXT      10 characters
   9 Ent:Date  DATE
  10 Phone     TEXT      13 characters

   Current number of rows:      9

R>_
```

Figure 9.12: CustNo redefined as a key column

speedy data entry more than you do error-trapping. In either case, the easiest way to delete rules is to use the REMOVE command. If you look at the syntax for the REMOVE RULE command in Figure 9.11, you'll notice that you need to know a rule's number (*rulenum*) before you can delete it. One way of finding a particular rule number is to type

LIST RULES

at the R> prompt, which will bring up the screen shown in Figure 9.13.

The first line of this display reminds you that rule-checking is on. Although active rule-checking is R:BASE's default, it can be turned off with the SET command. The next lines summarize the one rule associated with the Mail database. Notice that our rule is rule number one.

Another way of finding out a rule's number is to type

SELECT ALL FROM RULES

Your rules will be displayed in the form in which they're stored in R:BASE's RULES table. The leftmost column, Numrule, lists the rule numbers associated with each rule.

```
R>LIST Rules
(RULES     ) ON  Check data validation RULES
RULE 1           L:name IN Names EXISTS
      Message:You must enter a last name!
R>_
```

Figure 9.13: Reviewing your rules

To remove the rule you created in Chapter 2, type

REMOVE RULE 1

and press Enter. To verify that the rule was deleted, you could use any of several strategies. You could try to enter a new record with nothing in the L:Name field. You could also type LIST RULES or SELECT ALL FROM RULES again.

Although it's possible to edit rules by editing the RULES table, you need to understand how R:BASE encodes its rules in order to do this. Generally, when changes in rules need to be made, it's easiest to delete the rule that isn't working and create a new one.

Let's finish our overview of techniques for changing database structure now. In this chapter, you've learned several new commands for modifying the basic structure of a table in a database. You've graduated from managing a single-table database, and are now ready to work with a database that contains multiple tables.

Part 2

Working with Multiple Tables

Chapter 10

Increasing Your Database's Power with Multiple Tables

FAST TRACK

To add a new table to a database, 247
use Definition EXPRESS by typing **RBDEFINE** at the R> prompt, then selecting the following options:

1. Option 2, *Modify an existing database definition*
2. Option 1, Tables.
3. Option 1, *Add a new table to the database*

To define variables (expressions) 252
to display data from other tables and perform calculations on custom forms, use Forms EXPRESS.

To define rules 257
for rejecting invalid data before they are stored on a table, use **Definition EXPRESS.**

To help speed data entry, 264
use the SET AUTOSKIP command to control whether the Enter key must be pressed after each field on a custom form is filled in. Type **SET AUTOSKIP ON** at the R> prompt to have R:BASE skip automatically to the next field when the current field is full.

To design a database, 268
use the following step-by-step method:

1. Find out what information will be needed.
2. Group the data.
3. Determine the types of relationships among the tables.

4. Decide on the columns for each table.
5. Assign key columns.
6. Establish links between related tables.
7. Define the database.

IN THIS CHAPTER, WE'LL ADD A NEW TABLE TO THE Mail database and explore techniques for setting up a relationship between two tables. We'll set up a form that serves two tables simultaneously. We'll also discuss techniques for defining various types of *rules* to help catch errors before they are stored in a table. Finally, at the end of the chapter, we'll take another look at the process of database design.

DESIGNING RELATIONSHIPS INTO YOUR TABLES

Let's start expanding the Mail database so that it can serve as a sales-register system. To do so, we need to add another table to record individual charge transactions. For each charge, we want to record the amount of the charge, the date, and the items purchased.

Since it is likely that each customer will charge many purchases, it makes no sense to record the name and address along with every charge transaction. Instead, we need a *code* that relates numerous charge transactions to an individual in the Names table. We don't want to use last name as this code because it is not accurate enough. For example, if we recorded a charge made by "Smith," we'd have problems sending the bill to the correct individual if there were 20 Smiths listed in the Names table. We could use both first and last names to improve the accuracy, but even this is risky.

A better approach is to use the unique *customer number* that we assigned to each person in the Names table (we did this in the last chapter). Then the table for charge transactions needs to record only the customer number to set up a link that will eliminate any confusion in billing.

This approach of dividing the data into two separate tables within the database is known as recognizing a *one-to-many* relationship between the tables. This relationship is so named because for every *one* row on one table, there may be *many* related rows on another table. In this example, for every one individual in the Names table, there may be many individual sales-transaction records stored in the Charges table.

ADDING A NEW TABLE TO YOUR DATABASE

Take a moment to look at the structure for the Charges table, described below:

NAME	*TYPE*	*LENGTH*	*DESCRIPTION*
CustNo	Integer		Customer number
ProdNo	Text	8	Product number
Qty	Integer		Quantity purchased
U:Price	Currency		Unit price (as sold)
Tax?	Integer		Is item taxable?
Total	Currency		Calculated total
P:Date	Date		Date of purchase

The customer number (CustNo) will be the key field to relate data from the Charges table to individuals in the Names table. As in the Names table, its data type is INTEGER. The ProdNo column will store the product number of the item purchased. We could later add an Inventory table listing items in stock to our Mail database and use the ProdNo column to link the Charges table with items in the Inventory table. Each transaction would then reduce the quantity of the product shown to be in inventory. The ProdNo column is TEXT data with a length of eight characters. Using the TEXT data type will allow you to enter hyphenated numbers, such as A-111.

The Qty column is for recording the quantity of items purchased. The U:Price column is for the unit price of items purchased. Its data type is CURRENCY, which will cause numbers to be displayed with a leading dollar sign and two decimal places.

The Tax? column will contain a 1 for taxable items or a 0 for nontaxable items. The Total column will contain the total of the row—either the quantity times the unit price for nontaxable items or the quantity times the unit price plus 6 % sales tax for taxable items. R:BASE will calculate the total automatically, so you don't need to fill in this column when you're entering data. You might be tempted to make this field a TEXT field of length 1 in order to store the data in Y/N format. You'll see why we choose INTEGER format on the next page. The P:Date column will store the date of the purchase.

The easiest way to add this new table to a database is through Definition EXPRESS. Recall that you can enter Definition EXPRESS by entering the command RBDEFINE at the R> prompt or by selecting RBDEFINE from PBE's *Define or modify a database* menu. From the Definition EXPRESS Main menu, select option 2, *Modify an existing database definition.* If Mail isn't open, select it now. From the Database Definition menu, select option 1, Tables. From the Tables menu, select option 1, *Add a new table to the database.*

You've already entered column names and data types through Definition EXPRESS in earlier chapters, so you should have no trouble creating the Charges table now, although there are a few new twists that deserve some explanation.

Enter the table name Charges in the top box. When entering the column names discussed below, select No each time the screen asks if the column should be a key column. Enter **CustNo** as the first column name. R:BASE will automatically assign INTEGER as the data type, since the CustNo column name was previously defined in the Names table. Enter **ProdNo** as the second column name, and select TEXT as the data type and a length of eight characters. Enter **Qty** as the third column name, and select INTEGER as the data type. Enter **U:Price** as the fourth column name, and select CURRENCY as the data type. Enter **Tax?** as the fifth column name, and select INTEGER as the data type.

For the sixth column, enter **Total** as the column name. Select COMPUTED as the data type. R:BASE will ask that you

```
Enter expression value:
```

What R:BASE needs to know is how to compute the data in this column. If there were not a Tax? column in this table, the expression could simply be (Qty*U:Price) which means the Qty field times the U:Price field. When the item is taxable, then the total becomes ((Qty*U:Price)*1.06) assuming 6 % sales tax. However, we also need to find a way to tell R:BASE that if the item is not taxable, then the total for the row is indeed (Qty*U:Price).

We can use an R:BASE *function* to help solve this problem. First, we need to know how to determine whether an item is taxable, so let's make up a rule. If the Tax? column contains the number 0, the item is not taxable. If the Tax? column contains the number 1, the item is taxable.

Given this knowledge, we can use the IFEQ function to calculate the total for the transaction. The IFEQ function uses this syntax:

IFEQ(*this item*, = *this item*, *then this*, *else this*)

The exact expression that you would enter on the screen is

```
(IFEQ(Tax?,0,Qty*U:Price,(Qty*U:Price)*1.06))

CCompany = Company IN Names WHERE CustNo = CustNo
```

In English, this expression means, "If the Tax? column equals 0, calculate the quantity times the unit price; otherwise calculate the quantity times the unit price times the tax rate."

IFEQ is just one of many functions that R:BASE offers. We'll discuss other functions in Chapter 11. After you've entered the expression correctly, R:BASE asks that you select a data type for the computed result. Select CURRENCY.

Finally, enter **P:Date** as the last column name, and select DATE as its data type. When you are finished defining the table structure, your screen will look like Figure 10.1. Press the Esc key to work your way to (or back to) the R> prompt.

A FORM FOR TWO TABLES

Now that we've added a second table to the Mail database, let's create a form for entering information into the new Charges table. Rather than just creating a simple form, however, we'll discuss some more advanced techniques that you can use when creating forms with multiple tables and computed columns.

Use Forms EXPRESS to create a new form. Make sure that the Mail database is open, and enter the command

```
FORMS
```

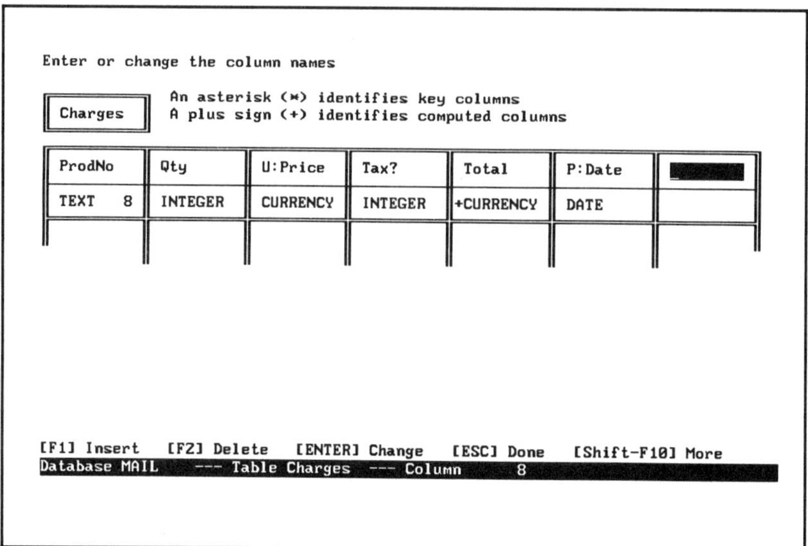

Figure 10.1: The Charges table defined on the screen

at the R> prompt. Select option 1 to create a new form. Then select New when asked to specify a form. Type in **ChrgFrm** as the name of the new form and press Enter. When asked about customizing the form characteristics, select No. Next, R:BASE will ask you to specify the associated table. Select Charges, and then select No when asked about customizing the table characteristics.

To enter the form layout, select Edit from the top menu. Type in each of the prompts listed below beginning at the row and column position listed in the left column:

POSITION	*PROMPT*
<2,3>	Enter/Edit Transactions
<5,1>	Customer Number:
<5,30>	Customer Name:
<6,36>	Company:
<8,1>	Product Number:
<8,30>	Taxable? (1 = Yes, 0 = No):

<10,1>	Qty:
<10,19>	Unit Price:
<10,47>	Total:
<12,1>	Date of Sale:
<15,3>	Highlighter and Cursor Movement
<17,5>	Next Item: ENTER or TAB
<17,40>	Previous Item: SHIFT-TAB
<18,5>	Cursor Right: →
<18,40>	Cursor Left: ←
<19,5>	Insert Space: INS
<19,40>	Delete Character: DEL

After typing in the prompts, you can draw some double-line boxes as in Figure 10.2. Remember, select Draw and Double Line from the top menu, and use the F4 key to raise and lower the "pen."

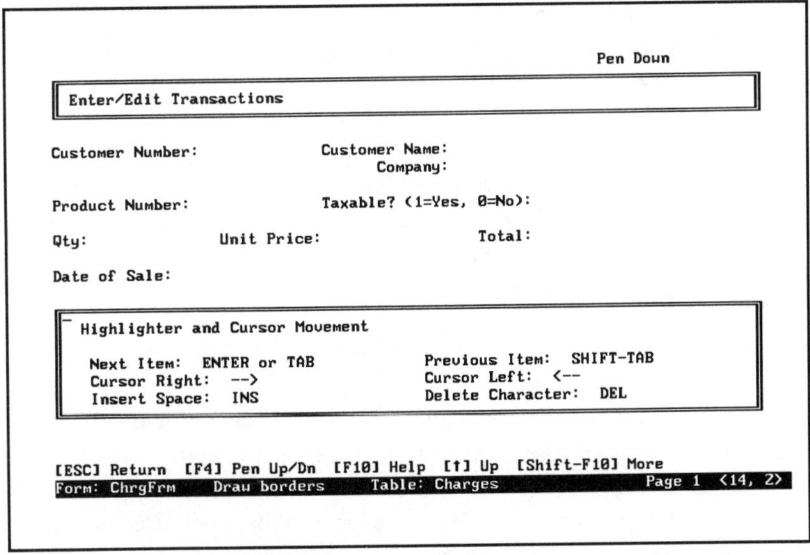

Figure 10.2: ChrgFrm with prompts and boxes

USING VARIABLES IN FORMS

As in reports, you can use variables (or expressions) to place information on the form that is not readily available from the table in use. We can use form variables in several ways in this form. First, when entering or editing data in the Charges table, you will need to enter a customer number. It would be helpful to display the associated person's name and company from the Names table on the form as verification that you've entered the correct customer number.

Second, even though R:BASE automatically calculates the total for the transaction on the database, this total will not automatically appear on the screen. Therefore, we'll create an expression to calculate and display the total directly on the form.

To begin entering expressions onto the ChrgFrm form, select Expression from the top menu and Define from the submenu. Enter the first expression exactly as shown below:

```
Name1 = F:Name IN Names WHERE CustNo = CustNo
```

Answer No when asked whether you want to customize lookup characteristics. The line above is a *lookup expression,* which states that the *lookup variable* Name1 will contain the contents of the F:Name column from the Names table where the customer number entered onto the form matches the customer number in the Names table. (Hence, if you enter 1001 onto the ChrgFrm, the variable Name1 will store the corresponding customer's first name.) Name1 is called a lookup variable because R:BASE must look up the appropriate customer number in the Names table to find the correct name.

Press Enter after typing in the first expression, and then type in the second expression exactly as shown below:

```
Name2 = L:Name IN Names WHERE CustNo = CustNo
```

Answer No again when asked whether you want to customize lookup characteristics. As you may have guessed, Name2 will contain the last name (L:Name) of the appropriate customer on the Names table. We need to create a third variable that contains both the first and last name with a space between. Enter the third expression exactly as it appears below:

```
CName = Name1 & Name2
```

CName is the actual variable that will eventually be located on the form.

The fourth expression to enter will store the company of the appropriate person in a variable named CCompany. Enter the fourth expression as

CCompany = Company IN Names WHERE CustNo = CustNo

and opt not to customize the lookup characteristics.

Notice that this formula uses the same basic syntax as the other lookup expressions, as follows:

variable = *column name* IN *table* WHERE +
+ > *column name* = *column name*

The fifth expression does not perform a lookup. Instead, it calculates the total sale using the same formula as the computed column, but it stores this result in a variable named ShowTot. Enter the fifth expression as shown below:

ShowTot = IFEQ(Tax?,0,Qty*U:Price,(Qty*U:Price)*1.06)

After you've entered all five expressions, press the Esc key. Your screen should look like Figure 10.3.

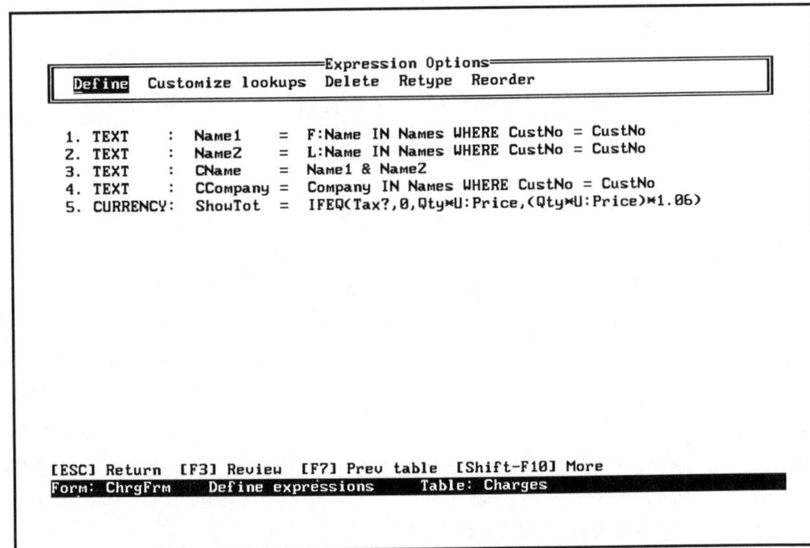

```
Expression Options
Define  Customize lookups  Delete  Retype  Reorder

1. TEXT     : Name1    = F:Name IN Names WHERE CustNo = CustNo
2. TEXT     : Name2    = L:Name IN Names WHERE CustNo = CustNo
3. TEXT     : CName    = Name1 & Name2
4. TEXT     : CCompany = Company IN Names WHERE CustNo = CustNo
5. CURRENCY: ShowTot   = IFEQ(Tax?,0,Qty*U:Price,(Qty*U:Price)*1.06)

[ESC] Return  [F3] Review  [F7] Prev table  [Shift-F10] More
Form: ChrgFrm     Define expressions     Table: Charges
```

Figure 10.3: Expressions defined for the ChrgFrm form

LOCATING VARIABLES AND COLUMNS

You've already had experience using the F6 key to locate column and variable names in reports and forms, so you should be able to do so now given only the start and end (S and E) coordinates for each location. Press Esc to bring back the top menu, and select Edit to move the cursor onto the form. Place each of the column and variable names listed in the left column below at the start and end locations listed in the right columns. For now, select No to answer the various questions about defining expressions and customizing field characteristics that appear while you are locating information on the screen.

COLUMN/ VARIABLE NAME	*START*	*END*
CustNo	<5,18>	<5,21>
CName	<5,45>	<5,75>
CCompany	<6,45>	<6,75>
ProdNo	<8,18>	<8,24>
Tax?	<8,54>	<8,54>*
Qty	<10,6>	<10,15>
U:Price	<10,31>	<10,43>
ShowTot	<10,54>	<10,64>
P:Date	<12,15>	<12,44>

*Only the E will be displayed here

Figure 10.4 shows the completed ChrgFrm form on the screen. For added convenience, you can place a default value into the Tax? field. To do so, move the cursor to the E on the Taxable? prompt <8,54> and press F6. Then select Yes in response to the question about customizing field characteristics. Move the highlight to the fourth question (...default value for this field?), type in **Y,** and press Enter to change the No to a Yes. Type in **1** as the default value, and press Enter. Press Esc to leave the Field Customization menu, and select No in response to the question about changing the field's location.

```
Enter/Edit Transactions

Customer Number: S  E        Customer Name: S                    E
                                   Company: S                    E

Product Number:  S    E      Taxable? (1=Yes, 0=No): E

Qty: S        E   Unit Price: S           E   Total: S        E

Date of Sale: S                               E_

  Highlighter and Cursor Movement

   Next Item:  ENTER or TAB                Previous Item:  SHIFT-TAB
   Cursor Right:  -->                      Cursor Left:  <--
   Insert Space:  INS                      Delete Character:  DEL

[ESC] Return  [F1] Insert  [F2] Delete  [F3] Review  [Shift-F10] More
Form: ChrgFrm    Edit              Table: Charges          Page 1  <12,45>
```

Figure 10.4: The completed ChrgFrm form on the screen

You can put in the current date as the default date for the P:Date column as well. Move the cursor between the S and E for the P:Date column <12,16>, and press F6. Change the answer to the fourth question on the Field Characteristics menu to Yes, and enter # DATE (current date) as the default value for the P:Date column. Press Esc and select No in response to the second question.

When you are done, press Esc to work your way back to the exit options, and select Save Changes. Then keep exiting the other menus to return to the R> prompt.

TESTING THE FORM

To test the form, enter the command

```
ENTER ChrgFrm
```

at the R> prompt. The form appears on the screen with only the default Taxable? and Date of Sale prompts filled in. Entering any valid customer number (for example, 1001..1009 at this point) immediately displays the customer's name and company on the form. You can press the ↑ key and change the customer number at any time, and the name and company will change accordingly.

To complete the transaction, fill in a product number, a taxable status (1 for Yes, 0 for No), a quantity, and a unit price. The total for the transaction appears on the screen immediately, and the cursor moves to the Date of Sale prompt. You can press the ↑ key to move back to previous prompts and make corrections (the total will be corrected as soon as you make the changes). Optionally, you can press Enter to accept the default date, or you can type in a new date and press Enter.

If you enter a customer number that isn't in the Name table, R:BASE will display the message

```
WARNING: No row found for lookup
```

and the highlighter will move down to the Product Number field. Should you fill out the rest of the form, R:BASE will add the data you entered to the Charges table, but you may not be able to collect on the charge, because you won't know who made it. There will be no record of the new customer in the Names table to check against. You'll learn how to create true multi-table forms that allow you to enter data into more than one table at once in Chapter 13.

Figure 10.5 shows a complete transaction on the screen. When you are finished entering transactions, press Esc (if the top menu is not already on the screen), and select Quit.

You can also use the form for editing transactions by entering the command

```
EDIT USING ChrgFrm
```

at the R> prompt. As usual, select Quit from the top menu when you have finished editing.

While the ChrgFrm in its current state is useful, there are a few weaknesses that can be corrected. For one, if you enter an invalid customer number (such as 9999), the form will accept your entry and store whatever you save on the Charges table with little or no warning. Later, when billing time comes, nobody will be billed for the transaction because there is no customer number 9999.

Also, if you accidentally enter an invalid tax code (such as 9), the form will accept it and consider the transaction to be for a nontaxable

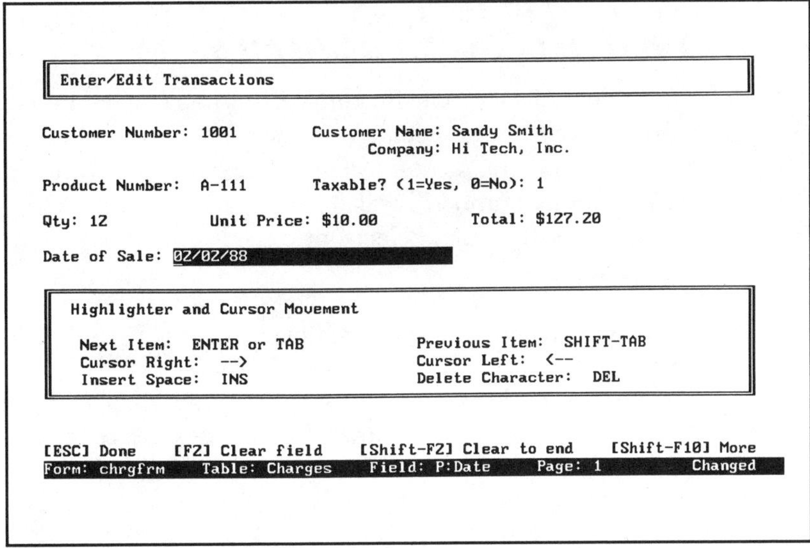

Figure 10.5: The completed transaction on the ChrgFrm form

item. We can ensure that errors such as these do not occur when entering transactions by defining *rules* for the form.

DEFINING MORE COMPLEX RULES

To define rules for a database, use Definition EXPRESS. As you may recall, the quickest way to reach Definition EXPRESS is to enter the command

RBDEFINE

at the R> prompt. To define rules for an existing database, select option 2, *Modify an existing database definition.* From the next submenu, select Rules. This brings up the Rules menu, which presents these self-explanatory options:

(1) Add a new rule
(2) Change an existing rule
(3) Remove a rule
(4) Return to the Database Definition Menu

RULE TO REJECT INVALID CUSTOMER NUMBERS

Our first rule will state that any transaction entered into the Charges table must contain a customer number that exists in the Names table. Otherwise, the transaction will be rejected and the error message "No such customer number!" will appear.

To create the rule, select option 1 from the Rules menu. The screen asks that you

```
Enter the error message for this rule:
```

This prompt asks for the message that you want to appear on the screen when the rule is violated. In this example, type in the message

```
No such customer number!
```

and press Enter.

Next the screen asks that you

```
Choose a table:
```

Since this rule is based on entries into the Charges table, select Charges. Next the screen asks that you

```
Choose a column to validate:
```

We want to make sure a valid customer number is entered, so select CustNo as the column to validate.

Next the screen asks that you

```
Choose an operator
```

and displays the following options. A brief description of each operator is also provided below:

OPERATOR	MEANING
EQ	Equal to a value
NE	Not equal to a value
GT	Greater than a value

GE	Greater than or equal to a value
LT	Less than a value
LE	Less than or equal to a value
EXISTS	Contains any value
FAILS	Contains no value
EQA	Equals any value in a column
NEA	Does not equal any value in a column
GTA	Greater than any value in a column
GEA	Greater than or equal to any value in a column
LTA	Less than any value in a column
LEA	Less than or equal to any value in a column

In our example, the rule is that the customer number entered into the Charges table must *equal any* customer number in the Names table, so you want to select EQA (equal any) for this rule.

The screen asks that you choose the table to be used for comparison. We want to check the Names table for valid customer numbers, so select Names. The screen asks that you

Choose the column to compare:

We're comparing customer numbers in this rule, so select CustNo. Now the rule is defined, and your screen should look like Figure 10.6. In English this screen says, "Display the error message 'No such customer number!' unless the customer number entered into the Charges table equals any customer number in the Names table."

The screen then asks that you

Choose a logical operator:

and presents the following options:

AND   OR   AND NOT   OR NOT   (Done)

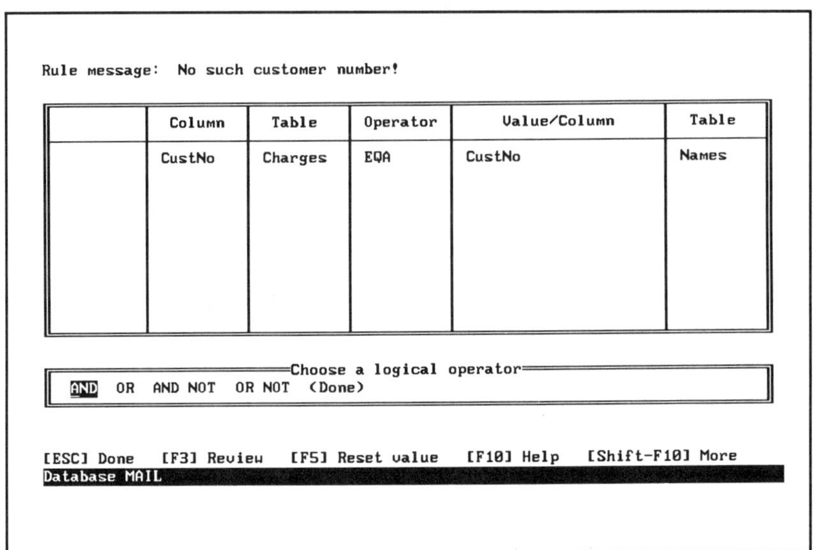

Figure 10.6: The rule to reject invalid customer numbers

We don't need any additional ANDs, ORs, or NOTs to further define this rule, so select Done. The Rules menu appears on the screen. Before testing this rule, let's define a few more rules.

RULE TO REJECT INVALID TAX CODES

Suppose we want a rule that displays the error message "Tax must be 1 or 0!" unless the Tax? column in the Charges table contains a one or a zero. Let's define such a rule now. Select option 1 to add a new rule.

As the error message for the rule, enter this sentence:

Tax must be 1 or 0!

When asked to choose a table, select Charges, since the Tax? column is part of the Charges table. When asked to choose the column to validate, select Tax?, since this is the column of interest in this rule. When asked to choose an operator, select EQ. We don't want EQA here because we're not searching an entire column for a valid Tax? entry; we just want to compare to a couple of predefined values (either 1 or 0). When asked to enter a value to be used for comparison, enter **1** and press Enter.

So far, the rule states that the Tax? column must equal one to be valid. Actually, either a one or a zero is a valid entry in the Tax? column. Therefore, we need to work on the rule some more.

The screen asks that you

Choose a logical operator

In this case, the Tax? column must equal one *or* zero, so select OR. The screen asks for the column to validate, and you select the Tax? column. The screen asks that you select an operator for this part of the expression. Select EQ. The screen asks that you enter a value to be used for comparison, so you enter **0**. Now the rule is defined, as shown in Figure 10.7.

In English, the screen says, "Display the error message 'Tax must be 1 or 0!' unless the Tax? column contains 1 or the Tax? column contains 0." Since you are finished with this rule, select Done from the bottom menu.

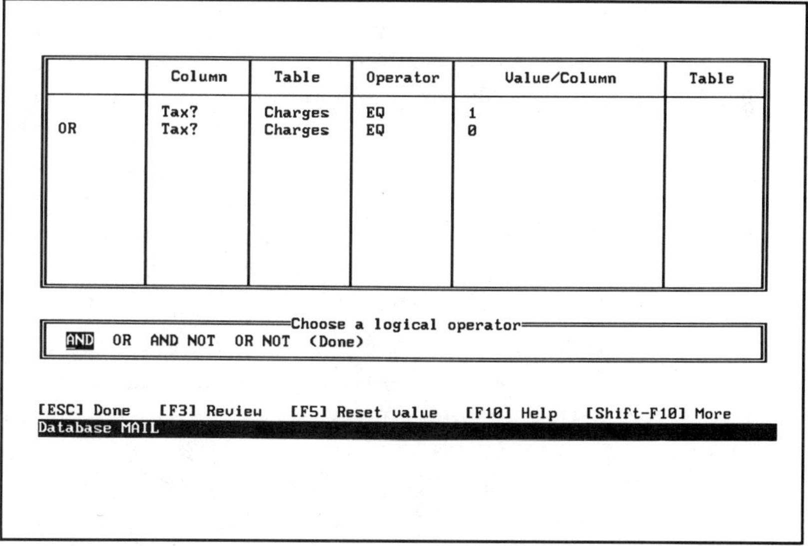

Figure 10.7: The rule to validate the Tax? entry

RULE TO REJECT DUPLICATE CUSTOMER NUMBERS

We created the CustNo column in both the Names and the Charges tables so that we could tell which customer each charge transaction referred to. This will only work if every customer in the Names table has a unique customer number. (Obviously, if two people in the Names table have the customer number 1001, then any transactions referring to customer number 1001 in the Charges table are going to create problems. You'd have to flip a coin to decide which customer number 1001 gets stuck with the bill for the charges.)

To ensure that every customer in the Names table has a unique customer number, we can define a rule that rejects duplicate customer numbers before they are added to the Names table.

To create such a rule, select 1 to add a new rule. Enter the sentence

```
Duplicate customer number!
```

as the error message, and press Enter.

When the screen asks that you choose a table, select Names (because it is the customer numbers on the Names table that we are concerned about). When the screen asks that you choose a column to validate, select CustNo. When you are asked to choose an operator, select NEA (Not Equal Any), because in order to be valid, a new customer number must not equal any existing customer numbers.

When asked to choose the table for comparison, select Names, because the new customer number must not equal any existing customer numbers in the Names table. When asked to choose the column for comparison, select CustNo again, obviously. The completed rule appears on the screen as in Figure 10.8.

In English the screen says, "Display the error message 'Duplicate customer number!' unless the new customer number does not equal any existing customer numbers in the CustNo column of the Names table."

Since you are finished with this rule, select Done from the bottom menu. You can exit Definition EXPRESS now and return to the R> prompt.

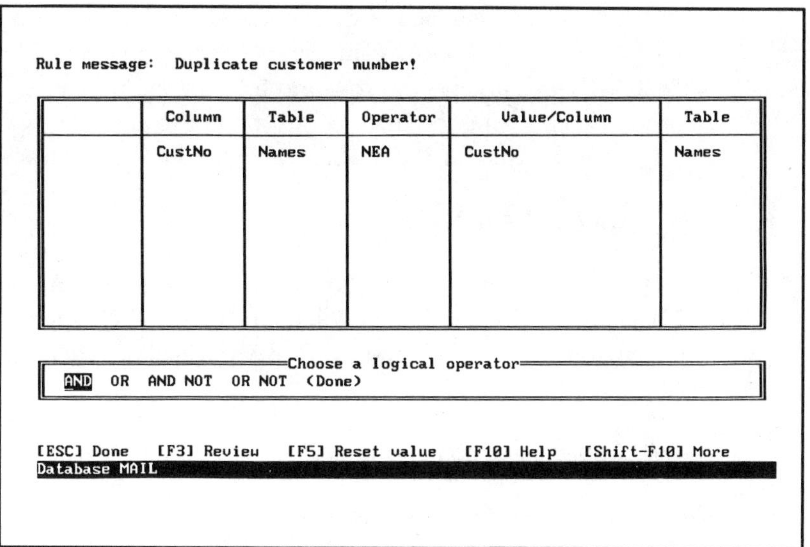

Figure 10.8: The rule for rejecting duplicate customer numbers

TESTING THE RULES

To test the rules for the Charges table, enter the command

ENTER ChrgFRM

at the R> prompt. When the form appears on the screen, fill out the form with an invalid customer number (such as 5555). As soon as you press Enter, R:BASE will warn you that no row was found for the lookup. It doesn't, however, display *your* error message yet. After filling in the form and pressing Esc to bring up the top menu, select Add to add the new data to the Charges table. You'll hear a beep and see your error message at the top of the screen:

"No such customer number!"

Enter a new customer number (such as 1001) into the CustNo field, and press Enter. Now enter an invalid tax code (such as 3). Press Esc and select Add again, and notice that you get the new error message

Tax must be 1 or 0!

You'll need to change the Tax? entry to either a one or a zero. Press Esc and select Add once again. Since no rules are violated by the new data, R:BASE accepts the row and asks for the next one. There's no need to keep testing the rules, so just press Esc and select Quit.

To test the rule for the Names table, enter the command

```
ENTER NamesFrm
```

at the R> prompt. Enter an existing customer number (such as 1001), and fill in any data you like for the rest of the form. When you select Add from the top menu, R:BASE displays the following error message:

```
Duplicate customer number!
```

You must fill in a new customer number (such as 1010), press Enter, then press Esc and select Add again to add the customer to the Names table.

When you are finished experimenting, select Quit from the top menu.

AUTOSKIP ON FORMS

R:BASE includes an Autoskip feature, which can help speed data entry. With the Autoskip feature off, you need to press the Enter key after filling in a highlighted item on the screen. With the Autoskip feature on, the highlighting automatically moves to the next item on the screen when the highlighted area is filled.

To use the Autoskip feature, from the R> prompt use the command

```
SET AUTOSKIP ON
```

Entering the command Set Autoskip Off will disable Autoskip. The Show command displays the current status of the feature. Next we'll add new rows to the Charges table. Leave Autoskip on to see how it works.

ADDING DATA TO THE CHARGES TABLE

We'll add data to the Charges table using the same procedure as we did for adding data to the Names table. Since we've already created a form for this table, simply enter the command

```
ENTER ChrgFrm
```

Enter the following data into the Charges table using the ChrgFrm form. We'll use these new data in next chapter.

CustNo	*ProdNo*	*Tax?*	*Qty*	*U:Price*	*P:Date*
1001	A-111	1	12	10.00	06/15/88
1001	B-222	1	5	12.50	06/15/88
1001	C-434	1	2	100.00	06/15/88
1004	A-111	1	5	10.00	06/15/88
1004	Z-1281	0	10	12.80	06/15/88
1007	A-111	1	10	10.00	06/15/88
1007	Z-128	0	10	12.80	06/15/88
1002	B-222	1	12	12.50	07/01/88
1002	A-111	1	10	10.00	07/01/88

After you've entered the new data, press Esc and select the Quit option from the menu. To verify your entries, enter the command

```
SELECT ALL FROM Charges
```

at the R> prompt. If necessary, you can enter

```
EDIT ALL FROM Charges
```

and make changes.

MANAGING MULTI-TABLE DATABASES

Although life may seem more complicated when you first start working with a multi-table database, there are some powerful tools that will make your work much easier. One of these tools is the *view*. You've seen views alluded to in syntax diagrams; now it's time to learn about them.

WHAT'S IN A VIEW?

Views are *pseudo-tables*—that is, they share many characteristics of tables but are not defined as tables—that can contain columns taken from up to five different related tables. Although a view is displayed like a table and can be manipulated with many of the commands you use for tables, it is not a table.

Views can be created using either Definition EXPRESS or the VIEW command. The prerequisite for constructing multi-table views is that you include the linking (or common) columns as you move from table to table. Furthermore, if you're constructing a view from tables that have different passwords, you'll have to identify yourself as the database owner first.

All view definitions are stored in the Views and Viewwher tables. This means that a view's actual data is not stored in a table of its own, taking up valuable disk space. It also means, however, that R:BASE assembles views "on the fly," which may result in somewhat slower performance. Views are most often used with the SELECT, COMPUTE, CROSSTAB, and TALLY commands, and as the basis for reports. By basing a report on a view, you can avoid defining elaborate lookup expressions. For example, if we wanted to create an invoice report for the Mail database with a combination of data from the Names and Charges tables, it would be easiest to do if we set up a view that contained all of the necessary columns.

Views inherit modify and read passwords from their parent tables. If the first (or source) table in a view has both a modify and a read password, those will be the view's passwords. If the first table only has a modify password, but the second table has both a modify and a read password, the view will have the first table's modify password and the second table's read password. View passwords, like table passwords, can be changed with the RENAME command. Judicious selection of columns to be included in a view combined with use of the WHERE clause allows you to protect any field from casual inspection. If a personnel table contained sensitive information about employee's bonuses that only the personnel director was supposed to see, a personnel view could be created using all but the bonus column from the personnel table. The single-table personnel view could be viewed and edited, much like a "real" table.

Views have their limitations, however. You can't EDIT or BROWSE with multi-table views. You can't add or delete rows to a view, which means you can't base a form on a view. You can't redefine columns that are in a view without deleting the view (with the REMOVE VIEW command). Worse yet, any changes you make in a table that has columns used in a view may corrupt the view.

GRANT AND REVOKE

Once you start working with a multi-table database, you may need to establish more sophisticated security than owner, modify, or read passwords, or even views provide. In that case, you should learn about the SQL GRANT and REVOKE commands.

Look at the syntax diagram for the GRANT command, as shown in Figure 10.9.

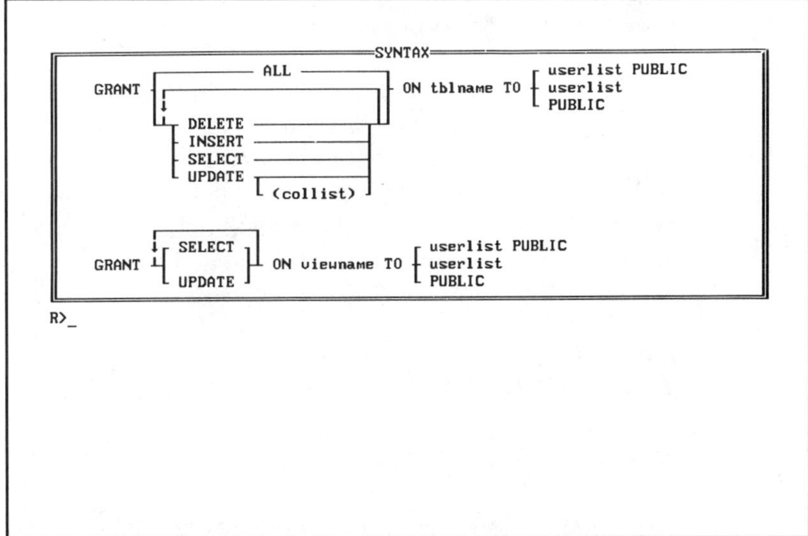

Figure 10.9: The syntax for R:BASE's GRANT command

As you can see, GRANT is used to fine-tune user access to any table or view. GRANT DELETE lets users delete data from a table or view; GRANT INSERT lets them add data; GRANT SELECT allows them only to view data; GRANT UPDATE allows them to edit data—even for a restricted list of columns! If you specify GRANT...TO PUBLIC, you are granting the indicated privileges to all users. If you want to give different users different privileges, you'll have to provide their passwords in the command, in the form of a *userlist*. You'll have to establish an owner password before you can use the GRANT command, just as an owner had to be established before modify or read passwords could be implemented. Users identify themselves using the same USER command, irrespective of the way in which the passwords were established.

With the single exception of forms that have their own passwords, passwords established via the GRANT command have priority over those established with the read/modify system.

The SQL REVOKE command is used to reverse privileges established under GRANT. LIST ACCESS can be used to review the SQL security that has been established for a given database. Although you may or may not want to experiment with the SQL GRANT and REVOKE commands now, you should recognize their potential in establishing tight database security.

DATABASE DESIGN REVISITED

Now that you've seen some of the techniques for using multi-table databases, many of you will want to set up your own. If you're not ready to do so, you may want to skip the rest of the chapter for now. In this section, we will give you a *pragmatic* approach to database design. But before we talk about good database design, we want to give you some examples of poorly designed databases and what their effects can be.

PROBLEMS RESULTING FROM POOR DATABASE DESIGN

If you try to use a poorly designed database, you may encounter any of the following problems:

- Your system simply won't work properly.
- Data is inaccurate or unreliable.

- Data is unstable.
- Performance is slow.
- Data entry personnel will be made to enter redundant data.

Imagine what would have happened to the Mail database if we had tried to include information about both customers and their charges in one table, with one row for each transaction. If we store information about the customer's name, address, city, state, ZIP code, and so forth with each charge transaction, then there will be a great deal of redundant data. This consequence of poor database design is called, reasonably enough, *data redundancy*.

For example, even though there are only three unique customers (Smith, Miller, and Jones) in the database in Figure 10.10, the table uses a lot of disk space because of all the redundant data in the L:Name, F:Name, and Address fields. Also, if a data-entry operator needs to type in the name and address of each customer repeatedly, he or she will certainly be wasting a lot of time. Finally, if one of the customers moves and changes their address, it is not going to be easy to change the address in the table, since the change will have to be made several times. However, failing to change all references to the old address would lead to conflicting data. This consequence of poor database design is called *data inconsistency* and results in loss of the database's integrity.

L:Name	F:Name	Address	Product	Qty	U_Price
Smith	Adam	123 A St.	A-111	10	1.22
Smith	Adam	123 A St.	B-222	5	12.34
Smith	Adam	123 A St.	C-444	1	45.67
Miller	Mandy	234 Oak St.	A-111	5	1.22
Miller	Mandy	234 Oak St.	C-444	10	45.67
Jones	Jake	PO Box 123	A-111	8	1.22
Jones	Jake	PO Box 123	B-222	15	12.34
Jones	Jake	PO Box 123	C-444	5	45.67

Figure 10.10: A database table containing data redundancy

You might then consider modifying the table's design so that it has several fields for charges. But doing so creates another set of problems. For example, look at an alternative table design in Figure 10.11.

The design shown is a poor one, for several reasons. First, it limits the number of transactions a particular customer can be assigned (120 in this example). Second, this design makes it virtually impossible to answer questions such as, "How many charge transactions this month involved part number A-123?" Third, there's a tremendous amount of wasted space associated with storing so many currency fields for each customer. Most customers won't have anywhere near 120 transactions per month.

#	Name	Type	Length	Key
1	LNAME	TEXT	12	
2	FRSNAME	TEXT	10	
3	COMPANY	TEXT	15	
4	ADDRESS	TEXT	15	
5	CITY	TEXT	15	
6	STATE	TEXT	5	
7	ZIP	TEXT	10	
8	PHONE	TEXT	13	
9	TRANS1	CURRENCY		
10	TRANS2	CURRENCY		
11	TRANS3	CURRENCY		
12	TRANS4	CURRENCY		
13	TRANS5	CURRENCY		
...				
...				
...				
128	TRANS120	CURRENCY		

Figure 10.11: A revised table design

It turns out that the best way to handle transactions relationally is to use at least two tables: a master table with the relatively permanent data and a transaction table that is linked to the master table. We'll talk about linking tables in a moment.

A PRAGMATIST'S GUIDE TO DATABASE DESIGN

Databases and the applications associated with them exist to provide accurate and timely information, which can then be used to answer questions. A good way to start designing a database is to make a list of the types of questions the database might be expected to answer.

STEP ONE: FIND OUT WHAT INFORMATION WILL BE NEEDED

To find out what the information requirements of an organization are, you need to talk to people. If a friend wants you to set up a database for his company that sells used books, you need to get to know how information flows within his company. There's a pretty obvious need for supplier, inventory, and sales data, but he may also want to keep track of advertising and seasonal market changes.

When you interview people about their information needs, ask to see current forms and reports. Don't hesitate to prompt them; you may see areas they have either forgotten or may not have even considered. Informal brainstorming sessions often work well. It's far better to find out at the beginning that, for example, sales need to be tracked by time of day.

STEP TWO: GROUP THE DATA

If this sounds like deciding what tables you need, you're right! By looking at the list of data requirements, it's usually pretty easy to spot categories such as inventory, suppliers, sales, customers, employees, expenses, and so on. Each table should have its own subject.

Probably the most important step here is to limit the scope of the database. Make sure everyone involved realizes the trade-off between development time and the sophistication of the application.

Frequently, you'll only need to answer part of an organization's data requirements; just be sure that everyone agrees on what is expected. We'll assume that for now your friend is only interested in tracking his sales.

STEP THREE: DETERMINE THE RELATIONSHIPS AMONG THE TABLES

This can be a difficult step for beginners. Basically, there are three types of relationships between database tables: one-to-one, one-to-many, and many-to-many. One-to-one relationships don't occur that frequently between different objects; when they do, you can often collapse the tables into a single one. For example, you might conceive of a database with one table for names and another for social security numbers. These tables have a one-to-one relationship: for every name, there is a single, matching social security number. It really doesn't make sense to keep the data in two separate tables.

One-to-many and many-to-many relationships are far more common. Good relational database design requires that you break many-to-many relationships into one-to-many relationships, so it's important to be able to distinguish them. In a one-to-many relationship, for each row in the first table, there are (or could be) many corresponding rows in the second table. The relationship between Names and Charges in the Mail database is a one-to-many relationship.

In a many-to-many relationship, for each row in the first table, there are (or could be) many corresponding rows in the second table. However, for each row in the second table, there are (or could be) many corresponding rows in the first table as well. Tables containing parents and children would have a many-to-many relationship.

Your friend seems to need to keep track of customers and sales. The question is, what sort of relationship exists between the two? We find that most people find it easiest to visualize pairs of lists. In our example, one list would contain all the customers; the other all the sales. Then, imagine drawing lines from one list to the other. For each customer, could there be more than one line going to the sales list? Sure. What about the other way? Would one sale be associated with more than one customer? No, of course not. So customer-to-sales is a *one-to-many* relationship.

Even when you have a far more complicated data model, this method still works. You simply plot it out for each pair of tables. Some tables won't have any direct relationship between them. Suppliers and sales, for example, wouldn't normally be directly related.

STEP FOUR: DECIDE ON THE COLUMNS FOR EACH TABLE

Deciding on the columns for each table is usually a pretty easy task, since you're just listing the important facts about each object. You might initially come up with something like the following:

SALES	*CUSTOMER*
Invoice#	CustNo
P:Date	L:Name
ProdNo	F:Name
Qty	Address
U:Price	City
Tax?	State
Total	Zip
	Phone

It might not be until you arrive at this step that you recognize a problem with your design. What if customers purchase several items at a time? One solution would be to have separate invoices for each item, but this probably wouldn't be desirable. You might, then, decide to include a third table with invoice details, and thus reorganize the Sales table as follows:

INVDET	*SALES*	*CUSTOMER*
ProdNo	Invoice#	CustNo
Qty	P:Date	L:Name
U:Price	Invtotal	F:Name

INVDET	*SALES*	*CUSTOMER*
Tax?		Address
		City
		State
		Zip
		Phone

Many people start thinking about data types and lengths at this point, too. Probably the most common error at this stage is to go wild and include data that really isn't needed. Keep in mind that the overhead associated with carrying unneeded data is heavy: more data entry, more disk space, and slower performance.

STEP FIVE: ASSIGN KEYS

Keys, you may remember from the last chapter, uniquely identify a row. If you know the key fact (or group of facts) about an entity in your table, you should be able to retrieve data about the entity quickly and efficiently. If you have a Customer table in your database, keyed on CustNo, you can expect R:BASE to find no more than one customer's record when you type

```
SELECT ALL FROM Customer WHERE CustNo = 1004
```

There ought to be a law stating that all well-designed tables shall have keys and that no entries in the table will be allowed without the key entry. Unfortunately, R:BASE doesn't enforce such laws; the burden is on you to establish keys and set up rules that make sure that data entered into key fields is unique.

As you assign keyed columns, the list of attributes associated with each table may change. This is normal. For example, you may need to add a column to a table to serve as its key. This adds an attribute (column) to that table's definition.

What keys might you use for the book sales database? The answers seem to be fairly obvious for the Sales and Customer tables: Invoice# and CustNo are good keys, since each customer and each invoice will bear unique numbers. However, what key should the Invdet table use? ProdNo won't do, because a given product type will be sold more than once. Perhaps Invoice# should be added to the Invdet table. However, Invoice# alone isn't a good key for the Invdet table either, because some invoices will have many items on them. You may want to key both Invoice# and ProdNo. Alternatively, you could add a column for the invoice item number. Either method will require modifying the original design of the Invdet table.

STEP SIX: ESTABLISH LINKS BETWEEN RELATED TABLES

Establishing links between related tables may seem hard at first, but it becomes intuitive with practice. So if you find this step tough, lean on our pragmatic rules at first.

When you establish links between related tables, you're providing the "glue" that makes the database relational. Links are columns that appear in more than one table. At first, it will go against your grain to add columns to tables, because it's contrary to the notion of minimizing redundancy. However, you will soon learn to accept the fact that links are necessary.

So what are the ground rules for selecting links? We can summarize them as follows:

- Links should also be keys, so that data is linked unambiguously.
- To link tables with a one-to-many relationship, put the key from the "one" side of the relationship into the table from the "many" side of the relationship. This will create a situation where you effectively have two keys in the "many" table. The link key, however, is referred to as a *foreign* key.
- To link tables that have a many-to-many relationship, create a new table that contains the keys from each side of the relationship. This new table may or may not correspond to any physical entity. It may simply be a product of good relational design.

Before we can use the above rules, we need to know about the relationships that exist among the tables. Since we've added a new table, we need to reevaluate the relationships. Customer to Sales is still a one-to-many relationship. Sales to Invdet is also a one-to-many relationship, since any given invoice can contain several items. Finally,

Customer and Invdet have another one-to-many relationship, but it is indirect, since Sales will link customers and their transactions.

The second rule above reminds us that the key from the Customer table needs to be in the Sales table and that the key from the Sales table needs to be in the Invdet table. The design might be modified as follows:

INVDET	*SALES*	*CUSTOMER*
Invoice#(key)	Invoice#(key)	CustNo(key)
ProdNo(key)	CustNo	L:Name
Qty	P:Date	F:Name
U:Price	Invtotal	Address
Tax?		City
		State
		Zip
		Phone

A common mistake is to create separate tables for separate items of information (which is a step in the right direction), but to forget to provide a common column that links them. If you hadn't put the CustNo column in the Sales table, you wouldn't be able to answer the question "Who bought 'Gone With the Wind' on Invoice 321?"

STEP SEVEN: SET UP THE DATABASE

At this stage, you still shouldn't have done any hands-on data entry. Only after having designed the database on paper, and worked out the keys and links, should you actually use Definition EXPRESS to set it up. And bear in mind that even after having gone through the design steps listed above, changes may still need to be made in your database design. The beauty of relational databases such as R:BASE is that it's easy to make changes.

COMMON ERRORS IN DATABASE DESIGN

What are some common errors in database design? Based on our experience, here is a list of a few:

- Having many-to-many relationships without a link table
- Setting up tables without keys (or without good keys)
- Not having rules set up to ensure entry of key values
- Putting the link column for one-to-many relationships in the wrong table
- Having tables that contain more than one emphasis, such as an orders table with supplier information alongside purchase order details
- Not taking advantage of calculated fields
- Having too many common columns relating a pair of tables

However, if you employ this step-by-step approach to database design, you should be able to avoid these errors.

In this chapter, we've added a new table and form to the Mail database. We've also created some rules to minimize the likelihood of erroneous data being entered into the database. Finally, we've looked at seven steps that lead to good database design. In the next chapter, you'll learn some new techniques for handling calculations using R:BASE's variables and SuperMath functions.

Chapter 11

Complex Calculations Using Variables and Functions

FAST TRACK

To store data in variables, 282

use the syntax SET VARIABLE *variable name* TO *value*.

To display all currently active variables, 282

use the SHOW VARIABLES command. Enter SHOW VARIABLE *variable name* to display the value of a single variable.

R:BASE's arithmetic operations 285

include +, −, *, /, **, %, and &.

To calculate variables, 286

use the syntax SET VARIABLE *variable name* TO *expression*. The *expression* may contain arithmetic operators and functions.

To predefine a variable's data type 288

explicitly, enter SET VARIABLE <*variable name*> <*data type*>. Otherwise, R:BASE automatically assigns variable data types based on the nature of the data being stored.

To pass data from tables 289

in an open database to variables, use the syntax SET VARIABLE *variable name* TO *column name* IN *table name* WHERE *condition*.

To store the results of table calculations 290

in variables, use the syntax COMPUTE *variable name* AS <*calculation*> <*column name*> FROM *table name* WHERE *conditions*.

To erase a single active variable, 293

enter CLEAR *variable name*. The CLEAR ALL Variables command erases all active variables except #DATE, #TIME, and #PI.

R:BASE offers 70 functions 295

that can be used with variables, in computed columns, in expressions for forms and reports, and in R:BASE commands.

To alter basic table data 315

in all or selected rows, use the CHANGE and UPDATE commands, in the form CHANGE *column name* TO *expression* IN *conditions*. *Conditions* can take the form of a column number, or a WHERE clause specifying criteria for column selection in a named table.

NOW THAT YOU'VE GRADUATED FROM THE R:BASE novice stage, you need to learn how to create and manage R:BASE *variables,* which are also referred to as *global variables.* The adjective refers to the fact that data in variables can be passed from one database to another, and hence are accessible, or "global," to all databases. Unlike information stored in databases and tables, variables are stored in the computer's random access memory (RAM), and they are normally used as temporary, or "scratch pad," data.

A variable is a character or word that holds a value that is subject to change. This definition is identical to the use of variables in basic mathematics. For example, if we state that X equals 10 and Y equals 15, then X plus Y equals 25, and Y minus X equals 5.

In this chapter, we'll explore techniques for creating and using R:BASE variables. We'll discuss the practical applications of variables in the following chapters.

CREATING VARIABLES

In R:BASE, you use the SET VARIABLE command (abbreviated to SET VAR or SET V) to store and manipulate variables. The SHOW VARIABLES command (abbreviated to SHOW VAR or SHO V) displays the current value of all the variables. You can also use the SHOW VARIABLE command to display a single variable. You enter these commands at the R> prompt; it does not matter whether a database is open at the time.

Here are some examples that you may want to try. First, from the R> prompt, enter the command

```
SHOW VARIABLES
```

You'll see three variables, #DATE, #TIME, and #PI displayed on the screen, as below:

VARIABLE	=	*VALUE*	*TYPE*
#DATE	=	06/19/88	DATE

#TIME	=	5:59:18	TIME
#PI	=	3.14159265358979	DOUBLE

These variables are always available in R:BASE and are sometimes referred to as *system variables.* We used the #DATE variable earlier when we printed dates on our database reports.

Now, enter the command

```
SET VARIABLE X TO 10
```

and then enter this command:

```
SET VARIABLE Y TO 15
```

If you now enter the command

```
SHOW VARIABLES
```

you'll see these two new variables added to the table of existing variables, as below:

VARIABLE	=	*VALUE*	*TYPE*
#DATE	=	06/19/88	DATE
#TIME	=	5:59:41	TIME
#PI	=	3.14159265358979	DOUBLE
X	=	10	INTEGER
Y	=	15	INTEGER

Notice that the new variables have the INTEGER,data type. R:BASE assigned this data type based on the nature of the values being stored (10 and 15).

Now, enter the command

```
SET VARIABLE A TO Hello
```

and then the command

```
SET VARIABLE B TO There
```

If you now enter the command

```
SHOW VARIABLES
```

you'll see the new A and B variables added to the list, as below:

VARIABLE	=	*VALUE*	*TYPE*
#DATE	=	06/19/88	DATE
#TIME	=	6:00:19	TIME
#PI	=	3.14159265358979	DOUBLE
X	=	10	INTEGER
Y	=	15	INTEGER
A	=	Hello	TEXT
B	=	There	TEXT

R:BASE assigned the TEXT data type to these new variables, again because it made an assumption based on the nature of the values being stored.

Next, enter each of the commands below individually at the R> prompt:

```
SET VARIABLE Today TO 6/20/88
SET VARIABLE Now TO 12:30:00
SET VARIABLE Salary TO 12345.67
SET VARIABLE DecNumb TO 1.0
```

Then enter the command

```
SHOW VARIABLES
```

You'll see that R:BASE made valid assumptions about the data types of each variable, as shown below:

VARIABLE	=	*VALUE*	*TYPE*
#DATE	=	06/19/88	DATE
#TIME	=	7:19:15	TIME
#PI	=	3.14159265358979	DOUBLE

X	=	10	INTEGER
Y	=	5	INTEGER
A	=	Hello	TEXT
B	=	There	TEXT
Today	=	06/20/88	DATE
Now	=	12:30:00	TIME
Salary	=	12345.67	DOUBLE
DecNumb	=	1.	DOUBLE

Note that each variable name (A, B, Today, Now, and so on) is purely arbitrary. You can use whatever variable names you like, as long as the name is no more than eight characters in length and does not contain spaces or punctuation marks. The number of variables that you can create is limited only by the amount of computer memory available. You should be able to use at least 40 variables, and the maximum is about 1000 variables.

Before taking a look at ways to manipulate variables, let's talk about R:BASE's arithmetic operators.

R:BASE'S ARITHMETIC OPERATORS

When you used the * operator in previous chapters to represent multiplication, you were using one of R:BASE's predefined arithmetic operators. Of course, R:BASE also provides operators for addition, subtraction, division, and percentages. These are shown in Table 11.1 in their order of *precedence.* Precedence refers to the order in which the calculations take place. For example, the formula 10 + 5 * 2 results in 20, because the multiplication takes precedence over (occurs before) the addition. You can use parentheses to change the order of precedence. For example, the formula (10 + 5) * 2 results in 30, because the operation inside the parentheses takes precedence.

R:BASE also offers many *functions* for performing advanced trigonometric and financial calculations that we'll talk about later in this chapter. Remember for now that parentheses and functions have higher precedence than any of the arithmetic operators.

Table 11.1: R:BASE's Arithmetic Operators

OPERATOR	FUNCTION	EXAMPLE
–, +	Unary minus or plus	– 10 means negative 10
**	Exponentiation	3**2 = 9 (3 squared) 27**(1/3) = 3
*, /	Multiplication, Division	3 * 5 = 15, 100 / 10 = 10
%	Percentage	50 % 100 = 50
+, –	Addition, Subtraction	2 + 2 = 4, 10 – 5 = 5
+, &	Concatenation, Concatenation (with space)	"ABC" + "DEF" = "ABCDEF", "ABC" & "DEF" = "ABC DEF"

MANIPULATING VARIABLES

We've already discussed the R:BASE operators that you can use for addition, subtraction, and other operations. You can use all of these operators to create and manipulate variables. For example, to find the cube root of 27, you could enter the command below:

```
SET VAR Cube TO (27**(1/3))
```

The two asterisks (**) represent the exponent sign, and the parentheses ensure that the division (1/3) will take place before the exponentiation. When you enter the SHOW VARIABLES command at the R> prompt, you'll see the answer 3. stored in the variable named Cube.

The expression above contains only *constants;* that is, 27 is a constant and (1/3) is a constant because they are numbers. Similarly, the expression below contains two constants, the text string "So" and the text string "Long":

```
SET VARIABLE ByeBye TO "So" & "Long"
```

After entering this command at the R> prompt, the variable ByeBye will contain the text "So long". (Use SHOW VARIABLES to see the results.)

Expressions can contain *variables* as well as constants. When using variable names in expressions, however, you should always precede the variable name with a period, in order to avoid confusing variables and constants. For example, recall that we created a variable named A, which contains the word "Hello". We also created a variable named B, which contains the word "there". To use these two variable names in an expression, precede each variable name with a period (or dot), as follows:

```
SET VAR Howdy TO .A & .B
```

If you enter the SHOW VARIABLES command after entering this command, you'll see that the variable Howdy now contains the TEXT string

```
Hello there
```

You can use the predefined (or *system*) variables in expressions (such as #DATE, #TIME, and #PI), although you should make a habit of preceding these variable names with periods as well. For example, you may recall from geometry that the area of a circle can be found using the formula π times the radius squared. Assuming that you know the radius is 5, the expression below can calculate the area of the circle and store the result in a variable named Area (note that the #PI variable is preceded with a dot):

```
SET VAR Area TO (.#PI * 5 ** 2)
```

The SHOW VARIABLES command displays the following result:

```
Area = 78.5398163397447 DOUBLE
```

You can manipulate dates in expressions just as you can manipulate text and numbers. For example, recall that we created a variable named Today a short time ago, and we assigned 6/26/88 to the date.

To find out what the date will be 90 days past the Today variable, you could enter the command

```
SET VARIABLE Ninety TO .Today + 90
```

and then enter the command

```
SHOW VARIABLE Ninety
```

You'll see the date 90 days beyond Today, as below:

```
09/24/88
```

When you mix data types, the results can be confusing. For example, if you add the X variable (which is an INTEGER data type) to the DecNumb variable (which is a DOUBLE number data type), as in:

```
SET VARIABLE Mix TO .X + .DecNumb
```

when you enter the command

```
SHOW VARIABLES
```

you'll see that the new variable Mix is the DOUBLE data type, as below:

VARIABLE	=	*VALUE*	*TYPE*
Mix	=	11	DOUBLE

Generally, when you mix an INTEGER data type with a DOUBLE or CURRENCY data type amount, the result will be the data type with the most decimal places. However, you can control the data type of a variable before defining a variable or performing a calculation, through a process known as *explicit data typing.*

EXPLICIT DATA TYPING

You can define a variable's type by using the SET VARIABLE command without the TO (or =)option, followed by a data type. For example, the command

```
SET VARIABLE JJ CURRENCY
```

creates an "empty" variable named JJ with the CURRENCY data type. The command

```
SET VARIABLE Later DATE
```

creates an empty variable named Later with the DATE data type. The data types for variables are the same as those for columns: INTEGER, DOUBLE, CURRENCY, TEXT, NOTE, DATE, REAL, and TIME. We'll see the value of explicit data typing in later chapters when we develop command files.

PASSING TABLE DATA TO VARIABLES

Variables can also be assigned values directly from a table in a database. To do so, you need to open the appropriate database first. Then you use a version of the SET VARIABLE command with the following syntax:

SET VARIABLE *variable name* TO *column name* IN *table name* +
+ > WHERE *condition*

We can try this one using the Names table in the Mail database. First, open the database from the R> prompt by entering the command

```
OPEN Mail
```

Now, if you enter the command

```
SET VARIABLE Name1 TO F:Name IN Names WHERE +
+ > CustNo = 1003
```

the Name1 variable will contain the first name of customer number 1003. If you then enter the command

```
SET VARIABLE Name2 TO L:Name IN Names WHERE +
+ > CustNo = 1003
```

the Name2 variable will contain the last name of customer number 1003. If you then enter the command

```
SET VARIABLE Name TO .Name1 & .Name2
```

the Name variable will contain the first and last name separated by a space. When you enter the command

```
SHOW VARIABLES
```

you'll see, among the existing variables, the new Name1, Name2, and Name variables, as below:

VARIABLE	=	*VALUE*	*TYPE*
.	.	.	.
.	.	.	.
.	.	.	.
Name1	=	Marie	TEXT
Name2	=	Miller	TEXT
Name	=	Marie Miller	TEXT

This technique is especially useful when developing sophisticated applications, as we'll see in the coming chapters.

THE COMPUTE COMMAND REVISITED

Variables can also be used to store the results of computations performed on a table. You may recall from Chapter 6 that the general syntax for the COMPUTE command is

COMPUTE *variable name* AS <*calculation*> <*column name*> + + > FROM *table name* WHERE *conditions*

The WHERE clause is optional. Although you used this powerful command in Chapter 6, you never stored the results.

Suppose, for example, that you want to compute the sum of the Total column in the Charges table and store the result in a variable named GrandTot. Enter the following command:

```
COMPUTE GrandTot AS SUM Total FROM Charges
```

When you enter the command

```
SHOW VARIABLE GrandTot
```

you'll see the total, as below:

```
$1,085.45
```

To compute the average unit price from the Charges table and store the result in a variable named AvgPrice, enter the command

```
COMPUTE AvgPrice AS AVE U:Price FROM Charges
```

To see the result, enter this command:

```
SHOW VARIABLE AvgPrice
```

R:BASE will display the average unit price of $21.18.

You can count the number of rows in a table and store this number in a variable using the ROWS option with the COMPUTE command, as below:

```
COMPUTE RowCount AS ROWS FROM Names
```

Enter the command

```
SHOW VARIABLE RowCount
```

to see that there are nine rows in the table, as the screen now shows.

The optional WHERE clause allows you to create COMPUTE commands that are more specific. For example, to compute the total sales from the Charges table for product number A-111 and store this value in a variable named ATot, enter the command

```
COMPUTE ATot AS SUM Qty FROM Charges WHERE +
+> ProdNo = A-111
```

Enter the command

```
SHOW VARIABLE ATot
```

to see the result, 37.

You can verify this calculation by entering the command

```
SELECT ALL FROM Charges WHERE ProdNo = A-111
```

which displays all product number A-111 transactions from the Charges table, as shown in Figure 11.1.

To determine the largest single transaction amount for product number A-111, enter the command

```
COMPUTE HiSale AS MAX Total FROM Charges WHERE +
+> ProdNo = A-111
```

To determine the lowest sale for product number A-111, enter this command:

```
COMPUTE LowSale AS MIN Total FROM Charges WHERE +
+> ProdNo = A-111
```

To count the number of rows in a table that meet a specific criterion, use the COMPUTE command with the COUNT option rather than with the Rows option. For example, the command

```
COMPUTE RowCount AS COUNT ProdNo IN Charges +
+> WHERE ProdNo = A-111
```

```
R>SELECT ALL FROM Charges WHERE ProdNo = A-111
 CustNo     ProdNo   Qty        U:Price          Tax?       Total
 ---------- -------- ---------- ---------------- ---------- ---------------
       1001 A-111            12           $10.00          1         $127.20
       1004 A-111             5           $10.00          1          $53.00
       1007 A-111            10           $10.00          1         $106.00
       1002 A-111            10           $10.00          1         $106.00
R>_
```

Figure 11.1: Product number A-111 transactions in the Charges table

counts the number of rows from the Charges table that have A-111 in the ProdNo column and then stores the result in a variable named RowCount.

If you now enter the command

```
SHOW VARIABLES
```

you'll see, among the other variables we've created in this chapter, those listed below:

VARIABLE	=	*VALUE*	*TYPE*
GrandTot	=	$1,085.45	CURRENCY
AvgPrice	=	$21.18	CURRENCY
ATot	=	37	INTEGER
HiSale	=	$127.20	CURRENCY
LowSale	=	$53.00	CURRENCY
RowCount	=	4	INTEGER

Note that the data types for the variables have been assigned the same data types as the columns that were computed. Again, R:BASE has made reasonable assumptions about the data types based on the type of data being computed.

CLEARING VARIABLES

When you exit R:BASE, all variables (except #DATE, #TIME, and #PI) are immediately erased, and they cannot be recalled other than to recreate them using the SET VARIABLE command. Prior to exiting, however, the variables are available in memory even as you open and close databases.

You also can eliminate variables using the CLEAR command. For example, the command

```
CLEAR Salary
```

erases the Salary variable. You can clear all variables (except #DATE, #TIME, and #PI) using the command

```
CLEAR ALL VARIABLES
```

MACRO SUBSTITUTION

You can also use variables as a portion of R:BASE commands using a technique often called *macro substitution.* An example will best demonstrate this technique. First, assume you create a TEXT variable named ColNames using the SET VARIABLE command, as below:

```
SET VARIABLE ColNames TO "CustNo L:Name F:Name +
+> Company"
```

Assuming that the Mail database is open, you could then use the ColNames variable as part of a command, as long as you precede the variable name with an ampersand (&) character. For example, entering the command

```
SELECT &ColNames FROM Names
```

displays the CustNo, L:Name, F:Name, and Company columns from the Names table, because R:BASE automatically substitutes the text stored in the variable ColNames into the command. In other words, R:BASE changes the command to

```
SELECT CustNo L:Name F:Name Company FROM Charges
```

by substituting the contents of the ColNames variable before executing the command. (The substitution takes place "behind the scenes," so you see only the final result and not the actual substitution.)

Macro substitution is an advanced, though often useful, technique used primarily in programming with the R:BASE programming language.

EXPRESSION LIMITATIONS

An expression in a SET VARIABLE command can be up to 160 characters long. Any expression can contain up to 50 operators and operands. *Operands* are the data that the operators act upon. For example, the expression below contains three operators: two multiplication signs (*) and one minus sign (–). The expression also contains four operands (.A, .X, .Y, and .Z).

```
.A * (.X - .Y) * .Z
```

THE POWER OF FUNCTIONS (SUPERMATH)

Most pocket calculators that you can purchase for more than 99 cents have a least a few *function* keys on them. The function keys are included to perform calculations that extend beyond simple arithmetic, such as square roots and logarithms.

R:BASE also offers a set of *functions* collectively referred to as SuperMath. In fact, R:BASE offers about 70 functions that you can use to perform sophisticated calculations with variables. These functions can also be used for defining expressions for computed columns in a database and for variables in reports and forms. (In earlier chapters, we've already seen how the IFEQ function can be used to calculate a total sale based on the status of the Tax? column in the Charges table.)

Functions can also be used in command lines, including ORDER BY and WHERE clauses. Furthermore, functions can also be used freely within the R:BASE programming language, a topic we'll discuss in Chapter 16.

Almost all functions require at least one *argument,* which is the information that the function operates on. For example, the SQRT function calculates the square root of a number and requires one argument. In the expression

```
SET VARIABLE Root TO SQRT(9)
```

the number 9 is the argument to the function. The result of the calculation is stored in the variable named Root.

The argument can be another variable. For example, the expression below stores the number 9 in a variable named StartNum:

```
SET VARIABLE StartNum TO 9
```

The next command calculates the square root of the value stored in the StartNum variable and replaces the prior value of Root:

```
SET VARIABLE Root TO SQRT(.StartNum)
```

In most cases, the argument to a function can also be a column name.

When using functions, you must be careful to use the correct data type in the argument. For example, the command

```
SET VARIABLE Root TO SQRT("Smith")
```

makes no sense, because you cannot possibly calculate the square root of a person's last name. If you try, R:BASE will respond with an error message.

Function arguments can also be expressions in themselves. For example, the command

```
SET VARIABLE Root TO SQRT(80 + 20)
```

stores the square root of 100 in the variable named Root. (One exception to this rule is TEXT functions, which do not allow expressions in TEXT string arguments.)

Functions other than TEXT (or *string*) functions may be nested within an expression, as long as there is an equal number of opening and closing parentheses in the expression. For example, the ABS function converts a negative number to a positive number, but leaves a positive number as positive. The square root function accepts only positive numbers. Therefore, you could use the ABS function inside the SQRT function to ensure that the argument to the SQRT function is positive.

In the example below, the negative number −49 is stored in a variable named NegNumb:

```
SET VARIABLE NegNumb TO -49
```

In the next expression, the square root of the absolute value of NegNumb is stored in the variable named Root. Notice that the parentheses are *balanced* (there are two opening parentheses and two closing parentheses):

```
SET VARIABLE Root TO SQRT(ABS(NegNumb))
```

Since the ABS function is nested inside the SQRT function, R:BASE first calculates the absolute value of the NegNumb variable, and then calculates the square root of that result. The resulting number, 7., is stored in the variable named Root.

The remainder of this chapter lists the R:BASE functions categorized by the types of calculations they perform. Each function is shown with the correct placement and data types of the argument(s) that the function operates on. The types of arguments include the following:

Number	A real, double-precision, or integer number
Real	Either a real or double-precision number
Date	The DATE data type
Time	The TIME data type
Integer	The INTEGER data type
Text	The TEXT data type
Angle	An angle measurement expressed in radians
List	A list of column names, variables, constants, or expressions

A few other examples of arguments are also included in the summary that follows. These are explained in more detail when they are used.

An example of each function is also included. To verify that the function performs as expected, or to experiment with new values, use the SET VARIABLE and SHOW VARIABLE commands at the R> prompt on your own computer. For instance, the example shown in the SQRT function is

```
SQRT(81) is 9.
```

To try this, enter the command

```
SET VARIABLE Test TO SQRT(81)
```

(Of course, Test is just a sample variable name; you can use any variable name you like.) To see the result, enter the command

```
SHOW VARIABLE Test
```

or enter the command

```
SHOW VARIABLES
```

and you'll see that the variable named Test does indeed contain the number 9.

The examples all assume that the variable name used has not already been assigned a data type, either through explicit data typing or through previous use. If you use the same variable name repeatedly, your results may be inconsistent with the examples given. To rectify any discrepancies caused by existing data types, use the CLEAR ALL VARIABLES or CLEAR VARIABLE *variable list* command before entering the SET VARIABLE command.

Several additional examples of using R:BASE functions are included at the end of this chapter.

ARITHMETIC AND MATHEMATICAL FUNCTIONS

The arithmetic and mathematical functions that follow perform common calculations on numbers and are used in both scientific and business applications.

ABS(*Number*)

Absolute Value—Converts a negative number to a positive number, or leaves a positive number as positive. Examples: ABS(– 2) equals 2, as does ABS(2).

DIM(*Number,Number*)

Positive Difference—Subtracts the second *Number* from the first. The result is either a positive number or zero. Examples: DIM(12,10) is 2. DIM(10,12) is 0.

EXP(*Number*)

Inverse of Logarithm—Raises the constant *e* (2.71828) to the power of *Number*. Example: EXP(1) is 2.71828.

LOG(*Number*)

Natural Logarithm—Computes the logarithm base *e* of *Number*, where *Number* is positive. Example: LOG(2.71828) equals 1.

LOG10(*Number*)

Logarithm Base 10—Returns the logarithm base 10 of *Number*, where *Number* is positive. Example: LOG10(100) is 2.

SQRT(*Number*)

Square Root—Returns the square root of *Number*, where *Number* is positive. Example: SQRT(81) is 9.

AVE(*List*)

Average—Computes the average of the numbers in *List*. Example: AVE(9,3,4.5,11,15) is 8.5.

MAX(*List*)

Highest Value—Finds the largest number in the specified *List* of values. Example: MAX(2, −3,87,99,16) is 99.

MIN(*List*)

Lowest Value—Finds the smallest number in the specified *List* of values. Example: MIN(2, −3,87,99,16) is −3.

MOD(*Number,Number*)

Modulus—Returns the remainder after dividing the first *Number* by the second *Number*. Examples: MOD(6,4) is 2. MOD(10,5) is 0, because 10 is evenly divisible by 5.

SIGN(*Number,Number*)

Sign Transfer—Transfers the sign of the second *Number* to the first *Number*. Example: SIGN(12, −7) is −12.

TRIGONOMETRIC FUNCTIONS

The trigonometric functions are used primarily in scientific and engineering applications. If your work generally does not require the use of these functions, you can probably skip these. Note that all trigonometric angle measurements are in radians, not degrees. Also,

R:BASE will typically display the results of trigonometric functions with 14 decimal places of accuracy, although we'll show only five decimal places in these examples.

ACOS(*Number*)

Arccosine—Computes the arccosine of *Number,* where *Number* is a value in the range −1 to 1. The result is an angle, in radians, between zero and pi. Example: ACOS(−0.5) is 2.09439.

ASIN(*Number*)

Arcsine—Computes the arcsine of *Number,* where *Number* is in the range −1 to 1. The result is an angle expressed in radians. Example: ASIN(−0.75) is −0.84806.

ATAN(*Number*)

Arctangent—Computes the arctangent of *Number,* with the result being an angle expressed in radians. Example: ATAN(1) returns 0.78540.

ATAN2(*Number*)

Arctangent of Coordinate Angle—Computes the arctangent of *Number,* where *Number* is a coordinate angle expressed in radians. Example: ATAN2(1,1) returns 0.78540.

COS(*Angle*)

Cosine—Computes the cosine of *Angle,* where *Angle* is expressed in radians. Example: COS(0.78) is 0.71091.

SIN(*Angle*)

Sine—Computes the sine of *Angle,* where *Angle* is expressed in radians. Example: SIN(0.78) returns 0.70328. *Angle* can also be expressed as a fraction of the #PI function. Example: SIN (.#PI/4) returns 1.

TAN(*Angle*)

Tangent—Computes the tangent of *Angle,* expressed in radians. Example: TAN(0.78) is 0.98926.

COSH(*Angle*)

Hyperbolic Cosine—Computes the hyperbolic cosine of *Angle*. Example: COSH(1.047) results in 1.60004.

SINH(*Angle*)

Hyperbolic Sine—Computes the hyperbolic sine of *Angle*. Example: SINH(1.047) returns 1.24905.

TANH(*Angle*)

Hyperbolic Tangent—Computes the hyperbolic tangent of *Angle*. Example: TANH(0.785) returns 0.65556.

CONVERSION FUNCTIONS

The conversion functions modify the data types of variables and are generally used only in programming. The R:BASE data types are described in Chapter 2 of this book.

AINT(*Real*)

Truncates Real Number—Truncates the decimal portion of a real (or double-precision) number, returning only the integer portion in the DOUBLE data type. Example: AINT(1.8888) returns 1., where 1. is a double precision number.

ANINT(*Real*)

Rounds Real Number—Rounds the *Real* number to a double precision value. Example: ANINT(1.888) results in 2., where 2. is a double precision number.

INT(*Real*)

Converts Real to Integer Number—Converts a *Real* number to the Integer data type by truncating the decimal portion of the number. Example: INT(9.999) returns 9, where 9 is an integer.

NINT(*Real*)

Rounds Real to Integer Number—Converts a *Real* number to an integer by rounding the decimal portion to the nearest whole number. Example: NINT(9.999) returns 10 as an integer.

FLOAT(*Integer*)

Converts Integer to Real Number—Converts an integer to the DOUBLE data type. Example: FLOAT(9) returns 9 as a double precision number.

CTXT(*Number*)

Converts Number to Text String—Converts *Number* to a text string. Example: CTXT(1.2345) returns "1.2345" as the TEXT data type.

ICHAR(*Text*)

ASCII Code for Character—Returns the ASCII code for a character of *Text*. Example: ICHAR(A) returns 65 as an integer (the ASCII code for the uppercase letter A).

CHAR(*Integer*)

Character for ASCII Code—Returns the character associated with the *Integer* code. Often used to store printer control codes. Examples: CHAR(27) codes the "Escape" character that often initiates a series of printer-control codes. Can be used after the OUTPUT PRINTER command in conjunction with WRITE to send printer control codes directly to your printer.

STRING-MANIPULATION FUNCTIONS

The string-manipulation functions operate on TEXT data. They allow you to manipulate (and change) uppercase and lowercase, pad text with blank spaces, trim blank spaces from the text, and move sections of text. Many of these functions are used for "tricky" programming techniques. Even though they seem uninteresting or meaningless to beginners and nonprogrammers, they are worth skimming over because you may find them useful occasionally. When you see them, be sure to enclose the entire string function in parentheses, as in this example:

```
SEL ALL FROM NAMES
WHERE (SGET(LiName,1,1))
CONT "m"
```

Here are the string-manipulation functions:

SFIL(*Text,Number*)

Fill Character String—Creates a text variable consisting of *Text* characters, *Number* characters long. Example: SFIL("-",80) creates a text variable consisting of 80 hyphens.

SGET(*Text,Number,Location*)

Get from Text—Selects *Number* characters from a *Text* string starting at *Location.* Example: SGET(CatDogFish,3,4) results in *Dog,* because *Dog* is three letters long, and it begins at the fourth character in the "CatDogFish" character string.

SLEN(*Text*)

Length of String—Returns the length of a *Text* string. Example: SLEN(Snowball) returns 8.

SLOC(*Text,Smaller*)

Location of Text—Searches the *Text* string for the *Smaller* string and returns to the starting location of the smaller string within the larger string. If the smaller string is not found inside the larger string, the result is zero. Example: SLOC(CatDogFish,Dog) returns 4, because the word Dog starts at the fourth character in "CatDogFish". SLOC(CatDogFish,MooMoo) returns 0, because there is no MooMoo inside CatDogFish.

SMOVE(*Text,Position 1, Number, String, Position 2*)

Moves Text into String—Moves the characters in *Text,* starting at numeric *Position 1,* for a length of *Number* characters into *String,* starting at numeric *Position 2.* Example: SMOVE (ddogg,2,3,ABCDE,2) returns "AdogE".

SPUT(*Text,String,Location*)

Puts Text into String—Moves a *String* of characters in *Text* starting at *Location.* Example: SPUT(ABCDE,mm,3) returns "ABmmE".

STRIM(*Text*)

Trims Trailing Blanks—Removes any trailing blank spaces from the *Text* variable. Example: If a variable named Test contains the characters "This is a test   " (notice the *trailing blanks* in front of the closing quotation mark), then STRIM(Test) produces "This is a test" (with the trailing blanks removed).

ULC(*Text*)

Converts Uppercase to Lowercase—Converts all uppercase letters in *Text* to lowercase. Example: ULC(Hi There) returns "hi there".

LUC(*Text*)

Converts Lowercase to Uppercase—Converts all lowercase letters in *Text* to uppercase. Example: LUC(Give me a break) returns "GIVE ME A BREAK".

ICAP1(*Text*)

Uppercases First Letter Only—Converts *Text* to a text string with a capital letter on the first character of the first word only. Example: ICAP1(this Is It) produces "This is it".

ICAP2(*Text*)

Uppercases All First Letters—Converts *Text* to a text string with a capital letter on the first character of each word. Example: ICAP2(ADAM P. JONES, JR.) produces "Adam P. Jones, Jr.". ICAP2(this is a test) produces "This Is A Test".

CTR(*Text*,*Width*)

Centers Text—Centers *Text* within the specified *Width*. Example: CTR(Best,10) produces "   Best   ".

LJS(*Text*,*Width*)

Left-Justifies Text—Left-justifies *Text* within the specified *Width*. Example: LJS(Best,10) produces "Best   ".

RJS(*Text*,*Width*)

Right-Justifies Text—Right-justifies *Text* within the specified *Width*. Example: RJS(Best,10) produces "   Best".

DATE AND TIME FUNCTIONS

The Date and Time functions operate on data stored as the DATE or TIME data type. These functions can convert TEXT data to DATE and TIME data and can isolate portions of dates and times. These can be particularly useful in WHERE clauses. For example, the TDWK function isolates the day of the week as text. Therefore, the command

```
SELECT ALL FROM Charges WHERE TDWK(P:Date) = +
+ > "Wednesday"
```

displays the seven rows from the Charges table in which the date falls on a Wednesday.

Note that when operating on dates that are not already stored in columns or variables defined as DATE data, the *Date* argument in the function must be enclosed in double quotation marks as shown in the examples below:

RDATE(*Mon,Day,Year*)

Converts to Date Data Type—Where *Mon* is an integer from 1 to 12, *Day* is an integer from 1 to 31, and *Year* is an integer representing a year, creates a variable of the DATE data type. Example: RDATE(12,31,1988) creates a DATE data type containing the date 12/31/1988.

RTIME(*Hrs,Min,Sec*)

Converts to Time Data Type—Where *Hrs* is an integer from 1 to 24, *Min* is an integer from 1 to 60, and *Sec* is an integer representing seconds, creates a variable of the TIME data type. Example: RTIME(12,59,30) creates a TIME data type containing the time 12:59:30.

JDATE(*Date*)

Julian Date—Converts *Date* to a Julian date in the range of 1 (for 01/01/1900) to 99365 (for 12/31/1999). Example: JDATE("1/1/1900") produces 1.

IDAY(*Date*)

Day of the Month—Returns the day of the month (1–31) of *Date* as an integer. Example: IDAY("12/31/88") produces 31.

IDWK(*Date*)

Integer Day of the Week—Returns the day of the week (1–7) of *Date* as an integer, where Monday is 1. Example: IDWK("12/31/1988") produces 6 (Saturday).

TDWK(*Date*)

Text Day of the Week—Returns the day of the week of *Date* as text. Example: TDWK("12/31/1988") produces "Saturday".

IMON(*Date*)

Integer Month—Returns the month (1–12) of *Date* as an integer, where January is 1. Example: IMON("12/31/1988") produces 12.

TMON(*Date*)

Text Month—Returns the month of *Date* as text. Example: TMON("12/31/1988") produces "December".

IYR(*Date*)

Integer Year—Returns the year of *Date* as an integer. Example: IYR("12/11/88") returns 88.

IHR(*Time*)

Integer Hour—Isolates the hour from *Time* data as an integer. Example: IHR(11:59:00) produces 11.

IMIN(*Time*)

Integer Minute—Isolates the minute from *Time* data as an integer. Example: IHR(11:59:00) produces 59.

ISEC(*Time*)

Integer Second—Isolates the second from *Time* data as an integer. Example: IHR(11:59:22) produces 22.

FINANCIAL FUNCTIONS

The financial functions perform numerous financial calculations that can be used in a variety of business settings. The main trick to using the financial functions is making certain that you do not confuse yearly and monthly data. For example, to find the *monthly* payment for a $150,000 loan, given a term of 20 *years,* and a 9.37% *annual* interest rate, you must first convert the years to months (multiplying by 12) and then convert the annual interest rate to a monthly interest rate (by dividing by 12). You can do so within the function argument. The formula below calculates the *monthly* payment ($1,385.49) on the loan described above:

```
SET VARIABLE MonPay TO Pmt1(.0937/12,20*12,150000)
```

Note that the interest rate (the first argument) is divided by 12 and the term (second argument) is multiplied by 12.

When calculating values in which interest is compounded daily, you can divide the annual interest rate by 365 and multiply the term by 365. The examples below will demonstrate these conversions.

FV1(*Pmt,Int,Per*)

Future Value of Payments—Computes the future value of a series of regular equal payments of the amount specified in *Pmt* and the per-period interest rate specified in *Int* for the number of periods given in *Per.* Example: If you deposit $250 monthly into an account that pays 8% annual interest, how much money will be in the account after ten years? The expression FV1(250,.08/12,10*12) returns the answer, $45,736.51.

FV2(*Dep,Int,Per*)

Future Value of Deposit—Computes the future value of a single deposit in the amount specified in *Dep* and the per-period interest rate specified in *Int* for the number of periods given in *Per.* Example: Suppose you deposit $10,000 in an account that pays 8% interest (compounded monthly) for ten years. How much money will be in the account after ten years? The answer is given by the expression FV2(10000,.08/12,10*12), which computes the result $22,196.40.

PV1(*Pmt,Int,Per*)

Present Value of Cash Flow—Computes the present value of a series of equal payments of the amount specified in *Pmt* at the periodic interest rate specified in *Int* for the number of periods specified in *Per.* Example: You purchase an annuity into which you pay $200 a month, at an annual interest rate of 10%, for ten years. What is the present value of the annuity? The answer is given by the expression PV1(200,.10/12,10*12), which returns $15,134.23.

PV2(*Fv,Int,Per*)

Present Value—Computes the present value based on the future value given in *Fv* at the periodic interest rate specified in *Int* for the number of periods specified in *Per.* Example: You want to have $10,000 in a savings account at the end of ten years. The interest rate, compounded daily, is 8%. How much money must you invest now to ensure $10,000 in the future? The answer is given with the expression PV2(10000,.08/365,10*365), which returns $4493.68.

PMT1(*Int,Per,Prin*)

Payment on Loan—Calculates the payment required to pay off a loan with the principal specified in *Prin* at the per-period interest rate given in *Int* for the number of payment periods specified in *Per.* Example: You wish to borrow $5000 dollars for three years at 2.9% interest to buy a car. What will the monthly payment on the loan be? The answer is given by the expression PMT1(.029/12,3*12,5000), which displays the monthly payment $145.19.

PMT2(*Int,Per,Fv*)

Payments to Reach Future Value—Calculates the regular payment required to accumulate the future value given in *Fv* at the per-period interest rate given in *Int* for the number of periods given in *Per.* Example: You want to accumulate $10,000 in ten years in an account that pays 7% interest compounded monthly. How much must you pay each month to reach your goal? The answer is given by the expression PMT2(.07/12,10*12,10000), which returns $57.78.

RATE1(*Fv,Pv,Per*)

Required Interest Rate—Calculates the interest rate required for the sum of money given in *Pv* to reach the future value given in *Fv* in the term given in *Per.* Example: You have $5000 to invest for ten years. What interest rate will you need to double your money within that time? The answer given with the expression RATE1(10000,5000,12*10) is the monthly interest rate (about 0.0058) or when multiplied by 12, 0.0695, or a little under 7% annual interest rate.

RATE2(*Fv,Pmt,Per*)

Required Interest Rate—Calculates the interest rate required for a series of regular payments given in *Pmt* to reach the future value given in *Fv* in the number of payment periods given in *Per.* Example: You wish to deposit $250 per month into an account for five years. What interest rate is required to accrue $20,000 at the end of the five years? The expression RATE2(20000,250,5*12) returns the answer, 0.00936 monthly interest, or about 11% annual interest.

RATE3(*Pv,Pmt,Per*)

Required Interest Rate—Calculates the periodic interest rate required for an annuity with the value given in *Pv* to return a series of future cash flows given in *Pmt* for the number of periods given in *Per.* Example: You want to purchase a $100,000 annuity that will pay $1500 monthly for a period of ten years. What interest rate is required to reach your goal? The answer is given in the expression RATE3(100000,1500,10*12), which yields 0.01093 monthly interest, or about 12% annual interest.

TERM1(*Pv,Int,Fv*)

Required Term—Computes the term required for the present value specified in *Pv* to reach the future value given in *Fv* given the periodic interest rate in *Int.* Example: You want to invest $5000 in an account that pays 10% annual interest. How long will it take to double your money? The expression TERM1(5000,.10/12,10000) gives the answer 84 months (or 7 years).

TERM2(*Pmt,Int,Fv*)

Required Term—Calculates the number of compounding periods for a number of equal payments given in *Pmt* at the periodic interest rate given in *Int* to reach the future value given in *Fv*. Example: You want to deposit $250 a month at 10% annual interest. How long will it take until you accumulate $10,000? The expression TERM2(250,.10/12,10000) gives the answer, 35 months.

TERM3(*Pmt,Int,Pv*)

Computed Term—Calculates the number of periods that an annuity will last, given the payment you wish to receive in each term (*Pmt*), the periodic interest rate for the annuity (*Int*), and the present value of the annuity (*Pv*). Example: You wish to purchase a $20,000 annuity that pays 8% annual interest. How long will the annuity last (before reaching 0) if you receive $250 monthly payments from the annuity? The expression TERM3(250,.08/12,20000) gives the answer, 115 months (or about 9½ years).

LOGICAL FUNCTIONS

The logical functions make decisions based on two alternatives. We've seen several examples of the IFEQ function in earlier chapters, with the expression

```
IFEQ(Tax?,0,Qty*U_Price,(Qty*U:Price)*1.06)
```

This expression calculated the total of a transaction, excluding tax if the column named Tax? contained a zero. Otherwise, the total is calculated as the quantity times the unit price times 1.06 (to add 6% sales tax).

In the logical functions, all arguments are assumed to be numeric. For example, the following expression is not allowed:

```
IFEQ(L:Name,"Smith","Yes","No")
```

because L:Name is not a numeric column, and "Smith", "Yes", and "No" are all Text data.

IFEQ(*N1,N2,Yes,No*)

If Equal—Returns the value, or the result of the expression, given in the argument *Yes,* if *N1* equals *N2*. If *N1* does not equal *N2,* then the value or result of the expression specified in the argument *No* is returned. Example: IFEQ(10,10,0,100) returns 0, because 10 is equal to 10. The expression IFEQ(10,9,0,100) returns 100, because 10 does not equal 9.

IFLT(*N1,N2,Yes,No*)

If Less Than—Returns the value, or the result of the expression, given in the argument *Yes,* if *N1* is less than *N2.* If *N1* is greater than or equal to *N2,* then the value or result of the expression specified in the argument *No* is returned. Example: IFLT(– 1,0,0,100) returns 0, because – 1 is less than 0. The expression IFLT(10,9,0,100) returns 100, because 10 is not less than 9.

IFGT(*N1,N2,Yes,No*)

If Greater Than—Returns the value, or the result of the expression, given in the argument *Yes,* if *N1* is greater than *N2.* If *N1* is less than or equal to *N2,* then the value or result of the expression specified in the argument *No* is returned. Example: IFGT(99,50,0,100) returns 0, because 99 is greater than 50. The expression IFGT(2,99,0,100) returns 100, because 2 is not greater than 99.

EXPERIMENTS WITH FUNCTIONS

The easiest way to experiment with functions is to try a few in conjunction with the SELECT command. For example, if the Mail database is open and the R> prompt is on the screen, you can enter the command

```
SELECT Company = 15 LUC(Company) = 15 +
+ > ULC(Company) = 15 ICAP1(Company) = 15 +
+ > ICAP2(Company) = 15 FROM Names
```

to view the Company column from the Names table in its current state, and after treatment with the LUC, ULC, ICAP1, and ICAP2 functions. (For a good fit on the screen, the width is set to 15 characters in each column.) The Company column from each record will be displayed, although the listing below shows only a single row:

ABC Co.   ABC CO.   abc co.   Abc co.   Abc Co.

The commands below set the date format to MM/DD/YY, and then display the P:Date column, the day of the week (TDWK), the month (TMON), and the Julian date (JDATE) of the date from the Charges table:

```
SET DATE "MM/DD/YY"
SELECT P:Date TDWK(P:Date) TMON(P:Date) JDATE(P:Date) +
+ > FROM Charges
```

A portion of the resulting display is shown below:

P:Date	COMPUTED	COMPUTED	COMPUTED
06/15/88	Wednesday	June	88167
07/01/88	Friday	July	88183

FUNCTIONS IN COMPUTED COLUMNS

You can use functions in computed columns. For example, Figure 11.2 shows a table named Loans that consists of the columns named Princ, APR, Years, MoPmt, and TotBack.

MoPmt is a computed field with the expression

```
PMT1(((APR/100)/12),(Years*12),Princ)
```

The first argument inside the PMT1 function, ((APR/100)/12), divides the annual interest rate by 100 (so that when the APR is entered as 9.375, it is correctly converted to the decimal 0.09375), and then divides the annual interest rate by 12 for the monthly interest rate. The second argument, (Years*12), multiplies the years in the loan by 12 to calculate the months. The third argument is the principal of the loan. Hence, for each row entered into the table, R:BASE automatically calculates the monthly payment.

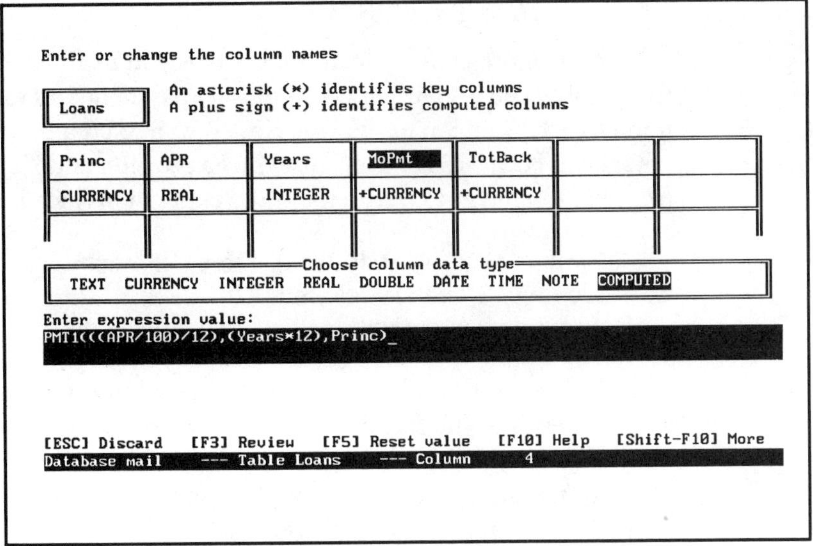

Figure 11.2: The table definition for the Loans table

You may notice that immediately after entering the formula, R:BASE changes it to the following:

```
PMT1((('APR'/100)/12),('Years'*12),'Princ')
```

R:BASE automatically places single quotation marks around the existing column names when you enter computed field expressions.

The TotBack column is also a computed column, and it calculates the entire payback on the loan using the expression

```
(12*Years)*MoPmt
```

which is the term of the loan in months (for example, the number of years times 12) times the monthly payment (already calculated in the MoPmt column). Again, R:BASE automatically adds single quotation marks around column and variable names as below:

```
(12*'Years')*'MoPmt'
```

As with any table with computed fields, each time you enter or edit data on the Loans table, R:BASE will automatically calculate the payment on the loan and the total payback on the loan.

FUNCTIONS IN FORMS

If you want to create a form that allows you to enter data into the Loans table and also display the monthly payment and total payback immediately, you can use Forms EXPRESS to create the form.

Once in Forms EXPRESS, use the Expression and Define options from the top menu to create the three expressions listed below:

```
MoPymt = PMT1(((APR/100)/12),(Years*12),Princ)
TotBack = ((12*Years)*MoPymt)
Hold    = Use arrow keys to change, or press Enter
```

Then use the Edit option to place text, column names, and variable names onto the form using the usual arrow and F6 keys. The Hold variable should be located near the bottom of the screen, below all column names and other variable names. When given the opportunity to customize field characteristics for the Hold variable, select Yes, and change the answer to the first questions to Yes, as below:

```
Will new data be entered in the field? .................................. [Yes]
Can the user change the data displayed in the field? ............ [Yes]
```

Changing these answers to Yes ensures that the highlight cursor will move into the Hold variable and wait for an entry, thereby giving you time to view the results of the calculations and to modify the data on the screen. (Be sure to place the S and E locations wide enough apart to accommodate the entire message stored in the Hold variable.)

Figure 11.3 shows a Loans form in use. The principal, interest, and term have already been typed onto the screen, and the monthly payment and total payback have been calculated automatically. The highlight is currently on the Hold variable, waiting for the next keystroke.

FUNCTIONS IN REPORTS

Functions can be used in reports in the same fashion that they are used in forms. For example, suppose the Loans table consisted of only the Princ, APR, and Years columns, without computed columns for the monthly payment and total payback.

You could easily create a report using Reports EXPRESS to calculate and display the payment and payback. Once in Reports

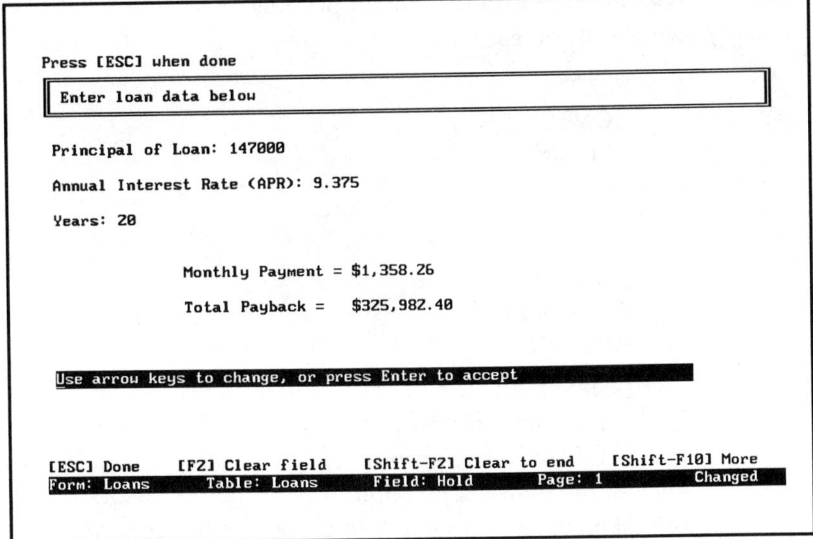

Figure 11.3: A Loans form in use

EXPRESS, use the Expression and Define options from the top menus to create the appropriate expressions, as below:

```
MoPmt = PMT1(((APR/100)/12),(Years*12),Princ)
TotBack = (12*Years)*MoPmt
```

When locating column and variable names on the report format, include the MoPmt and TotBack variables in the detail lines of the report. You can even use functions in break footings to group data. We'll explore breakpoints in the next chapter.

USING FUNCTIONS WITH THE CHANGE OR UPDATE COMMANDS

You can use functions with the CHANGE (see Figure 11.4) or UPDATE commands to modify existing data in a database. For example, suppose you had initially entered all the names in the

Names table with the Caps Lock key on so that all of the last names were in uppercase, as below:

```
SMITH
JONES
MILLER
ADAMS
MILLER
BAKER
MILLER
TEASDALE
MARTIN
```

To convert those names to initial capital letters, use the ICAP1 function in the CHANGE command. (Note: When using functions in the CHANGE command, particularly with a TEXT column, enclose the entire expression in parentheses so that the expression is not taken as the actual text to place into the column):

```
CHANGE L:Name TO (ICAP1(L:Name)) IN Names +
+ > WHERE L:Name EXISTS
```

or

```
UPDATE Names SET L:Name = (ICAP1(L:Name)) WHERE +
+ > L:Name EXISTS
```

When you use the command

```
SELECT L:Name FROM Names
```

to view the last name column after entering the CHANGE command, you'll see that the last names have been converted to initial capital letters, as below:

```
Smith
Jones
Miller
Adams
Miller
Baker
Miller
Teasdale
Martin
```

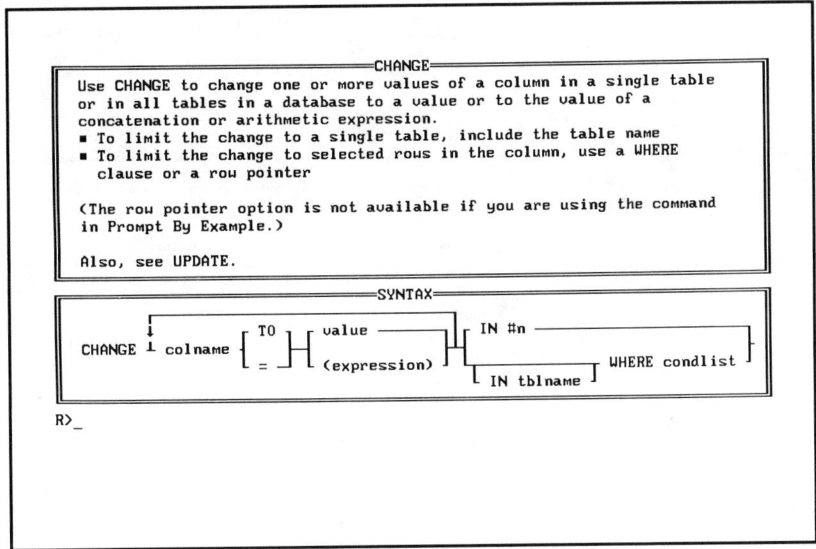

Figure 11.4: The syntax for the CHANGE command

The CHANGE and UPDATE commands make permanent changes to a table immediately and should be used with care. When using functions to change data in columns, it would probably be a good idea to use the PROJECT command to make a copy of the table first, and then practice and experiment with the copied table. To make a copy of the Names table, type

```
PROJECT Temp FROM Names USING ALL
```

Then, experiment with the table Temp. (You'll learn more about the PROJECT command in Chapter 14.)

As an alternative to changing the data in the column, you can always use the appropriate function in a report expression and locate the variable instead of the original column. If you defined

```
Rptlname = (LUC(L:Name))
```

as a report variable, you could locate it at those points where you wanted last names to be printed. All last names would then appear in uppercase on the report, but would remain unchanged in the Names table.

Now that you have a basic knowledge of R:BASE variables and functions, we can move to the next step in building complex applications: creating *command files*.

Chapter 12

Refining Your Reports

FAST TRACK

To define variables for totals and subtotals, **325**
use the SUM OF operator when defining report variables.

To define column names from other tables **326**
as lookup variables, use the syntax *variable name* = *column name* IN *table name* WHERE *conditions*.

The report heading (RH) and Footing (RF) **329**
each appear once, at the top and the bottom of the entire report.

Page headings (PH) and footings (PF) **330**
appear at the top and bottom of each page in the report.

Breakpoint headings and footings (H1...H10 and F1...F10) **330**
appear each time there is a subtotal or subheading break in the report. Breakpoints are determined by a change in the contents column that you specify.

To organize data in a report visually, **337**
design a report containing no subtotals associated with a breakpoint. R:BASE will group and sort report data based on the break column.

To avoid defining report lookup variables, **338**
create a view to be used as the report's driver "table."

To correct a mistake made while locating columns or variables, 340
use Shift-F2 or F6. If you have located fields on a line that has the wrong code associated with it, you can even change the code along the vertical bar.

To format TEXT and NOTE fields to wraparound 341
when you locate them on a report, use the W operator to set a right margin for the field. You can also specify a maximum number of lines to be printed in the wrapped text.

IN THIS CHAPTER, WE'LL DESCRIBE SOME ADVANCED reporting techniques, such as displaying totals and subtotals, as well as techniques for using data from multiple tables. We'll develop a report named Sales that shows charge transactions, subtotals for each individual, and a grand total at the end of the report. Figure 12.1 shows a sample of the report.

ADVANCED DESIGN TECHNIQUES

When designing more sophisticated reports, it is important that you mark the heading, footing, and detail lines on a rough draft of the report, as shown in Figure 12.2.

Notice that there are several headings and footings specified, as described below:

Report heading	Appears on the first page of the report only.
Page heading	Appears once at the top of each page in the report.
Break heading	Appears at the top of each subtotal break.
Detail	Data printed once for each row within a subtotal section.
Break footing	Displayed at the bottom of each subtotal break.
Report footing	Displayed once at the end of the entire report.

Although we haven't included one here, a report can also contain a page footing, which is printed once at the bottom of each page.

ADVANCED USE OF REPORT VARIABLES

The next step in designing a report is to determine what variables you will need. We'll need the usual .#DATE and .#PAGE for the report date and page numbers. We'll also need variables for the totals

Charge Transactions

Date: 07/15/88 **Page: 1**

Customer

Prod #	**Qty**	**Unit Price**	**Total**	**Date**
1001 Sandy Smith: Hi Tech, Inc.				
A-111	12	$10.00	$127.20	06/15/88
B-222	5	$12.50	$66.25	06/15/88
C-434	2	$100.00	$212.00	06/15/88
			________	
Subtotal:			$405.45	
1002 Mindy Jones: ABC Co.				
A-111	10	$10.00	$106.00	07/01/88
B-222	12	$12.50	$159.00	07/01/88
			________	
Subtotal:			$265.00	
1004 Bart Adams: Dataspec Inc.				
A-111	5	$10.00	$53.00	06/15/88
Z-128	10	$12.80	$128.00	06/15/88
			________	
Subtotal:			$181.00	
1007 Monica Miller: Acme Development				
A-111	10	$10.00	$106.00	06/15/88
Z-128	10	$12.80	$128.00	06/15/88
			________	
Subtotal:			$234.00	
			________	
Grand Total:			$1085.45	

Figure 12.1: A sample of the Sales report

		Charge Transactions				
Report Heading	**Date: 07/15/88**				**Page: 1**	
Page Heading	**Customer**					
	Prod #	**Qty**	**Unit Price**	**Total**		**Date**
Break Heading	1001 Sandy Smith—Hi Tech, Inc.					
Detail Lines	A-111	12	$10.00	$127.20		06/15/88
	B-222	5	$12.50	$66.25		06/15/88
	C-434	2	$100.00	$212.00		06/15/88
				———		
Break Footing	SubTotal:			$405.45		
Report Footing	Total:			$1085.45		

Figure 12.2: A rough draft of the Sales report

and subtotals. In English, we can define these variables as follows:

SubTotal	Sum of the Total column for each individual
GrandTot	Sum of the Total column in all rows

In this example, most of the data will be from the Charges table, but we'll need to get the name and company for each individual from the Names table. In simple English, we can define the necessary variables as follows:

FullName	First and last names from the Names table
NameCo	Full name plus company from the Names table

After you've sketched a rough draft of the final report on paper, you can begin using Reports EXPRESS to lay out the report format. Recall that you can enter Reports EXPRESS by entering the command

```
REPORTS
```

at the R> prompt. Open Mail if you haven't already and select option 1 from the Report Options Menu to Edit/Create a report. Select New and enter

```
Sales
```

as the report name. When asked to select the associated table, select Charges.

ADDING SYSTEM VARIABLES

We'll begin by defining the variables to be used in the report. Select Expression from the top menu and Define from the submenu. The report date and page number variables are simple to define. Type in the first expression

```
RepDate = .#DATE
```

and press Enter. Enter the page number variable by typing in the expression

```
PgNo = .#PAGE
```

THE GRANDTOT AND SUBTOTAL VARIABLES

The GrandTot and SubTotal variables are entered using the SUM OF operator in the expression. Since the SubTotal variable for each customer is the sum of the Total column from the relevant rows in the Charges table, enter the command as

```
SubTotal = SUM OF Total
```

The GrandTot variable is also the sum of the Total column, so enter the expression

```
GrandTot = SUM OF Total
```

It may seem odd that both of these variables use the same expression, but the difference between them will be determined later by configuration settings. We'll tell R:BASE to clear the SubTotal variable and to reset it to zero after each customer subtotal block.

You can define report variables by using any of the operators shown in Table 12.1.

USING LOOKUP VARIABLES TO ACCESS DATA FROM OTHER TABLES

Next we need to enter some variables that will insert some of the data from the Names table into the Sales report. The general syntax for defining columns from other tables is

variable = *column name* IN *table name* WHERE *expression list*

Define a variable called Name1, which is the first name from the Names table. The expression to enter is

Name1 = F:Name IN Names WHERE CustNo = CustNo

The WHERE clause expression CustNo = CustNo tells R:BASE which name to get from the Names table. In English, the formula reads, "The Name1 variable is the first name from the Names table,

Table 12.1: Operators Used When Defining Report Variables

OPERATOR	FUNCTION
+	Sum of columns or variables (or links two text strings with no space)
–	Difference of columns or variables
*	Product of columns or variables
/	Quotient of columns or variables
%	Percent of columns or variables
&	Links two text strings with a space inserted
SUM OF	Computes the sum of a column
**	Raises column to a power

where the customer number in the Names table equals the customer number in the Charges table."

We also need the last name from the Names table. Enter the expression

Name2 = L:Name IN Names WHERE CustNo = CustNo

Now we need the company data from the Names file. The expression is

CompName = Company IN Names WHERE CustNo = CustNo

Finally, we'll store the name and company combined in a variable called NameCo by entering the following expression:

NameCo = Name1 & Name2 + ":" & CompName

After you've defined all the variables, press Esc. Your screen should look like Figure 12.3. Press the Esc key again to return to the Report Definition menu.

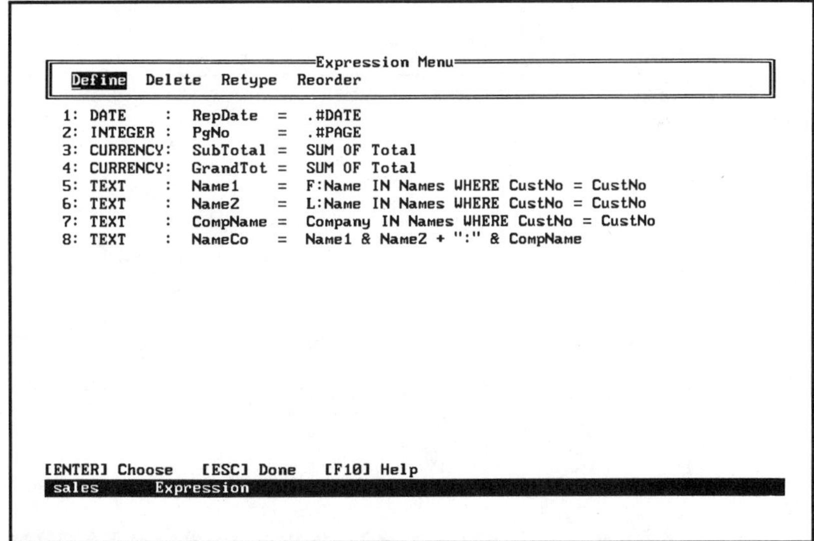

```
Expression Menu
Define  Delete  Retype  Reorder

1: DATE      :  RepDate  =  .#DATE
2: INTEGER   :  PgNo     =  .#PAGE
3: CURRENCY:    SubTotal =  SUM OF Total
4: CURRENCY:    GrandTot =  SUM OF Total
5: TEXT      :  Name1    =  F:Name IN Names WHERE CustNo = CustNo
6: TEXT      :  Name2    =  L:Name IN Names WHERE CustNo = CustNo
7: TEXT      :  CompName =  Company IN Names WHERE CustNo = CustNo
8: TEXT      :  NameCo   =  Name1 & Name2 + ":" & CompName

[ENTER] Choose   [ESC] Done   [F10] Help
sales     Expression
```

Figure 12.3: Variables defined for the Sales report

CONFIGURING BREAKPOINTS

The next step is to define the *breakpoints* for the report. Breakpoints indicate where one group or subtotal of data ends and another begins. From the top menu, select Configure, which brings up the screen shown in Figure 12.4.

The first four options on the configuration screen are not relevant at the moment; however, the columns under the Breakpoints heading are. You can move the cursor to this section of the screen using the arrow keys.

In our sample report, we want to print a subtotal for each customer in the Charges table. Therefore, CustNo is the break column in the table. To supply the configuration screen with this information, move the highlighter to the default [None] prompt just to the right of the Break1 prompt. Type in **CustNo** as the name of the column, and then press the Tab key to move to the Variable Reset column.

When using subtotals in a report, you need to reset the subtotal variable to zero at the end of each section so that it can start accumulating the next subtotal from zero. Therefore, you should type in **Y** to change the default [NO] to [YES]. The screen will ask which variable(s) to reset within this breakpoint. You want to reset the SubTotal

```
Lines Per Page .................:   60
Remove Initial Carriage Return..:  [NO ]
Manual Break Reset .............:  [NO ]
Page Footer Line Number.........:    0

               BREAKPOINTS                FORM FEEDS
            Break     Variable        Header          Footer
            Column    Reset       Before After    Before After
            --------  ------      ------ ------   ------ ------
 Report                           [NO ]  [NO ]    [NO ]  [NO ]
 Page                 [NO ]
 Break1     [None]    [NO ]       [NO ]
 Break2     [None]    [NO ]       [NO ]
 Break3     [None]    [NO ]       [NO ]
 Break4     [None]    [NO ]       [NO ]
 Break5     [None]    [NO ]       [NO ]
 Break6     [None]    [NO ]       [NO ]
 Break7     [None]    [NO ]       [NO ]
 Break8     [None]    [NO ]       [NO ]
 Break9     [None]    [NO ]       [NO ]
 Break10    [None]    [NO ]       [NO ]

[↑] Up  [↓] Down   [F10] Help   [ESC] Done
 sales       Configure
```

Figure 12.4: The configuration screen

variable, so select SubTotal. The screen will prompt you to reset other variables. Just press Esc to indicate that you don't want to reset any other variables in conjunction with Break1.

At this point you've made CustNo the break column and specified SubTotal as the variable to clear and reset to zero after each customer subtotal is displayed. The section of the screen that defines the Break1 break column should look like this:

```
Break1                  CustNo                  [YES]
```

Now that you've told R:BASE that there will be subtotals based on the CustNo column, you can begin laying out the report format. Press Esc to bring back the top menu.

LAYING OUT THE FORMAT

To begin laying out the report format, select Edit from the top menu. The blank screen will appear with a report heading (RH) symbol on the first line.

REPORT HEADING

To fill in the report heading, move the cursor to <1,30> and type

```
Charge Transactions
```

Press Enter to begin the second RH line. At <2,1> type in

```
Date:
```

With the cursor on <2,7> press F6, enter **RepDate** as the variable name, and mark <2,7> as the start location and <2,36> as the end location.

Move the cursor to <2,60> and enter the heading

```
Page:
```

Move the cursor to <2,66> and press F6. Enter PgNo as the variable name, <2,66> as the start location, and <2,70> as the end location. Press Enter to create another blank RH line. (This line will appear as a blank line on the printed report.)

PAGE HEADING

To begin the page heading, press F8 so that the PH symbol appears. At <4,1> type in

    Customer

and press Enter. The start locations for the remaining column titles for the page heading are listed below. Move the cursor to the position in the left column, and type in the text in the right column.

LOCATION	*TEXT*
<5,5>	Prod #
<5,15>	Qty
<5,23>	Unit Price
<5,42>	Total
<5,55>	Date

Press Enter after typing in all the column headings.

BREAK HEADING

Press F8 to start the next section, H1 in this case. Because we have already defined CustNo as our Break1 variable, R:BASE gives us the chance to make entries on break header lines and footer lines associated with the customer grouping. To place the customer number, name, and company in the break heading, move the cursor to <7,1>. Press F6 and enter CustNo as the column name. Start the location at <7,1> and end it at <7,5>. Move the cursor to <7,7>, press F6, enter NameCo as the variable name, and press Enter. Mark <7,7> as the start location and <7,50> as the end location. Press Enter to put in a blank break heading (H1) line.

This H1 heading will appear at the top of each subtotal group (each customer in this example) when the report is printed.

DETAIL LINES

You'll only need one detail line for this report. Press F8 to begin the next section. A detail (D) line will appear.

When locating currency data on the report format, the screen will ask

Print in check format? Yes No

If you answer Yes, the currency data in the printed report will be displayed with leading asterisks as below:

********$123.45

Since this is unnecessary on this report, you can always answer No to this prompt while placing column names on the Sales report format. Locate column names at the start and end locations listed below, using the F6, arrow, S, and E keys.

COLUMN NAME	*START*	*END*	*CHECK FORMAT?*
ProdNo	<9,5>	<9,12>	
Qty	<9,14>	<9,17>	
U:Price	<9,23>	<9,32>	No
Total	<9,37>	<9,46>	No
P:Date	<9,55>	<9,70>	

After placing all the column names, you can press Ctrl-← to bring the cursor back to column 1.

BREAK FOOTING

A break footing appears once at the end of each subtotal group. When using subtotals, the break footing should include the variable name that contains the subtotal. You can also add text and underlines, as we'll do in this example.

First, press F8 to start the first break footing. The F1 symbol appears in the left margin. Move the cursor to <10,35> and type in 12 hyphens. Press Enter, and move the cursor to <11,5>. Type in the word

    Subtotal:

Move the cursor to <11,35>, press F6, and enter **SubTotal** as the variable name. Start the SubTotal variable at <11,35> and end it at <11,46>. (Again, you can select No in response to printing the subtotal in check format.) Press Enter to create a blank line in the break footing.

REPORT FOOTING

All we need now is the grand total to appear at the bottom of the report. Since this needs to appear only once at the end of the report, this will be a report footing. Press F8 twice to start an RF section. Move the cursor to <13,35> and type in 12 hyphens. Press Enter, and move the cursor to <14,1>. Type in the words

    Grand Total:

Move the cell pointer to <14,35>, press F6, and locate the variable GrandTot. Start the variable at <14,35> and end it at <14,46>. Again, answer No to the prompt about printing in check format.

When you are finished, your screen should look like Figure 12.5. You can press Esc twice to work your way back to the Save options, and select Save Changes. Exit all of the subsequent menus to return to the R> prompt.

PRINTING THE REPORT

Now you can print the report using the PRINT command. For example, enter the command

    PRINT Sales

The report will resemble Figure 12.1 at the beginning of this chapter. Notice that the report is automatically sorted on the breakpoint column (CustNo). This is a handy feature of breakpoints.

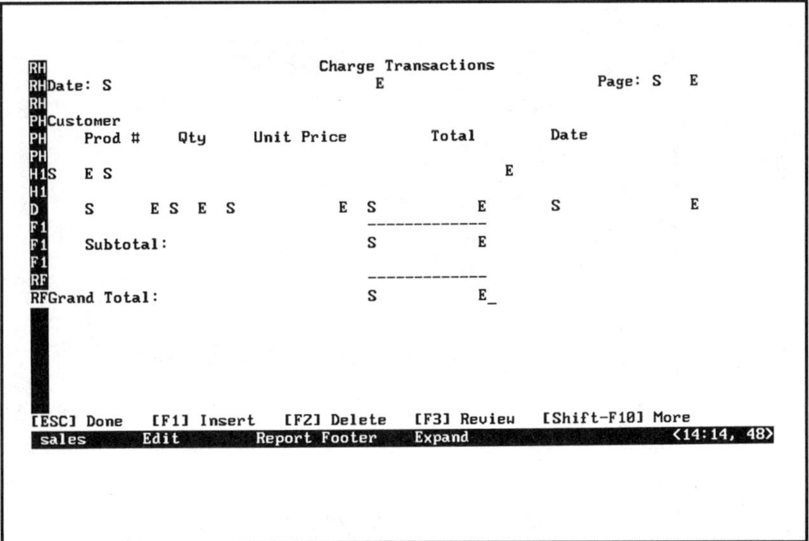

Figure 12.5: The format for the Sales report

You can use the ORDER BY and WHERE clauses to sort and filter the report. Use the OUTPUT command to direct the report to the printer or a file.

NESTED SUBTOTALS

In the sample Sales report, we used only a single breakpoint column: Customer Number. R:BASE will let you define up to ten breakpoints for a single report. For example, you could create a report format that presents subtotals for each customer, and within each customer, subtotals by product code. The sample Charges table is too small to demonstrate this, but the hypothetical report in Figure 12.6 shows how such a format might appear. Notice that a subtotal appears for each customer. Furthermore, a subtotal for each product purchased appears within each customer listing. Notice also that the various report sections are written onto the sample report.

To create such a report, you would need to define two subtotaling variables using the Expression and Define options in Reports

Charge Transactions

Date: 07/15/88					**Page: 1**
Customer					
	Prod. #	**Qty**	**Unit Price**	**Total**	**Date**
1004 Bart Adams: Dataspec Inc.					
	A-111	5	$10.00	$ 53.00	06/15/88
				———	
Subtotal for product A-111				$ 53.00	
	Z-128	10	$12.80	$128.00	06/15/88
	Z-128	1	$12.80	$ 12.80	07/01/88
				———	
Subtotal for product Z-128				$140.80	
				═══	
Total for customer 1004				$193.80	
1007 Monica Miller: Acme Development					
	A-111	10	$10.00	$106.00	06/15/88
	A-111	10	$10.00	$106.00	07/15/88
				———	
Subtotal for product A-111				$212.00	
	Z-128	10	$12.80	$128.00	06/15/88
	Z-128	10	$12.80	$128.00	07/01/88
				———	
Subtotal for product Z-128				$256.00	
				═══	
Total for customer 1007				$468.00	
				———	
Grand total of all customers:				$661.80	

Figure 12.6: A report with two subtotal breakpoints

EXPRESS. You'd probably still want a GrandTot variable for the grand total, as below:

SubTot1 SUM OF Total
SubTot2 SUM OF Total
GrandTot SUM OF Total

Using the Configure options from Reports EXPRESS, you would want CustNo to be the Break1 column and ProdNo to be the Break2 column. Each of these columns must reset the appropriate subtotaling variable. In this example, Break1 is based on the CustNo column and resets the SubTot1 variable. Break2 is based on the ProdNo column and resets the SubTot2 variable. Figure 12.7 shows the configuration screen with two breakpoints defined.

When laying out the report format, Reports EXPRESS will give you the opportunity to define two break headings (H1 and H2) and two break footings (F1 and F2). These multiple break headings and footings should surround the detail lines and be nested within one another as shown below:

RH Report Header
PH Page Header

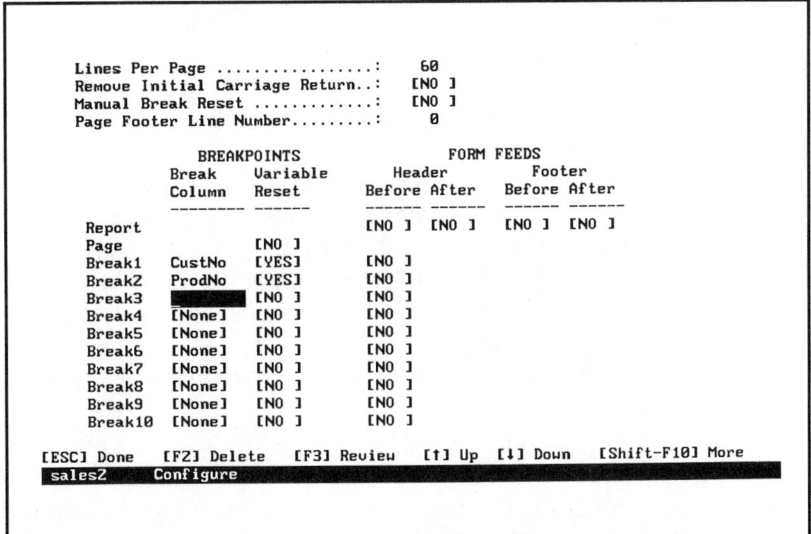

```
Lines Per Page .................:     60
Remove Initial Carriage Return..:    [NO ]
Manual Break Reset .............:    [NO ]
Page Footer Line Number.........:     0

              BREAKPOINTS                  FORM FEEDS
           Break     Variable         Header          Footer
           Column    Reset         Before After    Before After
           --------  ------        ------ ------   ------ ------
Report                             [NO ]  [NO ]    [NO ]  [NO ]
Page                 [NO ]
Break1     CustNo    [YES]         [NO ]
Break2     ProdNo    [YES]         [NO ]
Break3               [NO ]         [NO ]
Break4     [None]    [NO ]         [NO ]
Break5     [None]    [NO ]         [NO ]
Break6     [None]    [NO ]         [NO ]
Break7     [None]    [NO ]         [NO ]
Break8     [None]    [NO ]         [NO ]
Break9     [None]    [NO ]         [NO ]
Break10    [None]    [NO ]         [NO ]

[ESC] Done   [F2] Delete   [F3] Review   [↑] Up   [↓] Down   [Shift-F10] More
sales2     Configure
```

Figure 12.7: Two breakpoints defined for a report

H1 Break Header 1 (customer number)
H2 Break Header 2 (product codes)
D Detail Lines
F2 Break Footer 2 (with SubTot2 variable to show subtotal by product)
F1 Break Footer 1 (with SubTot1 variable to show subtotal by customer)
PF Page Footing
RF Report Footing (including the GrandTot variable if any)

Figure 12.8 shows the report format used to print the sample report in Figure 12.6 above. Variable and column names are shown between the appropriate S and E locations (though these, of course, do not appear on your screen).

The same basic structure can be used with any number of headings. For example, if a report contained five levels of subtotaling, then you would need to define five subtotaling variables. Each of these would need to be reset at each breakpoint.

When laying out the report format, you'd still want to nest the various break headings and footings within one another, as follows:

RH Report Header
PH Page Header
H1 Break Header 1
H2 Break Header 2
H3 Break Header 3
H4 Break Header 4
H5 Break Header 5
D Detail Lines
F5 Break Footer 5 (and subtotaling variable)
F4 Break Footer 4 (and subtotaling variable)
F3 Break Footer 3 (and subtotaling variable)
F2 Break Footer 2 (and subtotaling variable)
F1 Break Footer 1 (and subtotaling variable)
PF Page Footing
RF Report Footing (and grand total variable if any)

Any section in the report, be it a heading, a detail line, or a break header or footer, can consist of any number of lines and any number of variables or table columns. If you wish to display a cumulative total along with (or in place of) a subtotal, don't reset the variable. (In

```
RH                      Charge Transactions
RH Date:  S  RepDate            E              Page: S PgNo E
RH
PH Customer
PH       Prod. #     Qty  Unit Price        Total    Date
PH
H1 S CustNo E S NameCo E
H2
D        S ProdNo ES  Qty ES  U:Price ES    Total ES    P:Date E
F2                                          __________
F2       Subtotal for product S ProdNo E    S SubTot1 E
F1                                          ==========
F1       Total for customer S CustNo E      S SubTot2 E
F1
RF                                          __________
RF       Grand Total of all customers:     S GrandTot E
```

Figure 12.8: The report layout for a report with two breakpoints

other words, leave the Variable Reset column of the configuration sheet at the default [NO] setting for the appropriate breakpoint and variable.)

A breakpoint doesn't have to have a subtotal variable associated with it. For example, you might want to put breakpoints for State and City in a report format for the Names table. Doing so will display the names grouped by state and grouped by city within each state. The grouping, in this case, is only for organization and therefore you need not define subtotal variables.

BOXES AND LINES ON REPORTS

As in Forms EXPRESS, you can draw boxes and lines on reports with the Draw option from the top menu. The lines and boxes will appear on the screen when you print the report, but may not appear on the printed report (it depends on your particular printer). Your best bet is to draw a simple box on a report format with the Draw options from the menu, save the report, and then print a copy of the report with the OUTPUT PRINTER and PRINT commands.

If the box does not appear properly on the printed report, you can erase it using the Erase option on the Draw menu in Reports EXPRESS. Even if the custom boxes don't work with your report, you can still use hyphens and the underscore character on your keyboard to draw underlines on your report. (These will show up on any printer's output.)

CREATING A REPORT BASED ON A VIEW

Earlier in this chapter you created a Sales report that contained information from two tables: Charges and Names. Why did we base the report on the Charges table rather than the Names table? This sort of question is often hard to answer and merits some discussion.

Since the Sales report is designed to print details about charges, the Charges table provides the most logical *base*, or *driver* table. You can see this clearly if you visualize the data in the Names table: there's only one row for each customer. Now visualize data in the Charges table: most customers have more than one row, since they have made multiple purchases. We want a report that summarizes information about charges by customer, so we use the Charges table. S's and E's located in the Detail section of the report can then correspond to individual rows in the driver table.

The drawback to using the Charges table as a driver table is that we have to define three lookup variables (Name1, Name2, and CompName) to get data from the Names table. An alternative approach would be to define a view that contains all the necessary data in one "table."

Recall from Chapter 10 that a view can contain columns from up to five different tables. The Sales report needs only the following columns:

FROM NAMES	***FROM CHARGES***
CustNo	CustNo
L:Name	ProdNo
F:Name	Qty
Company	U:Price
	Total
	P:Date

Sometimes you'll make lists like these only to discover that your lists don't contain common columns. If, for example, we didn't want to print customer numbers, we wouldn't have included CustNo on our lists. However, when you establish a view, you must include the common, or link, columns in your view, even if you don't plan to use that data.

See if you can define a view for an alternative sales report by using Definition EXPRESS. Call your view Salesrpt and include the columns from the two tables listed above. (You won't have to specify CustNo twice; R:BASE will realize it's the common column.) Press the Esc key when asked to select a column for validation. Once you have established the view, start Reports EXPRESS and define a Salesrpt report based on the Salesrpt view. Then define the Repdate, PgNo, SubTot, and GrandTot variables, as you did for the original Sales report. Do not define variables for Name1 or Name2, since that data is directly available through the view. Define NameCo as

```
NameCo = F:Name & L:Name + ":" & Company
```

Then, use the Configure option to set up CustNo as the break column for Break1, as you did before. Change the Variable Reset to Yes, and select SubTot as the variable to reset, as you did before. Continue by typing in the text and locating the columns and variables in Edit mode. Save the new report and test it.

Using a view as the driver table for a report can be a real time-saver when the alternative is defining a lot of lookup variables.

ADDITIONAL TIPS AND TECHNIQUES FOR REPORTS

Locating and relocating columns and variables can be confusing at first. Remember that the F3 and F6 keys are both sensitive to the cursor location. If you press the F3 key when the cursor is inside the bounds of a located field, you'll get information about that field's identity on the top line of the report edit screen. Otherwise, pressing F3 will yield a list of the columns and variables associated with the report. If you press F6 when the cursor is within the bounds of an SE pair, R:BASE assumes that you want to make changes to the located field.

What are your options when you make a mistake in locating a field? (Or, rather, what do you tell your friends if they make a mistake in locating *their* fields?) Here are some solutions:

- If you want to delete an SE pair, move the cursor to within the offending field's SE pair and press Shift-F2.
- If you want to relocate an SE pair, or customize an individual field's characteristics, move the cursor to within the field's SE pair and press F6.
- If you have located columns and variables, but the code on the line is the wrong one (for example, H1 instead of D), try moving the cursor to the first column of the work area on the line whose report code needs changing. Make sure EXPAND is on. Use F7 or F8 until the code is the one you want the line to be. Then, press Shift-Tab to move the cursor into the Mark area. Finally, use the cursor arrows to expand the marking section as needed. Press the Tab key to return to the work area. This technique, although complex, can save you deleting and relocating time.

DEFAULT WIDTHS

As you locate your fields, you may not understand what the process is behind the default location of the E's. The table below summarizes what is occurring:

DATA TYPE	ALIGNMENT	DEFAULT WIDTH
DATE	Left	8–30*
TIME	Left	8–20*
CURRENCY	Right	26
TEXT	Left	1
INTEGER	Right	10
REAL	Right	8
DOUBLE	Right	22
NOTE	Left	1

*Depending on selected display format.

DECIMAL POINT ALIGNMENT

You can control decimal alignment for REAL and DOUBLE data types by placing a decimal point at the desired location within the SE pair. Of course, it's your responsibility to make sure the defined field is wide enough to handle the data that will be printed. When EXPRESS doesn't have enough room to display a number according to the decimal alignment you have defined, it will either print a leading % in front of the incomplete number, or print all the digits to the left of the decimal point, and then round the digits to the right of the decimal point to fit in the remaining space. The result will depend on whether extra space is needed to the left or the right of the decimal point.

LOCATING TEXT AND NOTE FIELDS

Although the Mail database doesn't have any NOTE fields, you may want to set up reports that contain both TEXT and NOTE data. Locating TEXT and NOTE fields is a bit more complicated than locating other fields. For one thing, the default length of one character (see above) is rarely acceptable. On top of that, you'll have to decide whether you want to implement wraparound to print long fields like paragraphs. If you do, you can establish a right margin, so to speak, by typing a W rather than an E. R:BASE will then prompt you to

```
Press [T] for end line or [ESC]
```

If you only want to devote three lines to the long field, for example, you would move your cursor down two lines from the W and type a T (for Truncate). This would tell R:BASE to print three lines worth of data from the field and to break at a space. Something like "and th" would not be printed; the line would end with "and". If you press Esc, EXPRESS will use as many lines as necessary to print the entire field.

Figure 12.9, for example, displays a report layout for a vocabulary database. Its only table, Vocab, has two columns: Word and Def. Def is defined as a NOTE field to accommodate widely varying definition lengths. In the report, the W tells R:BASE to wrap the definition around onto the next line. Part of the VocabRep report is shown in Figure 12.10.

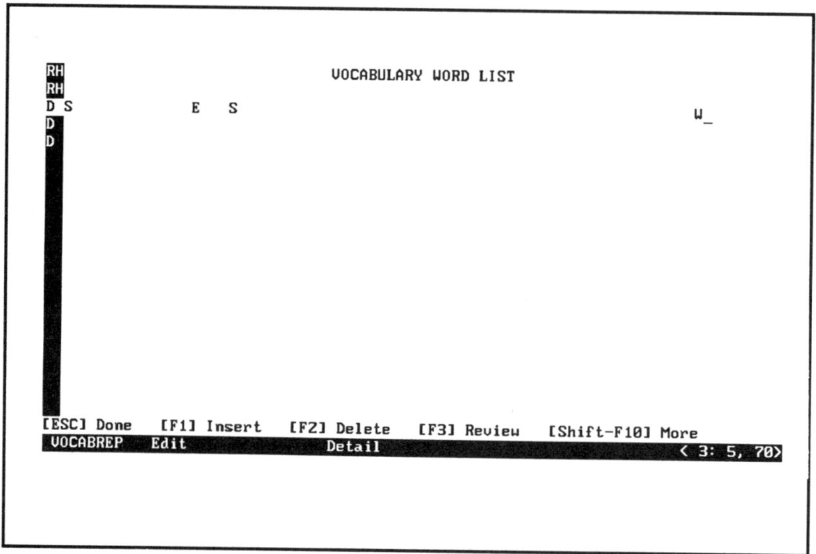

Figure 12.9: The report layout for the vocabulary database

Finally, Reports EXPRESS gives you the option of indenting or outdenting any wrapped fields. If you want indenting, type an I to the *right* of the S; if you want outdenting, type it to the *left*. If you don't want either, you can press Esc.

This completes our look at wraparound in reports.

CREATING A REPORT WITHOUT DETAIL LINES

Although most reports will have at least one line marked D for Detail, it's not necessary to have them. It's quite possible to set up a summary report that prints only subtotal variables associated with break footers.

R:BASE has a powerful report generator, and you've learned a good deal about its advanced features in this chapter. You're probably feeling overwhelmed, but remember, the more you practice, the easier it becomes. The techniques we've used in this chapter illustrate the variety of formats you can use for reports; now we'll turn to some advanced formats and techniques available for forms.

```
                        VOCABULARY WORD LIST

abat-jour          A device, as a skylight or reflector, for diverting
                   light into a building

abulia             Abnormal lack of ability to act or to make
                   decisions

accoutrement       An article of equipment or dress, especially when
                   used as an accessory

acerbate           To excite impatience, anger, or displeasure in;
                   exasperate

ad hoc             For this (special purpose) only; with respect to
                   this (subject or thing)

adagio             A love-duet sequence in ballet; a duet or trio
                   emphasizing difficult feat

adduce             To offer as example, reason, or proof in discussion
                   or analysis

adiabatic          Occurring without gain or loss of heat e.g. the
                   power and compression strokes of a gasoline engine

adjuration         A solemn oath; an earnest urging or advising

adumbration        A sketchy representation or outline; a vague
                   foreshadowing; intimation

adventitious       Associated with something by chance, extrinsic
```

Figure 12.10: The report layout for the vocabulary database

Chapter 13

Refining Your Data-Entry Forms

FAST TRACK

To create a region on a form, 350
use the F8 key to attach the new table. Then answer Yes to the prompt about customizing table characteristics and Yes to the question about defining a region.

To place text and column names in a region, 353
use the arrow keys and the F6 key to mark the start and end locations for each column name.

To duplicate a series of column names 354
(called *tiers*) in a region, use Shift-F4.

To edit and enter data simultaneously 356
in a form that serves multiple tables, create a master lookup expression with the syntax *column* = *column* IN *table* WHERE *id* = id.

To access a form that serves multiple tables, 356
use either the ENTER or the EDIT USING command followed by the name of the form.

To change the size of a region, 359
enter Forms EXPRESS. You can then use F1 to add lines to the region, F2 to delete lines, and F9 and the arrow keys to change the overall size.

To prevent changes to a column, 361
edit your form and place the cell pointer anywhere between the S and E for the chosen column. Press F6 and select Yes, and then answer No when prompted whether users should be allowed to change data in the field.

To reordder field names, 362

select the Customize and *Field order* options in Forms EXPRESS. You can change the order in which F9 cycles through the tables in a form by selecting Customize, Table, and Reorder in Forms EXPRESS.

ONE OF THE MOST POWERFUL FEATURES OF R:BASE IS its ability to display data from multiple tables on a single form and to allow data to be entered into and edited on many tables simultaneously. Now that you've learned a bit about database design, you know that tables often contain columns whose only purpose is to link them to other tables. If you've been bothered by the prospect of entering redundant data associated with common columns into many tables, worry no more. You only have to enter data for common columns once when you use multi-table data-entry forms. Another advantage of multi-table forms is that you can usually design screens that look like existing paper forms. If data-entry personnel will be transcribing data from paper forms into R:BASE, this will make life easier.

In Chapter 10, we introduced you to some of the more advanced features of Forms EXPRESS when you created the ChrgFrm form. You may want to look at it to refresh your memory. It is based on the Charges table and includes a number of lookup variables and an automatic date-entry feature. If the Mail database is open and you type

```
ENTER ChrgFrm
```

at the R> prompt, R:BASE will display the form on the screen. If you enter an actual customer number next to the Customer number prompt, R:BASE will automatically display that person's name and company.

In this chapter, we're going to explore multi-table forms, which allow you to enter data into or edit data from two or more tables. The ChrgFrm form, by comparison, was only designed to let you enter new data into the Charges table. But before we proceed, let's take a moment to discuss a general approach to designing and creating a complex form.

THE PRAGMATIST'S GUIDE TO FORM DESIGN AND IMPLEMENTATION

O.K., so you're ready to create a form. What now? Start Forms EXPRESS? No! Before you do any hands-on programming with R:BASE, you should do some hands-on work with your paper and pencil.

Common sense dictates that you should plan your form. You want it to be easy-to-use, pleasant to look at, and have fields located in a logical fashion. You may need the screen form to look like an existing paper form. You'll probably want to minimize the number of keystrokes the data-entry person will have to make, and also make it easy for that person to correct mistakes.

You should also think about your form's general characteristics. Is the form going to be used for data entry, editing, data display, or some combination of activities? What tables are involved? R:BASE will let you create a form that serves up to five tables. Will part of the form display background (or lookup) information? Will you want to enter several rows of data into one form, as in the case of multi-item invoices? R:BASE lets you define *regions* where many rows of data can be entered at once; we'll explore such regions later in the chapter. Is case consistency desirable? You may want to use some of R:BASE's *functions* to ensure that data is entered into your tables in a consistent fashion.

Next, you should make a preliminary sketch of the form. Remember that R:BASE lets you use up to five screens for your forms, so you don't need to pack all the necessary data onto one screen.

After you've sketched the form, you're ready to start setting it up. The next steps should be done in order, one table at a time. Generally, it's best to set up your expressions before entering text and prompts onto the form, because you may encounter problems with the expressions that force you to rethink your form's basic design.

In Chapter 10 you created the ChrgFrm form and defined variables that "looked up" data from other tables for display on the form. Your Name1, Name2, and CompName variables are referred to as *standard lookups* because they access data from the Names table.

R:BASE also lets you define what's referred to as a *master lookup*. Master lookups are used to look up data in the current table—not another table. For example, we'll create a form that lets you enter data both into the Names and Charges tables. When a new customer makes a transaction, you'll want to enter basic customer information (for the Names table) *and* details about the charge (for the Charges table). However, if a customer is already on record in the Names table you don't want to have to enter his or her data again. You'll establish a master lookup expression, so that when you type in an existing customer's number, all the current data about that customer will be displayed automatically.

The next step is to place the columns and variables. Once you've finished placing columns and variables, you'll want to fine-tune your form by customizing table and field characteristics. After doing that, you'll move on to the next table. Ready to try out some of these techniques?

Rather than create an entirely new form to demonstrate this capability, we'll modify a copy of the NamesFrm form created earlier. To make the copy, make sure the Mail database is open, and enter the command

```
FORMS
```

at the R> prompt to enter Forms EXPRESS.

From the opening Forms EXPRESS menu, select option 3 to copy a form. The screen asks that you

```
Enter name of the form to copy:
```

Type in **NamesFrm** and press Enter. The screen asks that you

```
Enter the new form name:
```

Type in Both and press Enter. Now there are two identical forms in the Mail database, named NamesFrm and Both.

To begin changing the Both form to serve two tables, select 1 to Edit/Create a form. When requested, select Both as the name of the form to edit, and then select Edit to move the cursor onto the form.

We'll place a region for displaying data from the Charges table near the bottom of the screen. Use the ↓ key to move the cursor down to the bottom box (at <16,1>), and press F2 seven times to erase the box and its contents. The bottom portion of the screen is now empty, giving you room to create a region. A *region* is an area on a form that can display data from a group of rows. The region for Both allows you to enter multiple charges for a given customer on one screen. Also, by defining a region, you'll be able to scroll through *all* of a given customer's charges.

CREATING THE REGION

Notice that the words *Table: Names* appear in the middle of the status bar at the bottom of the screen. This indicates that the form is currently "attached to" the Names table. To create a region on the form for the Charges table, you first need to attach the form to the Charges table. To do so, press the F8 key. The screen asks for the name of the new table to attach to. Select Charges from the menu. (Note that the status bar at the bottom of the screen indicates that the form is now attached to the Charges table.)

The first question to appear on the screen is the following:

Do you want to customize table characteristics?

Select Yes and take a look at the Table Characteristics menu. Notice the question

Do you want to define a region?

Move the highlighter to this question, and change the answer to Yes (by typing the letter **Y** and pressing Enter).

The form will reappear on the screen, along with the request to

Move the cursor to locate a corner of the region—press [ENTER]

Now you can "draw" the region where you want rows from the Charges table to appear. Move the cell pointer to <16,1> and press Enter. The screen now asks that you

Move the cursor to paint the region's area—press [ENTER] when done.

Press the down arrow key six times to move the highlighter to <22,1>; then press the right arrow key to stretch the highlighter all the way to the right, to <22,80>. Your screen should look like Figure 13.1.

Press Enter after highlighting the region area. The screen displays the message

Region created. Press any key to continue

When you press any key, the Table Characteristics menu reappears on the screen.

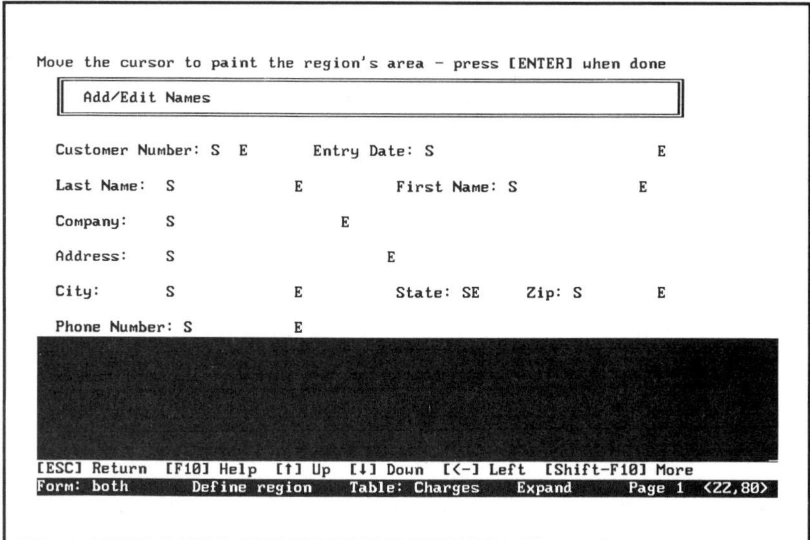

Figure 13.1: A region area highlighted on the form

A couple of questions on the menu refer to the appearance of the region on the form. The first question—

Do you want a border around the region?

—controls whether or not there will be a border around the region so that it stands out on the form. The choice is yours, but generally the form will look better with the border, so Yes, the default, is the preferred answer. The second question

How many lines in the border: Enter 1 or 2

lets you determine whether the border is displayed with a single line or a double line. For this example, 2 is preferred because it will match the existing box near the top of the screen. (Again, however, this is purely an aesthetic decision.) Notice that R:BASE defaults to double-lined borders.

If you have a color monitor, you can also define colors for the region by answering the appropriate questions on the Table Characteristics menu. When you are finished, press Esc until you see the Form Definition menu, and then select Edit.

LOCATING TEXT AND PROMPTS IN THE REGION

Now you can place text and column names from the Charges table inside the region. The procedure for doing so is the same as for any form. For typing in text, position the cursor with the arrow keys and type in the text. For this example, place the cursor at each of the start locations in the left column below, and type in the text listed in the right column:

START LOCATION	*TEXT*
<17,2>	Cust #
<17,10>	Prod #
<17,19>	Tax?
<17,25>	Qty
<17,32>	Unit Price
<17,51>	Total
<17,63>	Date of Sale

You can locate column names with the F6 key and arrow keys. When locating columns, the screen will ask the usual questions, such as

Do you want to define an expression for <*column name*>?

For the current form, you can select No each time this question appears. The screen will also ask

Do you want to customize field characteristics?

Generally, you can just answer No to each of these questions. However, you might want to put the default value of 1 in the Tax? column and the default #DATE in the P:Date column, as we've done before.

Using the F6 key and the arrow keys, place the column names listed below at the start and end locations listed to the right of each column name:

COLUMN NAME	*START*	*END*
CustNo	<18,2>	<18,5>
ProdNo	<18,10>	<18,17>

Tax?	<18,20>	<18,20>
Qty	<18,24>	<18,27>
U:Price	<18,30>	<18,41>
Total	<18,43>	<18,55>
P:Date	<18,58>	<18,79>

When you are finished, your screen should look like Figure 13.2.

Since there may be many rows in the Charges table associated with a single row in the Names table, you'll want to duplicate the column locations in the region. That way, when a particular customer is displayed on the screen, you'll be able to scroll through and edit any of the transactions.

COPYING TIERS IN A REGION

Your form's region currently has one tier. A *tier* is the area, which can include text, as well as S's and E's, associated with a single row. However, we've made the region large enough to accomodate several tiers. The process for doing so is simple. First, press Shift-F4 (hold down the Shift key and press F4). The screen asks that you

Move cursor to locate a corner of the area to be duplicated—press [ENTER]

Using the arrow keys, move the cursor to the left column of the area to copy (<18,2> in this example), and press Enter. Next the screen asks that you

Move cursor to paint the area to be duplicated—press [ENTER]

Using the → key, extend the highlighter to <18,79> to "paint over" all the column name locations. Press Enter when you are finished. Automatically, the entire region will be filled with the column name locations, as in Figure 13.3.

At this point you've finished creating the screen portion of the new form named Both. Before testing it, however, we can add another feature called a *master lookup*. Press Esc to get to the Form Definition menu.

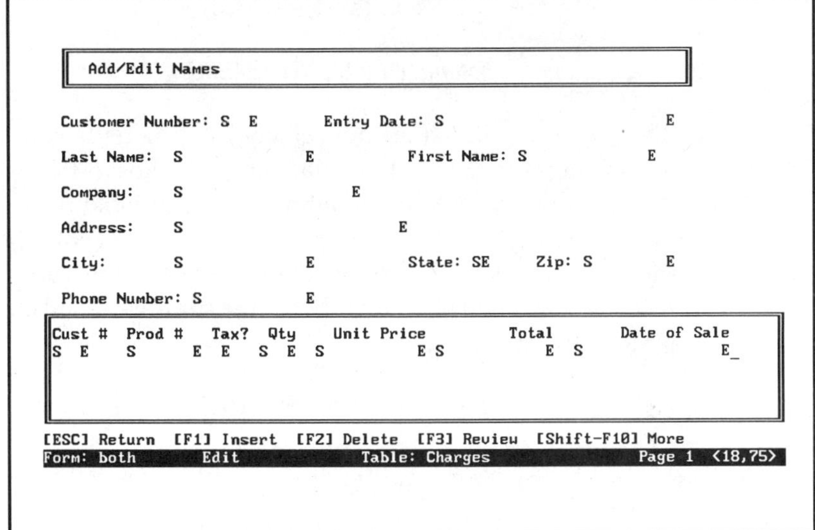

Figure 13.2: Text and column names located in the region

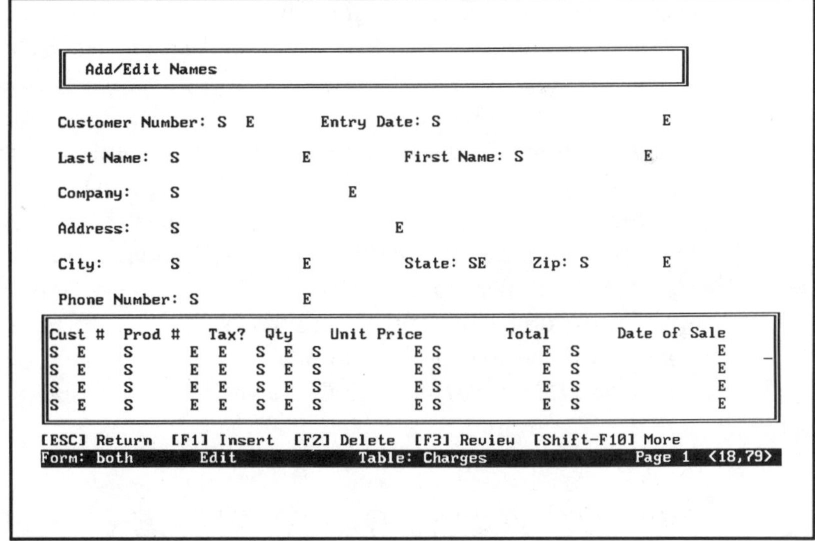

Figure 13.3: Tiers copied in the Charges region

DEFINING A MASTER LOOKUP EXPRESSION

A master lookup expression is used in forms that serve multiple tables to display the data from a particular row in one of the tables.

Generally, the expression takes the form

column = *column* IN *table* WHERE *id* = *id*

The *column* portion is the name of any column in the named *table*. The *id* portion is the name of the matching columns in the two tables. In this example, you want to define a master lookup for the Names table. Press F7 to make Names the active table (note the change in the status bar along the bottom of the screen.) Then select Expression from the top menu and Define from the submenu, and enter the master lookup expression

L:Name = L:Name IN Names WHERE CustNo = CustNo

When the screen asks if you want to customize lookup characteristics, select No.

When using the form later, you will enter a customer number in the first field. R:BASE will use your master lookup expression to match up the customer number entered onto the form to customer numbers in the Names and Charges tables. L:Name in this case is simply an arbitrary column; you could have used F:Name, Company, Address, or any of the others. The purpose of the expression is not to look up a particular L:Name. Actually, the overall purpose is to attempt to find out if the customer number entered onto the form already exists. If it does, *all* the remaining fields in the Names portion of the form will automatically display that customer's data.

We'll see the effects of this master lookup expression in a moment, and this will, perhaps, shed more light on this expression.

For the time being, we're finished creating the form. Press the Esc key until the exit options appear on the screen, and select Save Changes. Then exit all the higher-level menus to work your way back to the R> prompt.

USING YOUR MULTI-TABLE FORM

You can use the new form with either the EDIT or the ENTER command. To try out the new form in the edit mode, enter the command

EDIT USING Both

at the R> prompt.

You'll notice right away that the form displays both the first row in the Names database and all the charges associated with that name, as in Figure 13.4.

You can select Next or Previous to scroll through the names in the Names table and watch how the form displays data.

To edit data in either table, select Edit from the top menu as usual. Once the cursor is inside the form, you can use the following keys in addition to the Enter, arrow, and Tab keys:

F9 Switch from one region (or table) to the next

F7 Skip back one row

F8 Skip forward one row

For example, if you press F9 while the cursor is still in the Names region of the screen, the cursor will jump down to the Charges region. Once inside the Charges region, you can press F8 and F7 to scroll up and down through the rows (that contain data) in the Charges region. Pressing F9 again brings the cursor back up to the Names portion of the form.

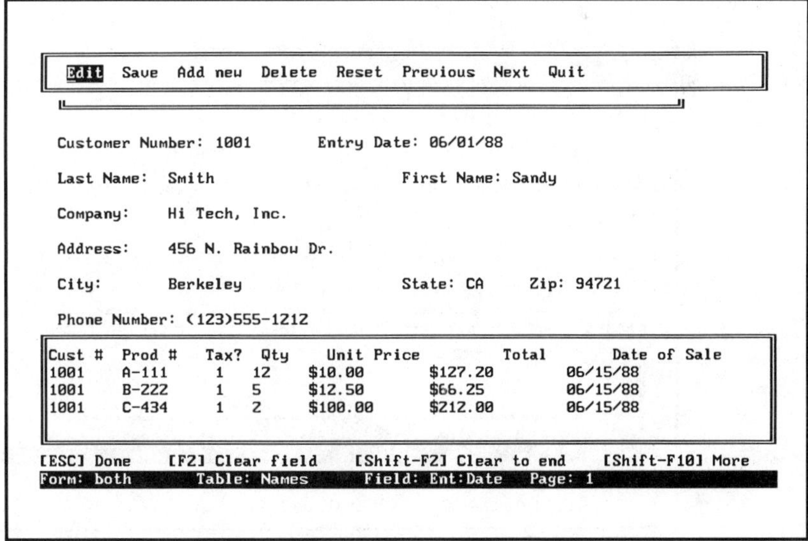

Figure 13.4: Data displayed from both the Names and Charges tables

Of course, you can change any data on the form that you wish. When you are finished editing, press Esc and select Quit from the top menu.

To enter new data through the form, enter the command

```
ENTER Both
```

at the R> prompt. The form appears with no data in it (except for the default date), ready to accept new data.

Here is where the master lookup expression comes in. Normally, when entering data into a database, R:BASE will accept any entry you type in, or it will check the rules (if any) to see if a violation took place. But with the master lookup expression defined, R:BASE will simply display existing data if you enter an existing customer number.

For example, if you enter customer number 1003 onto the form and press Enter, the screen will display all existing data for customer number 1003 as shown in Figure 13.5. You can simply press F9 to move to the Charges region of the form and then type in new charges for this customer. If you have customized the Tax? and Date of sale fields, data is already displayed in them. After entering the new charges, press Esc and select Add.

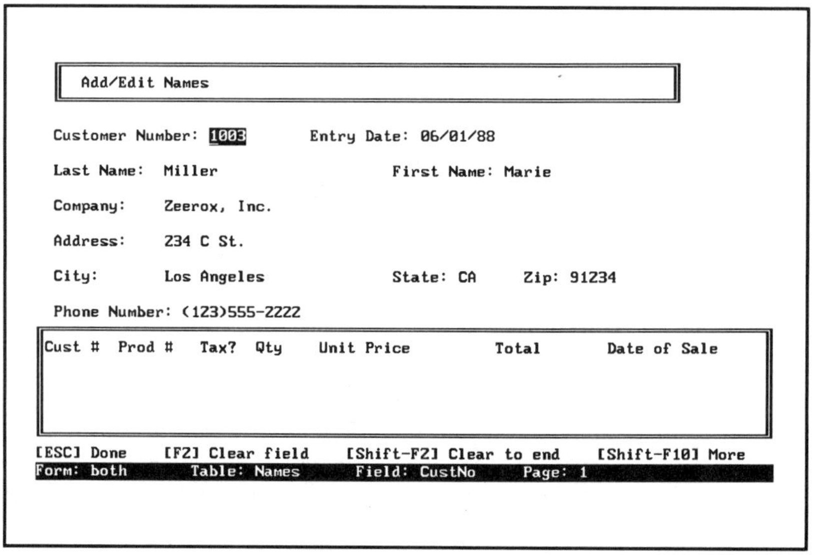

```
 Add/Edit Names

Customer Number: 1003        Entry Date: 06/01/88

Last Name:  Miller                   First Name: Marie

Company:    Zeerox, Inc.

Address:    234 C St.

City:       Los Angeles              State: CA     Zip: 91234

Phone Number: (123)555-2222

Cust #  Prod #   Tax?  Qty   Unit Price        Total       Date of Sale



[ESC] Done    [F2] Clear field    [Shift-F2] Clear to end    [Shift-F10] More
Form: both         Table: Names        Field: CustNo      Page: 1
```

Figure 13.5: Existing data displayed automatically for customer number 1003

If, for your next data entry, you enter a new customer number (such as 9999) and press Enter, the top portion of the screen will display the message

```
Master lookup row not found—Press [ENTER] to add, [ESC] to continue
```

R:BASE is telling you that the customer number you entered does not exist yet in the Names table, and it gives you two options. If you press Enter, a row for the new customer number will be created on the Names table, and you can fill in the remaining data (including data on the Charges table) for this new customer. If you press Esc, R:BASE will reject the new customer number and let you enter another one.

As usual, press Esc and select Quit when you are finished entering new data.

With some experience entering and editing data through a form that serves multiple tables, you'll soon find this method convenient for managing several tables.

MAKING CHANGES IN THE FORM

Rarely will your first attempt at setting up a form be perfect. Some of you may have noticed that in Edit mode, the data in the region doesn't line up quite right (see Figure 13.5). When you establish boundaries for a field with S's and E's, R:BASE will display any data starting at the S. To change the form so that the alignment looks better, you'll have to return to Forms EXPRESS. If you type

```
FORMS Both
```

at the R> prompt, you'll go directly to your form in Forms EXPRESS.

Once in Forms EXPRESS, select Edit, and press F8 to make the Charges table the active one. Then move your cursor to <18,25> (between the S and E for Qty), and press F6. Normally, when you press F6 and your cursor is inside a located SE pair, R:BASE asks you two questions: whether you want to customize the field's characteristics, and whether you want to relocate the field. Although we want to relocate several fields, R:BASE won't let us, because we have multiple tiers of the same row. R:BASE is going to make us remove the tiers before we can make changes in fields' locations. To start this process, press any key.

Now press Shift-F4. R:BASE asks you if you want to remove all the duplicate rows. Answer Yes. As fast as you can blink, all your tiers have disappeared. Don't worry; it'll be easy to duplicate them again.

Try again to relocate the Qty field. Make sure your cursor is inside the bounds of the S and E associated with Qty, and press F6. Answer No when asked about customizing the field's characteristics, but Yes when asked about relocating the field. Locate the S at <18,25> and the E at <18,27>. Continue relocating fields as follows:

COLUMN NAME	*START*	*END*
U:Price	<18,33>	<18,41>
Total	<18,49>	<18,57>
P:Date	<18,65>	<18,72>

After you've done that, copy the tier again by pressing Shift-F4 and painting the area between <18,2> and <18,79> as you did before. Press Esc twice, save your changes, return to the R> prompt, and observe the fruits of your effort with the command

```
EDIT USING Both
```

The data should be displayed in a much more aesthetically pleasing way, as shown in Figure 13.6. As usual, select Quit to return to the R> prompt.

TIPS AND TECHNIQUES FOR MULTI-TABLE FORMS

Before concluding this chapter, there are a few more tips and techniques that you should know about forms and regions.

CHANGING A REGION'S SIZE

You can change the size, location, or appearance of a region using Forms EXPRESS. When the appropriate form is on the screen, you

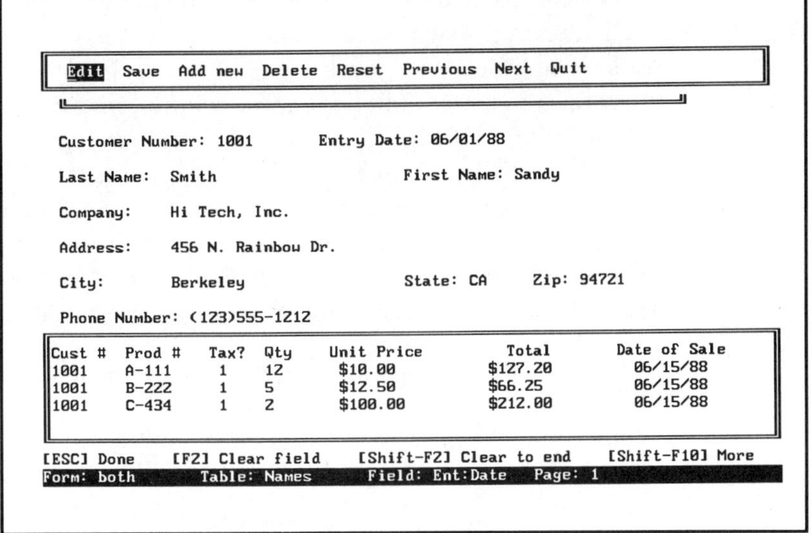

Figure 13.6: The data reformatted for better alignment

can insert lines above or beneath the region using the F1 key (assuming that there is room on the form to insert new lines). You can also delete lines above or beneath the region using the F2 key. (The F2 key will only delete lines that do not have column names or variables located. If necessary, use Shift-F2 to delete column and variable names, and then use F2 to delete the line.)

To change the size of a region, first make sure that the table the region serves is the active table and that duplicate tiers have been removed. When the name of the table associated with the region appears in the status bar, press F9. The cursor moves to the upper-left corner of the region, and the entire region is highlighted. You can then alter the size of the region with the arrow keys.

After you've made your changes to the column locations and text inside the region, you can use the Shift-F4 key again to copy the tier.

PREVENTING CHANGES TO THE CUSTOMER NUMBER

When using the form with multiple tables and the ENTER command, the user can enter any customer number. If the customer number exists, the data are displayed on the screen. At this point, the user could change the customer number, but the results of doing so could cause problems, because the corresponding existing charges on the Charges table will not automatically be updated to reflect the new customer number.

To prevent changes to the CustNo column, you can enter Forms EXPRESS and edit the form named Both. Make sure the Names table is the active table (press F7 if Charges is active). Move the cell pointer anywhere between the S and E for the CustNo column for the Names table (in this example, <5,18>) and press F6. When the screen asks if you want to customize field characteristics, select Yes. On the Field Characteristics menu you'll see the question

Can the user change the data displayed in the field?

If you change the answer to this question to No, the user will not be allowed to change the number of an existing customer.

REORDERING FIELD AND TABLE NAMES

If you noticed that your cursor was jumping around erratically in your form during data entry, remember that you can change the field order in Forms EXPRESS. Once in Forms EXPRESS, you should select Customize from the menu, and then Field order. R:BASE gives you the choice of either cycling through or reordering the current field order. Make sure the table that has the field order problem is the active table before you select Reorder. Then, simply type in the number of the field that needs reordering and enter the position it should be on the list. R:BASE will immediately update the field order list. You can continue to make as many changes as you need to.

If in the future you create a form that serves more than two tables, you may want to change the order in which the F9 key cycles through the tables in the form. To do so, select Customize from the top menu in Forms EXPRESS. From the submenus select Table and Reorder. The screen will display instructions for changing the order of the tables in the database. (The technique is virtually identical to that used for changing the order of expressions.)

In this chapter, you've seen how easy it is to create sophisticated forms that let the user enter data into several tables from one form.

You've also learned how Forms EXPRESS provides several levels of customization, which allow you to specify default values for fields and have existing data displayed for the user's convenience. In the next chapter we'll look at some *relational* commands for combining and summarizing multiple tables.

Chapter 14

Expanding Your Tables by Combining and Copying Data

FAST TRACK

To copy a table or a portion of a table *368*
to a new table, use the PROJECT command. By specifying column names, you can rearrange the order of columns or reduce the number of columns in the copied table. The WHERE clause allows you to limit the number of rows passed to the copied table, and the ORDER BY clause allows you to specify a sort order for the copied table.

To copy all or some rows from a table and append them *373*
to the bottom of another table, use the APPEND command.

To create a third table using all or some *379*
of the columns from two other tables, use the UNION command. The existing tables must have a common column (one with identical names, data types, and widths). Common columns are merged into a single column, and all rows are copied from both tables.

To create a third table from all or part of two existing tables, *383*
use the INTERSECT command. Like the UNION command, the INTERSECT command requires that the tables have at least one common column. Common columns are merged into a single column, and only common rows are copied to the new table.

To create a third table composed of rows that do not match *386*
from two existing tables, use the SUBTRACT command.

To merge two tables that do not have a common column name, *387*
use the JOIN command. The columns used for comparison must have the same data type and length.

To view data from multiple tables simultaneously, 392
without creating a report format to do so, create a *view* using Definition EXPRESS. Views can contain columns from up to five different tables. The tables in the view must have at least one column in common.

To create form letters in Forms EXPRESS, 399
locate columns and variables in the body of a letter created in Edit mode.

To back up your database, 401
use the COPY command. Back up large databases with the BACKUP command, making sure you have a sufficient supply of floppy disks available before directing the output to a file.

To squeeze unused disk space 403
from your database files, use the RELOAD command. (Use RELOAD only if you have enough room on your hard disk for another copy of your files.) Use the PACK command to optimize disk space only after backing up your files.

R:BASE OFFERS SIX COMMANDS FOR COMBINING AND copying tables in a database: PROJECT, APPEND, UNION, INTERSECT, SUBTRACT, and JOIN. Like all commands, these can be entered directly at the R> prompt. Alternatively, you can build from these commands by selecting the *R:BASE and operating system utilities*, and then *All commands* options from PBE.

Before trying the sample operations in this chapter, make sure that the Mail database is open and the R> prompt is on the screen. Keep in mind that your results may differ if your Names or Charges table contains data other than those used in the sample operations.

COPYING TABLES WITH THE PROJECT COMMAND

The PROJECT command makes a copy of all or part of a table, creating a new table in the process. It is useful for making backup copies of tables, creating summary tables, and reordering columns and rows in a table. The basic syntax for the project command is

```
PROJECT new table name FROM existing table name USING +
+ > column names ORDER BY column names WHERE +
+ > conditions list
```

The ORDER BY and WHERE clauses are optional with this command, and ALL can be used in place of individual column names. An example of the operation of the PROJECT command is shown in Figure 14.1.

Let's suppose that you want to create a list of names, telephone numbers, and entry dates for everyone in the Names table whose entry dates are between June 1 and June 15, 1988. Furthermore, you want to store the list in order by telephone number. To create a new table named PhoneLst for these data, enter the command

```
PROJECT PhoneLst FROM Names USING Phone +
+ > L:Name F:Name Ent:Date ORDER BY Phone WHERE +
+ > Ent:Date > 5/31/88 AND Ent:Date < = 6/15/88
```

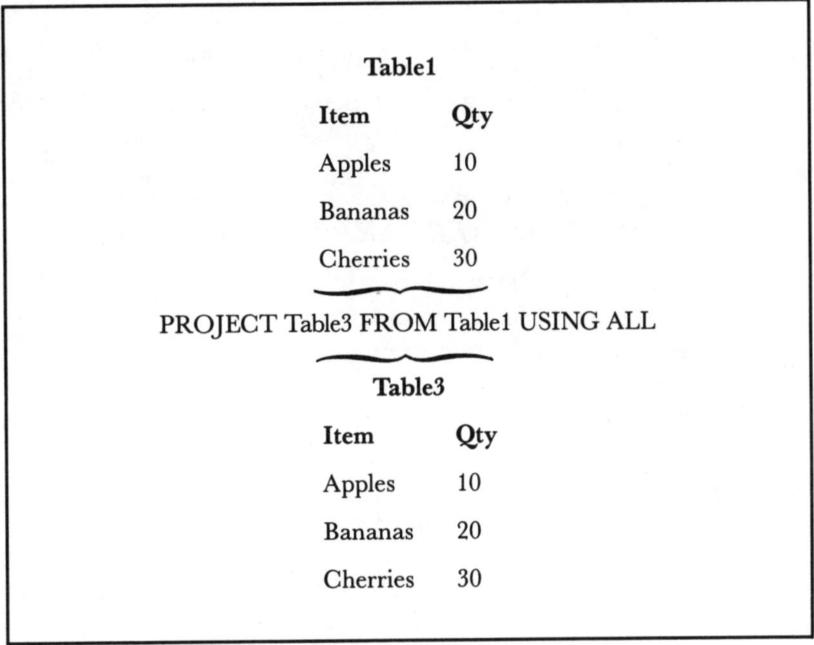

Figure 14.1: An example of the PROJECT command

After performing the requested task, R:BASE responds with this message:

```
Successful project operation     6 rows generated
```

To see the contents of the new PhoneLst table, use the SELECT command, as follows:

```
SELECT ALL FROM PhoneLst
```

R:BASE displays the new PhoneLst table, as below:

PHONE	*L:NAME*	*F:NAME*	*ENT:DATE*
(123)555-1010	Jones	Mindy	06/15/88
(123)555-1212	Smith	Sandy	06/01/88
(123)555-2222	Miller	Marie	06/01/88
(213)123-4567	Adams	Bart	06/15/88

PHONE	L:NAME	F:NAME	ENT:DATE
(213)234-5678	Miller	Anne	06/01/88
(345)678-9012	Baker	Robin	06/15/88

USING THE PROJECT COMMAND TO REARRANGE COLUMNS

Let's take a look at how you can use the PROJECT command to rearrange columns in a table (don't, however, try this out on-line—let's retain the column arrangement we already have). Suppose that you want to rearrange the columns in the Names table so that Ent:Date is the column farthest left and CustNo is the column farthest right. First, you would need to copy the Names table to a temporary table (named Temp in this example), specifying all the column names in the order that you want them, as below:

```
PROJECT Temp FROM Names USING Ent:Date L:Name +
+ > F:Name Company Address City State Zip Phone CustNo
```

When you leave out the ORDER BY and WHERE clauses, you retain the original sort order and ensure that all the rows from the Names table are copied to the Temp table. To ensure that the PROJECT command was correctly executed, you could look at the Temp table by entering

```
SELECT ALL FROM Temp
```

Next, you would need to remove the original Names table using the REMOVE command, as below:

```
REMOVE TABLE Names
```

Finally, you would change the name of the Temp table to Names, using the RENAME command, as follows:

```
RENAME TABLE Temp TO Names
```

R:BASE would respond with

```
Table Temp renamed to Names
```

If you then looked at the Names table by entering

SELECT ALL FROM Names

you'd see that the Ent:Date column was indeed in the position farthest left, as shown in Figure 14.2. Using the LIST command with the table name would display the new column order, as shown in Figure 14.3.

```
R>SELECT ALL FROM Names
 Ent:Date L:Name          F:Name          Company              Address
 -------- --------------- --------------- -------------------- ---------------
 06/01/88 Smith           Sandy           Hi Tech, Inc.        456 N. Rainbow D
 06/15/88 Jones           Mindy           ABC Co.              123 A St.
 06/01/88 Miller          Marie           Zeerox, Inc.         234 C St.
 06/15/88 Adams           Bart            DataSpec Inc.        P.O. Box 2890
 06/01/88 Miller          Anne            Golden Gate Co.      2313 Sixth St.
 06/15/88 Baker           Robin           Peach Computers      2311 Coast Hwy.
 07/15/88 Miller          Monica          Acme Development     355 Torrey Pines
 07/01/88 Teasdale        Trudy           Atomic Ovens, Inc.   321 Microwave St
 07/01/88 Martin          Mary            Atomic Ovens, Inc.   321 Microwave St
R>_
```

Figure 14.2: Columns rearranged in the Names table

USING THE PROJECT COMMAND TO REARRANGE ROWS

Although the ORDER BY clause allows you to arrange rows in any order that you wish, you might want to use a quicker (and more permanent) method when you're working with a large table. If this is the case, you can use the PROJECT command to rearrange all the rows in a table.

For example, suppose you regularly send letters in ZIP-code order to the individuals listed in the Names table. You can create a sorted version of the Names table by first using the PROJECT command to

```
R>LIST Names

   Table: names            No lock(s)
   Read Password: No
   Modify Password: No

   Column definitions
   # Name     Type      Length          Key    Expression
   1 Ent:Date DATE
   2 L:Name   TEXT      15 characters
   3 F:Name   TEXT      15 characters
   4 Company  TEXT      20 characters
   5 Address  TEXT      25 characters
   6 City     TEXT      15 characters
   7 state    TEXT       2 characters
   8 Zip      TEXT      10 characters
   9 Phone    TEXT      13 characters
  10 CustNo   INTEGER

   Current number of rows:       9

R>_
```

Figure 14.3: New column arrangements for the Names table

make a copy of the Names table sorted in ascending order by ZIP code, as in the command below (again, don't try this on-line now):

PROJECT Temp FROM Names USING ALL ORDER BY Zip = A

At this point, the table named Temp has the same information as the Names table; however, the Temp table data are sorted into ZIP-code order. You can verify this with the command

SELECT Zip L:Name F:Name FROM Temp

Next, you can remove the Names table using the command

REMOVE TABLE Names

Then change the name of the Temp table to Names, using the command

RENAME TABLE Temp TO Names

Now you could use the SELECT command without an ORDER BY clause, and the rows in the Names table would be displayed in ZIP-code order, as Figure 14.4 shows.

```
R>SELECT Zip CustNo L:Name F:Name Company FROM Names
 Zip        CustNo     L:Name          F:Name          Company
 ---------- ---------- --------------- --------------- --------------------
 12121            1009 Martin          Mary            Atomic Ovens, Inc.
 12121            1008 Teasdale        Trudy           Atomic Ovens, Inc.
 54821            1007 Miller          Monica          Acme Development
 91234            1003 Miller          Marie           Zeerox, Inc.
 92111            1004 Adams           Bart            DataSpec Inc.
 92112            1006 Baker           Robin           Peach Computers
 92122            1002 Jones           Mindy           ABC Co.
 94711            1005 Miller          Anne            Golden Gate Co.
 94721            1001 Smith           Sandy           Hi Tech, Inc.
R>_
```

Figure 14.4: The new Names table in ZIP-code order

USING THE PROJECT COMMAND TO MAKE A BACKUP COPY

To make a backup copy of a table within the same database, use the PROJECT command with the USING ALL option, as below:

```
PROJECT Backup FROM Names USING ALL
```

In summary, the PROJECT command makes a copy of all or part of a table, creating an entirely new table.

ADDING ROWS WITH APPEND

The APPEND command copies rows from one table onto the bottom of another table. Only the columns that have identical names, types, and widths in the two tables are copied. An example of the APPEND command is shown is Figure 14.5.

Table2

Item	Price
Apples	0.25
Bananas	0.50
Cherries	0.75
Rutabaga	1.00

Table3

Item	Qty
Apples	10
Bananas	20
Cherries	30

APPEND Table2 TO Table3

Table3

Item	Qty
Apples	10
Bananas	20
Cherries	30
Apples	-0-
Bananas	-0-
Cherries	-0-
Rutabaga	-0-

Figure 14.5: An example of the APPEND command

The APPEND command is often used for managing *transaction* tables and *history* tables, particularly in inventory and accounting systems. For example, the Charges table in the Mail database could grow indefinitely throughout the course of the year. However, most businesses bill monthly, so there is no need to keep all the transactions of the year on the Charges table.

Instead, after the customers have been billed at the end of the month, you could move all of that month's transactions to a history table for later reference, emptying the Charges table to make room for the following month's transactions.

Let's try using the APPEND command with the Charges table. Figure 14.6 shows the current contents of that table. (Remember that

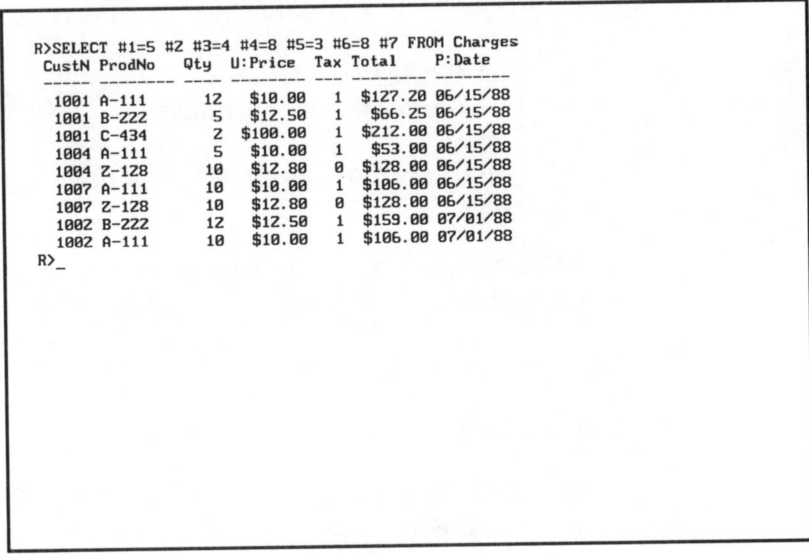

```
R>SELECT #1=5 #2 #3=4 #4=8 #5=3 #6=8 #7 FROM Charges
 CustN ProdNo    Qty  U:Price  Tax Total     P:Date
 ----- -------- ---- -------- --- -------- --------
  1001 A-111      12   $10.00   1  $127.20 06/15/88
  1001 B-222       5   $12.50   1   $66.25 06/15/88
  1001 C-434       2  $100.00   1  $212.00 06/15/88
  1004 A-111       5   $10.00   1   $53.00 06/15/88
  1004 Z-128      10   $12.80   0  $128.00 06/15/88
  1007 A-111      10   $10.00   1  $106.00 06/15/88
  1007 Z-128      10   $12.80   0  $128.00 06/15/88
  1002 B-222      12   $12.50   1  $159.00 07/01/88
  1002 A-111      10   $10.00   1  $106.00 07/01/88
R>_
```

Figure 14.6: The current contents of the Charges table

you can substitute column numbers for columns names, as we have done.)

Now we'll create a table named History for storing transactions, and we'll give it the same structure as the Charges table. You can easily copy the *structure* of the Charges table with the Project command, as below:

```
PROJECT History FROM Charges USING ALL WHERE CustNo +
+ > FAILS
```

or

```
PROJECT History From Charges USING ALL WHERE COUNT = 0
```

R:BASE responds with the message

```
-WARNING- No rows satisfy the WHERE clause
Successful project operation      0 rows generated
```

Even though no rows were copied, a History table now exists with the same structure as the Charges table. If you use the SELECT

ALL command to view the History table, you'll see this:

```
SELECT ALL FROM History
-WARNING- No data exists for this table
```

At the end of June, to move June transactions to the History table, enter the following:

```
APPEND Charges TO History WHERE P:Date > = 6/1/88 +
+ > AND P:Date < = 6/30/88
```

R:BASE responds with this message:

```
Successful append operation      7 rows added
```

Using the SELECT command to view the contents of the History table verifies that it now contains June transactions, as Figure 14.7 shows.

```
R>SELECT #1=5 #2 #3=4 #4=8 #5=3 #6=8 #7 FROM History
 CustN ProdNo   Qty  U:Price  Tax Total    P:Date
 ----- -------- ---- -------- --- -------- --------
  1001 A-111      12   $10.00   1  $127.20 06/15/88
  1001 B-222       5   $12.50   1   $66.25 06/15/88
  1001 C-434       2  $100.00   1  $212.00 06/15/88
  1004 A-111       5   $10.00   1   $53.00 06/15/88
  1004 Z-128      10   $12.80   0  $128.00 06/15/88
  1007 A-111      10   $10.00   1  $106.00 06/15/88
  1007 Z-128      10   $12.80   0  $128.00 06/15/88
R>_
```

Figure 14.7: June transactions in the History table

With these transactions listed in the History table, you can use the DELETE command with a WHERE clause to delete them from the Charges table, as follows:

```
DELETE FROM Charges WHERE P:Date >= 6/1/88 +
+> AND P:Date <= 6/30/88
```

R:BASE replies

```
7 row(s) have been deleted from Charges
```

If you use the SELECT command to view the contents of the Charges table, you'll see that only the July transactions remain, as shown in Figure 14.8.

```
R>SELECT #1=5 #2 #3=4 #4=8 #5=3 #6=8 #7 FROM Charges
 CustN ProdNo   Qty  U:Price  Tax Total     P:Date
 ----- -------- ---- -------- --- -------- --------
  1002 B-222      12   $12.50   1  $159.00 07/01/88
  1002 A-111      10   $10.00   1  $106.00 07/01/88
R>_
```

Figure 14.8: July transactions in the Charges table

When the end of July rolls around, you can append the July transactions to the History table using this command:

```
APPEND Charges TO History WHERE P:Date >= 7/1/88 +
+> AND P:Date <= 7/31/88
```

R:BASE displays the following message:

```
Successful append operation     2 rows added
```

If you use the SELECT command to view the contents of the History table now, you'll see that it contains both the June and July transactions, as shown in Figure 14.9.

```
R>SELECT #1=5 #2 #3=4 #4=8 #5=3 #6=8 #7 FROM History
 CustN ProdNo    Qty  U:Price  Tax Total      P:Date
 ----- --------- ---- -------- --- --------- --------
  1001 A-111      12   $10.00   1  $127.20 06/15/88
  1001 B-222       5   $12.50   1   $66.25 06/15/88
  1001 C-434       2  $100.00   1  $212.00 06/15/88
  1004 A-111       5   $10.00   1   $53.00 06/15/88
  1004 Z-128      10   $12.80   0  $128.00 06/15/88
  1007 A-111      10   $10.00   1  $106.00 06/15/88
  1007 Z-128      10   $12.80   0  $128.00 06/15/88
  1002 B-222      12   $12.50   1  $159.00 07/01/88
  1002 A-111      10   $10.00   1  $106.00 07/01/88
R>_
```

Figure 14.9: June and July transactions in the History table

To clear the transactions from the Charges table, use the command

DELETE ROWS FROM Charges WHERE P:Date >= 7/1/88 +
+> AND P:Date <= 7/31/88

If you attempt to view the Charges table with the SELECT command, you'll see that it is empty, as below:

SELECT ALL FROM Charges
-WARNING- No data exists for this table

Now the Charges table is clear for adding new transactions for August, and the History table has a record of all June and July transactions.

If you've followed along on-line through these exercises, let's delete the History table and put the Charges table back into its original condition. First, remove the now empty Charges table with the command

```
REMOVE TABLE Charges
```

Then, change the name of the History table to Charges with the following command:

```
RENAME TABLE History TO Charges
```

Everything should now be as it was before we started these exercises.

COMBINING TWO TABLES WITH THE UNION COMMAND

The UNION command allows you to combine all or part of two existing tables into a new third table. The UNION command requires that the two tables have at least one common column (a key field). Common columns are those that have identical names, data types, and widths. An example of the UNION command is shown in Figure 14.10.

The basic syntax for the UNION command is the following:

UNION *table1* WITH *table2* FORMING *table3* USING *columns*

The UNION command will combine common columns into a single column on the new table. If you specify ALL in the USING portion of the command, the new table will include all the columns from the two original tables. If you specify only certain column names in the USING portion, the new table will contain the named columns in the order that you specified.

Suppose that you want a listing of the product numbers, customer numbers, names, quantities, and unit prices from the Charges and

Table1

Item	Qty
Apples	10
Bananas	20
Cherries	30

Table2

Item	Price
Apples	0.25
Bananas	0.50
Cherries	0.75
Rutabaga	1.00

UNION Table1 WITH Table2 FORMING Table3

Table3

Item	Qty	Price
Apples	10	$0.25
Bananas	20	$0.50
Cherries	30	$0.75
Rutabaga	-0-	$1.00

Figure 14.10: An example of the UNION command

Names tables. You could create a new table (named Temp in this example) with the appropriate information using the command below:

```
UNION Charges WITH Names FORMING Temp USING +
+ > ProdNo CustNo L:Name F:Name Qty U:Price
```

R:BASE responds as follows:

```
Successful union operation   14 rows generated
```

If you then enter the command

```
SELECT ProdNo = 6 CustNo = 5 L:Name = 10 F:Name = 7 +
+ > Qty = 4 U:Price = 8 FROM Temp
```

R:BASE displays the contents of the new Temp table, as shown in Figure 14.11.

```
R>SELECT ProdNo=6 CustNo=5 L:Name=10 F:Name=7 Qty=4 +
+>U:Price=8 FROM Temp
 ProdNo CustN L:Name     F:Name  Qty  U:Price
 ------ ----- ---------- ------- ---- --------
 A-111   1001 Smith      Sandy     12   $10.00
 B-222   1001 Smith      Sandy      5   $12.50
 C-434   1001 Smith      Sandy      2  $100.00
 A-111   1004 Adams      Bart       5   $10.00
 Z-128   1004 Adams      Bart      10   $12.80
 A-111   1007 Miller     Monica    10   $10.00
 Z-128   1007 Miller     Monica    10   $12.80
 B-222   1002 Jones      Andy      12   $12.50
 A-111   1002 Jones      Andy      10   $10.00
 -0-     1003 Miller     Marie   -0-  -0-
 -0-     1005 Miller     Anne    -0-  -0-
 -0-     1006 Baker      Robin   -0-  -0-
 -0-     1008 Teasdale   Trudy   -0-  -0-
 -0-     1009 Martin     Mary    -0-  -0-
R>_
```

Figure 14.11: The results of the UNION command

Notice that several rows have a null character in the ProdNo column. These null characters indicate that those individuals were not listed in the Charges table (because they didn't make any purchases). When one table has rows that do not match the second table, the UNION command will copy those rows to the new table and add null characters to the columns in nonmatching rows.

Let's use the UNION command to combine the Names and Charges tables in another way. Suppose that you want a listing of all customer numbers and company names, followed by a list of items purchased. Although we could just create a new table, for this example we'll remove the existing Temp table with the command

REMOVE TABLE Temp

Then, we'll create a new Temp table using the UNION command, with the Names table entered first and with the appropriate column names listed in the USING portion, as below:

UNION Names WITH Charges FORMING Temp +
+ > USING CustNo Company ProdNo Qty U:Price

R:BASE responds with the following:

```
Successful union operation      14 rows generated
```

To view the contents of the new Temp table, enter this command:

```
SELECT ALL FROM Temp
```

You should see the display shown in Figure 14.12.

```
R>SELECT ALL FROM Temp
 CustNo     Company                                ProdNo   Qty        U:Price
 ---------- ------------------------------------ -------- ---------- ---------------
       1001 Hi Tech, Inc.                          A-111           12          $10.00
       1001 Hi Tech, Inc.                          B-222            5          $12.50
       1001 Hi Tech, Inc.                          C-434            2         $100.00
       1002 ABC Co.                                B-222           12          $12.50
       1002 ABC Co.                                A-111           10          $10.00
       1003 Zeerox Inc.                            -0-      -0-         -0-
       1004 Dataspec Inc.                          A-111            5          $10.00
       1004 Dataspec Inc.                          Z-128           10          $12.80
       1005 Golden Gate Co.                        -0-      -0-         -0-
       1006 Peach Computers                        -0-      -0-         -0-
       1007 Acme Development                       A-111           10          $10.00
       1007 Acme Development                       Z-128           10          $12.80
       1008 Atomic Ovens                           -0-      -0-         -0-
       1009 Atomic Ovens                           -0-      -0-         -0-
R>_
```

Figure 14.12: The results of the second UNION command

Again, notice how the UNION command handled nonmatching rows. Since the Charges table showed no transactions for customers 1003, 1005, 1006, 1008, and 1009, these rows were displayed in the Temp table with null values in the ProdNo, Qty, and U:Price columns. As you'll see, the Intersect command handles this situation differently.

Go ahead and enter the command

```
REMOVE TABLE Temp
```

to delete the Temp table, and we'll experiment with the INTERSECT command.

COMBINING TABLES WITH THE INTERSECT COMMAND

The INTERSECT command is similar to the UNION command, except that it does not generate rows with null values. For example, when combining the Charges and Names tables with the UNION command, rows from the Names table that were not listed in the Charges table appear in the Temp table with null values. With the INTERSECT command, nonmatching rows are not added to the new table.

Like the UNION command, the INTERSECT command requires that the two tables have at least one common column (with identical names, data types, and widths). An example of the INTERSECT command is shown in Figure 14.13. The general syntax for the INTERSECT command is identical to the syntax for the UNION command, as shown below:

Table1

Item	**Qty**
Apples	10
Bananas	20
Cherries	30

Table2

Item	**Price**
Apples	.25
Bananas	.50
Cherries	.75
Rutabaga	1.00

INTERSECT Table1 WITH Table2 FORMING Table3

Table3

Item	**Qty**	**Price**
Apples	10	$0.25
Bananas	20	$0.50
Cherries	30	$0.75

Figure 14.13: An example of the INTERSECT command

INTERSECT *table1* WITH *table2* FORMING *table3* USING +
+ > *columns*

If you combine the Names and Charges tables using the INTERSECT command, as below:

INTERSECT Charges WITH Names FORMING Temp USING +
+ > ProdNo CustNo L:Name F:Name Qty U:Price

R:BASE will respond with this message:

Successful intersect operation 9 rows generated

If you then enter the command

SELECT ProdNo CustNo L:Name = 10 F:Name = 10 Qty = 4 +
+ > U:Price = 8 FROM Temp

you'll see the contents of the Temp table, as shown in Figure 14.14. As the figure shows, only the customers that appear in both the Names and Charges tables are included in the new table.

```
R>SELECT ProdNo CustNo L:Name=10 F:Name=10 Qty=4 U:Price=8 FROM Temp
 ProdNo   CustNo     L:Name     F:Name     Qty  U:Price
 -------- ---------- ---------- ---------- ---- --------
 A-111          1001 Smith      Sandy        12   $10.00
 B-222          1001 Smith      Sandy         5   $12.50
 C-434          1001 Smith      Sandy         2  $100.00
 A-111          1004 Adams      Bart          5   $10.00
 Z-128          1004 Adams      Bart         10   $12.80
 A-111          1007 Miller     Monica       10   $10.00
 Z-128          1007 Miller     Monica       10   $12.80
 B-222          1002 Jones      Andy         12   $12.50
 A-111          1002 Jones      Andy         10   $10.00
R>_
```

Figure 14.14: The results of the first INTERSECT command

Let's try another example. First, enter

REMOVE TABLE Temp

to eliminate the Temp table. Now we'll create a table with customer numbers and company names, followed by product numbers, quantities, and unit prices. Enter the command

INTERSECT Names WITH Charges FORMING Temp USING +
+ > CustNo Company ProdNo Qty U:Price

If you use the SELECT command to view the results of the INTERSECT command, as below:

SELECT ALL FROM Temp

you'll see that only the customers listed in both the Names and Charges tables made it to the Temp table, as Figure 14.15 shows.

```
R>SELECT ALL FROM Temp
 CustNo     Company                          ProdNo   Qty         U:Price
 ---------- -------------------------------- -------- ---------- ---------------
       1001 Hi Tech, Inc.                    A-111            12          $10.00
       1001 Hi Tech, Inc.                    B-222             5          $12.50
       1001 Hi Tech, Inc.                    C-434             2         $100.00
       1002 ABC Co.                          B-222            12          $12.50
       1002 ABC Co.                          A-111            10          $10.00
       1004 Dataspec Inc.                    A-111             5          $10.00
       1004 Dataspec Inc.                    Z-128            10          $12.80
       1007 Acme Development                 A-111            10          $10.00
       1007 Acme Development                 Z-128            10          $12.80
R>_
```

Figure 14.15: The results of the second INTERSECT command

We've seen that the UNION command transferred all the rows from both the Names and Charges table to the new table, including those that did not have common customer numbers. The result was that we could see the purchases made by various customers, as well as see the customers who made no purchases. The INTERSECT command, however, copied only those rows that had common values in both the Names and Charges tables; we thus saw a listing of purchases made by various customers, without seeing the customers who didn't make purchases.

Suppose you wanted to see a listing of only those customers who didn't make any purchases (the opposite of what the INTERSECT command provided). In this case, you could use the SUBTRACT command. Again, remove the Temp table so that we can use it for the next exercise by entering

```
REMOVE TABLE Temp
```

VIEWING DIFFERENCES WITH THE SUBTRACT COMMAND

The SUBTRACT command forms a new table of rows that do not match on two existing tables. An example of the SUBTRACT command is shown in Figure 14.16. The general syntax for the command is

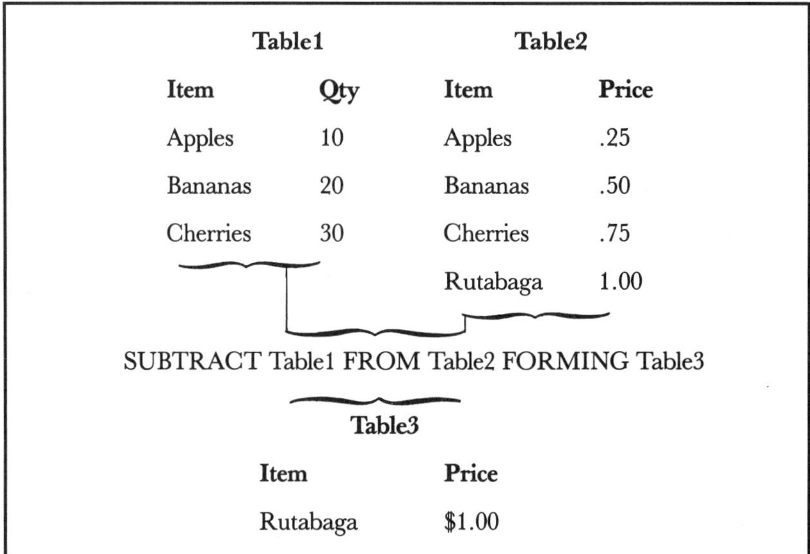

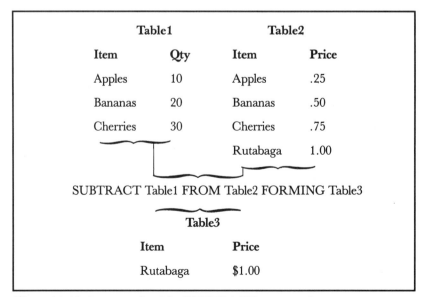

Figure 14.16: An example of the SUBTRACT command

```
SUBTRACT small table FROM large table FORMING +
+ > new table USING column names
```

The *small table* is not necessarily physically smaller than the *large table,* but instead it might be a subset of the other table. For example, even if the Charges table contained 1000 rows, it would be the smaller table in this example because it might not contain every customer number. The Names table is the *large table* because it does contain every customer number.

To find out which customers in the Names table did not make purchases (that is, the ones that do not appear on the Charges table), subtract the Charges table from the Names table using the command

```
SUBTRACT Charges FROM Names FORMING Temp
```

R:BASE responds with the following:

```
Successful subtract operation      5 rows generated
```

When you enter the command

```
SELECT ALL FROM Temp
```

you'll see the five customers who are not included in the Charges table, as shown in Figure 14.17.

Note that if you do attempt to subtract a large table from a smaller one, you'll end up with no rows on the new table, as below (note the message "0 rows generated"):

```
SUBTRACT Names FROM Charges FORMING Temp
Successful subtract operation      0 rows generated
```

COMBINING TABLES WITH THE JOIN COMMAND

The JOIN command works in much the same way as the UNION command, except for two important differences:

- The JOIN command allows you to compare column data from two tables using any of the various operators, such as equal, not equal, greater than, and less than.

```
R>SELECT ALL FROM Temp
 CustNo      L:Name           F:Name           Company              Address
 ----------  ---------------  ---------------  -------------------- --------------
       1003  Miller           Marie            Zeerox, Inc.         234 C St.
       1005  Miller           Anne             Golden Gate Co.      2313 Sixth St.
       1006  Baker            Robin            Peach Computers      2311 Coast Hwy
       1008  Teasdale         Trudy            Atomic Ovens, Inc.   321 Microwave
       1009  Martin           Mary             Atomic Ovens, Inc.   321 Microwave
R>_
```

Figure 14.17: The results of the SUBTRACT command

- The columns used for comparing the two tables may have different names; however, the two columns must be of the same data type and length.

The general syntax for the JOIN command is

JOIN *table1* USING *column name* WITH *table2* USING +
\+ > *column name* FORMING *table3* WHERE *operator*

The operator used with the WHERE clause may be any of the following:

OPERATOR	***MEANING***
EQ	Equal
NE	Not equal
GT	Greater than
GE	Greater than or equal to
LT	Less than
LE	Less than or equal to

Figure 14.18 gives an example of the JOIN command used with the EQ operator. Since the Names and Charges tables both have a column named CustNo, we'll demonstrate this command with a hypothetical database.

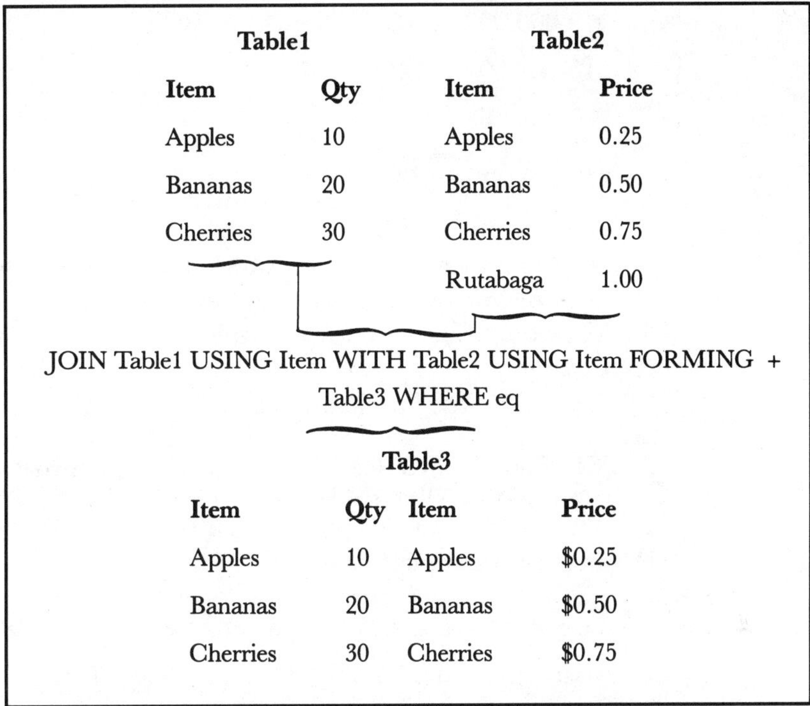

Table1

Item	**Qty**
Apples	10
Bananas	20
Cherries	30

Table2

Item	**Price**
Apples	0.25
Bananas	0.50
Cherries	0.75
Rutabaga	1.00

JOIN Table1 USING Item WITH Table2 USING Item FORMING +
Table3 WHERE eq

Table3

Item	**Qty**	**Item**	**Price**
Apples	10	Apples	$0.25
Bananas	20	Bananas	$0.50
Cherries	30	Cherries	$0.75

Figure 14.18: An example of the JOIN command with the EQ operator

Suppose that you have a database with two tables: one named Sales and the other named Commiss. The Sales table contains salespersons' names and sales amounts, as below:

NAME	***SALE***
Andrews	$12,500.00
Baker	$17,000.00
Carlson	$10,000.00
Edwards	$ 5,000.00
Davis	$45,000.00

The Commiss table contains commission rates and cutoff values, starting with a base rate of 15% for any sale that's at least $10,000, and adding another 2% of the total for larger sales, as below:

SALESAMT	*C:RATE*
$10,000.00	0.15
$15,000.00	0.02
$20,000.00	0.02
$25,000.00	0.02

We want to use the JOIN command to combine the Sales table, using the Sale column for comparison, with the Commiss table, using the SalesAmt column for comparison, to form a new table named Rates, and we want to use the greater than or equal to operator for the comparison.

To do this, we use the command

```
JOIN Sales USING Sale WITH Commiss USING SalesAmt +
+ > FORMING Rates WHERE GE
```

The resulting Rates table is listed below:

NAME	*SALE*	*SALESAMT*	*C:RATE*
Andrews	$12,500.00	$10,000.00	0.15
Baker	$17,000.00	$10,000.00	0.15
Baker	$17,000.00	$15,000.00	0.02
Carlson	$10,000.00	$10,000.00	0.15
Davis	$45,000.00	$10,000.00	0.15
Davis	$45,000.00	$15,000.00	0.02
Davis	$45,000.00	$20,000.00	0.02
Davis	$45,000.00	$25,000.00	0.02

Notice that Mr. Andrews receives a 15% commission for his $12,500 sale; Mr. Baker receives 15%, plus another 2%, for his $17,000 sale; and Mr. Davis receives 15%, plus another 6% (2% three times) for his

$45,000 sale. Displaying this table without the SalesAmt column, but instead displaying the total commission, makes the table clearer, as shown in Figure 14.19.

```
R>SELECT Name Sale C:Rate (Sale * C:Rate) FROM Rates
 name     sale             c:rate   COMPUTED
 -------- ---------------- -------- ----------------
 Andrews       $12,500.00      0.15        $1,875.00
 Baker         $17,000.00      0.15        $2,550.00
 Baker         $17,000.00      0.02          $340.00
 Carlson       $10,000.00      0.15        $1,500.00
 Davis         $45,000.00      0.15        $6,750.00
 Davis         $45,000.00      0.02          $900.00
 Davis         $45,000.00      0.02          $900.00
 Davis         $45,000.00      0.02          $900.00
R>_
```

Figure 14.19: Rows from the Rates table, including a computed column

Notice that the JOIN command creates a row for each comparison that satisfies the WHERE operator. Davis is listed four times because his $45,000 sale is greater than or equal to all of the SalesAmt figures in the Commiss table. However, Edwards's $5000 sale was not included in the Rates table, because it was not greater than or equal to any of the SalesAmt cutoff values in the Commiss table.

Finally, note that you could also use the SUBTRACT command to determine lackluster sales performance. By subtracting the Rates table from the Sales table, using the command

```
SUBTRACT Rates FROM Names FORMING Temp
```

you can isolate those salespeople who do not appear on the Rates table in a new table named Temp. Edwards is the only entry in the Temp table, since he hasn't made a sale big enough to merit a commission.

CONSTRUCTING VIEWS

We've already talked about views in general terms in chapters 10 and 12, but because of their usefulness, we should spend a bit more time going over them in depth now. A *view,* you will remember, is a *pseudo-table* that, rather than containing data of its own, displays data from up to five related tables. The tables in a view must have at least one key column (with the same column name, width, and data type) in common. Once you have created a view, you can view data through it as you would any other table. For example, you can use the view with the SELECT command and the ORDER BY and WHERE clauses. You can also use the view as a table for creating report formats in Reports EXPRESS.

There are limitations on views, however. Since a view only displays data from existing tables, you cannot enter data directly into it. Nor can you edit data through the view except in the special case of single-table views. For that matter, you cannot create forms for a view at all. Instead, you'll want to enter and edit data through the actual tables from which the view gets its data. Nonetheless, a view is a convenient and dynamic tool for viewing data from multiple tables quickly and easily.

For this exercise, we'll create a view that displays the customer number, product number, quantity, tax status, unit price, transaction total, and date of sale from the Charges table, along with the appropriate last name, first name, and company from the Names table. To further demonstrate the power of views, we'll limit the view to customers in the state of California (although R:BASE does not require that you place such limits on views). We'll name the view CaTrans (for California Transactions).

DEFINING A VIEW

To define a view, enter Definition EXPRESS by entering the command

```
RBDEFINE
```

at the R> prompt. From the Definition EXPRESS Main menu, select option 2 to *Modify an existing database definition.* From the options submenu, select option 2, Views. You'll see the Views menu with the options below:

(1) Add a new view to the database
(2) Change an existing view
(3) Remove a view from the database
(4) Return to the Database Definition Menu

To create a new view, select option 1. You'll see a screen that resembles the one in which you create a new table. The screen asks that you

Enter the name for this view:

Like tables, a view can have a name with up to eight letters. (It must begin with a letter and include no spaces or punctuation.) For this example, type in the name

CaTrans

and press Enter.

The screen asks for the name of the first table to be used in the view. In this example, we're primarily interested in rows from the Charges table (that is, we want to view every transaction in the Charges table). Therefore, select Charges from the list of table names.

Next, the screen asks which column from Charges you want to include in the view. For this example, select ALL, though you could select only certain column names. All the column names fill in on the main part of the screen, as shown in Figure 14.20. (The CustNo column is off the left edge of the screen.)

Next, press the Enter key to select the next table for the view. From the menu of table names that appears, select Names. The column names for the Names table appear on a menu at the bottom of the screen.

From the Names table, we'll want the L:Name, F:Name, Company, and State columns. To select a column name, move the highlighter to the appropriate name and press Enter. (We need the State column in this example because we're going to place a WHERE clause in the view that limits the view to California residents. You can select any other column names that you wish for the view.)

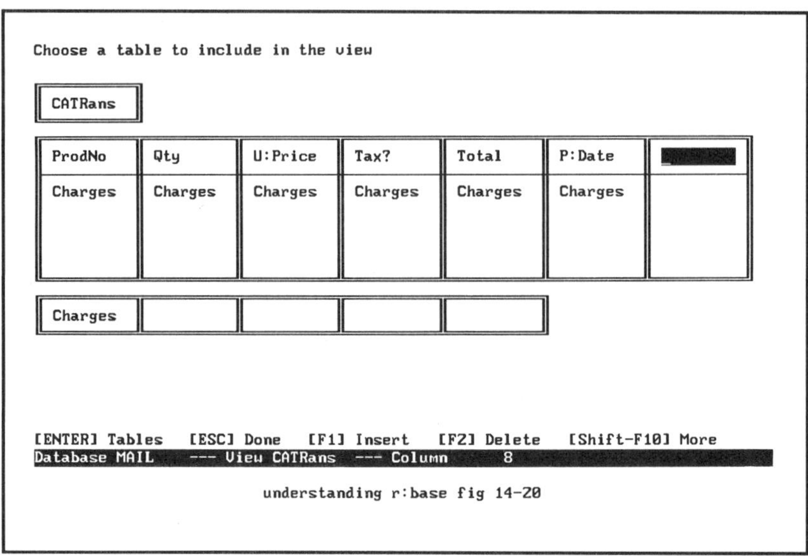

Figure 14.20: All column names from Charges selected for the view

After you select the column names, they appear in the table portion of the screen, as in Figure 14.21. (Most of the column names from the Charges table have been pushed off the left edge of the screen.) Press Esc twice to continue constructing the view.

Choose a table to include in the view

CaTrans

Total	P:Date	L:Name	F:Name	Company	state	
charges	charges	names	names	names	names	

charges | names

Choose the columns to include from names
Address City Zip Ent:Date Phone (Reset)

[ENTER] Choose [ESC] Done [F1] Insert [F2] Delete [Shift-F10] More
Database mail --- View CaTrans --- Column 12

Figure 14.21: Column names from the Names table in the view

BUILDING CONDITIONS FOR THE VIEW

After selecting the columns for the view, you'll see a screen asking you to choose a column to validate. This amounts to including a WHERE clause in the view. You can leave this blank (thereby not limiting the view to any particular rows) by pressing the Esc key. In this example, however, we'll limit the view to California residents.

The screen asks that you

Choose column to validate:

Select State, since this is the column of interest. The screen then asks that you select an operator and presents the following (now familiar) operators:

EQ NE GT GE LT LE CONTAINS EXISTS FAILS

For this example, select EQ (for equals). The screen asks that you

Enter value to be used for comparison:

Since we want this view to be limited to California residents, type in CA and press Enter. The completed WHERE clause definition appears on the screen, along with options for extending the clause, as in Figure 14.22.

You can select a logical operator (such as AND or OR) to add conditions to the WHERE clause. However, for this example, just select (Done). That completes the view definition. Now select options 4, 5, and 3 from the higher-level menus to leave Definition EXPRESS and return to the R> prompt.

At the R> prompt, type **LIST** to see the tables in your database. Note that there are two new tables: VIEWS and VIEWWHER. These are the tables that R:BASE uses to keep track of your view definition and conditions.

You also have a new "table" called CaTrans. If you type

```
LIST CaTrans
```

you'll see a list of all the columns in the view. The current number of rows, however, is listed as N/A, reminding you that no actual rows are stored in this view. When you use the view, R:BASE assembles the view by getting up-to-date data from its underlying tables.

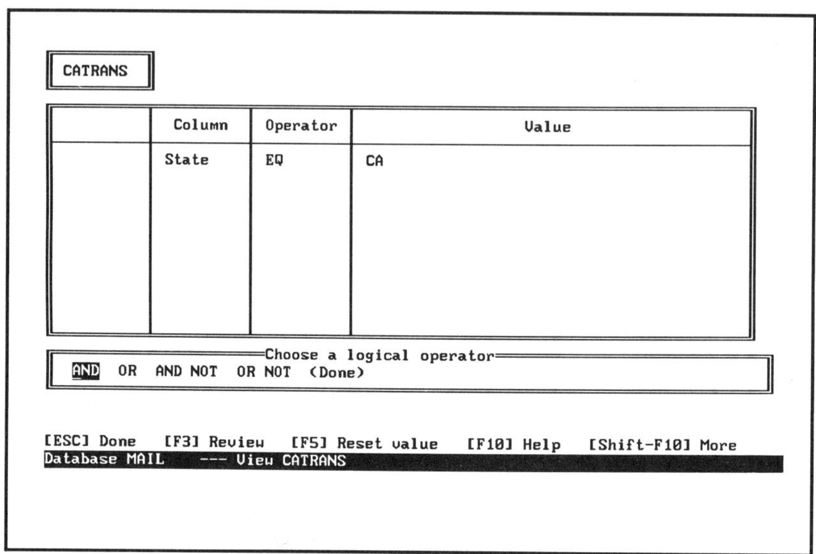

Figure 14.22: Your view limited to California residents

USING THE VIEW TO DISPLAY DATA

You can use the SELECT command in the usual way with the view, using the name of the view (that is, CaTrans) in place of a particular table name. For example, suppose you want to see all the transactions for California residents, with name, company, and state for each transaction, sorted into ascending product number order and descending total order. Entering the command below will show the information you want:

```
SELECT ProdNo=6 Qty=4 U:Price=8 Total=8 +
+> CustNo=6 L:Name=7 F:Name=7 Company=15 State +
+> FROM CaTrans ORDER BY ProdNo Qty=D
```

The results of this SELECT command are shown in Figure 14.23.

To see a list of customer numbers and company names with product numbers, quantity purchased, and date of sales, enter the command

```
SELECT CustNo Company=15 ProdNo Qty Total P:Date +
+> FROM CaTrans
```

```
R>SELECT ProdNo=6 Qty=4 U:Price=8 Total=8 CustNo=6 L:Name=7 F:Name=7 Company=+
+>15 State FROM CaTrans ORDER BY ProdNo Qty=D
 ProdNo Qty  U:Price  Total    CustNo L:Name  F:Name  Company         state
 ------ ---- -------- -------- ------ ------- ------- --------------- --------
 A-111    12   $10.00  $127.20   1001 Smith   Sandy   Hi Tech, Inc.   CA
 A-111    10   $10.00  $106.00   1002 Jones   Mindy   ABC Co.         CA
 A-111     5   $10.00   $53.00   1004 Adams   Bart    DataSpec Inc.   CA
 B-222    12   $12.50  $159.00   1002 Jones   Mindy   ABC Co.         CA
 B-222     5   $12.50   $66.25   1001 Smith   Sandy   Hi Tech, Inc.   CA
 C-434     2  $100.00  $212.00   1001 Smith   Sandy   Hi Tech, Inc.   CA
 Z-128    10   $12.80  $128.00   1004 Adams   Bart    DataSpec Inc.   CA
R>_
```

Figure 14.23: A display from the CaTrans view

The results will appear on your screen as in Figure 14.24.

```
R>SELECT ALL FROM Newview
 custno     company              prodno   qty        U:price
 ---------- -------------------- -------- ---------- ---------------
       1001 Hi Tech, Inc.        A-111            12          $10.00
       1001 Hi Tech, Inc.        B-222             5          $12.50
       1001 Hi Tech, Inc.        C-434             2         $100.00
       1004 DataSpec Inc.        A-111             5          $10.00
       1004 DataSpec Inc.        Z-128            10          $12.80
       1007 Acme Development     A-111            10          $10.00
       1007 Acme Development     Z-128            10          $12.80
       1002 ABC Co.              B-222            12          $12.50
       1002 ABC Co.              A-111            10          $10.00
R>_
```

Figure 14.24: Another display from the CaTrans view

To use the view as the basis for a report, enter Reports EXPRESS in the usual fashion. When asked to supply the name of the table that the report is to display data from, select CaTrans, as though it were a table.

VIEWS COMPARED WITH INTERSECT TABLES

Some of you may have wondered about the relationship between a view and tables created with the INTERSECT or UNION commands. At the beginning of the chapter you saw the difference between the INTERSECT and UNION commands when you created a new table with the ProdNo, CustNo, L:Name, F:Name, Qty, and U:Price columns. The UNION command was more comprehensive, yielding a new table that included all rows from both tables. On the other hand, the new table created with INTERSECT only included rows if there was matching data from both of the parent tables. How does a view work?

To make the comparison, let's create a view that parallels these tables. You can do that either with RBDEFINE or directly from the R> prompt. Let's try the latter this time. You can use either the standard R:BASE or R:BASE SQL syntax for creating a view from the R> prompt:

```
VIEW viewname WITH column list FROM table list WHERE +
+ > conditions
```

or

```
CREATE VIEW view name AS SELECT column list FROM +
+ > table list WHERE conditions
```

To create a view called Newview, type the following:

```
VIEW Newview WITH ProdNo CustNo L:Name F:Name Qty +
+ > U:Price FROM Names Charges
```

R:BASE should respond with a message that 9 rows have been created. To see if they match the rows created with the parallel INTERSECT command, typc

```
SELECT ALL FROM Newview
```

If you compare the rows with those in Figure 14.10, you'll see they're the same.

Although a view seems to yield the same result as an INTERSECT command, there is one important difference. When you create a new table with INTERSECT, you are in effect taking a snapshot of the two parent table's contents at a given moment. If you make additions to either of the parent tables, you'll have to give another INTERSECT command if you need to have the new data in a single table. A view, however, is dynamic. Any changes in the parent tables are automatically recognized by the view.

You may want to remove the view Newview at this time by typing

```
REMOVE VIEW Newview
```

or

```
DROP VIEW NewView
```

You can also remove a view from within Definition EXPRESS or PBE.

USING A VIEW TO CREATE A FORM LETTER REPORT

Let's assume that your friend in the book business wants to follow up on a new product line he's been marketing. His company wants to write each of its California customers a personal letter to see how they like the products they've purchased. This is a job for Reports EXPRESS. However, before jumping into the report, you need to choose the table or view upon which the report will be based. We need the following information: client name, address, city, state, ZIP, and the types of products purchased by that client. The CaTrans view has everything we need except the address, city, and ZIP. Why not just modify it? No problem. Views, like tables, can be modified in Definition EXPRESS.

MODIFYING A VIEW

To add needed columns to your view, type **RBDEFINE** at the R> prompt, and select option 2, *Modify an existing database definition*, 2,

Views, and 2, *Change an existing view*. Select CaTrans. Then press Enter to accept the current view name, and press the End key to move the highlighter to a new column. Press Enter to select a table, and select Names. It should be the only one listed. Then select the Address, City, and Zip columns. When you are finished, press the Escape key. R:BASE is now giving you the opportunity to change the view's conditions. If you wanted to delete the current WHERE clause limiting the view to California residents, you could press the F2 function key. However, simply press Esc again to accept the current condition, and exit Definition EXPRESS by pressing Esc three times.

Now you're ready to create the form letter report.

MAILMERGING WITH R:BASE

Start Reports EXPRESS by typing **REPORTS** at the R> prompt. Select option 1, *Edit/Create a report*, and select New. Call your report CaLetter, and tell R:BASE that it will be based on the CaTrans view. Then choose Expression and define the following expressions:

```
Rptdate = .#DATE
Holname = (F:Name & L:Name)
Holname2 = (.Holname + ":")
```

Return to the Report Definition menu by pressing the Escape key twice, and from there select Configure. We're going to need to establish breakpoints.

The report is based on a view that has multiple rows for customers who've ordered more than one item, but we don't want to send customers multiple copies of the letter. However, we do want to list the items they've purchased. What can we do? One solution is to make CustNo the first breakpoint and to locate most of the letter on the H1 and F1 lines. Then we can locate ProdNo on a single Detail line. The report will then print a single letter for each customer, but list all the items they've charged. Go ahead and enter CustNo in the area for the Break1 column, and set *Form Feed Before Header* to Yes so that each letter is printed on a separate page.

You may want to add your own flourishes to the letter, which has been squeezed in Figure 14.25, but you'll get the general idea by studying it. Rptdate is located in the upper-right corner of the report; Holname, Address, City, State, and Zip are in the address area; and Holname2 is located after the salutation. ProdNo is located on the Detail line.

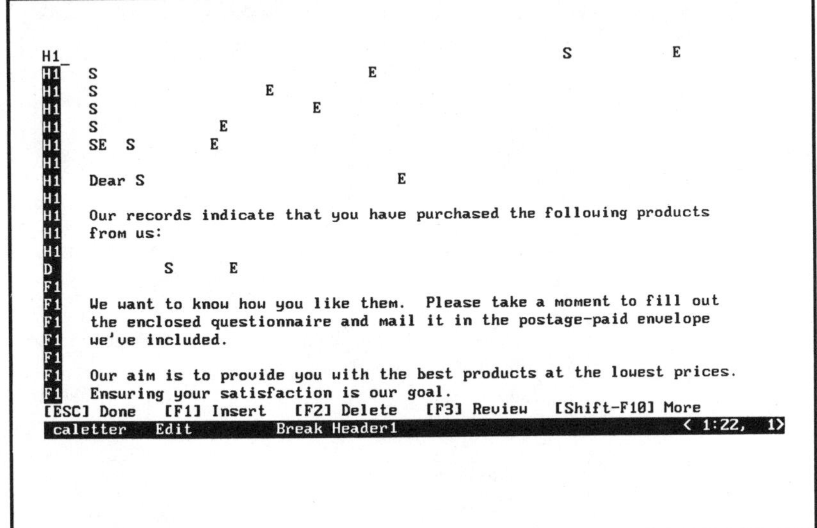

Figure 14.25: The form letter report for mailmerging

Once you've created the report, exit Reports EXPRESS and test it by typing

PRINT CaLetter

A sample letter is displayed in Figure 14.26. Note that the date is displayed in long format, rather than simply as MM/DD/YY. That's because the DATE FORMAT display was changed to MMM + DD, YYYY prior to printing the report.

DATABASE MAINTENANCE

Those of you who have done the exercises in this chapter may have noticed that your Mail2.RBF file has grown considerably. That's because when you remove a table from a database, R:BASE doesn't automatically free the disk space that was used by the data. For that

02/19/88

Sandy Smith
Hi Tech, Inc.
456 N. Rainbow Dr.
Berkeley
CA 94721

Dear Sandy Smith:

Our records indicate that you have purchased the following products from us:

A-111
B-222
C-434

We want to know how you like them. Please take a moment to fill out the enclosed questionnaire and mail it in the postage-paid envelope we've included.

Our aim is to provide you with the best products at the lowest prices. Ensuring your satisfaction is our goal.

Sincerely,

Bob Smith, President
ABC Company

Figure 14.26: A sample letter from the CaLetter report

matter, it doesn't free the disk space used by rows that have subsequently been deleted from a table, either. R:BASE provides two different commands that squeeze unused disk space from your database, but before you use either of them, you should back up your database.

BACKING UP AND RESTORING A DATABASE

In Chapter 6 you learned to use the COPY and BACKUP commands to back up your database, either from within R:BASE or directly from the operating system. To decide which command to use, you should look at the size of your database files and compare them with the capacity of your floppy disks. (Generally, it's not a good idea to back up a database onto the same hard disk it's already on, because this wouldn't help if your hard disk "crashed.") If none of your database files is larger than the capacity of a floppy disk, it's easiest simply to back up your database onto floppies with the COPY command.

If your database is too large for floppies, you'll have to use either R:BASE's or DOS's BACKUP command. We recommend R:BASE's, because it is optimized to back up R:BASE databases. To back up your open database, prepare a stack of formatted floppy disks (not system disks, just disks formatted using FORMAT A:, for example), put one of them into your floppy drive, and type the following:

```
SET NULL -0-
OUTPUT filespec (for example, OUTPUT A:Names.BAK)
BACKUP ALL
OUTPUT SCREEN
```

If your database is large, you'll be prompted to insert additional disks. Be sure to number your disks as Backup disk #1, Backup disk #2, and so on. Don't be surprised if the backed up version of your database takes up less space than you expected—the database files are compressed during the BACKUP procedure.

If you need to use the backed up version of your database, erase the existing version of the database from your hard disk, put Backup disk #1 in your floppy drive, and from the R> prompt type the following:

```
SET NULL -0-
RESTORE filespec (for example, RESTORE A:Names.BAK)
```

As before, R:BASE will prompt you to change disks if necessary.

RECOVERING UNUSED DISK SPACE

You have two methods for recovering unused disk space that results from DELETE and REMOVE commands. The easiest, PACK, is also the riskiest, because PACK acts on the actual database files you specify. For example, if you have one copy of the Mail database on your hard disk, and want to squeeze unused disk space out of it, you could type

```
OPEN Mail
```

and then

```
PACK
```

Generally, R:BASE would simply pack the database as instructed, without problem. The result would be a new version of the Mail database that takes up less space. However, if an error or machine malfunction occurred during the PACK, you might end up with an unusable version of Mail. If you didn't have a backup copy of Mail, you'd be out of luck. The virtue of the PACK command is that it is fast, and doesn't require much free space on your hard disk to execute the command.

The second method is to use R:BASE's RELOAD command. Since RELOAD makes an entirely new copy of the database, you need to have sufficient hard disk space to accommodate the new copy of the database. The RELOAD command differs from the PACK command in another way, too. RELOAD not only removes unused disk space from your database files; it also optimizes them, placing, for example, all rows from a given table in a single area on your hard disk. If you wanted to RELOAD your mail database, you could type

```
OPEN Mail
```

and then

```
RELOAD Mailbak
```

R:BASE would create a database called Mailbak in the default directory. Before erasing the Mail files, however, you should OPEN Mailbak, and use the LIST and SELECT commands to be sure the Mailbak database is intact. Then you could use the RENAME command to change the names of the Mailbak1.RBF file to Mail1.RBF, Mailbak2.RBF to Mail2.RBF, and Mailbak3.RBF file to Mail3.RBF.

In this chapter, we've looked at R:BASE's six relational commands: PROJECT, APPEND, UNION, INTERSECT, SUBTRACT, and JOIN. We've also looked at some new techniques for views, mailmerging, and backing up files. With the next chapter, we'll start developing all of our techniques so far into a unified application.

Chapter 15

Developing Your Own Applications

FAST TRACK

- Delete a menu option.
- Add a new menu option to any menu.
- Insert a menu option between existing options.
- Change the method of exiting a menu.
- Add or modify Help screens.
- Change the actions associated with a menu option.
- Add actions to any menu option, either before or after existing actions.

To customize the application environment— 432
screen colors, message display, or the use of the beep during errors—select option 3 from the Application menu.

BEGINNING IN THIS CHAPTER, WE'LL LEARN TECHniques for organizing all the tables, forms, and reports in a database into a unified *application*. While R:BASE is a general database-management system, an application is a system of menus that manages all aspects of a specific database for a particular task. For example, an application may manage a mailing, accounts-receivable, general-ledger, or inventory system.

The real advantage of an application is that it allows even a novice user to manage a database by using a series of menus, rather than by typing commands. As we'll learn in this chapter, R:BASE applications are easy to develop. In fact, you can create applications more quickly and efficiently with R:BASE than you can with most database-management systems.

The best way to understand the concept of an application is to develop one and use it. In this chapter, we'll develop a sample application using the familiar Mail database.

DESIGNING AN APPLICATION

Once you've designed and developed the tables, forms, and reports that you want to use in a database, designing the application simply involves defining a hierarchical structure of menus. Figure 15.1 shows the menu structure that we'll use to manage the Names and Charges tables in the Mail database.

The Main menu in the figure presents three options: 1, Manage Customer List (meaning the Names table); 2, Manage Charges List (meaning the Charges table); and 3, Exit (meaning that you want to return to the R> prompt). If the user selects menu option 1, Sub-Menu 1 is displayed on the screen. From this menu, the user can select from several options to add new data to the Names table, edit the table, print any of three different reports, or return to the Main menu. Similarly, if the user selects option 2, a submenu for managing the Charges table is displayed on the screen.

You can design your menu system in any way that you wish. For example, you could include an option on the Main menu for printing reports, and group all the various report options under a separate menu. Also, you can create sub-submenus below submenus. Finally,

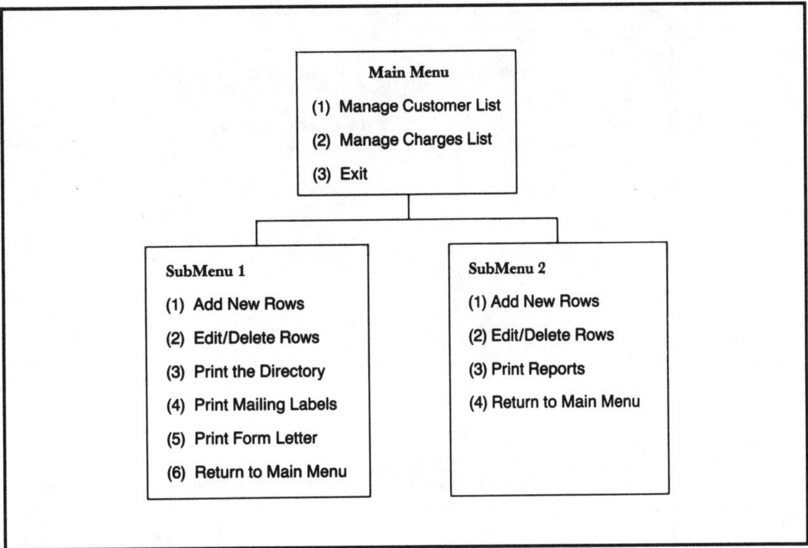

Figure 15.1: The menu structure for an application

and perhaps most importantly, you can always change your mind and redesign your application at any time. You can add new menus, change menu items, and even insert new options into existing menus. This is important because application development is usually an iterative process, and perfecting an application usually involves a series of increasing enhancements and refinements.

DEVELOPING AN APPLICATION

Once you've sketched the menus for your application, you can use Application EXPRESS to start building the application. As with Forms and Reports EXPRESS, you can enter Application EXPRESS from either of two methods. Type in the command EXPRESS at the R> prompt, and press Enter; or select option 2, *Create or modify an R:BASE application* from the PBE Main menu.

The Application EXPRESS Main menu appears on the screen as in Figure 15.2. Options 1 and 2 let you create or modify an application. Option 3 exits Application EXPRESS back to wherever you started from.

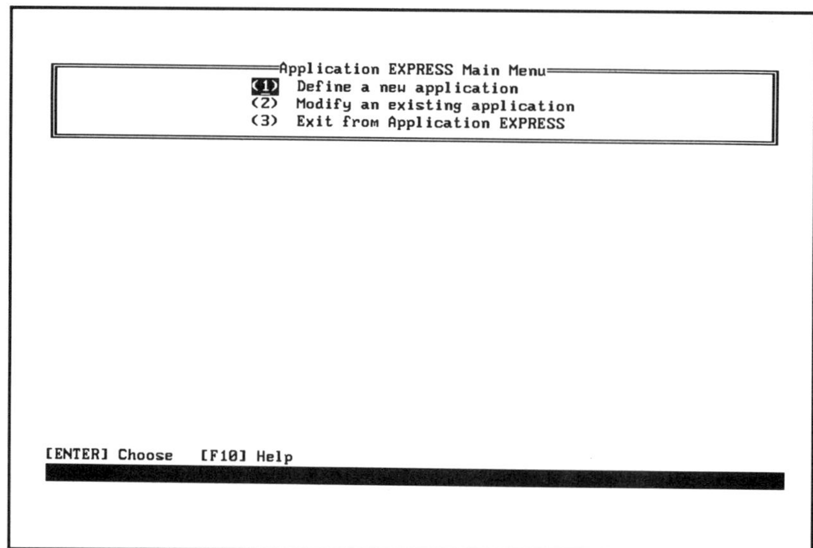

Figure 15.2: The Application EXPRESS Main menu

To create a new application now, select option 1. If there is no database currently open, the screen will ask you to choose a database and present the names of existing databases. If necessary, select Mail as the database name for this application. (Note: If at any time you feel lost and want to exit Application EXPRESS without saving your work, press the break keys. On some IBM keyboards, you hold down the Ctrl key and press Scroll Lock to break; on others you hold down the Ctrl key and press Break.)

Next, R:BASE asks for a name for the application. The name cannot be longer than eight characters or contain any blank spaces or punctuation marks. For this example, enter the name **MailSys** and press Enter. R:BASE then asks for a name for the Main menu. Again, the name needs to be limited to eight characters. R:BASE suggests the name Main, which is a good suggestion, so press the Enter key.

Now the screen displays options for displaying the menu vertically or horizontally. A vertical menu provides more flexibility, so select the Vertical option by pressing the Enter key.

Next, R:BASE asks for a title for the Main menu. Unlike the menu name, which R:BASE uses to store the program information, the menu title is displayed on the screen and can be of any length with spaces and punctuation marks. This is the title that application users will see. Type in the title **Main Menu**, and press Enter. R:BASE automatically centers the title. Then it asks for the text for the first menu option. Type in the phrase

Manage Customer List

and press Enter. R:BASE then asks for the text for menu option 2. Type in

Manage Charges List

and press Enter. R:BASE asks for the text for the third option. Type in the word

Exit

You've just developed the first menu as it will appear on the screen later when you use the application. Your screen should look like Figure 15.3. Press the Esc key to continue developing the MailSys application.

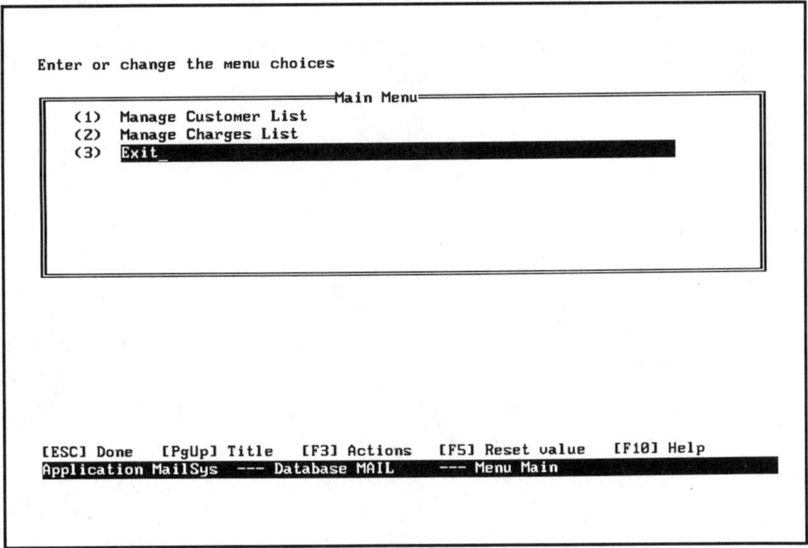

Figure 15.3: The first menu designed for the MailSys application

Next, R:BASE wants to know if the Esc key should be used to exit the menu. Select the Yes option by pressing the Enter key. (Although option (3) on the Main menu provides for exiting, there is certainly no harm in allowing the Esc key to be used to exit the menu as well.)

R:BASE then asks if you want to develop a custom help screen for this menu. We can add that later, so for now select the No option.

R:BASE needs to know what actions should be associated with the first menu option. Several options are displayed on the screen, as shown in Figure 15.4. The actions that you can associate with a menu option are listed below:

OPTION	*ACTION*
Load	Enter new data into a table.
Edit	Edit and delete data using a predefined form.
Delete	Globally delete rows from a table.
Modify	Edit and delete rows using an edit screen.
Select	Look up specific information in a table.
Print	Print a report.
Custom	Develop a custom action for this menu choice.
Macro	Use a predefined custom action.
Template	Access a custom procedure.
Menu	Build a submenu for this menu option.
Password	Initiate a password.
Exit	Exit this menu.

Some of the more advanced options displayed, such as *Custom, Template, Macro,* and *Password* will be more meaningful to you after we discuss the R:BASE programming language in the next chapter. For now, however, the other options are sufficient for developing the MailSys application.

In this example, you want menu option 1 to branch to a submenu for managing the Names table. Press the down arrow to move the highlighting to the Menu choice and press Enter. When R:BASE asks for a name for the submenu, type in the name **SubMenu1** and press Enter. Select the Vertical option.

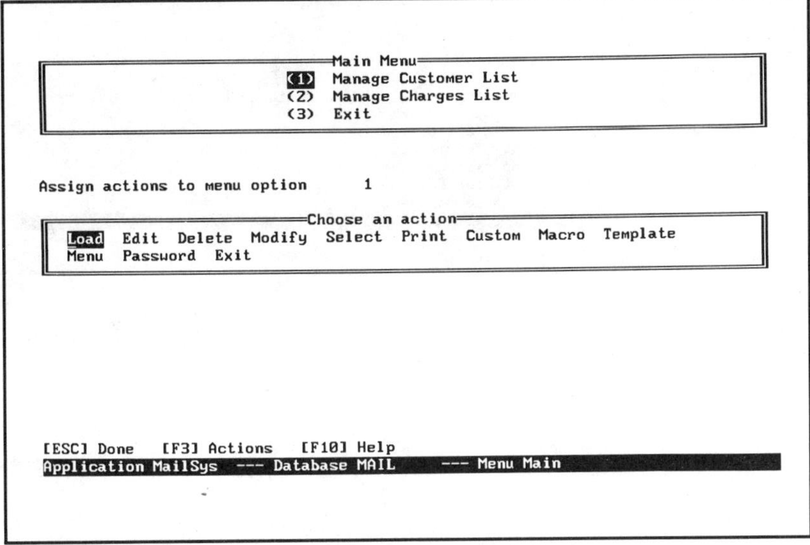

Figure 15.4: The screen for selecting actions for menu options

R:BASE needs to know what this submenu should look like. The screen will ask that you fill in a title for this submenu. Type in the title

Manage Customer List

and press Enter. Next, type in the menu text shown below. Press Enter after typing in each option.

1. **Add New Customers**
2. **Edit/Delete Customers**
3. **Print the Directory**
4. **Print Mailing Labels**
5. **Print Form Letter**
6. **Return to Main Menu**

When you're finished, your screen should look like Figure 15.5. (It doesn't matter whether or not you press Enter after typing the last menu item.) Press Esc after you've filled in the menu options. R:BASE returns you to the Main menu and displays the prompt

Do you want another action for the current menu option? Yes No

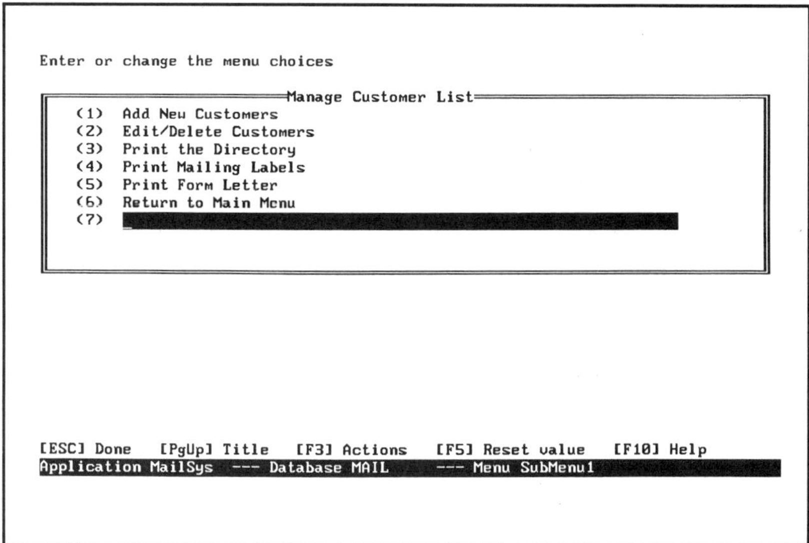

Figure 15.5: SubMenu1 defined on the screen

If you select Yes, you can add additional actions to this menu item. For this example, select No.

Next, R:BASE allows you to define actions for option 2 of the Main menu. Since we want this option to branch to another menu, select the Menu choice, and name the new submenu **SubMenu2**. Select the Vertical option, and fill in the menu title **Manage Charges List**. Then type in the options listed below. When you're finished, your screen should look like Figure 15.6.

1. **Add New Charges**
2. **Edit/Delete Charges**
3. **Print Charges**
4. **Return to Main Menu**

Press Esc after entering the four menu options. R:BASE will ask if you want to define another option for the new submenu. Select the No option.

Next, R:BASE asks if you want to assign actions to option 3 of the Main menu. Since this option simply allows the user of the application to exit, select Exit from the choices on the screen.

```
Enter or change the menu choices

                         Manage Charges List
    (1)  Add New Charges
    (2)  Edit/Delete Charges
    (3)  Print Charges
    (4)  Return to Main Menu
    (5)

[ESC] Done   [PgUp] Title   [F3] Actions   [F5] Reset value   [F10] Help
Application MailSys  --- Database MAIL     --- Menu SubMenu2
```

Figure 15.6: SubMenu2 defined on the screen

MANAGING THE NAMES TABLE

Now R:BASE is ready to find out what actions you want to assign to the first submenu's options. You'll see the entire menu on the screen, along with the prompt

Do you want [ESC] to exit this menu? Yes No

Select Yes. Then R:BASE asks

Do you want to create a help screen for this menu?

Select No for now. R:BASE is then ready to assign an action to submenu option 1. Since this option allows the user to add new rows to the Names table, select Load from the choices on the screen. R:BASE asks which table to load, and it displays the names of the various tables in the database. Highlight the Names option and press Enter.

Next, R:BASE asks for the name of the form to use when adding new rows. Select the NamesFrm option, since this is the form we developed earlier for adding and editing data in the Names table. If you had not already defined a form for the Names table, or if you wanted to develop a new form, you could select the New option and develop a form on the spot with Forms EXPRESS. Since you've selected an existing form in this case, R:BASE asks

Do you want to edit the form?

There is no need to edit the form here, so you can select No. (Optionally, you could select Yes to move straight to Forms EXPRESS with the NamesFrm form on the screen ready for editing.) R:BASE asks if you want to assign any more actions to this first submenu choice. Select No.

Now it's time to define actions for submenu option 2. Since this option allows the user to edit and delete data from the Names table, select Edit from the choices on the screen. Select the Names table from the choices presented and the NamesFrm as the form to be used for editing. Again, the screen asks if you want to edit the form. There is no need to do so now, so select No. R:BASE asks how you want the data to be sorted while editing. For this example, select L:Name and Ascending, and then press Esc.

Now you will be given an opportunity to construct a WHERE clause that can be used to locate a particular record to edit when the application is put to use. Let's suppose that we want this option to ask the user for the last name of the customer to edit prior to displaying the list of customers on the edit screen. Select the L:Name option. R:BASE asks for the operator to be used when filtering the table (equal, not equal, less than, and so on). Select the EQ (equal) option.

The next prompt you'll see is the following:

Do you want the user to enter a comparison value? Yes No

This means "Do you know what rows to filter right now, or should we find out when we actually use the application later?" Select the Yes option. R:BASE asks for the text for the prompt message. Type in the line below:

Enter last name of customer to edit:

and press Enter. Later, we'll see how this option actually works. As with any WHERE clause, you can add a logical operator (such as AND or OR) to add more conditions. In this example, the single condition is sufficient, so just select Done.

Since we don't need to define any more actions for this menu option, select No when you see the next prompt.

For submenu option 3, we want the application to print the directory. Select the Print option from the choices on the screen; then select the Names table from the next list of choices displayed. We'll use the Director report we created earlier, so highlight Director and press Enter. The screen asks

```
Do you want to edit the report?
```

Answering Yes to this question will move you directly to Reports EXPRESS where you can change the format of the report immediately. To use the report format as it stands, select No.

For sort order, select the L:Name option and Ascending, select the F:Name option and Ascending, and then press Esc. (This will sort the customers into last- and first-name order.) To print all customers, press Esc rather than selecting columns to filter rows. Finally, select No when you're asked if you want to add more actions.

Assign actions to the fourth submenu option using the same procedure described above. Select the Print option and the Names table. Select the Labels option as the report format to use and No to the question about editing the report format. Select Zip as the sort order and Ascending. Press Esc twice when you're done. Select No when prompted for additional actions.

For form letters, select the Print option and the Names table once again. Select the Letter1 report format and No to the question about editing the report format. Then select Zip and Ascending as the sort order. Press Esc twice and select No when you're asked about adding more actions.

Of course, you could have selected filtering criteria for the directory, form letters, and mailing labels, just as we did while developing the action for the Edit option. You may want to add some filtering criteria later. We'll discuss techniques for modifying an application later in this chapter.

For the last submenu option, select the Exit choice from the screen. When this option is selected from the submenu, R:BASE will display the SubMenu2 menu.

MANAGING THE CHARGES TABLE

Now R:BASE is ready to assign actions to the second submenu. You'll see this submenu appear on the screen. Select Yes when you see the prompt about using the Esc key to exit. Select No to the prompt about defining help screens.

For the first submenu option, select the Load choice, the Charges table, and the ChrgFrm form. Again, the screen will ask if you want to edit the form using Forms EXPRESS. There is no need to do so now, so select No. Select No when you're asked about defining more actions for this submenu option.

For submenu option 2, select Modify. This will display an edit screen when the application is put to use. Select the Charges table and the All option to allow editing of all columns. Select CustNo as the sorting column and Ascending as the sorting direction. We don't need to filter the table for editing the Charges table, so press the Esc key twice rather than defining searching columns. Answer No to the prompt about adding more actions.

For submenu option 3, select Print from the choices on the screen. Select the Charges table name. Select the Sales option, since this is the report we developed to display data from the Charges table. You can modify the current report format by selecting Yes to the next prompt about editing the report. In this case, just select No. Select CustNo as the column to sort by and Ascending as the direction; then press Esc twice to bypass the questions about searching. Select No when asked about adding more actions.

For submenu option 4, select Exit from the choices on the screen and No when asked about more actions. At this point, all of the menus are developed, and actions have been assigned to all menu options. The screen asks if you want to change the EXPRESS default settings. For the time being, you can just select No. You'll see the message

```
Writing application files–Please wait
```

appear on the screen.

R:BASE will then write a long *program* based on the answers you've provided throughout this exercise. It may take a few minutes, but when you see the program you'll probably be glad that R:BASE wrote it for you. (Most database-management systems require that you write these programs yourself, which is why R:BASE is easier and faster for developing application systems.)

The last prompt to appear on the screen will be

```
Do you want to create an initial command file? ([F10] for help)
```

If you answer Yes to this question, the MailSys application will be run automatically when you start R:BASE. Select No for now, since we won't necessarily want to run the application every time we use R:BASE.

When all the basic tasks of creating the application are completed, the Application EXPRESS Main menu will reappear on the screen. Select option 3 to exit Application EXPRESS. Before using the application, you'll need to get back to the R> prompt. (You may need to press Esc at this point to exit the PBE menu.)

RUNNING THE APPLICATION

To use an application, you must enter the RUN command at the R> prompt using the general syntax

RUN *application name* IN *application name.*APX

For this example, at the R> prompt, enter the command

```
RUN MailSys IN MailSys.APX
```

The Main menu for the MailSys application will appear on the screen, as shown in Figure 15.7. The rest is easy. To manage the Names table, select option 1. The submenu we created will appear, as shown in Figure 15.8.

To add new customers, select option 1. You'll see the custom NamesFrm screen for adding rows. As usual, press Esc and select Quit after you've added new names. You'll be returned to the submenu. To edit the list of customers, select option 2. You'll see the prompt

```
Enter last name of customer to edit:
```

Type in a last name (**Smith**, for example) and press Enter. You'll see the data for Smith on the screen, ready for editing, as shown in

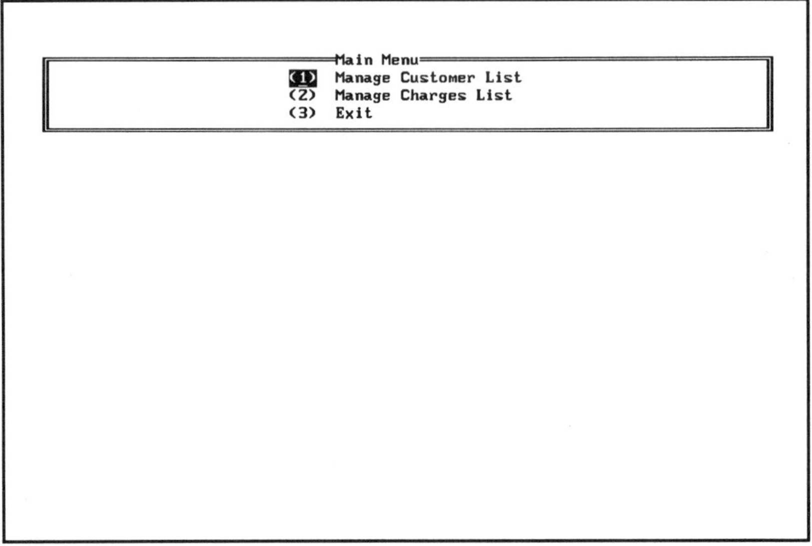

Figure 15.7: The MailSys Main menu

Figure 15.9. When you're finished with the edit screen, select the Quit option to return to the submenu.

When you select menu items that print reports, the screen will display the options

Screen Printer Both

Highlight the option you want and press Enter. The report will be displayed accordingly, and then you'll be returned to the submenu.

To exit the submenu, select option 6 or press the Esc key. The Main menu will reappear on the screen.

If you select option 2 from the Main menu, you'll see the submenu for managing the Charges table, as shown in Figure 15.10. Notice that when you select option 2, all the data appear on the screen, ready for editing, as shown in Figure 15.11.

A full edit screen appeared because we selected the Modify choice, rather than Edit, when we defined the submenu's options. Press Esc when you're finished editing. To return to the Main menu, select option 4 from the Charges submenu.

To exit the entire MailSys application, select the Exit option from the Main menu. You'll be returned to the R> prompt. From there,

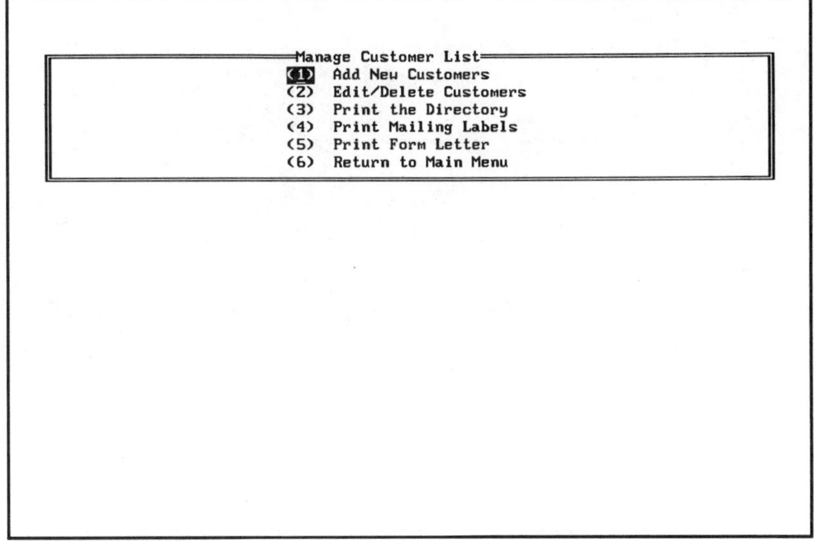

Figure 15.8: The menu for managing the Names table

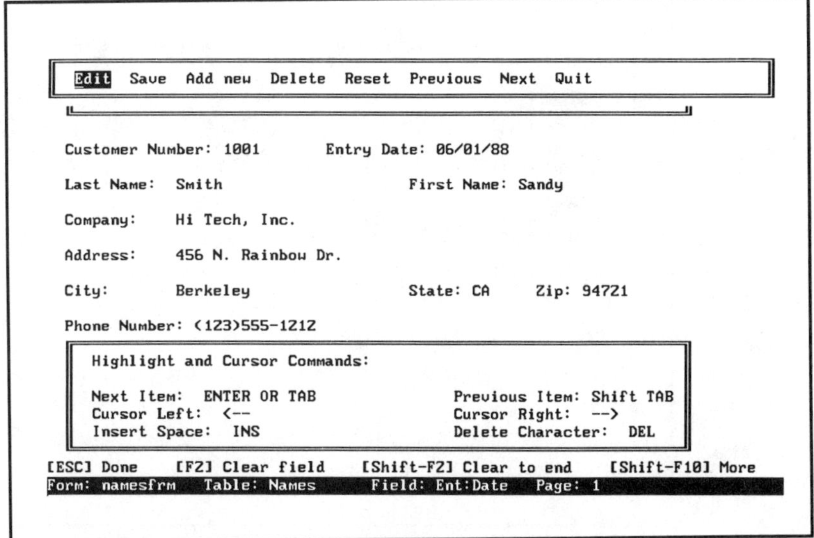

Figure 15.9: Data for Smith ready to be edited

you can use the R:BASE command mode commands to manage the data. To run the application again, enter the command

```
RUN MailSys IN MailSys.APX
```

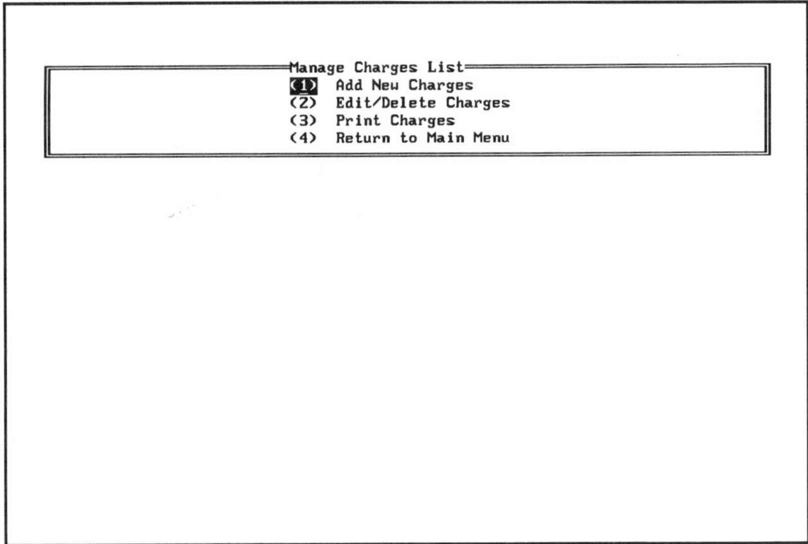

Figure 15.10: The submenu for managing the Charges table

Press [ESC] when done, [F2] to delete, [F5] to reset More→

CustNo	ProdNo	Qty	U:Price	Tax?	Total	P:Date
1001	A-111	12	$10.00	1	$127.20	06/15/
1001	B-222	5	$12.50	1	$66.25	06/15/
1001	C-434	2	$100.00	1	$212.00	06/15/
1002	B-222	12	$12.50	1	$159.00	07/01/
1002	A-111	10	$10.00	1	$106.00	07/01/
1004	A-111	5	$10.00	1	$53.00	06/15/
1004	Z-128	10	$12.80	0	$128.00	06/15/
1007	A-111	10	$10.00	1	$106.00	06/15/
1007	Z-128	10	$12.80	0	$128.00	06/15/

Figure 15.11: The Edit screen for the Charges table

Take a moment to review all the steps we've used to create the MailSys application and the end result that we've just tested. Remember that we created a Main menu and two submenus, and the application presented these menus in a vertical format.

Each of the submenus included an option for adding new rows to a table. On SubMenu1 we placed the option Add New Customers. On SubMenu2 we placed the option Add New Charges. When assigning actions in Application EXPRESS, we chose Load as the action to associate with each of the menu options. Now, when we actually use the application (by entering the RUN command at the R> prompt), these two menu options for entering data appear on the MailSys application's submenus. Selecting either option from the MailSys application lets you add new rows to either the Names or the Charges table.

We also defined two submenu items: Edit/Delete Customers and Edit/Delete Charges. While developing the application, we chose Edit as the action for SubMenu1 and Modify as the action for SubMenu2. The Edit option requires that a form be used, whereas Modify doesn't. Later, when we actually used the MailSys application, selecting either of these options allowed us to make changes to either the Names or the Charges table.

Similarly, we created the menu options Print the Directory, Print Mailing Labels, Print Form Letter, and Print Charges. We assigned Print as the action to each of these menu options and specified particular reports to print for each. Later, when using the application, we could print any of these reports simply by selecting the appropriate menu option from the application's menus.

Of course, we also included options to exit each of the menus, and assigned Exit as the action to each of these options. Furthermore, we opted to allow the user to exit any menu by pressing the Esc key. Therefore, when using the MailSys application, you can either select Exit or press Esc to leave the menu that is currently displayed on the screen.

You may want to experiment with the MailSys application for a while. Chances are, you'll come up with some ideas for changes and improvements. We'll discuss techniques for modifying an application in the next section.

MODIFYING THE APPLICATION

To modify an existing application, enter the Application EXPRESS menu in the usual manner and select option 2, to change an existing application. From there, you can perform any of the following tasks:

- Change the name of the application.
- Remove a menu from the application.

- Change a menu title.
- Change the text in any menu.
- Delete a menu option.
- Add a new menu option to any menu.
- Insert a menu option between existing options.
- Change the method of exiting a menu.
- Add or modify help screens.
- Change the actions associated with a menu option.
- Add actions to any menu option, either before or after existing actions.

When you first select option 2 from the Application EXPRESS menu, the screen will display the names of all the existing applications. Select the application that you want to modify by highlighting it and pressing Enter. In this example, select MailSys. R:BASE then displays the prompt

```
Do you want to change the application name? Yes No
```

Select No to use the same name or Yes to change the name. If you select Yes, R:BASE will prompt you for the new name. Next, R:BASE will display a message telling you that it is "reading" your application files. You'll then see a new menu, the Application menu, as shown in Figure 15.12.

The first option on the Application menu allows you to make changes, and the second option allows you to remove entire menus from the application. The third option allows you to change some of the application environmental settings, such as screen colors and beeping. We'll discuss these options later in the chapter. We'll work through a few changes to the MailSys application just for the practice. But since the general procedure for making changes does not vary much, we'll just describe most of the options briefly.

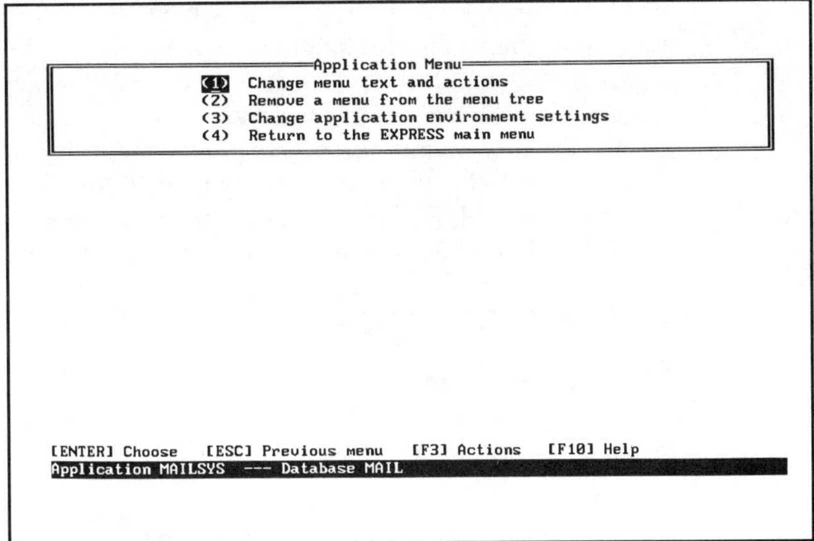

Figure 15.12: Options for modifying an existing application

CHANGING MENU OPTIONS AND ACTIONS

To change menu options and actions, select option 1 from the *Choose a menu to change* menu. The screen will display a list of menus, as follows:

MAIN SubMenu1 SubMenu2

Highlight the name of the menu that you want to change and press Enter. In a little while, we'll make some changes to the menu for managing the Names table, so highlight SubMenu1 and press Enter. The menu is displayed on the screen, ready for editing.

To change the title, type in the new title and press Enter. To retain the original title, just press Enter.

To change the text in a menu option, move the highlighting to the option and type in the new text.

You can also add and insert new menu items. You add a new menu option by pressing the End key. The highlighting will move to the bottom of the menu. Then, you just type in the text for the new menu option and press Enter. To insert a new menu option between existing options, move the highlighting to the option that you want the new item to appear before, and press the F1 key. All the menu options below the highlighting will move down one row. Type in the text for the new menu option and press Enter. To delete a menu option, move the highlighting to the appropriate option and press F2.

When you finish making changes to the menu text, press the Esc key. R:BASE will display the following prompt:

Do you want to change ESC or HELP action: Yes No

Select Yes if you want to change the Esc key option for exiting the menus or if you wish to add or modify help screens. If you are following along on-line, select Yes, and we'll add some Help screens.

CHANGING THE ESCAPE ACTION

When you select Yes to the prompt above, R:BASE first asks

Do you want [ESC] to exit this menu: Yes No

Select Yes to retain the Esc key method of exiting. You can select No to disable the Esc key if you wish, but generally it is a good idea to keep the Esc key as a way to exit from menus.

ADDING A CUSTOM HELP SCREEN

After you answer the prompt about the Esc key, R:BASE displays the message

Do you want to create a help screen for this menu? Yes No

Since we're going to add a Help screen to the MailSys application, select the Yes option. R:BASE asks that you enter a name for the new Help screen. As usual, the name cannot be more than eight characters long and cannot contain any spaces or punctuation marks. For this example, enter the name **SubHelp1**.

You'll see a blank screen for entering the Help screen text. You can use the arrow keys to move the cursor, just as you did when creating custom forms and reports. Figure 15.13 shows a Help screen, which you can type in now if you are following along on-line. Press Esc after you've filled in the Help screen text.

```
                                               < 23, 31>  [ESC] to exit

                      Manage the Customer List

Menu options are:

(1) Add new customers to the customer list

(2) Edit/Delete customers.  When prompted, type in the last name of the
    customer to edit, and then press Enter.  Select Edit from the top
    menu to make changes.  Select Next from the top menu to view more
    customers with the same last name.  Press F2 to delete a customer,
    but remember, this will not automatically delete the charges that
    may be associated with the customer in question.  To do that, you'll
    have to select Edit/Delete charges from the Manage Charges List
    menu.

(3) Print the Customer Directory in alphabetical order.

(4) Print Mailing Labels in zip code order.

(5) Edit and print form letters.

(6) Return to the Main Menu._
```

Figure 15.13: The Help screen for the MailSys application

Later, when you run the application, you can press the F10 key to view the Help screen. Keep in mind that when you develop Help screens for an application, each screen must be assigned a unique name.

CHANGING MENU ACTIONS

Next, you'll be given the opportunity to change the actions that you originally assigned to the menu options in your application. The screen asks

Do you want to change the actions assigned to this menu?

If you answer No, you'll be given an opportunity to change another menu or to return to the Application EXPRESS Main menu. If you answer Yes, the screen will ask

Do you want to review all the actions?

Answering Yes takes you step-by-step through each of the menu options and the actions assigned to them. If you answer No, the screen will display the current application menu (SubMenu1 in this example) and the prompt

Choose a menu option to change

You can move the highlighter to any option on your custom menu and press Enter to change the action associated with that menu option. For example, if you highlight option 2, Edit/Delete Customers, the screen will show you that the current action assigned to this option is to edit data, using the NamesFrm form, as shown below:

ACTION—Edit using form: NamesFrm
Do you want to insert an action before the current action:

You can insert another action above this action (which means that the newly inserted action will take place first), by selecting Yes in response to the question on the screen. If you select No, the screen asks what you want to do with the current action, as below:

Choose an option for this action
Keep Replace Delete

Selecting Keep leaves the menu action as it stands. Selecting Replace allows you to enter a new action in place of the currently defined action. Selecting Delete deletes the currently defined action (but not the associated menu option from the menu itself).

Once you've opted to Keep, Replace, or Delete the current action, the screen asks

Do you want another action for the current menu option?

If you answer Yes to this question, you'll be given the opportunity to add another action, which will take place immediately after the existing action(s). If you answer No, you'll see the question

Do you want to change another menu action?

If you answer Yes, you'll see all the options for the current application menu (still SubMenu1 in this example), and you can select the same option or another menu option to change. Doing so will repeat the process just described for the newly selected menu option. If you answer No to the question about changing another menu action, the screen will ask

Do you want to change another menu?

If you wanted to change something on the Main menu or SubMenu2, you could select Yes. Again, you'd be asked which menu to change and which items on that menu to change. When you do not opt to change another menu, the screen displays the following message:

Changes to application MAILSYS are complete
Press [ENTER] to save changes—Press [ESC] to discard them

You can either press the Enter key to save any changes you made to the application or press the Esc key to discard them. In this case, press Enter to save the custom Help screen. You'll see the new version of the application whiz by on the screen as R:BASE rewrites the entire application. When done, the screen asks

Do you want to create an initial command file?
([F10] for help)

For now, just select No. This will bring back the Application EXPRESS Main menu, from which you can select option 4 to return to the R> prompt.

Return to the R> prompt, and we'll test the Help screen we added in this exercise. Enter the command

```
RUN MailSys IN MailSys.APX
```

Select option 1 from the Main menu to manage the customer list. When the submenu appears, press F10 to view the custom Help screen (shown in Figure 15.14). Press any key after you're finished viewing the Help screen.

```
                    Manage the Customer List

   Menu options are:

   (1) Add new customers to the customer list

   (2) Edit/Delete customers.  When prompted, type in the last name of the
       customer to edit, and then press Enter.  Select Edit from the top
       menu to make changes.  Select Next from the top menu to view more
       customers with the same last name.  Press F2 to delete a customer,
       but remember, this will not automatically delete the charges that
       may be associated with the customer in question.  To do that, you'll
       have to select Edit/Delete charges from the Manage Charges List
       menu.

   (3) Print the Customer Directory in alphabetical order.

   (4) Print Mailing Labels in zip code order.

 More output follows - press [ESC] to quit, any key to continue_
```

Figure 15.14: The custom Help screen for SubMenu1

APPLICATION ENVIRONMENTAL SETTINGS

Whenever you create or modify an application, the Application menu includes the opportunity to

(3) Change application environment settings

If you select this option, you'll see the Settings menu below:

(1) Set messages
(2) Set error messages
(3) Set colors
(4) Set bell

If you select option 1, the screen will ask

> Do you want to display R:BASE messages?

If you change this option to Yes, your application will display various R:BASE messages, such as "Successful PROJECT operation", as appropriate. If you select the default No option, these messages will not be displayed while the application is running.

Option 2 presents the prompt

> Do you want to display R:BASE error messages?

R:BASE normally displays messages on the screen when an error occurs. If you select Yes for this option, your application will display these messages. If you select No, your application will not display these R:BASE error messages. The default is No.

Option 3 allows you to select foreground and background colors for the application. Background colors include

> Black Blue Green Cyan Red Magenta Brown Gray

The current background color is highlighted. After selecting a background color, you can select a foreground color from the following:

> Blue Green Cyan Red Magenta Brown Gray
> Light Black Light Blue Light Green Light Cyan
> Light Red Light Magenta Yellow White

Selecting option 4 displays the prompt

> Do you want your application to beep at errors?

Selecting Yes will ensure that any errors that occur while your application is in use will be accompanied by an audible beep. Selecting No, the default, suppresses this beep.

Press Esc to return to the Application menu.

DELETING MENUS AND APPLICATIONS

Although we won't work through a specific example, you can delete a menu using the following procedure. From the Application menu, select option 2 to remove a menu from the menu tree. Highlight the name of the submenu that you wish to delete and press Enter. You cannot remove the Main menu, because R:BASE needs it to get to the submenus.

To delete an entire application, use the ERASE command from either the R> prompt or your operating system prompt. Applications are stored in three files with the extensions .APP, .APX, and .API. If you wanted to remove the entire MailSys application, you would enter the following commands separately:

```
ERASE MailSys.APP
ERASE MailSys.APX
ERASE MailSys.API
```

If you are sure that only these three files have the file name MailSys, you can erase all three simultaneously by entering

```
ERASE MailSys.AP?
```

Don't do so now, however, unless you want to rebuild the entire application.

In this chapter, we've developed our first application. In the remaining chapters, we'll discuss techniques for building more complex applications.

Chapter 16

Automating Your Applications with R:BASE Macros and Programs

Fast Track

To record keystrokes in an Exec file, **440**

press **Shift-F7** and enter a valid file name. When you are finished recording keystrokes, press **Shift-F7** again.

To play back the keystrokes **441**

recorded in an Exec file, press **Shift-F8** and enter the name of the Exec file to play back.

To create your own function key definition, **442**

press **Shift-F1**, enter the keystroke combination you wish to define, and type in the command or portion of command to be associated with that keystroke combination. Press **Shift-F1** again to end your definition.

To create or edit a command file, **443**

enter the command RBEDIT followed by the name of the command file.

To run a command file, **446**

enter the **RUN** command at the R> prompt.

To create an interactive user interface **448**

by displaying messages, pausing for input, and receiving values for variables from the keyboard, use the WRITE, PAUSE, and FILLIN commands.

To set up loops **454**

for repeating commands in a command file, use the WHILE and ENDWHILE commands.

To allow for decision making 460

within a command file, use the IF, ELSE, and ENDIF commands.

To terminate programs containing WHILE or IF 462

commands, use the QUIT command.

To allow for branching capability 462

in a command file, use the GOTO and LABEL commands.

To pass information to subroutines, 464

use the syntax RUN *command file* USING *parameter list*. The parameters in the subroutine are accessed through the %1, %2, %3, . . ., %9 variables.

To simplify the debugging 466

of command files, use the SET ECHO, SET MESSAGES, SET ERROR MESSAGES, and SHOW VARIABLES commands.

THE APPLICATION EXPRESS FEATURE PROVIDES A quick and easy way to develop applications, but there are limits to its flexibility. As an enhancement, you can write your own R:BASE programs to use in conjunction with those generated by the Application EXPRESS feature, or even use your programs as entirely separate tools.

An R:BASE program is called a *command file* because it is a file stored on disk (like a table or database) that contains a series of commands to be carried out. This means that you can store an entire group of commands in a file and process them all with a single command, rather than typing in each command individually at the R> prompt.

For example, suppose you regularly print the Director and Sales reports from the Mail database. Each time you do so, you have to type in the following six commands individually at the R> prompt:

```
OPEN Mail
OUTPUT PRINTER WITH SCREEN
PRINT Director SORTED BY L:Name F:Name
NEWPAGE
PRINT Sales SORTED BY CustNo
OUTPUT SCREEN
```

You could instead create a command file that contained all these commands in order and have R:BASE automatically perform all six tasks using a single RUN command.

But there is much more to creating and using command files than simply storing commands. Command files allow you to perform tasks that are otherwise not possible within R:BASE. In this chapter, we'll discuss some of the basic constructs used in creating command files. (Note: Throughout this chapter, we'll use the terms *command file* and *program* interchangeably.)

RECORDING KEYSTROKES

Before we get into the nitty-gritty of creating and running command files, we'll discuss a technique whereby you can create simple *Exec* files by recording keystrokes as you type them. The Exec files you can create through recorded keystrokes are not as powerful as the command files we'll develop later in the chapter. Nonetheless, the technique of recording and playing back keystrokes can save you from repeatedly typing in all the commands necessary to perform a task that you perform often.

Some of you will prefer to think of Exec files as *macros* (stored sequences of keystrokes), but R:BASE uses the term macro a little differently, to refer to command files.

To begin recording keystrokes, press Shift-F7 (hold down the Shift key and press the F7 key). The screen asks for the

```
Name of file to record to:
```

Type in a valid file name (remember, eight characters without spaces or punctuation). You can add a three-letter extension preceded by a period after the file name. For this example, type in the file name

```
Labels.EXC
```

and press Enter.

Now, type in each of the commands below, pressing the Enter key after each one:

```
CLS
OPEN Mail
OUTPUT SCREEN
PRINT LABELS ORDER BY Zip
CLOSE
```

After typing in the last command, CLOSE, and pressing Enter, press Shift-F7 to stop recording the keystrokes.

To play back the recorded keystrokes, press the Shift-F8 key. The screen asks for the

```
Name of file to play back:
```

Type in the name of the Exec file (Labels.EXC in this example), and press Enter. You'll see all the commands that you recorded played back on the screen, and R:BASE will execute all of the commands as they are played back.

One of the nice things about Exec files is that they can be recorded at the R> prompt, in Application EXPRESS, in Definition

EXPRESS, in Forms EXPRESS, in Reports EXPRESS, and also in the modules RBEDIT, CodeLock, and FileGateway that we'll be discussing later in the book. Exec files are stored in your default directory (usually \DBFILES), not as part of any particular database's definition. That means that you could theoretically create a general-purpose Exec file and use it while working with any database. Exec files can be deleted with the ERASE command either from R:BASE or from the operating system level.

To view the Labels.EXC file, you can enter the command

```
TYPE Labels.EXC
```

at the R> prompt; it will contain all the commands you typed in. You can also edit exec files with RBEDIT, R:BASE's editor that you'll be using extensively later on this chapter.

Although simple Exec files act much like command files, you cannot include the programming commands such as WHILE, IF, FILLIN, and others that we'll discuss in this chapter in an Exec file.

DEFINING YOUR OWN FUNCTION KEY ACTIONS

R:BASE also lets you define single-command actions to be associated with the ten function keys (F1 through F10) when they are pressed in combination with either Ctrl or Alt. Function key definitions, however, are only active during the session in which they were defined and can only accommodate a total of 256 keystrokes. However, these function key definitions can be set up from any R:BASE module.

Since most of us use the SELECT ALL FROM command frequently, let's see how a function key could be set up to save us keystrokes. First, press Shift-F1 (hold down the Shift key and press the F1 key). When R:BASE prompts you for a key combination, press the Ctrl and F10 function keys simultaneously. If, by chance, Ctrl-F10 already has a definition, we will be replacing the old definition now.

Then, type

```
SELECT ALL FROM
```

and press the spacebar. To tell R:BASE this is the end of the function key definition, press Shift-F1 again. Then, after making sure a database is open, press Ctrl-F10. SELECT ALL FROM should appear as though you had typed it yourself. All you need to do is supply a table name and press Enter. Remember, though, that function key maps, as they are called, are only stored in RAM and must be redefined for each R:BASE session.

CREATING COMMAND FILES WITH RBEDIT

You can create command files, or write a program, using the R:BASE RBEDIT editor. (You can also use external word processors such as WordStar, Word, or WordPerfect as long as you use a nondocument mode or save the program in an unformatted ASCII file.) You can access RBEDIT from PBE by selecting option 8, R:BASE and operating system utilities and then RBEDIT or you can type the command

```
RBEDIT
```

at the R> prompt.

Let's try a simple exercise to practice creating and running command files. From the R> prompt, type in the command

```
RBEDIT
```

and press Enter. You'll see the short menu of options below:

```
Old File     New File     Quit
```

The New file option allows you to create a new command file, the Old file option allows you to modify an existing command file, and Quit returns you to the R> prompt. Select the New file option.

You'll see a blank screen for composing your command file. At the upper-right corner of the screen you'll see

```
<1,1> [ESC] to exit
```

The <1,1> indicates the row and column position of the cursor, and the [ESC] message reminds you that you can press the Esc key to quit RBEDIT. Table 16.1 lists the keys that you can use while creating and editing command files.

CREATING YOUR FIRST COMMAND FILE

Type in the command file (or program) shown in Figure 16.1. Press the Enter key after typing in each line. Remember, you can use the

Table 16.1: Keys Used with RBEDIT

KEY	FUNCTION
Enter	Finish the current line and move down one line
↓	Move down one line
↑	Move up one line
→	Move right one character
←	Move left one character
Tab	Move right ten characters
Shift-Tab	Move left ten characters
Ctrl →	Move to the end of the line
Ctrl ←	Move to the beginning of the line
F1	Insert a line above the current line
F2	Delete the current line
F4	Enter and exit repeat mode
Ins	Insert a blank space
Del	Delete a character
Home	Display the first page of text
End	Display the last page of text
PgUp	Move up one page
PgDn	Move down one page
Shift F6	Mark the beginning and end of a block
Shift F4	Copy indented block
Shift F2	Delete marked block

arrow keys to move the cursor and correct errors as you type. Use the Ins and Del keys to insert and delete characters and the F1 and F2 keys to insert and delete lines if you need to while making any corrections.

SAVING THE COMMAND FILE

Once you've typed in the entire command file, press the Esc key. You'll see the menu

```
Edit again    Save file    Next File    Quit
```

Select the Save file option to store a copy of the command file on disk. R:BASE will display the prompt

```
Name of new file to save:
```

You can use any valid file name that you wish. A valid file name is no more than eight characters long, without spaces, followed by a period and an optional three-letter extension. Typically, command files are stored with the extension .CMD, so type in the file name

```
Sample1.CMD
```

and press Enter.

```
                                          < 7,  6> [ESC] to exit
OPEN Mail
NEWPAGE
PRINT Director ORDER BY L:Name F:Name
NEWPAGE
CLEAR ALL VARIABLES
PRINT Sales ORDER BY CustNo
CLOSE_
```

Figure 16.1: A sample command file typed in with RBEDIT

Now select the Quit option, and you will be returned to the R> prompt.

RUNNING THE COMMAND FILE

Once you've saved the command file, use the RUN command with the name of the file to run the program. In this example, enter the command

```
RUN Sample1.CMD
```

and press Enter. You'll see the message "Database exists" briefly as the program opens the Mail database. Then the screen will clear, and after a brief pause, you'll see the Director report displayed in alphabetical order by last and first names. Then the screen will clear again (because of the NEWPAGE command), and you'll see the Sales report printed in order by customer number. When the command file is finished, you'll see the message

```
Switching input back to keyboard
```

which means that R:BASE will be expecting the next command to come from the keyboard, rather than from the command file.

EDITING A COMMAND FILE

To edit an existing command file, use the RBEDIT editor. As a shortcut, you can enter the name of the command file along with the RBEDIT command, as below:

```
RBEDIT Sample1.CMD
```

Let's add a couple of commands to clear the screen and then print mailing labels. Move the cursor to the bottom of the command file, just under the C in CLOSE, like so:

```
CLOSE
```

Press the F1 key twice to insert two blank lines, so the command file looks like Figure 16.2.

```
                                                       < 7,  1>  [ESC] to exit
OPEN Mail
NEWPAGE
PRINT Director ORDER BY L:Name F:Name
NEWPAGE
CLEAR ALL VARIABLES
PRINT Sales ORDER BY CustNo
_

CLOSE
```

Figure 16.2: Blank lines added to the Sample1.CMD command file

Next, type in the command

NEWPAGE

Press Enter and type in the command

PRINT Labels ORDER BY Zip

When you are finished, your command file should look like Figure 16.3.

Press Esc after making the changes. Again, select the Save File option. R:BASE will display the prompt

Name of new file to save [Sample1.CMD]:

To use the Sample1.CMD file name again, press the Enter key. You'll be returned to the R> prompt.

To run the modified command file, once again enter the command

RUN Sample1.CMD

You'll see the Director, Sales, and Labels reports printed on the screen, and then you'll see the message

Switching input back to keyboard

```
                                        < 8, 26>  [ESC] to exit
OPEN Mail
NEWPAGE
PRINT Director ORDER BY L:Name F:Name
NEWPAGE
CLEAR ALL VARIABLES
PRINT Sales ORDER BY CustNo
NEWPAGE
PRINT Labels ORDER BY Zip_
CLOSE
```

Figure 16.3: The edited Sample1.CMD command file

which means that you are once again back to the normal R:BASE command mode.

As you can see, creating a command file is as easy as calling up the RBEDIT editor, typing in the commands that you want to process, saving the command file, and then running it with the RUN command. With RBEDIT, you can create command files with about 750 command lines (depending on available memory).

With the addition of input/output, looping, decision making, and a few other tricks of the trade, you can build command files that go far beyond a simple list of commands and perform more sophisticated tasks. We'll discuss these techniques in the remainder of this chapter.

INPUT/OUTPUT COMMANDS

The input/output commands allow you to display messages, pause for a response, and assign values to variables from within a command file. The three primary input/output commands for R:BASE are WRITE, PAUSE, and FILLIN.

DISPLAYING MESSAGES WITH THE WRITE COMMAND

The WRITE command uses the general syntax

```
WRITE "message" AT <row> <column>
```

The AT portion is optional. Most screens contain 24 rows and 80 columns; the upper-left corner is row 1, column 1, and the lower-right corner is row 24, column 80.

To try the command, create a simple command file named IO1.CMD by entering

```
RBEDIT IO1.CMD
```

at the R> prompt. Fill in the lines

```
NEWPAGE
WRITE "This is the first message . . . "
```

Press Esc when you're done writing the command file, and select the Save file option. Press Enter to use the file name IO1.CMD. When the R> prompt reappears, run the command file by typing in the command

```
RUN IO1.CMD
```

and pressing Enter. The command file will clear the screen and display the message

```
This is the first message . . .
```

before returning to the R> prompt on the top line of your screen.

You can use the optional AT command with the WRITE command to specify the exact row and column position for displaying information on the screen. To test this, try using RBEDIT to create a command file named IO2.CMD. Enter the two command lines below into the command file (note that CLS and NEWPAGE both act to clear the screen):

```
CLS
WRITE "This is the middle" AT 12,31
```

Press Esc and select Save file to save the file with the file name IO2.CMD. Then, from the R> prompt, enter the command

```
RUN IO2.CMD
```

and press Enter to see how the command file works.

COMBINING TEXT AND NUMBERS

Sometimes, you may want to display a message from within a command file that contains both text and numeric data, such as the following message:

```
You just won $100,000.00!
```

Normally, you cannot directly combine textual and numeric data in a variable for display. However, by using the CTXT function to convert the numeric data to textual data, you can indeed combine the two types of data. Here is an example.

Use RBEDIT to create a command file named IO3.CMD. Enter the following lines into the command file:

```
CLEAR ALL VARIABLES
SET VARIABLE Prize CURRENCY
SET VARIABLE Prize TO 100000.00
SET VARIABLE Msg TO "You just won" & CTXT(Prize) + "!"
WRITE .Msg AT 20,1
```

Save the command file by pressing Esc and selecting Save file from the menu. When the R> prompt reappears, enter the command RUN IO3.CMD and press Enter. You'll see the message "You just won $100,000.00!" appear at row 20, column 1 on the screen, and then the R> prompt will reappear. Let's discuss why.

The first line in the command file, CLEAR ALL VARIABLES, simply erases any existing variables. Then the command

```
SET VARIABLE Prize CURRENCY
```

creates an empty variable named Prize, which is predefined as the Currency data type.

The next line

```
SET VARIABLE Prize TO 100000.00
```

stores the number $100,000.00 in the variable named Prize. The next line

```
SET VARIABLE Msg TO "You just won" & (CTXT(Prize)) + "!"
```

concatenates (joins) the numeric Prize variable to the text string "You just won", and then the concatenates the character "!" to the end of the variable.

Normally, these items could not be strung together because the Prize variable is numeric and the characters in quotation marks are text. However, the CTXT function converts the Prize variable to TEXT data within the SET VARIABLE command, so R:BASE accepts the concatenation. (Remember, however, that concatenation only allows you to join textual data.)

The last line in the command file

```
WRITE .Msg AT 20,1
```

displays the entire .Msg variable at row 20, column 1 on the screen.

Another example of using the CTXT function would be the following:

```
SET VARIABLE today TO "Today is" & (CTXT(.#DATE))
```

In this case, R:BASE changes date data to text data prior to concatenation.

PAUSING EXECUTION WITH THE PAUSE COMMAND

The PAUSE command temporarily causes R:BASE to stop processing the commands in a command file until the user presses a key. The PAUSE command is usually used with a message displayed with the WRITE command. For example, use RBEDIT to create a command file named IO4.CMD, and type in the commands below:

```
NEWPAGE
WRITE "Press any key to continue " AT 12,30
PAUSE
WRITE "Thank you" AT 23,5
```

Save the command file, and then run it by entering

```
RUN IO4.CMD
```

The screen will clear, and you will see the following:

```
Press any key to continue
```

After you press a key, R:BASE will continue processing commands, and you'll see the message

```
Thank you
```

near the bottom of the screen.

WRITING INTERACTIVE PROGRAMS WITH THE FILLIN COMMAND

The FILLIN command pauses program execution and waits for some data to be entered by the user. Whatever the user types in on the screen is stored in a variable. Generally, it is a good idea to define the data type for the variable explicitly before using the FILLIN command.

The general syntax for the FILLIN command is as follows:

```
FILLIN variable name USING "message" AT <row> <column>
```

To try the command, use RBEDIT to create a command file named IO5.CMD. Type in the lines shown below:

```
NEWPAGE
SET VARIABLE YourName TEXT
FILLIN YourName USING "Enter your name: " AT 12,5
NEWPAGE
```

```
SET VARIABLE Reply TO "Hello " & .YourName
WRITE .Reply AT 12,30
```

Note that the command file first clears the screen (NEWPAGE) and creates an empty variable named YourName of the TEXT data type. The FILLIN command displays the message "Enter your Name: " at row 12, column 5 and waits for a value to be entered from the keyboard. Then the command file clears the screen and creates a variable named Reply that consists of the word "Hello", followed by the YourName variable. The last line of the program displays the Reply variable at row 12, column 30.

When you run the command file, it will first ask for your name. Type in your name and press Enter. You'll then see the message "Hello", followed by your name, as below:

```
Hello Joe
```

PROGRAMMER COMMENTS

You can add comments to your programs (command files). These comments are never displayed and do not affect the program in any way. Generally, the purpose of these comments is to write helpful notes to yourself within a program. If you ever need to go back and modify a program many weeks or months later, the comments can help you translate the commands into English.

Comments in R:BASE programs must begin with an asterisk and an opening parenthesis and end with a closing parenthesis. For example, the line below is a valid program comment:

```
*(This is a program comment)
```

To make comments more visible in a program, programmers often add extra asterisks or hyphens, as in the two examples below:

*(****************************** Program to display menus)
*(- -Update the master file)

You must remember to add the closing parenthesis to a comment; otherwise R:BASE might think that the entire program is a comment and ignore all commands. When that happens, you'll be returned to the command mode with the +> prompt showing. To correct the problem, type in a closing parenthesis next to the +> prompt and press Enter. Then use RBEDIT to find the faulty comment and rectify it.

Figure 16.4 shows the IO5.CMD command file with some programmer comments added. Note that the first two comments provide the name of the command file, as well as a brief description of what the program does. Additional comments describe individual routines within the command file.

```
*(******************************** IO5.CMD)
*(--------------- Test the FILLIN command)
*(Clear the screen and initialize YourName variable)
NEWPAGE
SET VARIABLE YourName TEXT
*(-- Ask for user's name, and store in YourName variable)
FILLIN YourName USING "Enter your name: " AT 12,5
NEWPAGE
*(-- Create variable named Reply, and display it)
SET VARIABLE Reply TO "Hello" & .YourName
WRITE .Reply AT 12,30
```

Figure 16.4: The command file with comments

We'll use comments throughout the remaining sample programs in this book to help clarify various commands and routines.

LOOPING WITH WHILE AND ENDWHILE

One of the most common techniques used in programming is the *loop*. A loop allows a command file to repeat a single command, or several commands, as long as some condition exists. The general syntax for the WHILE and ENDWHILE commands is

WHILE *condition* THEN
  do this command
  and this command
ENDWHILE

Keep in mind that every WHILE command in a program *must* have an ENDWHILE command associated with it. Programmers typically indent instructions that are typed between WHILE and

ENDWHILE statements to highlight these WHILE/ENDWHILE pairs and to make it easy to identify the commands that are going to be executed over and over within the loop. Figure 16.5 shows a sample program with a WHILE loop in it.

Let's look at the logic of the program, line by line. The first two lines are simply programmer comments. The NEWPAGE command then clears the screen, as follows:

```
*(****************************************** Loop1.CMD)
*(- - - - - - - - - - - - - - - - Program to test a WHILE Loop)
NEWPAGE
```

Next, the program creates a variable named Counter and assigns it the value 1, as follows:

```
*(- - - - - - - - - - - - - - - Create a variable named Counter)
SET VARIABLE Counter TO 1
```

The next line starts a loop that will repeat all commands between the WHILE and ENDWHILE commands, as long as the Counter variable is less than or equal to 10:

```
*(- - - - - - - - - - - - - - - - - - - - - Repeat loop 10 times)
WHILE Counter < = 10 THEN
```

Within the WHILE loop, these lines create a variable named Progress, which contains the text "Loop Number" and the current value of the Counter variable converted to text. The WRITE command

```
*(************************************** Loop1.CMD)
*(---------------- Program to test the WHILE loop)
NEWPAGE
*(---------------- Create variable named Counter)
SET VARIABLE COUNTER TO 1
*(---------------- Repeat loop 10 times)
WHILE Counter <= 10 THEN
      *(---------- Create a prompt and display it)
      SET VARIABLE Progress TO "Loop Number " & (CTXT(.Counter))
      WRITE .Progress
      *(---------- Increment Counter variable by 1)
      SET VARIABLE Counter TO .Counter + 1
ENDWHILE *(Bottom of WHILE loop)
*(----------------- End of program)
QUIT
```

Figure 16.5: A sample program with a WHILE loop

then displays this message on the screen:

```
*(- - - - - - - - - - - - - - - - Create a prompt and display it)
SET VARIABLE Progress TO "Loop Number" & CTXT(.Counter)
WRITE .Progress
```

Next, the program increments the Counter variable by one by adding a 1 to its current value:

```
*(- - - - - - - - - - - - - - - - - - - Increment Counter by 1)
SET VARIABLE Counter TO .Counter + 1
```

The line below marks the end of the WHILE loop:

```
ENDWHILE *(- - - - - - - - - - - - - - - - End of WHILE loop)
```

The last line, QUIT, ends the program and returns control to the R> prompt. R:BASE uses portions of memory to manage WHILE loops, and the QUIT command frees up this memory. Therefore, it is a good idea to end a program that contains WHILE loops with the QUIT command.

```
*(- - - - - - - - - - - - - - - - - - - - - - - - - - End program)
QUIT
```

You can use RBEDIT to create the command file. When you run the program, you'll see the following on the screen:

```
Loop Number = 1
Loop Number = 2
Loop Number = 3
Loop Number = 4
Loop Number = 5
Loop Number = 6
Loop Number = 7
Loop Number = 8
Loop Number = 9
Loop Number = 10
Switching INPUT back to KEYBOARD
```

Notice that the WRITE command within the WHILE loop repeated ten times, and each time through, the Counter variable incremented by one.

You can use variables to determine how many times the WHILE loop should repeat. For example, the command file Loop2.CMD in Figure 16.6, when run, displays the prompt

```
How high shall I count?
```

and waits for a response. After you enter a number, the WHILE loop will repeat the appropriate number of times. For example, if you enter a 5, you'll see the following on the screen:

```
Loop Number = 1
Loop Number = 2
Loop Number = 3
Loop Number = 4
Loop Number = 5
Switching INPUT back to KEYBOARD
```

Notice in the program that the commands

```
SET VARIABLE Done INTEGER
FILLIN Done USING "How high shall I count?: " AT 9,5
```

create a variable named Done. The FILLIN command displays the prompt "How high shall I count?:" and waits for a response from the user. The user's response is then stored in the Done variable. The

```
*(************************************** Loop2.CMD)
*(---------------- Program to test the WHILE loop)
*(------------ Create Counter and Done variables)
SET VARIABLE COUNTER TO 1
SET VARIABLE Done INTEGER
*(------------- Ask how high to count)
NEWPAGE
FILLIN Done USING "How high shall I count?: " AT 9,5
NEWPAGE
*(---------------- Repeat loop until Counter > Done)
WHILE Counter <= .Done THEN
      *(---------- Create a prompt and display it)
      SET VARIABLE Progress TO "Loop Number " & (CTXT(.Counter))
      WRITE .Progress
      *(---------- Increment Counter variable by 1)
      SET VARIABLE Counter TO .Counter + 1
ENDWHILE *(Bottom of WHILE loop)
*(----------------- End of program)
QUIT
```

Figure 16.6: A program to test the WHILE command with a variable

WHILE loop repeats as long as the Counter variable is less than or equal to the Done variable, as follows:

```
WHILE Counter < = .Done THEN
```

THE SET POINTER COMMANDS

With the use of the SET POINTER command, a WHILE loop can also step through a table a single row at a time. The general syntax of the SET POINTER command is

```
SET POINTER #<n> <variable> FOR table name ORDER BY +
+ > column list WHERE conditions
```

The ORDER BY and WHERE clauses are optional. The *n* can be any number from 1 to 3. Three pointers can be set up simultaneously. The *variable* is an integer that equals zero until there are no more rows in the table to process. The command

```
NEXT # <n> <variable>
```

is used to move the pointer to the next row in the table. If no ORDER BY or WHERE clause is specified, the NEXT command simply moves the pointer to the next row in the table. If an ORDER BY or WHERE clause (or both) is included, the pointer moves through the appropriate records in the selected sort order.

Figure 16.7 shows a sample command file that displays the first and last names of individuals in the Names table.

The command

```
OPEN Mail
```

opens the Mail database. The command

```
SET POINTER #1 Status FOR Names ORDER BY +
+ > L:Name F:Name
```

sets up pointer #1 and a variable named Status for the Names table. The WHILE loop continues processing as long as there are still rows

```
*(********************************** Loop3.CMD)
*(*********** Test WHILE loop through a table)
NEWPAGE
*(----------------- Open the Mail database)
OPEN Mail
*(------ Set up pointer into Mail database)
SET POINTER #1 Status FOR Names ORDER BY L:Name F:Name
*(------ Repeat loop until end of table encountered)
WHILE Status = 0 THEN
      SET VARIABLE Name1 TO F:Name IN #1
      SET VARIABLE Name2 TO L:Name IN #1
      SET VARIABLE Name TO .Name1 & .Name2
      WRITE .Name        *(--Display the name)
      NEXT #1 Status     *(--Skip to next row in table)
ENDWHILE
CLOSE        *(-- close the database)
QUIT         *(-- end of program)
```

Figure 16.7: A sample program with a WHILE loop and the SET POINTER command

in the Names table to process; that is, as long as the Status variable is zero, as below:

```
WHILE Status = 0 THEN
```

Then the SET VARIABLE and WRITE commands assign first and last names to variables. Note the use of #1 in the first two SET VARIABLE commands. Since the pointer has been defined as #1, the Names table is now referred to as #1, as follows:

```
SET VARIABLE Name1 TO F:Name IN #1
SET VARIABLE Name2 TO L:Name IN #1
SET VARIABLE Name TO .Name1 & .Name2
WRITE .Name    *(– Display the name)
```

The following command

```
NEXT #1 Status    *(– Skip to next row in table)
```

moves the pointer to the next row in the Names table (#1) that meets the criteria established in the SET POINTER #1 command, and the Status variable receives a new value—either zero if there is another row to process or a nonzero number (usually 406) if there are no more rows to process.

If you type in the command file and run it, the screen will show all the first and last names listed in the Names table, sorted alphabetically, as follows:

```
Bart Adams
Robin Baker
Mindy Jones
Mary Martin
Anne Miller
Marie Miller
Monica Miller
Sandy Smith
Trudy Teasdale
End-of-data encountered
Switching input back to keyboard
```

Remember that you can type SHOW VARIABLES from the R> prompt to see the contents of your variables. This can often help you locate a problem if your program isn't working as you expected.

We'll see a few more examples of the WHILE and SET POINTER commands in coming chapters.

DECISION MAKING WITH IF

Another commonly used programming technique is *decision making* using the IF, THEN, ELSE, and ENDIF commands. The general syntax for the IF command is

```
IF conditions THEN
   Do this command
   and this command
ELSE
   Do this command
   and this command
ENDIF
```

The ELSE portion is optional, so the IF command might also use the following simpler syntax:

```
IF conditions THEN
   Do this command
   and this command
ENDIF
```

With either syntax, each IF command in a command file *must* have an ENDIF command associated with it.

There can be any number of commands between the IF and ENDIF commands. The *conditions* portion can have up to ten expressions joined with the AND and OR operators.

Figure 16.8 shows a simple program that makes a decision on whether or not to display information on the printer, based upon the user's response to the question

Send message to the printer? (Y/N):

The FILLIN command displays the prompt, then waits for the user to enter an answer. This answer is stored in a variable named YesNo. The clause

```
*(– Decide whether to use printer or just screen)
IF YesNo = Y THEN
   OUTPUT PRINTER WITH SCREEN
ELSE
   OUTPUT SCREEN
ENDIF
```

will channel output to the printer and screen if the YesNo variable contains the letter Y. If this variable contains an N, output will be channeled to the screen only.

```
*(***************************** IF1.CMD)
*(----- Program to test the IF command)
NEWPAGE
*(------- Create variable to hold answer)
SET VARIABLE YesNo TEXT
*(------- Display prompt and get answer)
FILLIN YesNo USING "Send message to the printer? (Y/N) " +
   AT 12,2
*(------ Decide whether to use printer or just screen)
IF YesNo = Y THEN
   OUTPUT PRINTER WITH SCREEN
ELSE
   OUTPUT SCREEN
ENDIF
*(-- Display message)
WRITE "Here is the message"
OUTPUT SCREEN  *(-- back to normal screen display)
QUIT
```

Figure 16.8: A sample program to test the IF command

Note the use of the QUIT command to end the program. Like programs that contain WHILE commands, command files that contain IF commands should always end with a QUIT command.

THE DECLARE CURSOR AND FETCH COMMANDS

The R:BASE SQL commands DECLARE CURSOR and FETCH offer an alternative to SET POINTER and NEXT. Either pair of commands can be used in conjunction with a WHILE loop to step through a table a row at a time. As you might expect, there are several differences. For example, when you use the SET POINTER command, you generally set up a pointer variable (it was called Status in the Loop3.CMD program) to use in your WHILE loop as the control variable. The variable remains set to zero as long as there continue to be rows to process.

When you use DECLARE CURSOR, however, you have to set up your own loop control variable. You do this with a statement in the form

SET ERROR VARIABLE *variable name*

You should then provide a way out of the loop in the event that the error variable indicates there is a problem, such as the end of your data. The BREAK command does this. Another difference between SET POINTER and DECLARE CURSOR is that the FETCH command, used in conjunction with DECLARE CURSOR, acts like a combination of SET VARIABLE and NEXT. The DECLARE CURSOR...FETCH equivalent of the Loop3.CMD program is shown in Figure 16.9.

BRANCHING WITH GOTO

The GOTO and LABEL commands are used to pass over a group of commands in a command file and branch to another group of commands. The basic syntax for the GOTO command is

GOTO *label name*

```
*(****************************************************Loop4.CMD)
NEWPAGE
CLEAR ALL VARIABLES
*(------- Open the Mail database)
OPEN Mail
*(------- Set up a pointer to first and last name data from the Names table)
DECLARE #1 CURSOR FOR SELECT L:Name F:Name FROM Names
*(------- Set up an error variable to check for end of data)
SET ERROR VARIABLE Problem
*(------- Repeat loop as long as there is data)
WHILE Problem = 0 THEN
    *(---- Assign the contents of L:Name to Name2 and F:Name to Name1)
    FETCH #1 INTO Name2 Name1
    *(---- Check to see if there is more data; if there isn't, BREAK out )
    *(---- of IF and WHILE loops)
    IF Problem <> 0 THEN
       BREAK
    ENDIF
    *(---- Concatenate the Name1 and Name2 variables)
    SET VARIABLE HName to (.Name1 & .Name2)
    WRITE .HName  *(---Display the name on the screen)
ENDWHILE
CLOSE
QUIT
```

Figure 16.9: The DECLARE CURSOR...FETCH version of the Loop3 program

The syntax for the LABEL command is the following:

LABEL *label name*

The label name may be up to eight characters long. Figure 16.10 shows a sample command file that displays the prompt

Do you wish to exit R:base? (Y/N):

If the user answers Yes, the program branches to the routine labeled Done, and control is returned to the operating system. If the user answers No, all commands between the GOTO and LABEL commands are executed, rather than skipped over, and the Director report from the Mail database is displayed on the screen.

Branching has the disadvantage of slowing down the speed of command file execution considerably, and in most cases a WHILE or IF command can be used in place of the GOTO and LABEL commands. You should only resort to using a GOTO command when there appears to be no other way to accomplish a programming goal. As you learn more techniques throughout this book, you'll see that the GOTO command is rarely necessary.

```
*(************************************ GoTest.CMD)
*(-- Program to test the GOTO and LABEL commands)
NEWPAGE
SET VARIABLE YesNo TEXT
*(-------------- Ask if user wants to exit, rather than
                continuing.  Branch to Done label.)
FILLIN YesNo USING "Do you wish to exit now? (Y/N) " +
   AT 12,1
NEWPAGE
*(-------------- If exit requested, skip over all
                commands before LABEL Done.)
IF YesNo = "Y" THEN
   GOTO Done
ENDIF
*(--- If exit not requested, print Directory report.)
OPEN MAIL
PRINT Director ORDER BY CustNo
CLOSE
QUIT   *(Return to R> prompt)
*(--- Routine to leave R:BASE R> prompt)
LABEL Done
EXIT  *(----- Leave R:BASE)
```

Figure 16.10: A sample program with GOTO and LABEL commands

USING SUBROUTINES

Subroutines are command files that can be accessed from other command files. They save programming effort by allowing you to perform a task, which may require several commands, using a single RUN command in a command file.

Subroutines (sometimes called *procedures* or *macros*) have the additional advantage of *parameter passing*. This technique leaves certain aspects of the routine open-ended so that it is more flexible.

Figure 16.11 shows a simple subroutine named Area.CMD, which calculates the area of a rectangle using the formula Area = Length × Width. SET VARIABLE Area = %1 × %2 calculates the area by multiplying the first (%1) and second (%2) parameters passed to the subroutine and stores the result in a variable named Area.

```
*(******************************* Area.CMD
            Subroutine to calculate area)
SET VARIABLE Area REAL
SET VARIABLE Area = %1 * %2
RETURN *(-- return to calling program)
```

Figure 16.11: The Area.CMD subroutine

The RETURN command should be placed at the end of every subroutine. This ensures that control is returned either to the R>

prompt or to a calling command file after the subroutine is done. Be sure to place the RETURN command at the bottom of the subroutine (and *not* in the middle of an IF or WHILE clause).

After creating and saving a subroutine, using the same technique that is used for creating command files, you can run it and pass parameters to it with the USING option of the RUN command.

For example, to calculate the area using a length of 5 and a width of 10, you would enter the command

```
RUN Area.CMD USING 5 10
```

To see the results of the calculation, enter the command

```
WRITE .Area
```

and you'll see that the Area variable contains 50.

You also can pass variables to subroutines. For example, if you create the variables Length and Width, as below:

```
SET VARIABLE Length TO 5.543
SET VARIABLE Width TO 6.1234
```

you can use the command

```
RUN Area.CMD USING .Length .Width
```

When you write the Area variable, it will contain the results of the appropriate calculation.

You can pass up to nine parameters to a subroutine. The parameters are assigned numbers (for example, %1, %2, %3, and so on) from left to right. Separate each parameter with a blank space.

In some cases, you might want to pass a parameter to a subroutine that has spaces in it. For example, the subroutine in Figure 16.12 displays a title, the date, and the time at the top of the screen. The title to be printed is passed as a parameter (%1).

To print the title Accounts Receivable Main Menu using the Title subroutine, you would need to enclose the title in quotation marks, as follows:

```
RUN Title.CMD USING "Accounts Receivable Main Menu"
```

```
*(****************************** Title.CMD
            Subroutine to print a title)
NEWPAGE
WRITE .%1 AT 2,1
WRITE .#DATE AT 2,60
WRITE .#TIME AT 2,70
RETURN
```

Figure 16.12: A subroutine to print a title

If you use the SHOW VARIABLES command after you've passed parameters to subroutines, you'll notice that R:BASE adds a second digit to the parameters, as in the %1-0 and %2-0 variables below:

VARIABLE	=	*VALUE*	*TYPE*
#DATE	=	06/21/88	DATE
#TIME	=	4:04:11	TIME
%1-0	=	5.543	DOUBLE
%2-0	=	6.1234	DOUBLE
Area	=	33.94201	DOUBLE
Length	=	5.543	DOUBLE
Width	=	6.1234	DOUBLE

R:BASE performs this "housekeeping" task as a means of keeping track of the level at which a parameter was used. The parameters in this example have the extension -0 because they were called from the R> prompt. If they had been called from a command file, the extension would be -1. If they had been called from a command file that had been called from another command file, the extension would be -2. However, you need not concern yourself with these extensions, and you definitely should not add them yourself.

DEBUGGING COMMAND FILES

Quite often, when you first run a command file, it will not perform exactly as you had expected. Errors in programs are referred to as *bugs,* and the process of removing them is called *debugging.* There are several techniques that you can use to help debug programs.

USING THE SET ECHO ON COMMAND

If you enter the command SET ECHO ON at the R> prompt before running a command file, you'll see each line in the program as R:BASE processes it. If an error causes the program to stop running, you'll be able to see the exact line that caused the error. Then, you can use RBEDIT to correct the program and try running it again.

To disable the ECHO option, use the SET ECHO Off command.

SETTING MESSAGES

R:BASE will display general-purpose messages, such as "Database exists," while the command file is running. You can suppress messages by entering

```
SET MESSAGES OFF
```

at the top of a command file. However, if you find that you are having problems getting a command file to run, remove the SET MESSAGES OFF command from the command file and enter

```
SET MESSAGES ON
```

at the R> prompt. After correcting your program, you can replace the SET MESSAGES OFF command.

SETTING ERROR MESSAGES

You can enter the following command

```
SET ERROR MESSAGES OFF
```

at the top of a command file to suppress the display of R:BASE error messages. However, if your command file has a bug in it that causes control to be returned to the R> prompt, you won't see what the error was. To debug the program, remove the SET ERROR MESSAGES OFF command from the command file. From the R> prompt, enter

```
SET ERROR MESSAGES ON
```

before you run the command file again. After you find and correct any bugs, you can put the SET ERROR MESSAGES OFF command back into the command file if you wish.

TRACKING VARIABLES

You can enter the command SHOW VARIABLES at any time from the R> prompt. If your program uses variables, look closely at the variables displayed. Make sure that all of the variables your program needs have been created and that they are the appropriate data type. If you find that some variables have the incorrect data type, use explicit data typing near the top of your program to specify what type they should be; for example, enter a command like

```
SET VARIABLE YourName TEXT)
```

MAKING HARD COPY OF A COMMAND FILE

Another method that will help you to debug a command file is to make a printed (hard) copy of it. Use the OUTPUT PRINTER and TYPE commands at the R> prompt. For example, to print a copy of the IO5.CMD command file, enter the commands

```
OUTPUT PRINTER WITH SCREEN
TYPE IO5.CMD
```

at the R> prompt. Enter the OUTPUT SCREEN command after printing the program to return to normal screen mode.

If your program contains WHILE or IF commands, you might want to use a pen or pencil to draw connecting lines between all WHILE and ENDWHILE commands and all IF and ENDIF commands, as shown in Figure 16.13. Make sure that each WHILE and IF command has an associated ENDWHILE and ENDIF command.

Missing and misplaced ENDWHILE and ENDIF commands will definitely cause problems in a program. Drawing connecting lines can help find them, as well as help you see more clearly the commands contained within the WHILE and IF clauses.

```
*(********************************** Sample3.CMD
              Test a WHILE loop through a table)
NEWPAGE
*(------------ Open the Mail database)
OPEN Mail
*(------------ Set a pointer in Names table)
SET POINTER #1 Status FOR Names ORDER BY L:Name
*(-----------  Continue loop to end of table)
WHILE Status = 0 THEN
      SET VARIABLE Name1 TO F:Name IN #1
      SET VARIABLE Name2 TO L:Name IN #1
      IF Name2 EXISTS THEN
         SET VARIABLE Name TO .Name1 & .Name2
         WRITE .Name
      ENDIF
      NEXT #1 Status
ENDWHILE
QUIT
```

Figure 16.13: A sample program with connecting lines drawn in

STRUCTURED PROGRAMMING

One of the best debugging techniques is to try to avoid bugs in the first place. The technique of structured programming can help accomplish this feat, and it will greatly aid in the process of debugging, as well as in making future modifications to a program.

The two basic rules of thumb for structured programming are quite simple:

- Use highly visible programmer comments in the command file to make it easy to locate commands that perform a specific task.
- Indent program lines within WHILE loops and IF clauses so that you can easily see the beginning and ending points of these specific routines.

The programs we've developed in this chapter have adhered to this basic rule of thumb. Note that the program shown in Figure 16.14 does not follow the basic rules of structured programming. There are no comments and no indentations in the programming. To figure out what the program is supposed to do, you need to read every line in the command file.

As shown in Figure 16.15, the same command file can be made much easier to understand by inserting comments that describe the various tasks that the program performs. Furthermore, the indented

```
SET VARIABLE COUNTER TO 1
SET VARIABLE Done INTEGER
NEWPAGE
FILLIN Done USING "How high shall I count?: " AT 9,5
NEWPAGE
WHILE Counter <= .Done THEN
SET VARIABLE Progress TO "Loop Number " & (CTXT(.Counter))
WRITE .Progress
SET VARIABLE Counter TO .Counter + 1
ENDWHILE
QUIT
```

Figure 16.14: An unstructured program

lines between the WHILE and ENDWHILE commands make it easy to see the starting and ending points of the loop, as well as which commands are repeated within the loop. Indenting the program lines between the IF and ENDIF and the WHILE and ENDWHILE commands is especially beneficial because many program errors are caused by leaving out the necessary ENDIF and ENDWHILE commands. If you use indentations, a missing ENDIF or ENDWHILE command will be more noticeable.

A missing ENDIF or ENDWHILE command in a command file can make R:BASE behave strangely, even after you've returned to the R> prompt. Usually, R:BASE will seem to ignore every command that you enter, simply redisplaying the R> prompt after each command without taking any action. If this happens, first try entering the command ENDIF right at the R> prompt. Then try some other commands to see if R:BASE is back to normal.

If that doesn't work, enter the ENDWHILE command at the R> prompt and try again. Things should be back to normal by then, but just to be safe, also enter the QUIT command to free the memory used by these commands. Then, use RBEDIT to find the missing command and put it into the command file.

WHAT'S THE POINT?

You are probably wondering why you need to know about R:BASE programming. The sample programs you've created and run in this chapter aren't necessarily the sort of programs you'll want to run on their own. We have used them to introduce the R:BASE programming language to you, and to show you the kinds of situations in which the different programming commands prove useful.

```
*(*************************************** Loop2.CMD)
*(---------------- Program to test the WHILE loop)
*(------------ Create Counter and Done variables)
SET VARIABLE COUNTER TO 1
SET VARIABLE Done INTEGER
*(------------- Ask how high to count)
NEWPAGE
FILLIN Done USING "How high shall I count?: " AT 9,5
NEWPAGE
*(---------------- Repeat loop until Counter > Done)
WHILE Counter <= .Done THEN
      *(---------- Create a prompt and display it)
      SET VARIABLE Progress TO "Loop Number " & (CTXT(.Counter))
      WRITE .Progress
      *(---------- Increment Counter variable by 1)
      SET VARIABLE Counter TO .Counter + 1
ENDWHILE *(Bottom of WHILE loop)
*(----------------- End of program)
QUIT
```

Figure 16.15: A structured program

Generally, you'll want to incorporate the R:BASE programs you write into an application. In Chapter 15, when you worked with Application EXPRESS, you may have wondered about the Custom and Macro options on the Application EXPRESS Action menu. These refer to command files that you want to use at a particular point in your application. When you select Custom, R:BASE presents you with RBEDIT and allows you to write your own program "on the fly" from within Application EXPRESS. Although experienced programmers sometimes select this option, its disadvantage is that you won't be able to test the program on its own, outside of Application EXPRESS. To see if it works, you'll have to run your application.

If you select Macro, on the other hand, R:BASE asks for the name of the program file you have created. Presumably, you've already tested the program on its own to make sure it works properly.

In the next chapter, we'll show you how powerful command files can be used to keep an accounts-receivable system up-to-date. You'll create several command files, test them, and then insert them into an accounts-receivable application.

Chapter 17

A Working Accounts-Receivable System

FAST TRACK

To design custom applications efficiently, 475
create an outline of the system to break down the overall goal into smaller, more manageable goals.

The master table 479
in the accounts-receivable system maintains a list of customers and their current balances.

Transaction tables 479
are used in the accounts-receivable system to store individual charges and payments.

Through the process of updating, 479
balances in the master table are adjusted to reflect current charges and payments in the transaction tables. The CHANGE or SQL UPDATE command is used to make these adjustments.

History tables 480
are used in the accounts-receivable system to store "old" transactions that have been billed on a previous billing cycle.

To access custom command files or macros 493
from menus developed using Application EXPRESS, select Macro as the action for the menu option.

IN THIS CHAPTER, WE'LL DISCUSS SOME ADVANCED programming techniques with the R:BASE programming language and methods for integrating custom routines with applications developed by using the Application EXPRESS feature. While learning these new techniques, we'll develop a complete accounts-receivable system with monthly billing.

DESIGNING AN ACCOUNTS-RECEIVABLE SYSTEM

When developing a large system, it's a good idea to write down your basic goals on paper. Sometimes, an overall goal, such as to develop an accounts-receivable/billing system, is too vague for a starting point. Using an outline, we can break down this overall goal into smaller, more manageable goals, as below:

I. Develop an accounts-receivable/billing system

- A. Maintain a customer list with accounts-receivable balances
- B. Maintain an inventory list of items in stock
- C. Maintain a history of individual charge transactions
- D. Maintain a history of payments
- E. Print monthly bills

From this point, we can further define the tasks required to attain each main goal under the overall goal, as below:

I. Develop an accounts-receivable/billing system

- A. Maintain a customer list with accounts-receivable balances
  1. Add, edit, and delete customers
  2. Print customer list

B. Maintain an inventory list of items in stock

1. Add, edit, and delete inventory items
2. Print inventory list

C. Maintain a history of individual charge transactions

1. Add, edit, and delete charges
2. Print charge transactions

D. Maintain a history of payments

1. Add, edit, and delete payments
2. Print payment transactions

E. Print monthly bills

1. Print the bills
2. Update customer billing history

Looking at the project from this perspective makes things seem easier. Most tasks simply involve managing data and printing reports from tables.

Once you write down the basic goals of the project, you can begin designing the database structure.

DATABASE DESIGN

We'll need several tables in our accounts-receivable system database to meet the goals that we've defined. First, we'll need a table to record basic customer information, including the current, and 30-, 60-, 90-, and 120-day balances, as well as other relevant information. We'll name the database ARSYS, and name the table for recording customer information ARMain. The ARMain table will have the structure shown in Figure 17.1.

Next, we'll develop a table of products with product numbers, product names, prices, and so forth. This table will speed up data entry in the accounts-receivable system. The user will simply enter a product number, and R:BASE will automatically fill in the rest of the information for each charge transaction. The name of the inventory table is Inventry, and its structure is shown in Figure 17.2.

TABLE: ARMAIN

COLUMN DEFINITIONS

#	Name	Type	Length	Description
1	CustNo	INTEGER	1 value(s)	Customer number
2	L:Name	TEXT	12 characters	Last name
3	F:Name	TEXT	15 characters	First name
4	Company	TEXT	20 characters	Company
5	Address	TEXT	25 characters	Street address
6	City	TEXT	15 characters	City
7	State	TEXT	2 characters	State
8	Zip	TEXT	10 characters	ZIP code
9	Phone	TEXT	13 characters	Phone number
10	Curr:Bal	CURRENCY	1 value(s)	Current balance
11	Bal:30	CURRENCY	1 value(s)	30-day balance
12	Bal:60	CURRENCY	1 value(s)	60-day balance
13	Bal:90	CURRENCY	1 value(s)	90-day balance
14	Bal:120	CURRENCY	1 value(s)	120-day balance
15	Curr:Chr	CURRENCY	1 value(s)	Last total charge amount
16	Curr:Pay	CURRENCY	1 value(s)	Last payment amount
17	BillDate	DATE	1 value(s)	Last billing date

Figure 17.1: The structure for the ARMain table

We'll also need a table to record individual charge transactions. This table will have a structure similar to the Charges table in the Mail database. The name of the table is Charges, and its structure is shown in Figure 17.3.

Since accounts-receivable systems typically revolve around a monthly billing cycle, we'll move all transactions that have been billed to a *history* table at the end of each billing period. The CHistory table will hold the historical charge transactions, and its structure will be identical to the structure of the Charges table, as shown in Figure 17.4.

TABLE: INVENTRY

COLUMN DEFINITIONS

#	Name	Type	Length	Description
1	ProdNo	TEXT	5 characters	Product number
2	PartName	TEXT	20 characters	Product name
3	U:Price	CURRENCY	1 value(s)	Unit price
4	Tax?	INTEGER	1 value(s)	Taxable?
5	OnHand	INTEGER	1 value(s)	Quantity in hand
6	ReOrder	INTEGER	1 value(s)	Reorder point
7	Last:Upd	DATE	1 value(s)	Date of last update

Figure 17.2: The structure of the Inventry table

TABLE: CHARGES

COLUMN DEFINITIONS

#	Name	Type	Length	Description
1	CustNo	INTEGER	1 value(s)	Customer number
2	ProdNo	TEXT	5 characters	Product number
3	Qty	INTEGER	1 value(s)	Quantity purchased
4	U:Price	CURRENCY	1 value(s)	Unit price
5	Tax?	INTEGER	1 value(s)	Taxable?
6	T:Price	CURRENCY	1 value(s)	Total price
7	P:Date	DATE	1 value(s)	Purchase date

Figure 17.3: The structure of the Charges table

Individual payment transactions will be stored in the Payments table. The structure for the Payments table is shown in Figure 17.5.

As with the Charges table, payments that have already been recorded on a bill at the end of the month will be moved to a history table named PHistory. The structure for the PHistory table is identical to the structure of the Payments table, as shown in Figure 17.6.

TABLE: CHISTORY

COLUMN DEFINITIONS

#	Name	Type	Length	Description
1	CustNo	INTEGER	1 value(s)	Customer number
2	ProdNo	TEXT	5 characters	Product number
3	Qty	INTEGER	1 value(s)	Quantity purchased
4	U:Price	CURRENCY	1 value(s)	Unit price
5	Tax?	INTEGER	1 value(s)	Taxable?
6	T:Price	CURRENCY	1 value(s)	Total price
7	P:Date	DATE	1 value(s)	Purchase date

Figure 17.4: The structure of the CHistory table

TABLE: PAYMENTS

COLUMN DEFINITIONS

#	Name	Type	Length	Description
1	CustNo	INTEGER	1 value(s)	Customer number
2	Check:No	INTEGER	1 value(s)	Check number
3	Amount	CURRENCY	1 value(s)	Payment amount
4	Pay:Date	DATE	1 value(s)	Date of payment

Figure 17.5: The structure of the Payments table

Finally, to simplify the printing of bills, a special table named BillTemp will hold records of both the Charges and Payments transactions. (We'll explain the purpose of the BillTemp table later in this chapter.) The structure for the BillTemp table is shown in Figure 17.7.

The hierarchical relationship of the ARMain, Charges, Payments, and two History tables is shown in Figure 17.8. The ARMain table is a *master table* because it maintains ongoing balances of individual customers' credit activities. The Charges and Payments tables are *transaction tables* because they record individual transactions during the month. Through *updating,* the ARMain master table receives

TABLE: PHISTORY

COLUMN DEFINITIONS

#	Name	Type	Length	Description
1	CustNo	INTEGER	1 value(s)	Customer number
2	Check:No	INTEGER	1 value(s)	Check number
3	Amount	CURRENCY	1 value(s)	Payment amount
4	Pay:Date	DATE	1 value(s)	Date of payment

Figure 17.6: The structure of the PHistory table

TABLE: BILLTEMP

COLUMN DEFINITIONS

#	Name	Type	Length	Description
1	CustNo	INTEGER	1 value(s)	Customer number
2	ProdNo	TEXT	5 characters	Product number
3	Qty	INTEGER	1 value(s)	Quantity
4	U:Price	CURRENCY	1 value(s)	Unit price
5	Tax?	INTEGER	1 value(s)	Taxable?
6	T:Price	CURRENCY	1 value(s)	Total price
7	P:Date	DATE	1 value(s)	Purchase date
8	Check:No	INTEGER	1 value(s)	Check number
9	Amount	CURRENCY	1 value(s)	Payment amount
10	Pay:Date	DATE	1 value(s)	Payment date

Figure 17.7: The structure of the BillTemp table

data from the transaction tables to keep each customer's balances up-to-date. The PHistory and CHistory tables are *history tables,* which record "old" transaction data that have already been through the entire monthly billing cycle.

If you are following along on-line, go ahead and use Definition EXPRESS to create the new database named ARSys. Create each of

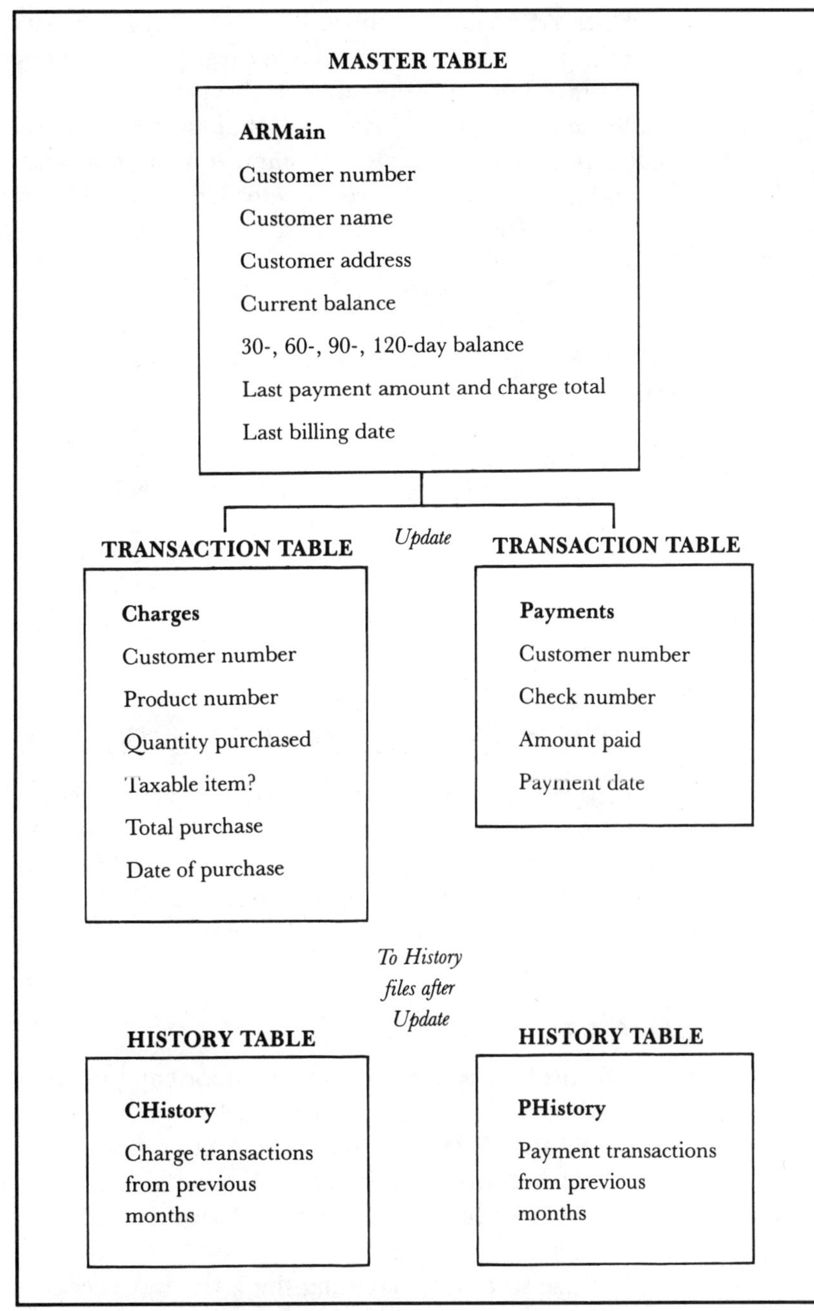

Figure 17.8: The relationship among the tables in the accounts-receivable system

the tables ARMain, Inventry, Charges, Payments, and BillTemp using the structures shown in the figures. (You don't need to define key columns for any of the tables at this point.)

After creating all five tables, exit Definition EXPRESS and return to the R> prompt. From the R> prompt, you can easily create the CHistory and PHistory tables by copying the Charges and Payments tables. First, open the new ARSys database by entering the command

```
OPEN ARSys
```

at the R> prompt. Then enter the two commands below at the R> prompt:

```
PROJECT CHistory FROM Charges USING ALL
PROJECT PHistory FROM Payments USING ALL
```

Once you've defined the tables, you can begin developing forms for entering and editing data.

FORMS FOR YOUR ACCOUNTS-RECEIVABLE SYSTEM

After you've created the accounts-receivable system tables, you can begin developing forms for entering and editing data. Bring up the Forms EXPRESS module, and open the ARSys database if necessary. (Remember, you can access Forms EXPRESS by entering the FORMS command at the R> prompt.)

THE CUSTOMER FORM

In Forms EXPRESS, create a form for entering and editing customer information. Assign the name Main to the form, and attach it to the ARMain table. You don't need to customize the table, form, or field characteristics on this form. Nor do you need to define any expressions for this form. Figure 17.9 shows a suggested format for the form.

Press Esc twice after creating the form and select *Save Changes* to save it.

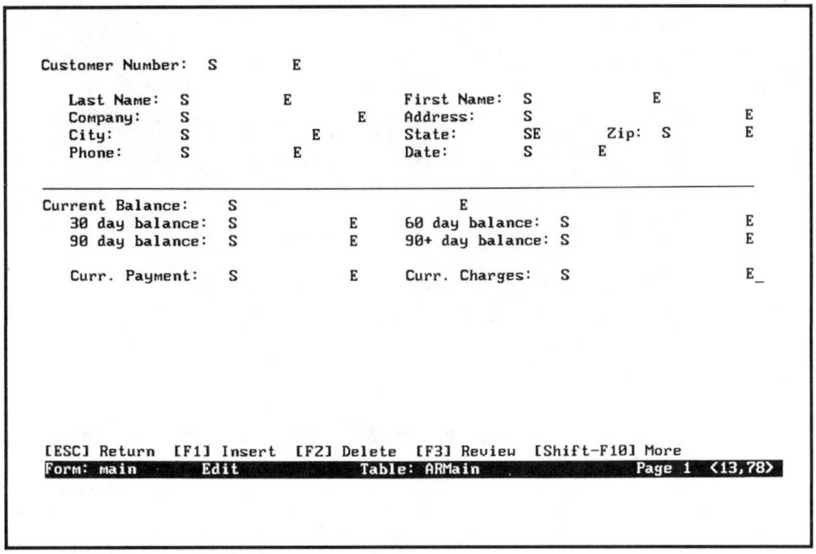

```
Customer Number:  S          E

    Last Name:   S          E              First Name:  S              E
    Company:     S                  E      Address:     S                          E
    City:        S             E           State:       SE        Zip:  S          E
    Phone:       S          E              Date:        S         E

Current Balance:      S                          E
    30 day balance:   S             E      60 day balance:  S                      E
    90 day balance:   S             E      90+ day balance: S                      E

    Curr. Payment:    S             E      Curr. Charges:   S                      E_

[ESC] Return  [F1] Insert  [F2] Delete  [F3] Review  [Shift-F10] More
Form: main          Edit              Table: ARMain                Page 1  <13,78>
```

Figure 17.9: The Main form on the screen

THE INVENTORY TABLE FORM

You can use Forms EXPRESS to create a form for entering and editing items in the inventory table. Name this form InvForm, and attach it to the Inventry table. You don't need to define any expression or customize any table or form characteristics for this form. Figure 17.10 shows a suggested format for the form. Once again, column names are shown on the figure, but these will not appear on your screen.

For added convenience, you may want to customize the field characteristics for the Tax? and Last:Upd fields. You can do so either while locating the column names with the F6 key or by returning the cursor to any place between the S and the E for the column names and pressing F6. Answer Yes to the question about customizing field characteristics. Change the answer to the question about displaying a default value to Yes. For the Tax? field, enter **1** as the default value. For the Last:Upd field, enter **#DATE** as the default value.

After creating the form, press Esc twice and select Save Changes to save the form.

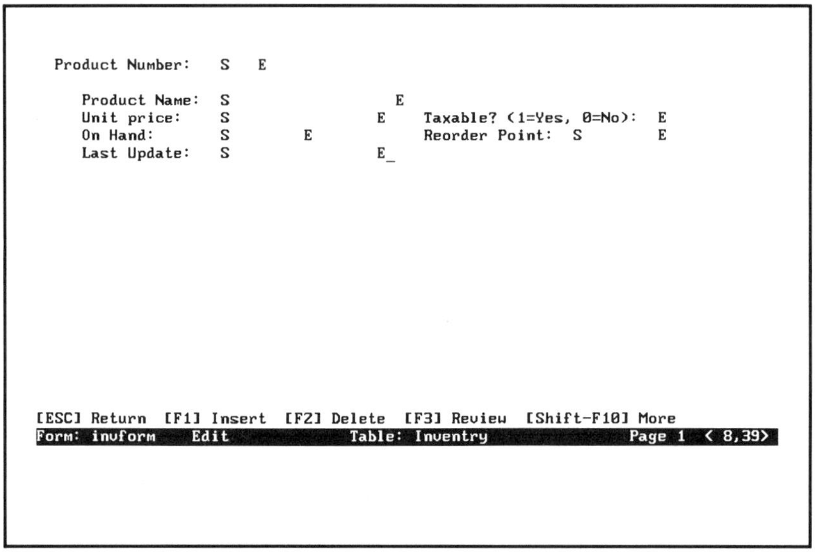

```
Product Number:   S   E

   Product Name:  S               E
   Unit price:    S             E    Taxable? (1=Yes, 0=No):  E
   On Hand:       S       E          Reorder Point:  S        E
   Last Update:   S             E_

[ESC] Return  [F1] Insert  [F2] Delete  [F3] Review  [Shift-F10] More
Form: invform    Edit             Table: Inventry              Page 1  < 8,39>
```

Figure 17.10: The InvForm form on the screen

THE CHARGES FORM

The form for entering and editing charges will be fancier than the Main and InvForm forms. For convenience, this form will automatically look up the customer name and company from the ARMain table when the user enters a customer number onto the form. These data will be displayed on the form so the user can verify that the correct customer number was entered.

As soon as the user enters a product number for the transaction, the form will look up the product name, unit price, and tax status on the Inventry table. These data will appear on the form immediately and will also be entered into the Charges table automatically. The user only needs to enter the quantity purchased, and the form will calculate and display the total sale.

Use Forms EXPRESS to create the form. Assign the name **ChrgFrm** to the form, and attach it to the Charges table. You don't need to customize any table or form characteristics for this form. From the top menu select Expression Define, and enter each of the expressions below:

```
Name1 = F:Name IN ARMain WHERE CustNo = CustNo
Name2 = L:Name IN ARMain WHERE CustNo = CustNo
```

```
VName = Name1 & Name2
VCompany = Company IN ARMain WHERE CustNo = CustNo
VPartNm = PartName IN Inventry WHERE ProdNo = ProdNo
U:Price = U:Price IN Inventry WHERE ProdNo = ProdNo
Tax? = Tax? IN Inventry WHERE ProdNo = ProdNo
T:Price = (IFEQ(Tax?,0,Qty*U:Price,(Qty*U:Price)*1.06))
```

Notice that the first four expressions look up information in the ARMain table based on the customer number entered onto the form. It stores the customer name and company from the ARMain table in the variables named VName and VCompany.

The last four expressions look up information in the Inventry table. The part name is stored in the variable named VPartNm. The unit price and tax are stored directly in the Charges table (because of the column names Tax? and U:Price, which are the actual column names in the Charges table). The total price (T:Price) is calculated using the IFEQ function to determine whether the item is taxable. T:Price is also a column name in the Charges table, and hence the results of this calculation are stored directly on the Charges table.

After defining the expressions for the form, press Esc twice and select Edit from the top menu to lay out the form. Figure 17.11 shows a suggested format for the ChrgFrm form. Again, column and variable names are displayed in the figure for clarity, but these will not appear on your screen.

For convenience, you can customize the field characteristics for the P:Date column and specify **#DATE** as the default value for the field. After creating the ChrgFrm form, press Esc twice and select Save Changes to save your work.

THE PAYMENTS FORM

The payments form lets the user enter and edit data on the Payments table. Use Forms EXPRESS as usual to create the form. Assign the name **PayForm** to the form, and attach the form to the Payments table.

From the top menu in Forms EXPRESS select Expression Define, and create the following expressions:

```
Name1 = F:Name IN ARMain WHERE CustNo = CustNo
Name2 = L:Name IN ARMain WHERE CustNo = CustNo
VName = Name1 & Name2
```

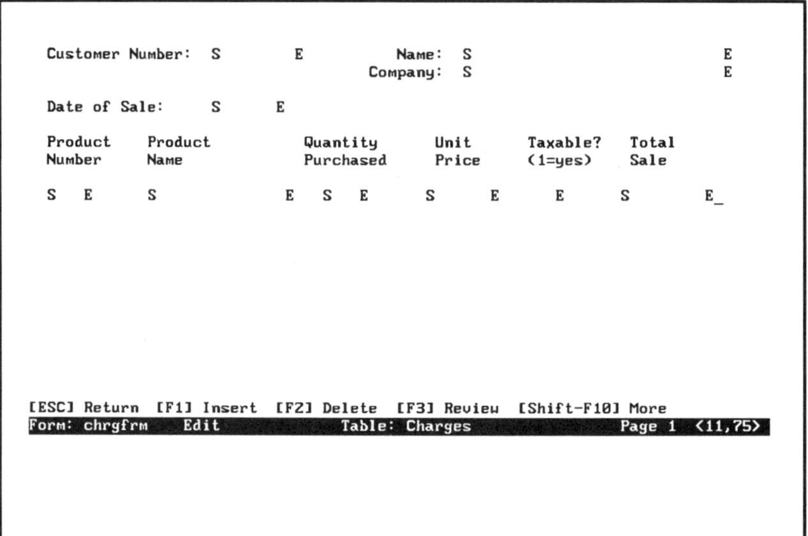
```
Customer Number:  S          E            Name:  S                                   E
                                       Company:  S                                   E

Date of Sale:     S       E

Product      Product               Quantity     Unit       Taxable?   Total
Number       Name                  Purchased    Price      (1=yes)    Sale

S    E       S                E    S    E       S      E       E      S          E_

[ESC] Return  [F1] Insert  [F2] Delete  [F3] Review  [Shift-F10] More
Form: chrgfrm      Edit              Table: Charges                    Page 1  <11,75>
```

Figure 17.11: The ChrgFrm form on the screen

VCompany = Company in ARMain WHERE CustNo = CustNo

Note that these expressions look up customer information in the ARMain table based on the customer number entered onto the form. The form will display this information for the user's convenience when the form is used to record or edit payment transactions.

After defining the expressions, press Esc twice and select Edit from the top menu to lay out the form format. Figure 17.12 shows a suggested format for the PayForm form. Again, column and variable names are included in the figure, but these will not appear on your screen.

For additional convenience, you can customize the field characteristics for the Pay:Date column by entering **#DATE** as the default date for the column.

After all four forms are created, you can exit Forms EXPRESS to return to the R> prompt.

RULES FOR YOUR ACCOUNTS-RECEIVABLE SYSTEM

To avoid entering duplicate customer numbers in the ARMain table and duplicate product numbers in the Inventry table, you can

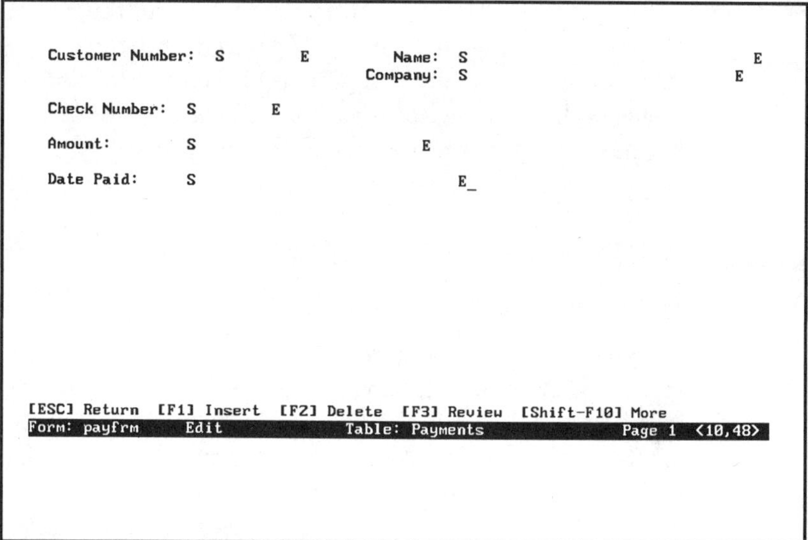

Figure 17.12: The PayForm form on the screen

create a few rules. Enter Definition EXPRESS to define the rules (you can get to Definition EXPRESS from the R> prompt by entering the command RBDefine).

From the Definition EXPRESS Main menu, select option 2, *Modify an existing database definition*. Select option 4, Rules, and option 1, *Add a New Rule*, to create some new rules.

To disallow duplicate customer numbers in the ARMain table, enter the message

Duplicate Customer Number!

when requested by the screen. Select ARMain as the table for the rule and CustNo as the column to validate. Select NEA (not equal any) as the operator and ARMain as the table to compare to. Select CustNo as the column to compare to, and select Done as the final logical operator.

To create a rule to disallow duplicate product numbers in the Inventry table, select option 1 from the menu once again to add a new rule. Enter the message

Duplicate Product Number!

when requested. Select Inventry as the table for the rule and ProdNo as the column to validate. Select NEA as the operator, Inventry as the table to compare to, and ProdNo as the column to compare to. Select Done as the final logical operator. After creating the rules, exit the various menus to return to the R> prompt.

REPORTS FOR YOUR ACCOUNTS-RECEIVABLE SYSTEM

You can create whatever reports you wish for the accounts-receivable system. In fact, you might want to develop reports similar to the Labels, Letter1, Director, and Sales reports that we developed for the Mail database. Also, simple reports displaying data from the Payments and Inventry table would be useful.

One of the primary reports for the accounts-receivable system will be the Aging report, which is shown in Figure 17.13.

```
                ACCOUNTS RECEIVABLE AGING REPORT

Date: 09/22/88                                  Page:  1
Current Bal.  30-Days    60-Days    90-Days   120-Days Payment

Customer Number: 1001   Stewart Smith
  $1,171.00    $56.00   $256.00     $0.00    $203.00    $100.00
Customer Number: 1002   Wanda Watson
    $696.00    $70.00    $80.00     $0.00    $296.00    $200.00
Customer Number: 1003   Zeppo Magillicuddy
    $200.00    $50.00    $85.00   $100.00      $0.00      $0.00
```

Figure 17.13: A sample Aging report from the accounts-receivable system

From the R> prompt, enter the command

```
REPORTS Aging
```

to begin designing the report layout. When prompted, enter the name **ARMain** as the table for the report. Select the Expression and

Define options and define the following report variables:

```
RepDate   = .#DATE
PgNo      = .#PAGE
Name1     = F:Name
Name2     = L:Name
FullName  = (Name1 & Name2)
```

Figure 17.14 shows a suggested format for the Aging report. Use the arrow, F7, F8, and F9 keys to enter text and create sections, and use the F6 key to locate column and variable names. Press Esc twice and select Save Changes when you are finished creating the report format.

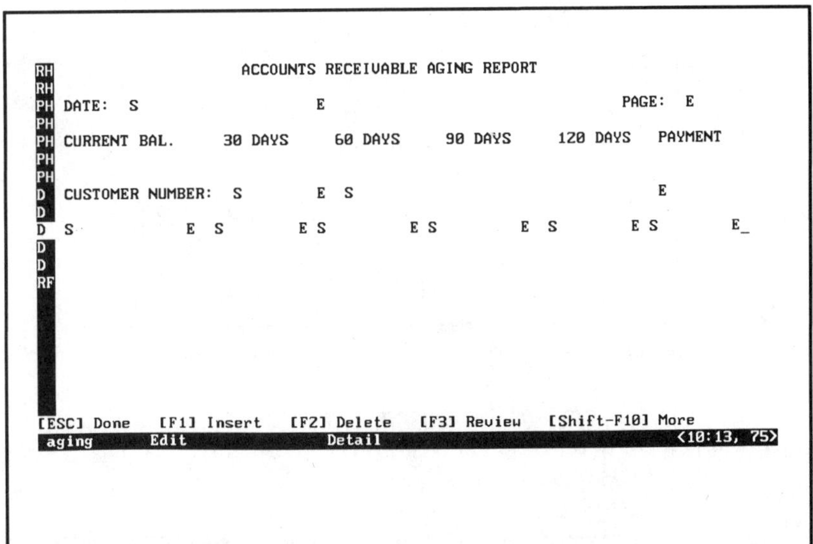

Figure 17.14: The Aging report layout on the Reports screen

The Bills report prints monthly statements, a sample of which is shown in Figure 17.15.

Enter the command

```
REPORTS Bills
```

to begin designing the Bills report format. The associated table name is **BillTemp**. Select the Expression and Define options, and create

Andy Adams
ABC Co.
123 A St.
San Diego CA 92111

Customer Number: 1001   Billing Date:06/26/88   Due Date:07/26/88

Product	Qty	Unit Price	Tax?	Total	Payment
A-111 Semiconductor	10	$ 1.56	1	$ 16.54	
B-100 RF Modulator	5	$34.56	1	$183.17	
A-111 Semiconductor	90	$ 1.56	1	$148.82	
					$50.00

Previous Balance:	$697.06
Total Charges:	$348.53
Total Payments:	$ 50.00
Current Balance:	$995.59

Figure 17.15: A sample bill printed by the accounts-receivable system

the report variables listed below:

```
RepDate   = .#DATE
PgNo      = .#PAGE
Name1     = F:Name IN ARMain WHERE CustNo = CustNo
Name2     = L:Name IN ARMain WHERE CustNo = CustNo
FullName  = (.Name1 & .Name2)
Comp      = Company IN ARMain WHERE CustNo = CustNo
Add       = Address IN ARMain WHERE CustNo = CustNo
C         = City IN ARMain WHERE CustNo = CustNo
S         = State IN ARMain WHERE CustNo = CustNo
Z         = Zip IN ARMain WHERE CustNo = CustNo
Comma     = ","
CSZ       = .C + .Comma & .S & .Z
B:Date    = .#DATE
```

```
D:Date      = B:Date + 30
PartNm      = PartName IN Inventry WHERE ProdNo = ProdNo
              AND ProdNo EXISTS
Prev:Bal    = Curr:Bal IN ARMain WHERE CustNo = CustNo
ChrgTot     = SUM OF T:Price
PayTot      = SUM OF Amount
Sub:Bal     = Prev:Bal + ChrgTot
Balance     = Sub:Bal - PayTot
```

Several of these variables warrant discussion. First, note that the Name, Company, Address, City, State, Zip, and Curr:Bal (current balance) variables are all taken from the ARMain table, using the option

```
IN ARMain WHERE CustNo = CustNo
```

Similarly, the product name is taken from the Inventry table using the expression

```
PartNm = PartName IN Inventry WHERE ProdNo = ProdNo +
+ > AND ProdNo EXISTS
```

(We used a technique similar to this when developing the Sales report in the Mail database.)

The B:Date (billing date) variable is assigned the current date (.#DATE), and the D:Date (due date) variable is calculated by adding 30 days to the billing date variable (B:Date + 30).

Balances for each bill are calculated by summing the total charges (ChrgTot = SUM OF T:Price) and summing the total payments (PayTot = SUM OF Amount), and then adding the total charges to the current balance (Sub:Bal = Prev:Bal + ChrgTot) and subtracting the total payments (Balance = Sub:Bal – PayTot).

After typing in all the expressions, press Esc and select Configure from the top menu. You'll want to make CustNo the breakpoint for each subtotal (and hence, for each invoice, since one invoice is printed for each customer). To do so, make CustNo the Break column for the Break1 point. Change the Variable Reset column to Yes, and select the following variables to reset:

```
ChrgTot
PayTot
```

Sub:Bal
Balance

Also, to ensure that each invoice is printed on a separate page, change the Header Before column under FORM FEEDS to [YES], so that the top portion of the screen looks like this:

	BREAKPOINTS		FORM FEEDS			
			Header		Footer	
	Break Column	Variable Reset	Before	After	Before	After
Report			[NO]	[NO]	[NO]	[NO]
Page		[NO]				
Break1	CustNo	[YES]	[YES]			

Press Esc after setting the configurations, and then select Edit to lay out the report format. Figure 17.16 shows a suggested report format. Column and variable names are shown between appropriate S and E locations, although these will not appear on your screen.

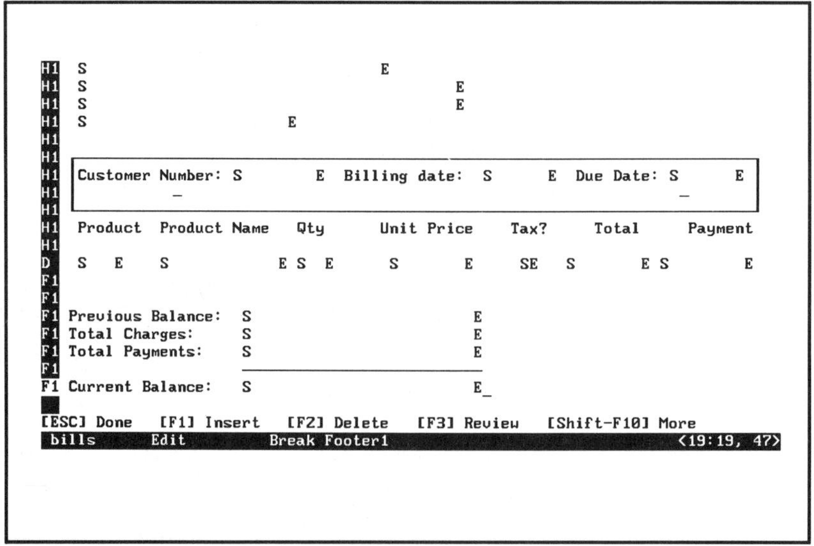

Figure 17.16: The layout for the Bills report

Since the Bills report gets its data from the BillTemp table, which is currently empty, we can't test it yet. In the next section we'll develop the appropriate command file to print the bills.

COMMAND FILES FOR YOUR ACCOUNTS-RECEIVABLE SYSTEM

Most of the command files for the accounts-receivable system can be created by using the Application EXPRESS menu. However, a few custom programs and subroutines will help refine the system. In this section, we'll develop these command files and subroutines, and we'll learn some advanced programming techniques along the way.

END-OF-MONTH PROCEDURES

Most accounting systems are based on a monthly schedule, whereby transactions are posted to a ledger at the end of each month. Our accounts-receivable system is no exception, and the tasks performed at the end of each month can be summarized as follows:

1. Print monthy statements (bills or invoices).
2. Shift all current and 30-, 60-, 90-, and 120-day balances back one month.
3. Add new charges to the current balance.
4. Subtract new payments from the current balance.

We can write a single command file to handle all of these tasks, and the user will be able to perform them simply by selecting a menu item. The command file to perform these tasks is named EndMonth.CMD, and it is displayed in Figure 17.17.

When first run, the command file displays the following message:

```
Bills are to be printed once a month only
Monthly updates are automatically performed after billing
Proceed with billing? (Y/N)
```

The purpose of this message is to give the user a chance to change his mind, since the procedure is only to be performed once a month. The message is stored in a separate file named Bills.MSG. To create the message file, enter

RBEDIT Bills.MSG

at the R> prompt; then type in the message exactly as it appears above. Save the file in the usual way.

```
*(*************************************** EndMonth.CMD)
*(------------------ Perform monthly billing and update)
NEWPAGE
DISPLAY Bills.MSG
SET VARIABLE YesNo TEXT
FILLIN YesNo USING " " AT 22,1
IF YesNo <> Y THEN
   GOTO Bailout
ENDIF *(yesno <> y)

NEWPAGE
WRITE "Prepare printer, then press any key to continue"
PAUSE

*(--- Set up the BillTemp Table)
NEWPAGE
WRITE "Working..."
SET RULES OFF
SET MESSAGES OFF
SET ERROR MESSAGES OFF
DELETE ROWS FROM BillTemp WHERE COUNT > 0
APPEND Charges TO BillTemp WHERE CustNo EXISTS
APPEND Payments TO BillTemp WHERE CustNo EXISTS

*(--- Print the invoices)
SET NULL " "
SET DATE "MM/DD/YY"
OUTPUT PRINTER
NEWPAGE
PRINT Bills
NEWPAGE
OUTPUT SCREEN
SET NULL -0-

*(--- Perform the update)
*(--- First, shift back Current, 30, 60, and 90 day balances)
CHANGE Bal:120 TO (Bal:120+Bal:90) +
 IN ARMain WHERE CustNo EXISTS
CHANGE Bal:90 TO Bal:60 IN ARMain WHERE CustNo EXISTS
CHANGE Bal:60 TO Bal:30 IN ARMain WHERE CustNo EXISTS
CHANGE Bal:30 TO Curr:Chr IN ARMain WHERE CustNo EXISTS

*(--- Set current charges and payments to zero.)
CHANGE Curr:Chr TO 0 IN ARMain WHERE CustNo Exists
CHANGE Curr:Pay TO 0 IN ARMain WHERE CustNo Exists

*(--- Next, update current balance from Charges and Payments)
RUN Update.MAC USING ARMain CustNo Curr:Chr Charges CustNo T:Price PLUS
RUN Update.MAC USING ARMain CustNo Curr:Pay Payments CustNo Amount PLUS

CHANGE Curr:Bal TO (Curr:Bal+(Curr:Chr-Curr:Pay)) +
 IN ARMain WHERE CustNo EXISTS
CHANGE BillDate TO .#DATE IN ARMain WHERE CustNo EXISTS
```

Figure 17.17: The EndMonth.CMD command file

```
*(--- Now move transactions to history files)
APPEND Charges TO CHistory
DELETE ROWS FROM Charges WHERE Count > 0
APPEND Payments TO PHistory
DELETE ROWS FROM Payments WHERE Count > 0

*(---- Now age the balances using the Age.CMD command file.)
RUN Age.CMD

*(--- Update complete)
NEWPAGE
SET MESSAGES ON
SET ERROR MESSAGES ON
WRITE "End of month procedures completed..."
SET RULES ON
RETURN

*(--- Bailout routine for immediate exit)
LABEL Bailout
WRITE "Returning to Main Menu without Update"
RETURN
```

Figure 17.17: The EndMonth.CMD command file (continued)

Now let's look at the EndMonth.CMD command file. The first lines include programmer comments and the command to clear the screen. The DISPLAY command displays the Bills.MSG file we just created with RBEDIT, and the FILLIN command waits for a response from the user on whether to proceed with the end-of-month procedures. If the user does not answer Y, control is passed to a routine named Bailout at the bottom of the command file:

```
*(************************************* EndMonth.CMD)
*(-------------- Perform monthly billing and update)
NEWPAGE
DISPLAY Bills.MSG
SET VARIABLE YesNo TEXT
FILLIN YesNo USING " " AT 22,1
IF YesNo <> Y THEN
   GOTO Bailout
ENDIF *(yesno <> y)
```

If the user chooses to go ahead with the monthly procedure, the command file displays the following prompt reminding him to prepare the printer and waits for him to press any key to continue:

```
NEWPAGE
WRITE "Prepare printer, then press any key to continue"
PAUSE
```

Next, the command file clears the screen and displays the message "Working . . .". The R:BASE rules and messages are then set off.

```
*(– Set up the BillTemp Table)
NEWPAGE
WRITE "Working . . ."
SET RULES OFF
SET MESSAGES OFF
SET ERROR MESSAGES OFF
```

Next, the command file prepares the BillTemp table for printing bills. The BillTemp table consists of both charges and payments. The two tables are combined into BillTemp for printing reports, because R:BASE only allows a single transaction table in a report. We could have used a single table like BillTemp to record both Charges and Payments throughout the system; but for general data management, it may be preferable to keep the two tables separate, as we have done in this example.

First, the command file deletes any rows currently in the BillTemp table, since any rows there are no doubt from last month's billings. The DELETE ROWS command below performs the deletions:

```
DELETE ROWS FROM BillTemp WHERE COUNT > 0
```

Next, the command file appends rows from the Charges and Payments tables onto the BillTemp table:

```
APPEND Charges TO BillTemp WHERE CustNo EXISTS
APPEND Payments TO BillTemp WHERE CustNo EXISTS
```

Next the command file prints the invoices. To keep null fields from being displayed as -0- symbols, the command file uses the command

```
SET NULL " "
```

to display all null values as blanks. The date format is set to the MM/DD/YY format, and output is channeled to the printer. The NEWPAGE command starts the printing on a new page, and the PRINT Bills command prints the invoices using the report format named Bills. After the invoices are printed, NEWPAGE again ejects the paper in the printer, sets the output back to the screen, and resets the null character to -0-, as follows:

```
*(– Print the invoices)
SET NULL " "
SET DATE "MM/DD/YY"
OUTPUT PRINTER
NEWPAGE
PRINT Bills
NEWPAGE
OUTPUT SCREEN
SET NULL -0-
```

Once the bills are printed, a series of CHANGE commands is used to shift the 90-day, 60-day, 30-day, and current balances back one month, as shown below:

```
*(– Perform the update)
*(– First, shift back Current, 30, 60, and 90 day balances)
CHANGE Bal:120 TO (Bal:120 + Bal:90) +
IN ARMain WHERE CustNo EXISTS
CHANGE Bal:90 TO Bal:60 IN ARMain WHERE CustNo EXISTS
CHANGE Bal:60 TO Bal:30 IN ARMain WHERE CustNo EXISTS
CHANGE Bal:30 TO Curr:Chr IN ARMain +
WHERE CustNo EXISTS
```

Since this is the start of a new month, the current charges (Curr:Chr) and current payments (Curr:Pay) are reset to zero in all the rows in the ARMain table, using a couple of CHANGE commands as follows:

```
*(– Set current charges and payments to zero.)
CHANGE Curr:Chr TO 0 IN ARMain WHERE CustNo Exists
CHANGE Curr:Pay TO 0 IN ARMain WHERE CustNo Exists
```

Next, a custom macro named Update.MAC (which we'll develop later) adjusts the current charges (Curr:Chr) and current payments (Curr:Pay) columns in the ARMain table to reflect charges and payments currently listed in the Charges and Payments tables:

```
*(– Next, update current balance from Charges and Payments)
RUN Update.MAC USING ARMain CustNo Curr:Chr Charges +
CustNo T:Price PLUS
```

```
RUN Update.MAC USING ARMain CustNo Curr:Pay +
Payments CustNo Amount PLUS
```

Next, a CHANGE command changes the current balance (Curr:Bal) column to reflect the previous month's balance, plus the current charges minus the current payments:

```
CHANGE Curr:Bal TO (Curr:Bal + (Curr:Chr – Curr:Pay)) +
IN ARMain WHERE CustNo EXISTS
```

The BillDate column in the ARMain table is changed in all rows to reflect the date of the invoices just printed (which is the same as the system date, .#DATE):

```
CHANGE BillDate TO .#DATE IN ARMain WHERE CustNo +
EXISTS
```

Once all of the updating is done, current transactions from both the Charges and Payments tables are appended onto the CHistory and PHistory tables and deleted from the Charges and Payments tables. This keeps the Charges and Payments tables small, which helps speed general processing.

```
*(– Now move transactions to history tables)
APPEND Charges TO CHistory
DELETE ROWS FROM Charges WHERE COUNT > 0
APPEND Payments TO PHistory
DELETE ROWS FROM Payments WHERE  COUNT > 0
```

The next step is to age the existing balances by incrementally subtracting the current payment from the current aged balances. This task is handled by a command file named Age.CMD, which we'll develop soon. The EndMonth.CMD calls upon Age.CMD to age the balances in the line below:

```
*(– Now age the balances using the Age.CMD command file.)
RUN Age.CMD
```

At this point, the end-of-month procedures are finished. The command file sets the normal messages back on, displays a prompt, and returns control to the calling program, as follows:

```
*(– Update complete)
NEWPAGE
```

```
SET MESSAGES ON
SET ERROR MESSAGES ON
WRITE "End of month procedures completed..."
SET RULES ON
RETURN
```

One last routine in the EndMonth.CMD command file is the Bailout routine, which is called if the user does not wish to perform the procedures. The Bailout routine is shown below:

```
*(– Bailout routine for immediate exit)
LABEL Bailout
WRITE "Returning to Main Menu without Update"
RETURN
```

AGING THE ACCOUNTS

The EndMonth.CMD command file already performed one aspect involved in aging the accounts receivable; that of shifting all the 30-, 60-, 90-, and over-90-day balances back one month (because, presumably, another 30 days have passed when the EndMonth.CMD command file is run). The EndMonth.CMD command file did so with a series of Change commands, as discussed earlier.

The Bal:120 column actually records (and accumulates) all balances over 90 days past due. (In other words, balances in the Bal:120 column are not shifted off to the right into oblivion.) However, for a true picture of the aged receivables, one should subtract the current payment from the aged balances, starting at the oldest period (Bal:120 in this case) and working toward the Bal:30 balance.

Incrementally subtracting the current payment from the aged balances is a large job and hence is handled separately in a command file named Age.CMD. Recall that the EndMonth.CMD "calls" Age.CMD to perform this task with the command

```
RUN Age.CMD.
```

The entire Age.CMD command file is shown in Figure 17.18. You can use the RBEDIT editor to key in this command file exactly as shown in the figure.

```
*(------------------------------------ Age.CMD
          Ages accounts receivable balances
          by incrementally subtracting current
          payment from existing balances.)

*(------------------ Set up variables.)
SET VARIABLE Remain CURRENCY
SET VARIABLE More INTEGER
SET VARIABLE NextBal INTEGER
SET VARIABLE BAL120 CURRENCY
SET VARIABLE BAL90 CURRENCY
SET VARIABLE BAL60 CURRENCY
SET VARIABLE BAL30 CURRENCY

*(----------------- Display opening messages)
NEWPAGE
WRITE "Aging the balances..." AT 1,1

*(----- Set up pointer for loop through table)
SET POINTER #1 Status FOR ARMain

WHILE Status = 0 THEN
   *(-- 0 is "false", 1 is "true" below)
   SET VARIABLE More TO 0
   SET VARIABLE NextBal TO 1
   SET VARIABLE Remain TO 0

   *(------- 90+ day balance)
   SET VARIABLE ThisPay TO Curr:Pay IN #1
   SET VARIABLE Bal120 TO Bal:120 IN #1
   IF Bal120 > 0 THEN
      SET VARIABLE Remain TO .ThisPay - .Bal120
      IF Remain >= 0 THEN
         CHANGE Bal:120 TO 0 IN #1
         SET VARIABLE More TO 1
      ELSE
         CHANGE Bal:120 TO (.Remain * -1) IN #1
         SET VARIABLE NextBal TO 0
      ENDIF
   ENDIF

   *(------- 90 day balance)
   SET VARIABLE Bal90 TO Bal:90 IN #1
   IF NextBal=1 AND Bal90 > 0 THEN
      IF More = 1 THEN
         SET VARIABLE Remain TO .Remain - .Bal90
      ELSE
         SET VARIABLE Remain TO .ThisPay - .Bal90
      ENDIF
      IF Remain >= 0 THEN
         CHANGE Bal:90 TO 0 IN #1
         SET VARIABLE More TO 1
      ELSE
         CHANGE Bal:90 TO (.Remain * -1) IN #1
         SET VARIABLE NextBal TO 0
      ENDIF
   ENDIF

   *(------- 60 day balance)
   SET VARIABLE Bal60 TO Bal:60 IN #1
   IF NextBal=1 AND Bal60 > 0 THEN
      IF More = 1 THEN
         SET VARIABLE Remain TO (.Remain - .Bal60)
      ELSE
         SET VARIABLE Remain TO (.ThisPay - .Bal60)
      ENDIF
      IF Remain >= 0 THEN
         CHANGE Bal:60 TO 0 IN #1
         SET VARIABLE More TO 1
      ELSE
         CHANGE Bal:60 TO (.Remain * -1) IN #1
         SET VARIABLE NextBal TO 0
      ENDIF
   ENDIF
```

Figure 17.18: The Age.CMD command file

```
*(------- 30 day balance)
SET VARIABLE Bal30 TO Bal:30 IN #1
IF NextBal=1 AND Bal30 > 0 THEN
   IF More = 1 THEN
      SET VARIABLE Remain TO (.Remain - .Bal30)
   ELSE
      SET VARIABLE Remain TO (.ThisPay - .Bal30)
   ENDIF
   IF Remain >= 0 THEN
      CHANGE Bal:30 TO 0 IN #1
      SET VARIABLE More TO 1
   ELSE
      CHANGE Bal:30 TO (.Remain * -1) IN #1
      SET VARIABLE NextBal TO 0
   ENDIF
ENDIF

   NEXT #1 Status
ENDWHILE

NEWPAGE
SET POINTER #1 OFF
WRITE "End of month procedures completed..."
RETURN
```

Figure 17.18: The Age.CMD command file (continued)

Let's briefly discuss how Age.CMD incrementally subtracts the current payment from the existing aged balances. First, numerous variables are created with predefined data types. The lines below set up the variable data types:

```
*(– – – – – – – – – – – – – – – – – – – – – – – Set up variables.)
SET VARIABLE Remain CURRENCY
SET VARIABLE More INTEGER
SET VARIABLE NextBal INTEGER
SET VARIABLE BAL120 CURRENCY
SET VARIABLE BAL90 CURRENCY
SET VARIABLE BAL60 CURRENCY
SET VARIABLE BAL30 CURRENCY
```

A pointer is created, as below, to move through the ARMain table one row at a time. (Whenever a new SET POINTER command is issued, the "pointer" always starts at the first row in the table.)

```
*(– – Set up pointer for loop through table)
SET POINTER #1 Status FOR ARMain
```

Then a WHILE loop is set up, as below, to access a row in the table repeatedly until the last row is processed (at which point the Status variable will no longer equal zero):

```
WHILE Status = 0 THEN
```

The variable Morc is used throughout the command file to determine whether the remainder to be subtracted from the next aged balance is greater than zero. (If More is one, then there is more to be subtracted. If More is zero, there is no more to be subtracted.)

The variable NextBal determines whether the next balance needs to be adjusted. (If NextBal is one, then the next balance needs to be adjusted. If NextBal is zero, the next balance does not need to be adjusted.) The Remain variable keeps track of the remainder of the current payment that needs to be subtracted from the next aged balance. These three variables receive their initial values in the commands below:

```
*(– 0 is "false", 1 is "true" below)
SET VARIABLE More TO 0
SET VARIABLE NextBal TO 1
SET VARIABLE Remain TO 0
```

Now the command file begins incrementally subtracting the current payment from the aged balances, starting at the Bal:120 (or over-90-day) balance. In the line below, a variable named ThisPay receives the value of the current payment in the row being analyzed:

```
*(– – – 90+ day balance)
SET VARIABLE ThisPay TO Curr:Pay IN #1
```

A variable named Bal120 receives the column value of the over-90-day balance in the current row, as follows:

```
SET VARIABLE Bal120 TO Bal:120 IN #1
```

If there is, indeed, a balance in the over-90-day category (that is, the Bal:120 column is greater than zero), then the Remain variable is set to the current payment minus the amount of the Bal:120 balance, as below:

```
IF Bal120 > 0 THEN
     SET VARIABLE Remain TO .ThisPay - .Bal120
```

If this remainder is greater than or equal to zero, then the balance in the Bal:120 column is set to zero, and the More variable is set to one ("true") to indicate that there is more payment to be subtracted from other balances.

```
IF Remain >= 0 THEN
     CHANGE Bal:120 TO 0 IN #1
     SET VARIABLE More TO 1
```

If the remainder is not greater than or equal to zero, then the over-90-day balance (Bal:120) is set to the absolute (positive) value of the Remain variable, and the NextBal indicator is set to zero ("false"), as follows:

```
   ELSE
      CHANGE Bal:120 TO (.Remain * -1) IN #1
      SET VARIABLE NextBal TO 0
   ENDIF
ENDIF
```

The same basic logic is used for the remaining aged balances. First, a variable named Bal90 receives the value of the Bal:90 column for the current row, as below:

```
*(--- 90 day balance)
SET VARIABLE Bal90 TO Bal:90 IN #1
```

If the "Next Balance" indicator is "true," and there is a value greater than zero in the Bal:90 column, as below, then the command file needs to decide what to do based on the status of the More variable.

```
IF NextBal = 1 AND Bal90 > 0 THEN
```

If the More variable is one ("true"), then the remainder equals itself minus the 90-day balance. If the More variable is not true, then the remainder is the current payment minus the 90-day balance, as follows:

```
IF More = 1 THEN
   SET VARIABLE Remain TO .Remain - .Bal90
ELSE
   SET VARIABLE Remain TO .ThisPay - .Bal90
ENDIF
```

Once that's decided, the command file decides what to do with the remaining payment amount. If this amount is greater than or equal to zero, then the 90-day balance is set to zero, and the More variable is set to one ("true"), as below:

```
IF Remain >= 0 THEN
   CHANGE Bal:90 TO 0 IN #1
   SET VARIABLE More TO 1
```

Otherwise, the 90-day balance is set to the absolute value of the remainder, and the NextBal indicator is set to zero ("false"), as follows:

```
   ELSE
      CHANGE Bal:90 TO (.Remain * -1) IN #1
      SET VARIABLE NextBal TO 0
   ENDIF
ENDIF
```

The same process is repeated for the 60- and 30-day balances.

The command below moves the pointer to the next row in the ARMain table and repeats the aging process for that row:

```
NEXT #1 Status
```

After all aged balances in the ARMain table have been aged, the command

```
SET POINTER #1 OFF
```

releases the pointer, and the command file prints a closing message and returns control to the EndMonth.CMD command file.

```
WRITE "End of month procedures completed..."
RETURN
```

There is one more command file (which is actually a *procedure* or *macro*) that needs to be written to complete the end-of-month procedures. This macro is the one named *Update.MAC* that updates the current charges and payments in the ARMain table from charges and payments in the Charges and Payments tables. Since updating is applicable to many databases (inventory, general ledger, and accounts payable, to name a few), we'll create this command file as a general-purpose macro that can easily be used in a variety of applications.

GENERAL-PURPOSE MACRO

The macro that we'll develop in this section can be used for any type of update. The syntax for using the Update.MAC macro will be the following:

```
RUN Update.MAC USING <master table name> +
+ > <master table common column> <master table update +
+ > column> <transaction table name> <transaction +
+ > table common column> <transaction table +
+ > update column> <type of update>
```

For example, to increment the current charges in the ARMain table by the T:Price amounts in the Charges table, you would use the command

```
RUN Update.MAC USING ARMain CustNo Curr:Chr Charges +
+ > CustNo T:Price PLUS
```

where ARMain is the name of the table to be updated, CustNo is the name of the common column on which to base the update, and Curr:Chr is the name of the column in the ARMain table to be updated. Charges is the name of the transaction table, CustNo is the common column, and T:Price is the column to add to the Curr:Chr column. The PLUS option tells the macro to add the quantities from the Charges table to the current balance.

To update the ARMain table from the Payments table, use the command

```
RUN Update.MAC USING ARMain CustNo Curr:Pay +
+ > Payments CustNo Amount PLUS
```

where, once again, ARMain, CustNo, and Curr:Pay are the name, common column, and column to be updated, respectively. Payments, CustNo, and Amount are the table name, common column, and column to perform the update from, respectively. The PLUS option tells the macro to add the amounts in the Payments table to the current balance in the ARMain table.

The Update.MAC macro is shown in Figure 17.19. Enter the command

```
RBEDIT Update.MAC
```

to create and save the macro, just as you would any standard command file.

Looking at the macro line by line, we see that it begins with many comments. When you're writing general-purpose macros, it's a good idea to list the meaning of the various parameters passed to the macro (%1 through %7 in this example), so that you can remember how to use the macro later.

```
*(*************************************** UPDATE.MAC)
*(- - - - Update a master table from a transaction table)
*( Parameters are: %1: Master table name
                   %2: Master table common column
                   %3: Master table update column
                   %4: Transaction table name
                   %5: Transaction table common column
                   %6: Transaction table update column
                   %7: PLUS MINUS or REPLACE)
```

The first commands in the macro clear the screen and then erase the variables PassVal and Compare. (Since the data type these variables contain from the most recent update may be incorrect for the current update, they are re-created later with the appropriate data type.)

```
NEWPAGE
CLEAR PassVal
CLEAR Compare
```

Next, the command file checks to make sure that the last parameter passed is a valid one. The parameter must be the word PLUS,

```
*(******************************************* UPDATE.MAC)
*(------ Update a master table from a transaction table)

*( Parameters are:    %1: Master table name
                      %2: Master table common column
                      %3: Master table update column
                      %4: Transaction table name
                      %5: Transaction table common column
                      %6: Transaction table update column
                      %7: PLUS MINUS or REPLACE)
NEWPAGE
CLEAR PassVal
CLEAR Compare
*(--- Make sure option %7 is valid)
IF %7 = PLUS OR %7 = MINUS OR %7 = REPLACE THEN
   WRITE "Performing update... Please wait"
   SET MESSAGES OFF
   SET ERROR MESSAGES OFF
ELSE
   WRITE "Invalid update option"
   WRITE "Must be PLUS, MINUS or REPLACE"
   WRITE "Press any key to try again..." AT 20 1
   PAUSE
   GOTO BailOut
ENDIF *(%7 option valid)

*(------------------ Set up pointer)
SET POINTER #1 Status1 FOR .%4 ORDER BY .%5
WHILE Status1 = 0 THEN
      SET VARIABLE PassVal TO .%6 IN #1
      SET VARIABLE Compare TO .%5 IN #1
      *(--- Update using PLUS)
      IF %7 = PLUS AND Compare EXISTS THEN
         SET VARIABLE CurrVal TO .%3 IN .%1 WHERE .%2 = .Compare
         SET VARIABLE NewVal TO (.CurrVal + .PassVal)
         CHANGE .%3 TO .NewVal IN .%1 WHERE .%2 = .Compare
      ENDIF (plus)

      *(--- Update using MINUS)
      IF %7 = MINUS AND Compare EXISTS THEN
         SET VARIABLE CurrVal TO .%3 IN .%1 WHERE .%2 = .Compare
         SET VARIABLE NewVal TO (.CurrVal - .PassVal)
         CHANGE .%3 TO .NewVal IN .%1 WHERE .%2 = .Compare
      ENDIF

      *(--- Update using REPLACE)
      IF %7 = REPLACE AND Compare EXISTS THEN
         SET VARIABLE NewVal TO .PassVal
         CHANGE .%3 TO .NewVal IN .%1 WHERE .%2 = .Compare
      ENDIF

      NEXT #1 Status1

ENDWHILE
WRITE "Update successful" AT 20 1
SET MESSAGES ON
SET ERROR MESSAGES ON
RETURN

*(------- Error encountered at outset.  Return)
LABEL BailOut
CLEAR %7
RETURN
```

Figure 17.19: The Update.MAC macro

MINUS, or REPLACE. If it is valid, the command file displays a prompt and sets the R:BASE messages off. If not, the command file displays an error message and branches control to a routine named Bailout, as follows:

```
*(- - - Make sure option %7 is valid)
IF %7 = PLUS OR %7 = MINUS OR %7 = REPLACE THEN
   WRITE "Performing update ... Please wait"
   SET MESSAGES OFF
   SET ERROR MESSAGES OFF
ELSE
   WRITE "Invalid update option"
   WRITE "Must be PLUS, MINUS or REPLACE"
   WRITE "Press any key to try again ..." AT 20 1
   PAUSE
   GOTO Bailout
ENDIF *(%7 option valid)
```

Now the command file begins the actual updating procedure. First, it sets up a pointer in the transaction table (%4 parameter) sorted by the common column (%5 parameter).

```
*(- - - - - - - - - - - - - - - - - - - - Set up pointer)
SET POINTER #1 Status1 FOR .%4 ORDER BY .%5
```

As long as there are still rows in the transaction table (the pointer variable Status1 equals 0), the command file performs the tasks in the WHILE loop below:

```
WHILE Status1 = 0 THEN
```

First, the program stores the value to be passed to the master table (%6) to a variable named PassVal. Then, it stores the common column name from the transaction table (%5) to a variable named Compare, as follows:

```
SET VARIABLE PassVal TO .%6 IN #1
SET VARIABLE Compare TO .%5 IN #1
```

If the user specified PLUS in the parameter list, the appropriate column in the master table (%3) is incremented by the amount stored in the PassVal variable, where the common column in the master table (%2) matches the common column in the transaction table (.Compare).

```
*(- - - Update using PLUS)
IF %7 = PLUS AND Compare EXISTS THEN
   SET VARIABLE CurrVal TO .%3 IN .%1 WHERE
      .%2 = .Compare
   SET VARIABLE NewVal TO (.CurrVal + .PassVal)
   CHANGE .%3 TO .NewVal IN .%1 WHERE .%2 = .Compare
ENDIF (plus)
```

If the user specified MINUS in the parameter list, the PassVal value is subtracted from the appropriate column in the master table, as below:

```
*(- - - Update using MINUS)
IF %7 = MINUS AND Compare EXISTS THEN
   SET VARIABLE CurrVal TO .%3 IN .%1 WHERE
      .%2 = .Compare
   SET VARIABLE NewVal TO (.CurrVal - .PassVal)
   CHANGE .%3 TO .NewVal IN .%1 WHERE .%2 = .Compare
ENDIF
```

If the user specified REPLACE, the item in the master table is replaced with the item in the transaction table, as follows:

```
*(- - - Update using REPLACE)
IF %7 = REPLACE AND Compare EXISTS THEN
   SET VARIABLE NewVal TO .PassVal
   CHANGE .%3 TO .NewVal IN .%1 WHERE .%2 = .Compare
ENDIF
```

Next, the pointer is moved to the next row in the transaction table, and the procedure is repeated until all the rows from the transaction table have been updated.

```
NEXT #1 Status1
ENDWHILE
```

When the macro is done, it returns to the calling command file below:

```
SET MESSAGES ON
SET ERROR MESSAGES ON
RETURN
```

The last routine in the Update.MAC macro is the Bailout routine, which is called in the event of an error at the beginning of the program. Before returning to the calling program, the routine clears the faulty update option (%7) from memory, as follows:

```
*(- - - Error encountered at outset. Return)
LABEL Bailout
CLEAR %7
RETURN
```

The Update.MAC macro is flexible, and it can be used for inventory-system updating, as well as for updating our accounts-receivable system. For example, to subtract the items that have been sold in the Charges table from the OnHand quantities in the Inventry table, you could simply enter the command

```
RUN Update.MAC USING Inventry ProdNo OnHand Charges +
+ > ProdNo Qty MINUS
```

That's the real benefit of a general-purpose macro. You need only write the macro once, and then you can use it repeatedly, just as though it were a regular R:BASE command.

TESTING THE ACCOUNTS-RECEIVABLE SYSTEM

Before integrating all of the parts of the accounts-receivable system through menus, you should check to see that all the parts work as expected directly from the R> prompt. You should also create whatever additional reports you want for the various tables using Reports EXPRESS. As mentioned earlier, you might want to add a directory listing, mailing labels, and perhaps form letters for the ARMain table, similar to the Director, Labels, and Letter1 report formats we developed in Chapter 7. You can also develop reports for displaying information from the Charges, Payments, and Inventry tables.

To enter some practice data for the system, enter the command

```
OPEN ARSys
```

at the R> prompt to open the database. Then use the command

```
ENTER Main
```

to enter a couple of sample customers. Use customer numbers that are easy to remember for the practice data, such as 1001 and 1002. You can fill in zeros for all the balances on the bottom half of the screen, because the system will automatically take care of these balances. Press Esc and select Quit after entering a couple of customers.

Enter a few sample records in the Inventry table as well. To do so, enter the command

```
ENTER InvForm
```

Use part numbers that will be easy to remember for the practice data, such as A-111 and B-222. You don't need to worry about the In Stock quantities, because the AR system, as designed, does not work on these directly. The column is only included in case you want to develop an inventory module later to manage the inventory database. Remember to enter either a 1 (for taxable) or 0 (for nontaxable) into the Tax? column.

After entering a couple of inventory records, press Esc and select Quit to return to the R> prompt.

Enter a few Charge transactions for each customer. To do so, first enter the command

```
ENTER ChrgFrm
```

Be sure to use only valid customer numbers and product numbers that you've already entered on the ARMain and Inventry tables. After entering a few Charge transactions, press Esc and select Quit.

Enter the command

```
ENTER PayForm
```

at the R> prompt to enter some payment transactions. Again, be sure to use only valid customer numbers from the ARMain table. Press Esc and select Quit after entering a couple of payment transactions.

To test the EndMonth.CMD, UpDate.MAC, and Age.CMD files, enter the command

```
RUN EndMonth.CMD
```

at the R> prompt. The files should print the invoices and then take a few minutes to perform all of the updating. If all runs smoothly, you'll be returned to the R> prompt without any error messages. At this point, all transactions from the Charges and Payments tables should be empty. To verify this, enter the commands

```
SELECT ALL FROM Charges
SELECT ALL FROM Payments
```

To verify that the old transactions were copied to the history files, enter the commands

```
SELECT ALL FROM CHistory
SELECT ALL FROM PHistory
```

These two tables should contain the data that were originally on the Charges and Payments tables.

If the Charges, Payments, and history tables do not contain the data you expected, then perhaps there is an error in the EndMonth.CMD command file, or in the UpDate.MAC or Age.CMD command file. Make sure you've keyed in the command files exactly as described in this chapter. You'll want to be sure to remove all the bugs from any command files, as well as from any forms or reports, before proceeding to the final step of integrating the accounts-receivable system through Application EXPRESS.

INTEGRATING THE ACCOUNTS-RECEIVABLE SYSTEM

The final step in creating a working accounts-receivable system is to link all the modules together through menus generated by Application EXPRESS. To start Application EXPRESS, enter the command

```
EXPRESS
```

at the R> prompt, or select Application EXPRESS from the RBSystem Main menu. From the Application EXPRESS Main menu, select option 1 to define a new application.

The screen will ask that you select a database for the new application. Select ARSys. The screen will ask that you enter a name for the application. Type in **AR** and press Enter. When the screen asks you to enter the name of the Main menu, press Enter to use the suggested name, Main. Select Vertical for the menu type.

ACCOUNTS-RECEIVABLE SYSTEM MAIN MENU

Type in the menu title and options for the Main menu. Figure 17.20 shows a suggested format for the Main menu. Press Esc after filling in the menu title and options.

For this menu (and all subsequent submenus), you can select Yes after the prompt

Do you want [ESC] to exit this menu?

You can select No in response to the prompt

Do you want a help screen for this menu?

Furthermore, for each submenu that you create in the following paragraphs, select Vertical as the menu type.

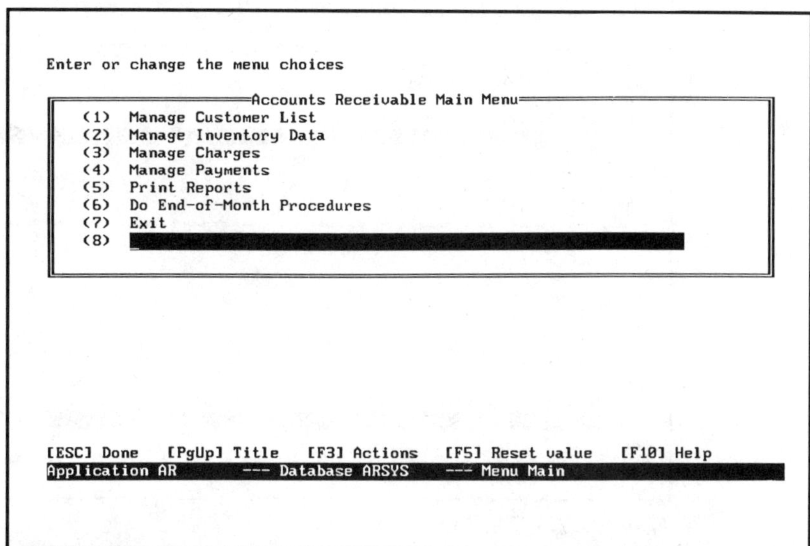

Figure 17.20: The accounts-receivable Main menu

Now you can begin assigning menu actions to items. For the action to menu option 1, select Menu from the list of choices, and enter the menu name **CustMenu**. Figure 17.21 shows a suggested format for the CustMenu submenu.

Press Esc after filling in the submenu title and options. Select No in response to the last prompt about assigning additional actions.

To assign actions to menu option 2, select Menu from the choices on the screen. Type **InvMenu** as the submenu name, and press Enter. Figure 17.22 shows a suggested format for the InvMenu submenu. Press Esc and select No after filling in the submenu title and options.

When asked to assign actions to Main menu option 3, once again select Menu from the list of options, and then enter **ChrgMenu** as the submenu name. Figure 17.23 shows a suggested format for the ChrgMenu submenu. Press Esc and select No after entering the menu title and options.

Next you'll be asked to assign actions to Main menu option 4. Once again, select Menu, and type in the name **PayMenu** for the submenu. Figure 17.24 shows a suggested format for the submenu. Press Esc and select No after filling in the menu title and options.

```
Enter or change the menu choices

              Manage Customer List
   (1)  Add New Customers
   (2)  Edit/Delete Customers
   (3)  Look Up Customer Data
   (4)  Return to Main Menu
   (5)  _

[ESC] Done   [PgUp] Title   [F3] Actions   [F5] Reset value   [F10] Help
Application AR      --- Database ARSYS      --- Menu CustMenu
```

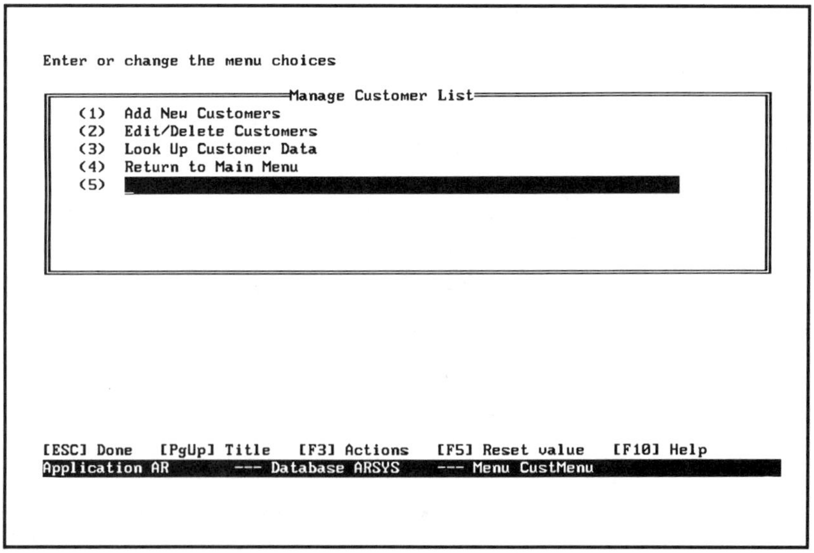

Figure 17.21: The CustMenu submenu

```
Enter or change the menu choices

                    Manage Inventory Data
  (1)  Add New Inventory Items
  (2)  Edit/Delete Inventory Items
  (3)  Look Up Inventory Data
  (4)  Return to Main Menu
  (5)  _

[ESC] Done   [PgUp] Title   [F3] Actions   [F5] Reset value   [F10] Help
Application AR        --- Database ARSYS     --- Menu InvMenu
```

Figure 17.22: The InvMenu submenu

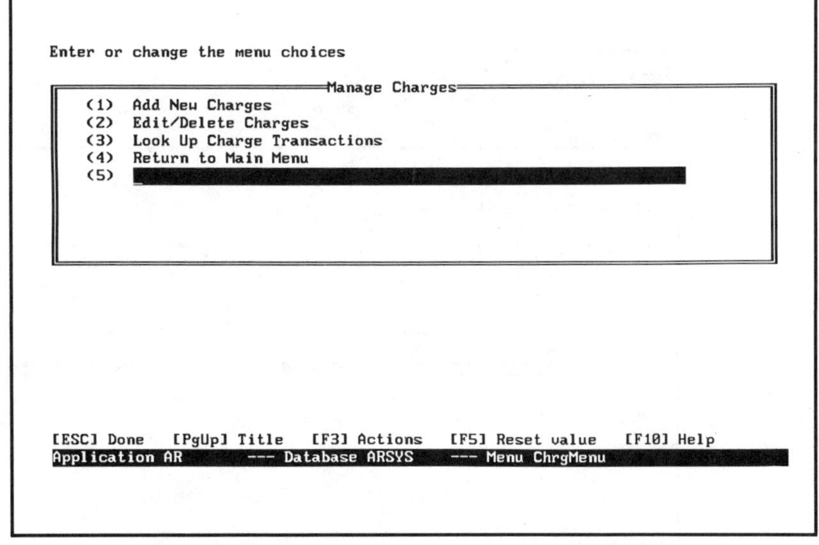

Figure 17.23: The ChrgMenu submenu

Next you can assign actions to menu option 5. Select Menu from the list of options, and enter **ReptMenu** as the submenu name. Create a menu to access the various reports that you've created for your accounts-receivable system (except for printing invoices, which are printed automatically by the EndMonth.CMD command file). Figure 17.25 shows suggested options for the ReptMenu submenu. Press Esc and select No after creating this submenu.

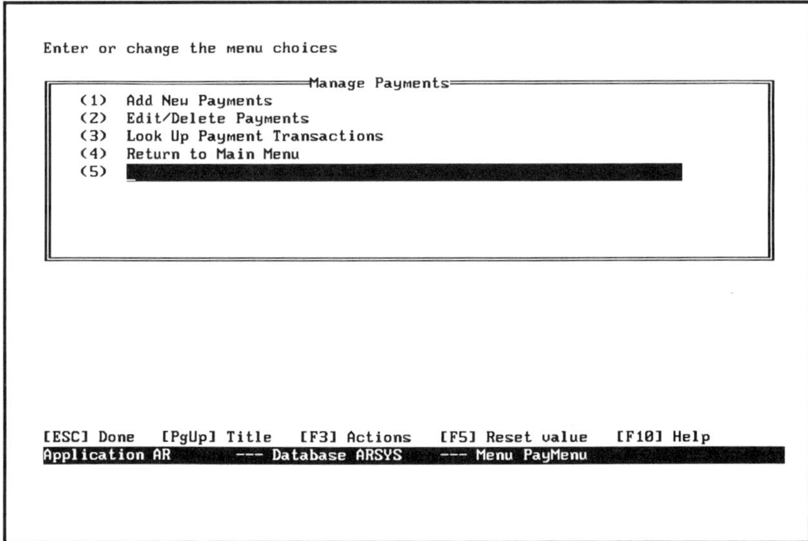

Figure 17.24: The PayMenu submenu

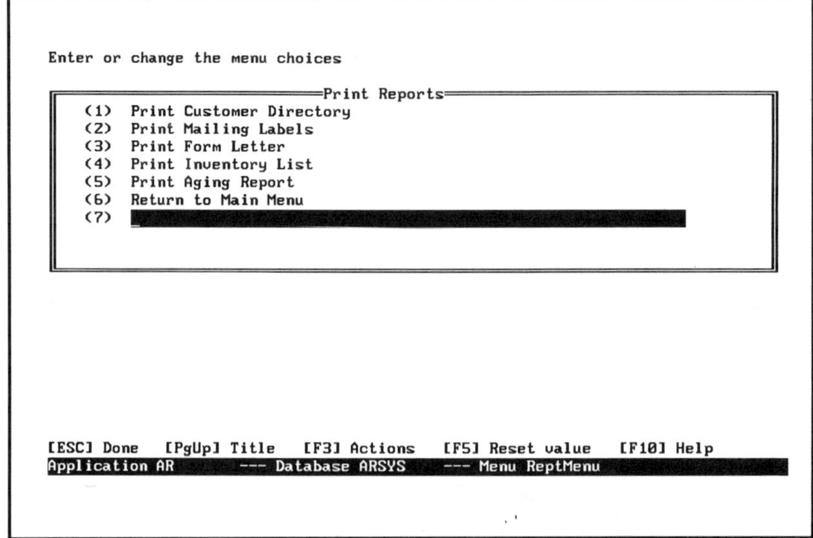

Figure 17.25: The suggested format for the ReptMenu submenu

Main menu option 6 performs the end-of-month procedures. These are all handled by the EndMonth.CMD command file and the other command files that EndMonth.CMD accesses. When asked to assign an action to Main menu option 6, select Macro from the list of options. (The Macro option will run an existing command file.) Type in the command file name **EndMonth.CMD**, and press Enter. Select No to continue.

Finally, you'll be asked to assign an action to Main menu option 7. Select Exit from the list of options, since this menu option allows the user to exit the accounts-receivable system.

CUSTOMERS SUBMENU ACTIONS

Next you'll be asked to select menu actions for the CustMenu submenu. For CustMenu option 1, select Load from the list of choices. Select ARMain as the table to load, and select Main as the name of the form to use. Choose No in response to the questions about editing the form and adding more actions.

When assigning menu actions to CustMenu option 2, select Edit from the list of choices. Select ARMain as the table to edit and Main as the form to use. When asked about sort orders, select CustNo and Ascending and press Esc. When asked for a column to validate, select CustNo as the column name and EQ (equal) as the operator. When asked if the user should enter the comparison value, select Yes. Type in the prompt message

```
Enter customer number
```

when requested, and press Enter. Select Done as the final logical operator. Choose No when asked about adding more actions.

To assign actions to CustMenu option 3, Look Up Customer Data, choose Select from the list of options and ARMain as the table to display data from. You can then choose columns to display. Select the particular columns you wish to display, or select All to display all columns. Of course, all the columns from the ARMain table will not fit on the screen simultaneously, so you might want to select a few important columns to display, such as CustNo, L:Name, F:Name, and Curr:Bal.

You can select CustNo and Ascending as the sort columns, and then press Esc. Select CustNo as the column to validate, EQ as the operator, and Yes in response to the question about having the user enter a comparison value. When prompted, type in the prompt message

Enter customer number

and press Enter. Select Done as the final logical operator, and select No when asked about assigning additional actions to the menu option.

To assign actions to CustMenu option 4, select Exit from the list of actions.

INVENTORY SUBMENU ACTIONS

The action for the Inventory submenu option 1 is Load, with Inventry as the name of the table to load and InvForm as the form to use. Select No to the prompts about editing the form and adding more menu actions.

For Inventory submenu option 2, select Edit as the action. Select Inventry as the table to edit and InvForm as the form to use. Select No when asked about editing the form. Select ProdNo and Ascending as sorting characteristics, and press Esc. For the column to validate, select ProdNo as the column, EQ as the operator, and Yes for having the user enter the comparison value. Enter the prompt message

Enter product number

when requested, and press Enter. Select Done as the last logical operator, and then select No.

For Inventory submenu option 3, choose Select from the list of possible actions. Specify Inventry as the table to display, and then select columns to display and a sort order. When requested, select ProdNo as the column to validate, EQ as the operator, and Yes in response to the user entering the comparison value. Enter the prompt

Enter product number

when requested, and then select Done as the final logical operator. Select No for additional actions.

For the Inventory submenu option 4, select Exit from the list of actions.

CHARGES SUBMENU ACTIONS

For the action to Charges submenu option 1, select Load and select Charges as the table to load. Select ChrgFrm as the form to use, and select No when asked to edit the form. Select No when asked about adding more actions.

The action for Charges SubMenu option 2 is Edit, with Charges as the table to edit and ChrgFrm as the form for editing. Select CustNo and Ascending as the sort order. Select CustNo as the column to validate, EQ as the operator, and Yes. Enter the prompt message

```
Enter customer number
```

when requested. Select Done as the final operator, and say No to the last prompt.

For Charges submenu option 3, choose Select as the action. Select Charges as the table to display, and then select the columns to display and a sort order to your liking. Select CustNo as the column to validate, EQ as the operator, and Yes, and then enter the prompt message

```
Enter customer number
```

Select Done as the final operator and then No.

For the last Charges submenu option, select Exit from the list of actions.

PAYMENTS SUBMENU ACTIONS

The Payments submenu is similar to the previous submenus. For option 1, select Load as the action, Payments as the table to load, and PayForm as the form to use.

For Payments submenu option 2, select Edit as the action, Payments as the table to edit, and PayForm as the form to use. Select CustNo and Ascending for the sort order. Select CustNo as the column to validate, EQ as the operator, and Yes. Enter the prompt

```
Enter customer number
```

and press Enter. Select Done and then select No.

For Payments submenu option 3, choose Select as the action, Payments as the table, All as columns to display, and CustNo and Ascending as the sort order. Select CustNo as the column to validate, EQ as the operator, and Yes. Enter the prompt message

```
Enter customer number
```

and press Enter. Select Done and No from the next prompts.

For Payments submenu option 4, select Exit.

REPORTS SUBMENU ACTIONS

Next you can assign actions to the Reports submenu. Select Print as the action for each of the menu options (except the last option), and select the appropriate report name for each menu option. You can, of course, select sort orders and search criteria for each report. (Generally, you'll want to leave the search comparisons blank for all the reports.)

For the last menu option on the Reports submenu, select Exit.

FINISHING UP

After you've defined all the actions for all the menu options, the screen will ask

```
Do you want to change EXPRESS default settings?
```

Select No. Then you'll see the message

```
Writing application files—Please wait...
```

After all the application files are written, you'll see the prompt

```
Do you want to create an initial command file?
```

Select No.

From this point, you'll be returned to the Application EXPRESS Main menu. Select option 3 to exit from Application EXPRESS.

USING THE ACCOUNTS-RECEIVABLE SYSTEM

To use the accounts-receivable system in the future, enter the command

```
RUN AR IN AR.APX
```

at the R> prompt. You'll see the Accounts-Receivable Main menu.

At any time during the month, you can enter new data or edit existing data. Before assigning charges or payments to a customer, the customer should be entered into the customer list with a unique customer number. To do so, select option 1, Manage Customer List, from the Accounts Receivable Main menu and option 1, Add New Customers, from the Customers submenu. You should enter zeros in all the balances on the bottom half of the screen when first entering a new customer.

You also need to add products to the inventory table before entering charges for that product. To enter or edit products, select option 2, Manage Inventory Data, from the Main menu and option 1, Add New Items, from the inventory submenu. Each item you enter must have a unique product number.

As customers charge items and make payments, record each transaction on the Charges and Payments tables. To record charges, select option 3, Manage Charges, from the Main menu and option 1, Add New Charges, from the submenu. To record payments, select option 4, Manage Payments, from the Main menu and option 1, Add New Payments, from the submenu.

You can make changes and corrections to the Charges and Payments tables any time *prior to performing the end-of-the-month procedures.* The Charges and Payments submenus each have options for editing and deleting transactions. (We'll discuss techniques for editing after the end-of-the-month procedures shortly.)

END-OF-THE-MONTH PROCEDURES

At the end of the month (or whenever you normally send bills), you can select option 6, Do End-Of-Month Procedures, from the Main menu to print the invoices and update all the balances in the

ARMain file. Be sure you have plenty of paper in the printer and that the printer is ready. Then select option 6 from the Main menu, and wait until the Main menu reappears. (If you add a report format for mailing labels, you can print mailing labels for the invoices as well.)

Once the end-of-the-month procedures are complete, you can no longer change that information on the Charges and Payments tables, because those transactions have now moved to the history files to make room for next month's charges and payments. The Inventry file is unchanged, and the ARMain table has updated balances for the start of the new month.

ADJUSTMENT TRANSACTIONS

Of course, errors will sneak through the end-of-month procedures from time to time. To fix those, you can add *adjustment transactions,* which not only correct the error, but also leave an *audit trail* to explain the change.

For example, if you overcharge a customer or a customer returns some merchandise for which she has already been billed, you can simply enter a payment transaction to credit the account. (In fact, you could add a "comment" column to the Payments table to add comments to each transaction to explain the reason for the adjustment.)

If you overcharged the customer $200.00 or the customer returned $200.00 worth of merchandise, just add a payment transaction in the amount of $200.00. The next time the end-of-month procedures are performed, the $200.00 will automatically be credited to the customer's account, and it will appear on the next invoice as a credit and be stored in the history file for future reference.

We've covered much advanced material in this chapter, and unless you are already a programmer who is fluent in some other database-management language, the techniques discussed in this chapter will probably take some study and practice to master. The time and effort you invest will be worthwhile—the techniques that we've used in this chapter are similar to the ones that you'll be using to develop your own custom applications.

Part 3

Advanced Application Techniques

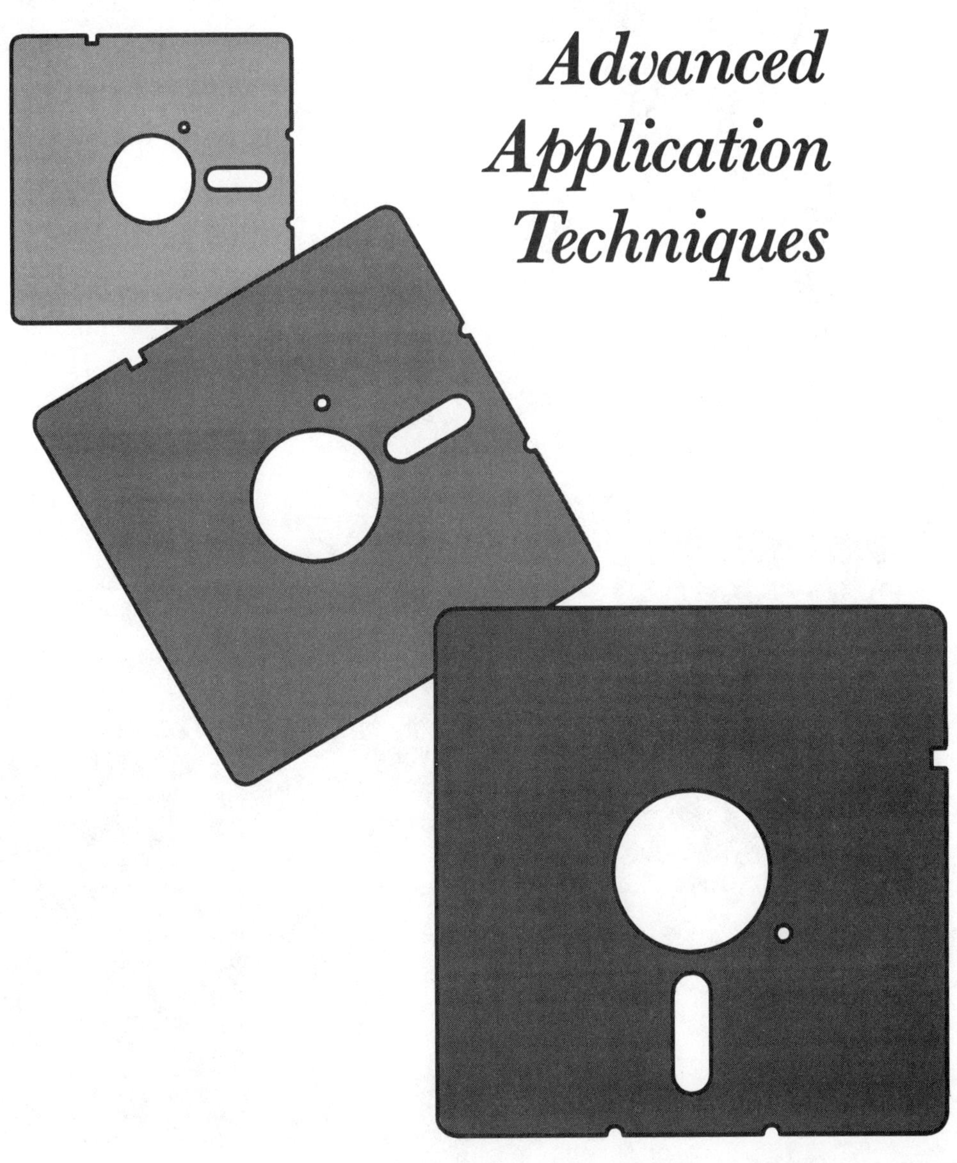

Chapter 18

Speeding Program Execution with CodeLock and Developer's EXPRESS

FAST TRACK

To convert ASCII command files to binary command files, **530**
as well as to group command, screen, and menu files into a single procedure file, use the CodeLock option. The options from the CodeLock Main menu are as follows:

- Option 1 converts an ASCII command file to binary format.
- Option 2 converts an ASCII command file to binary format and adds it to a procedure file. The RUN *block name* IN *procedure file name* syntax runs the compiled command file in the procedure file from the R> prompt or from a command file.
- Option 2 also compiles macros into procedure files. To run a compiled macro from the R> prompt or from a command file, use the syntax RUN *macro name* IN *procedure file name* USING *parameter list*.
- Option 3 adds a screen file to a procedure file. The DISPLAY *screen block* IN *procedure file* syntax displays the screen from the R> prompt or from a command file.
- Option 4 adds menu files to a procedure file. The syntax CHOOSE *variable name* FROM *menu name* IN *procedure file name* displays the menu from the R> prompt or from a command file, and stores the user's selection in the specified variable name.
- Option 5 converts an application file into a procedure file. Specify the file name with the .APP extension if you're converting a procedure file generated in Application EXPRESS.

To access R:BASE's pseudo-compiler **546**
with Developer's EXPRESS, run RCOMP directly from the operating system or by typing **ZIP ROLLOUT RCOMP** at the R> prompt. Select option 1, *Compile an ASCII file*, and specify your ASCII file.

To run an .APC file 550

generated by RCOMP, use RRUN directly from the operating system, or at the R> prompt with the syntax ZIP ROLLOUT RRUN *compiled application* .APC.

IN THIS CHAPTER, WE'LL DISCUSS CODELOCK AND Developer's EXPRESS, R:BASE modules that convert command files, which are normally stored as ASCII files, into binary format. ASCII files are stored in the format that you used to create the command file. Binary files are stored using special codes that are easily read by the computer, but not by people. One of the advantages of a command file stored in binary format is that it runs faster. When it runs binary files, the computer does not have to perform the work of converting the program from "English" (ASCII) to computer language (binary).

USING CODELOCK TO CONVERT YOUR FILES

You can convert the following five different types of ASCII files with CodeLock:

- Command files and macros created with RBEDIT (or any other text editor that stores files in ASCII format) into binary command files
- ASCII command files into binary procedure files
- Screen files, which display screens from within command files (such as the Bills.MSG file that we created in the last chapter) into binary procedure files
- Menu files, which display menus, into binary procedure files
- Application files

You can also combine up to 42 different files in a single procedure file using CodeLock. In this chapter, we'll experiment with converting the various types of files.

Before you can use CodeLock, you need to be sure you have it installed on your system. If you elected to install the entire R:BASE package, it will be in the directory with the other R:BASE files. If you bypassed installing R:BASE's utilities, you will need to go back and reinstall R:BASE in order to follow along on-line in this section.

CONVERTING COMMAND FILES

The simplest use of CodeLock is to convert a command file to binary format. In Chapter 16, we created a command file named Loop2.CMD to test the WHILE and ENDWHILE commands. Figure 18.1 shows the Loop2.CMD command file. Let's convert this program to a binary file.

As with most modules in R:BASE, you can start CodeLock in a variety of ways. You can start CodeLock from your operating system by typing **CodeLock.** Alternatively, you can start it from the PBE Main menu by selecting first option 8, *R:BASE and operating system utilities* and then CodeLock. If you are at the R> prompt, enter the command

```
CODELOCK
```

The CodeLock Main menu will appear on the screen, as shown in Figure 18.2.

Select option 1 to convert the command file. CodeLock asks for the

```
Name of the ASCII command file to convert:
```

For this example, enter the name **Loop2.CMD**. CodeLock then asks for the

```
Name of the backup file [Loop2.ASC]
```

```
*(************************************** Loop2.CMD)
*(---------------- Program to test the WHILE loop)
*(------------ Create Counter and Done variables)
SET VARIABLE COUNTER TO 1
SET VARIABLE Done INTEGER

*(------------- Ask how high to count)
NEWPAGE
FILLIN Done USING "How high shall I count?: " AT 9,5
NEWPAGE

*(---------------- Repeat loop until Counter > Done)
WHILE Counter <= .Done THEN
      *(---------- Create a prompt and display it)
      SET VARIABLE Progress TO "Loop Number " & (CTXT(.Counter))
      WRITE .Progress
      *(---------- Increment Counter variable by 1)
      SET VARIABLE Counter TO .Counter + 1
ENDWHILE *(Bottom of WHILE loop)

*(----------------- End of program)
QUIT
```

Figure 18.1: The Loop2.CMD command file

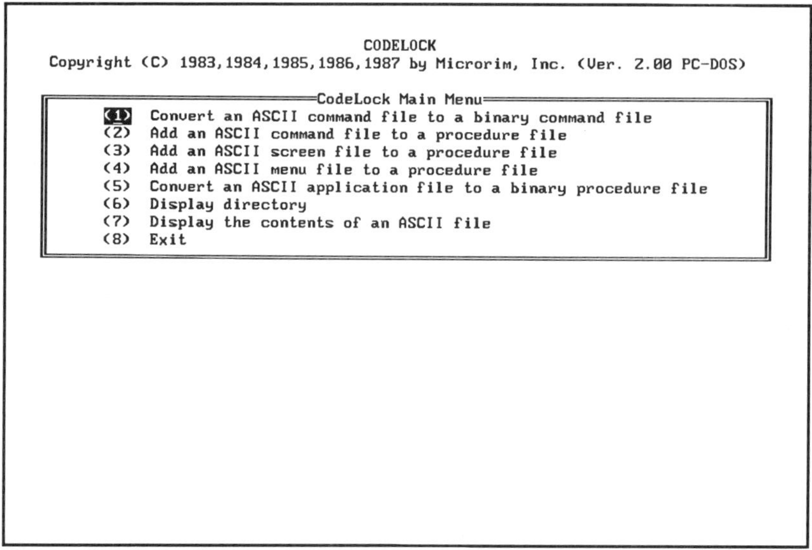

Figure 18.2: The CodeLock Main menu

This is the file that will contain the original, unconverted command file. CodeLock suggests the name Loop2.ASC (ASC is short for ASCII). To use the suggested name, press Enter. Next, CodeLock asks for the

```
Name of the binary command file [Loop2.CMD]:
```

CodeLock suggests the name Loop2.CMD. Press Enter to use the suggested name. As CodeLock converts the command file, it displays each line on the screen. When it's done, CodeLock displays the following prompt:

```
Press any key to continue
```

When you press any key, you'll be returned to the CodeLock Main menu.

To run the converted command file, exit CodeLock by selecting option 8 to return to the R> prompt. Then use the RUN command, as below:

```
RUN Loop2.CMD
```

You may not notice a major increase in speed when you're running this small command file, but as you begin converting larger command files, you will notice a significant improvement in your processing time.

You should always fully test and debug a command file before converting it. However, if you need to make changes to a command file, be sure to use the unconverted backup. In this example, you would use RBEDIT to modify the Loop2.ASC command file. Then, when reconverting with CodeLock, enter **Loop2.ASC** as the ASCII file to convert, **Loop2.ASC** as the backup file, and **Loop2.CMD** as the name of the binary file.

If you need to check which version of a command file is the ASCII version and which is the converted version, you can use the TYPE command from either the operating system prompt or the R> prompt, or by selecting CodeLock's option 7, *Display the contents of an ASCII file.* For example, after you've converted a command file, if you enter the command

```
TYPE Loop2.ASC
```

you'll see the ASCII file in its normal state. However, if you enter the command

```
TYPE Loop2.CMD
```

you'll see the binary file, which appears as a group of strange-looking characters including happy faces and umlauts. Never attempt to edit the binary file. Again, if you must make changes, edit the ASCII file and then reconvert it into a revised binary file.

PROCEDURE FILES

A *procedure file* is one that contains a group of previously separate files in a single binary file. The files within the procedure file can be command files, screen files, menu files, or macros. In this section, we'll develop a procedure file named TestProc.CMD for practice.

Adding Command Files to Procedure Files

To add a command file to a procedure file, select option 2 from the CodeLock Main menu. CodeLock will display this prompt:

```
Name of the ASCII command file to add:
```

Enter the name of the command file. (Be sure to use the name of the ASCII backup file if you've previously converted the command file.) For this example, enter the file name **Loop2.ASC**. CodeLock asks for the

```
Name of procedure file:
```

Enter the name **TestProc.CMD**. CodeLock displays the prompt

```
Name of the binary command block [Loop2]
```

suggesting the name Loop2. (Since the command file will be contained within a procedure file, you do not want to use file-name extensions.) Press Enter to use the suggested name.

CodeLock displays the command file as it converts the file and adds it to the procedure file. When it's done, you are prompted to press any key to continue. Before we try out the procedure file, let's add a screen file to it.

Adding Screen Files to Procedure Files

In the last chapter, we created a screen file named Bills.MSG. Let's add that screen file to the TestProc.CMD procedure file. Select option 3 from the CodeLock Main menu to add an ASCII screen file to a procedure file. CodeLock displays the prompt

```
Name of ASCII screen file to add:
```

Enter the name **Bills.MSG** and press Enter. CodeLock displays the prompt

```
Name of the procedure file [TestProc.CMD]:
```

suggesting the TestProc procedure file. Press Enter to use the suggested file name. CodeLock displays the following prompt:

```
Current blocks in the procedure file:
Loop2
Name of the binary screen block [Bills]:
```

Since each block in a procedure file must have a unique name, CodeLock displays the names of the blocks already in the file. Furthermore, CodeLock suggests the name Bills for the new block. Press Enter to accept the suggested name. You'll see the screen file displayed on the screen, and then you'll be prompted to press any key to continue. Press a key to return to the CodeLock Main menu.

We'll see how to access the screen in the procedure file shortly. First let's try adding a menu file to the procedure file.

Adding Menu Files to Procedure Files

A menu file is one that uses a specific format to display a menu. To create a menu file, you need to use the RBEDIT text editor (or your favorite ASCII word processor). If you're following along on-line, you'll need to exit CodeLock and then run the RBEDIT editor.

Figure 18.3 shows a sample menu file typed in with RBEDIT. Notice that the name of the menu, MENU1, is the first line in the file. The menu name must always be the first line, in the far-left column, of the menu file, and it cannot be more than eight characters long or contain spaces or punctuation marks.

```
MENU1
COLUMN Sample Menu
Add New Data
Edit/Delete data
Print Reports
```

Figure 18.3: A sample menu file

The second line of the menu file contains the word COLUMN, which specifies a vertical menu display. (Use the word ROW for a horizontal menu display.)

Next to COLUMN is the title of the menu, which is Sample Menu in this example. The menu title must always appear next to the menu type (COLUMN or ROW).

The last three lines in the menu file are menu options. When displayed on a vertical menu, the menu options will be numbered automatically.

After you've created the menu file, save it with any file name (**Menu1.ASC** in this example). Then, exit RBEDIT and return to the CodeLock Main menu.

To add the menu file to the TestProc.CMD procedure file, select option 4 from the CodeLock Main menu. CodeLock displays the prompt

```
Name of the ASCII menu file to add:
```

Enter the name of the menu file, which is **Menu1.ASC** in this example. CodeLock then displays the prompt

```
Name of the procedure file:
```

Enter the name of the procedure file, which is **TestProc.CMD** in this example. CodeLock displays the following:

```
Current blocks in the procedure file:
Loop2     Bills
Name of the binary menu block: [Menu1]:
```

to remind you of existing blocks in the procedure file. Press Enter to use the suggested block name, Menu1. CodeLock will display the menu file and ask you to press any key to continue. Press a key to return to the CodeLock Main menu, and then select option 8 to exit CodeLock.

ACCESSING PROCEDURES

Now that we've created a procedure file, let's look at ways to access the procedures within it. First, you'll need to return to the R> prompt. Then, use the RUN command with the procedure block name and the procedure file name in the following syntax:

RUN *command file block* IN *procedure file name*

To run the Loop2 procedure, enter the command

```
RUN Loop2 IN TestProc.CMD
```

The Loop2 command file will run its course, and you'll be returned to the R> prompt.

To display a screen block in a procedure file, use the DISPLAY command with the following syntax:

```
DISPLAY screen block name IN procedure file name
```

For this example, enter the command

```
DISPLAY Bills IN TestProc.CMD
```

You'll see the screen display appear, and then you'll be returned to the R> prompt.

If you were accessing this screen from within another command file, you'd probably use the commands

```
NEWPAGE
DISPLAY Bills IN TestProc.CMD
```

to clear the screen prior to displaying the screen block.

To access the menu in the procedure file, use the CHOOSE command with this syntax:

```
CHOOSE variable name FROM menu block name IN +
+ > procedure file
```

For this example, enter the command

```
CHOOSE MChoice FROM Menu1 IN TestProc.CMD
```

MChoice is an arbitrary variable name that will record the menu selection. You'll see the menu appear on the screen, as shown in Figure 18.4.

Select an item from the menu to return to the R> prompt. If you enter the command

```
SHOW VARIABLES
```

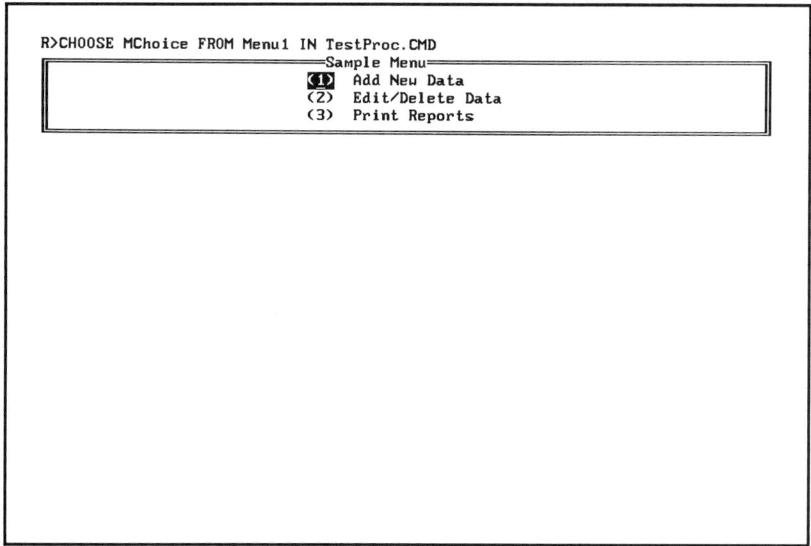

Figure 18.4: A sample menu displayed with the CHOOSE command

after returning to the R> prompt, you'll see that the MChoice variable contains your menu selection.

The variable used for storing the menu selection is always of the INTEGER data type. If you had pressed the Esc key, rather than selected a menu item, the variable would contain a zero. If you had pressed F10 rather than selected a menu item, the variable would contain −1. Figure 18.5 shows a sample command file, named MenuTest.CMD, that can be used to respond to a user's menu choice.

Note that if the user presses F10, the command file displays a screen named MenuHelp.SCN. (Note: We have not created such a screen file yet. If you want to test the MenuTest.CMD command file fully, use RBEDIT to create a screen file named MenuHelp.SCN.) Also, notice that the WHILE loop repeats as long as the MChoice variable does not equal zero. This means that the menu will be redisplayed until the user chooses to exit by pressing the Esc key.

If you develop the MenuHelp.SCN and MenuTest.CMD files, these, too, can be converted in the procedure file. You'll just need to change the line in the MenuTest.CMD command file that reads

```
DISPLAY MenuHelp.SCN
```

```
*(********************************************** MenuTest.CMD)
*(-- Test the menu1 block in the TestProc.CMD procedure file)
OPEN Mail

*(--- Set up loop for displaying menu)

SET VARIABLE MChoice TO 1
WHILE MChoice <> 0 THEN

   *(--- Clear screen and display menu. Store choice in MChoice)
   NEWPAGE
   CHOOSE MChoice FROM Menu1 IN TestProc.CMD

   *(--- Respond to menu selection)
   IF MChoice = 1 THEN
      ENTER NamesFrm
   ENDIF

   IF MChoice = 2 THEN
      EDIT ALL FROM Names
   ENDIF

   IF MChoice = 3 THEN
      PRINT Director
   ENDIF

   *(--- Display help screen if F10 selected)
   IF MChoice = -1 THEN
      NEWPAGE
      DISPLAY MenuHelp.SCN
      PAUSE
   ENDIF

ENDWHILE

NEWPAGE
WRITE "Exit Selected"
```

Figure 18.5: The MenuTest.CMD command file

to the following:

```
DISPLAY MenuHelp IN TestProc.CMD
```

If you add the MenuTest.CMD command file to the TestProc procedure file and you want to run it, enter the command

```
RUN MenuTest IN TestProc.CMD
```

at the R> prompt.

CONVERTING APPLICATION FILES

When you create an application file, such as the MailSys application that we created earlier, R:BASE generates three files with the extensions .APP, .API, and .APX, as shown below:

MailSys.APP

MailSys.API

MailSys.APX

When you're converting with CodeLock, use the .APP file as the name of the ASCII application file to convert.

To convert an application file, select option 5 from the CodeLock Main menu. When CodeLock asks for the

```
Name of ASCII application file to convert:
```

enter the name of the .APP file (**MailSys.APP**, for example). CodeLock will then display the prompt

```
Name of the procedure file:
```

You can add the application file to an existing procedure file if you wish. In this example, we'll create a new application file named MailSys.CMD. Enter the procedure file name **MailSys.CMD**.

CodeLock will display each line of the application file as it converts. When it's done, you can press any key to return to the CodeLock Main menu.

From the R> prompt, use the syntax

RUN *application name* IN *procedure file*

to run the converted application. In this example, you would enter the command

```
RUN MailSys IN MailSys.CMD
```

to run the converted MailSys application.

Since CodeLock and Application EXPRESS generate the same binary code, the above command is equivalent to the command you typed in Chapter 15:

```
RUN MailSys IN MailSys.APX
```

You may be puzzled about the need to convert application files created with Application EXPRESS. In fact, you'll rarely need to go through the procedure outlined above, because Application EXPRESS automatically creates binary files for you.

As we said above, Application EXPRESS generates three files every time you use it to create an application. The .APX binary file is the one that is actually run—recall from Chapter 15 that you type

```
RUN appname IN appname.APX
```

when you want to run your application. The .APP file is the "English" ASCII file that contains all the procedure blocks that Application EXPRESS creates for you, as well as any macros or custom sections you may have added. In essence, it's a long command file, which can be run by typing

```
RUN appname.APP
```

The .API file is the one that R:BASE uses to generate a new .APP file if you use Application EXPRESS to modify your application. In essence, the .API file is the only file that Application EXPRESS cares about.

What if you wanted to make some changes in your application but had lost or damaged its .API file? Since you wouldn't be able to use Application EXPRESS, the easiest solution would be to make changes in your .APP file and then use CodeLock to convert the existing .APP file to a binary procedure file. Since a binary procedure file is the same as an .APX file, the end result would be the same as if Application EXPRESS had generated the .APX file itself.

Finally, there will be those of you who like to do a lot of custom programming (working with ASCII files), but prefer to bypass Application EXPRESS; you will need to use CodeLock if you want your applications to run faster.

CONVERTING MACROS

Macros are particularly good candidates for procedure files. By combining (or *compiling*) macros, you can develop a library of general-purpose routines, stored together in a single file, that are readily accessible when you need them.

Figure 18.6 shows a macro named Summary.MAC, which you can use with the following syntax to summarize the data in a table:

RUN Summary.MAC USING *source table name* +
+ > *break column column to sum destination* +
+ > *table name*

For example, look at the data from the Mail database in the Charges table below:

CUSTNO	PRODNO	QTY	U:PRICE	TAX?	TOTAL
1001	A-111	12	$10.00	1	$127.20
1001	B-222	5	$12.50	1	$66.25
1001	C-434	2	$100.00	1	$212.00
1004	A-111	5	$10.00	1	$53.00
1004	Z-128	10	$12.80	0	$128.00
1007	A-111	10	$10.00	1	$106.00
1007	Z-128	10	$12.80	0	$128.00
1002	B-222	12	$12.50	1	$159.00
1002	A-111	10	$10.00	1	$106.00

The Summary.MAC macro can create a table from these data that displays the sum of the Total column for each customer. In this example, the *source table name* is Charges, the *break column* is CustNo (since we're summarizing for individual customers), and the *column to sum* can be any numeric column. (We'll use the Total column in this example.) The table that you are creating for the summary (the *destination table name* portion of the command) can have any table name. However, if a table with the same name already exists, it will be overwritten—so be sure to use a unique table name unless you want to replace an existing table.

Let's look at an example. Suppose that you open the Mail database and then wish to see a summary of totals for each customer in the Charges table. From the R> prompt, you could enter the command

RUN Summary.MAC USING Charges CustNo Total SumTable +
+ > Names

```
*(---------------------------------------- SUMMARY.MAC)
*(--------------------------- Summarize a table column)
*(Parameters:          %1: Name of table to summarize
                       %2: Key field to summarize on
                       %3: Column to total
                       %4: Name of summary table name
                       %5: Name of master table )
NEWPAGE
SET MESSAGES OFF
SET ERROR MESSAGES OFF
WRITE "Summarizing... Please wait" AT 1,1
CLEAR VAR Vsubtot Thisno

*(--------- Create empty table for summary data)
REMOVE .%4
PROJECT .%4 FROM .%5 USING .%2  ORDER BY .%2
EXPAND .%4 WITH Subtot CURR
*(--------- Set up a path through the new table)
SET POINTER #1 Status1 FOR .%4

*(--------- Loop through the rows one customer at a time)
WHILE Status1 = 0 THEN
   SET VAR Thisno = .%2 IN #1
   COMPUTE Vsubtot AS SUM .%3 FROM .%1 WHERE .%2 = .Thisno
   *(----------- Update the new table's column for subtotal)
   CHANGE Subtot TO .Vsubtot IN #1
   NEXT #1 Status1
ENDWHILE  *(checker = 0)
WRITE "Finished summarizing..." AT 21,1
SET MESSAGES ON
SET ERROR MESSAGES ON
NEWPAGE
RETURN
```

Figure 18.6: The Summary.MAC macro

The macro will create a table named SumTable that summarizes the totals for each customer, as below:

CUSTNO	*TOTAL*
1001	\$405.45
1002	\$265.00
1004	\$181.00
1007	\$234.00

To verify that the summary table exists, enter the command

SELECT ALL FROM SumTable

at the R> prompt.

Now suppose that you wish to put the Summary.MAC macro and the Update.MAC macro that we created in the last chapter into a single procedure file. From the CodeLock Main menu, select option

2 to add an ASCII command file to a procedure file. Enter the name of the macro (**Summary.MAC**, for this example), and name the procedure file when prompted (**GenProcs.CMD**, for this example). Use the default block name (Summary) when prompted.

After returning to the CodeLock Main menu, select option 2 again. Enter **Update.MAC** as the name of the ASCII command file and **GenProcs.CMD** as the procedure file. Use the suggested block name, Update.

Once the macros have been added to the GenProcs.CMD procedure file, they can be accessed from the R> prompt using the following syntax:

RUN *block name* IN *procedure file name* USING *parameter list*

For example, to run the Summary.MAC macro in the GenProcs.CMD procedure file to summarize the Total column by customer number in the Charges table, thereby creating a new table named SumTable, you would enter the command

```
RUN Summary IN GenProcs.CMD USING Charges CustNo +
+ > Total SumTable Names
```

To run the Update.MAC macro in the GenProcs.CMD procedure file, you would enter a command such as

```
RUN Update IN GenProcs.CMD USING ARMain CustNo +
+ > Curr:Bal Payments CustNo Amount MINUS
```

Of course, the parameters will vary depending on the tables involved and the type of update (PLUS, MINUS, or REPLACE). Also, be sure the appropriate database is open before you run the macro.

Remember, you can add up to 42 blocks to a procedure file, so you could develop a good collection of general-purpose macros and have them all readily accessible from a single file.

MODIFYING PROCEDURES

At some point, you may need to make changes to a file that has already been converted into a procedure file. To do so, use RBEDIT to change the *original* file. (Don't attempt to modify the procedure file.) Then, use CodeLock to add the file to the procedure file once again. When you specify the name of the modified file, CodeLock will display the warning

```
Duplicate name–overwrite (Y or N):
```

If you answer yes, the modified file will be added to the procedure file, and the existing procedure will be erased.

DISPLAYING THE DIRECTORY

Option 6 from the CodeLock Main menu allows you to view the files stored on disk. When you select this option, you'll see the prompt

```
Enter DOS drive and subdirectory:
```

Press Enter to display files on the current drive and directory.

To view the files on a separate drive or directory, include the drive specification and directory name; for example, enter B:\Newdbs or C:\Newdbs.

DISPLAYING THE CONTENTS OF ASCII FILES

To view the contents of a file before you compile it, select option 7 from the CodeLock Main menu. CodeLock will display the following prompt:

```
Enter the name of the file to be displayed:
```

Enter the name of the file (and the drive specification and directory name if necessary). For example, enter **Loop2.ASC** to display the contents of the Loop2.ASC file on the current drive and directory. Enter the file name **B:Loop2.ASC** to look for and display the Loop2.ASC file on drive B.

USING DEVELOPER'S EXPRESS TO IMPROVE PROGRAM PERFORMANCE

Now we'll turn to Developer's EXPRESS, a new module in R:BASE for DOS and R:BASE for OS/2 that can increase the performance speed of your applications. Like CodeLock, Developer's EXPRESS converts ASCII files into binary files. However, the binary files created by Developer's EXPRESS run even faster than the ones created by CodeLock.

We mentioned earlier that binary files, like the .APX file created by Application EXPRESS or the binary files generated by CodeLock, run faster than their equivalent ASCII files because R:BASE doesn't have to do so much translating in order to run them.

Developer's EXPRESS takes this idea one step further, creating binary files that run even faster in R:BASE. To achieve this, Developer's EXPRESS uses two distinct programs—a pseudo-compiler (RCOMP) and an execution module (RRUN).

THE PSEUDO-COMPILER

Before you can understand what a *pseudo*-compiler is, you need to know what a real compiler is. A real compiler is a program that translates programs written in a given language into what is called *machine language*. Machine language is the basic binary-level language your computer understands, and any program you run has to be ultimately translated into machine language. However, real compilers translate your original program only once and then save the result as a machine-language program, which can be run directly from the operating-system level. Because the compiled program is written in machine language, no additional translation is required, and the program runs very fast.

A real R:BASE compiler, then, would translate your application program into machine language. All you would have to do to run it would be to type the compiled program's name at the operating system prompt. You wouldn't have to start R:BASE in order to run your application; theoretically, you wouldn't even have to own R:BASE!

R:BASE's pseudo-compiler doesn't create a program that can be run from the operating system. Instead, it creates a binary program with a characteristic .APC extension that can be run by a special execution module of R:BASE called RRUN. You might want to think of RRUN as a stripped down version of R:BASE without the frills—think of RRUN as a speedway, and your .APC file as a dragster.

Before you can use RCOMP (the pseudo-compiler), you need to be sure you have it installed on your system. If you elected to install the entire R:BASE package, it will be in the directory with the other R:BASE files. If you bypassed installing the utilities, you will need to go back and reinstall R:BASE in order to follow along on-line in this section. In either case, you'll probably find it easier to have the RCOMP files in the same directory as your database files. Generally, the database files are in a subdirectory called \DBFILES.

You also need to have an ASCII file to "compile." The ASCII file can be the .APP file generated by Application EXPRESS or any other command file. Make sure you have tested the file you want to compile before actually compiling it.

You can run RCOMP either from the R> prompt by using the command

```
ZIP ROLLOUT RCOMP
```

or directly from the operating system. Whichever you choose, you should see the Developer's EXPRESS Compiler menu, as shown in Figure 18.7.

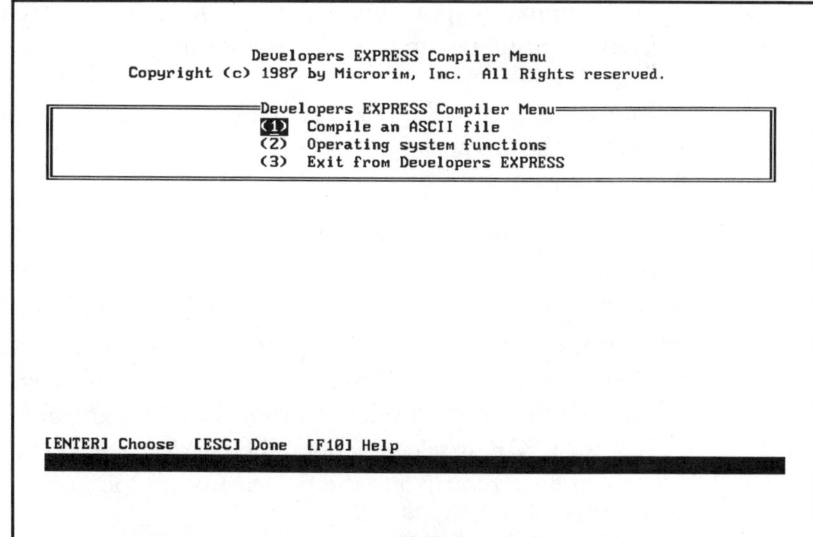

Figure 18.7: The Developer's EXPRESS Compiler menu

As you can see, using RCOMP is straightforward. Select option 1, *Compile an ASCII file*, and then select the application file name. If your application file isn't one of the ones listed on the *Choose an application* menu, it's probably because your file isn't in the default directory. Simply select Other and provide the file name along with its path, as follows:

c:\Apps*Appname*.APP

In the absence of error messages, compiling a program with RCOMP is as easy as that.

RCOMP may, however, display error messages. If it does, you'll have to read them, leave Developer's EXPRESS, and fix them. Some errors, however, won't be fixable.

THE LIMITATIONS OF THE PSEUDO-COMPILER

If you see the error message "Command not allowed" when you attempt to compile your program, you'll know that your application uses one or more commands that RCOMP can't deal with. You'll either have to modify your application so that it doesn't use the invalid command(s) or abandon your efforts to use RCOMP and RRUN. Commands that can't be used in compiled programs are listed in Table 18.1.

Another reality of RCOMP is that it's more rigorous in its syntax requirements. Go ahead and access RCOMP if you haven't already by entering

```
ZIP ROLLOUT RCOMP
```

at the R> prompt. Select option 1 and then specify Loop2.CMD as the file to compile. RCOMP will display an error message about ampersand variables not being allowed. But you don't have any ampersand variables in the Loop 2.CMD program! What's going on?

Exit RCOMP by selecting option 3, *Exit from Developer's EXPRESS*. Once you have returned to the R> prompt, type

```
RBEDIT Loop2.CMD
```

Table 18.1: Commands That Are Not Valid for Use with Developer's EXPRESS

ALTER TABLE	HELP	REDEFINE
CODELOCK	INPUT	RELOAD
COLUMNS	INTERSECT	REMOVE
CREATE TABLE	JOIN	RENAME
CREATE VIEW	LIST	REPORTS
DEFINE	OWNER	REVOKE
DROP TABLE	PASSWORDS	RULES
DROP VIEW	PROJECT	SUBTRACT
EXPAND	PROMPT	TABLES
EXPRESS	RBASE	UNION
FORMS	RBDEFINE	VIEW
GATEWAY	RBEDIT	ZIP ROLLOUT
GRANT		

You'll notice that there's only one & symbol in the program, used to join the two parts of the message that the program displays. Unfortunately, RCOMP has interpreted this as an ampersand variable, which is not allowed in RCOMP. To clarify the situation, we need to add parentheses around the line in question, as follows:

```
SET VAR Progress TO ("LOOP NUMBER " & +
+ > (CTXT(.COUNTER)))
```

Use the Ins key to make space for the opening parenthesis, add the closing one, and save the revised Loop2.CMD file.

If you try to compile Loop2.CMD again, it should work. Developer's EXPRESS won't give you any positive feedback to indicate that the compilation has been successful. Instead, if no error messages are displayed, you'll be returned to the *Choose an application* menu. Press Esc to return to the Developer's EXPRESS Compiler menu, and exit Developer's EXPRESS. Now that you've used RCOMP to generate an .APC file, you can use the execution module, RRUN, to run it.

USING RRUN

The RRUN module needs to be available on one of the PATHs you specified when you started R:BASE (or in your batch file) before you can actually run your compiled program. Again, it's generally easiest to have the RRUN files in the default subdirectory, which in most cases will be \DBFILES. RRUN, like RCOMP, can be run either from the R> prompt via ZIP ROLLOUT or from your operating system.

To test your Loop2.APC file, type the following command from the R> prompt:

```
ZIP ROLLOUT RRUN Loop2.APC
```

After a few seconds, R:BASE will ask you

```
How high shall I count?
```

If you enter **10** and press Enter, you'll see the same display you did when you ran the program as an ASCII file in Chapter 16, only the results will be displayed much faster. To see the comparison, try typing

```
RUN Loop2.CMD
```

when you have returned to the R> prompt. Note that in this simple example, the *overall* execution time isn't improved by using RRUN, since the ZIP ROLLOUT command took several seconds to execute. However, most applications aren't as simple as Loop2.CMD, and the extra time associated with ZIP ROLLOUT becomes insignificant.

In this chapter, you've seen how to use two of R:BASE's more advanced features: CodeLock and Developer's EXPRESS. Both are tools that you may want to use to increase R:BASE's performance. Keep in mind that both these programs provide an additional bonus, since they effectively encrypt your program. Binary files, for all practical purposes, can't be read by inquisitive humans. In Chapter 19, we'll focus on FileGateway, a marvelous tool for importing and exporting files.

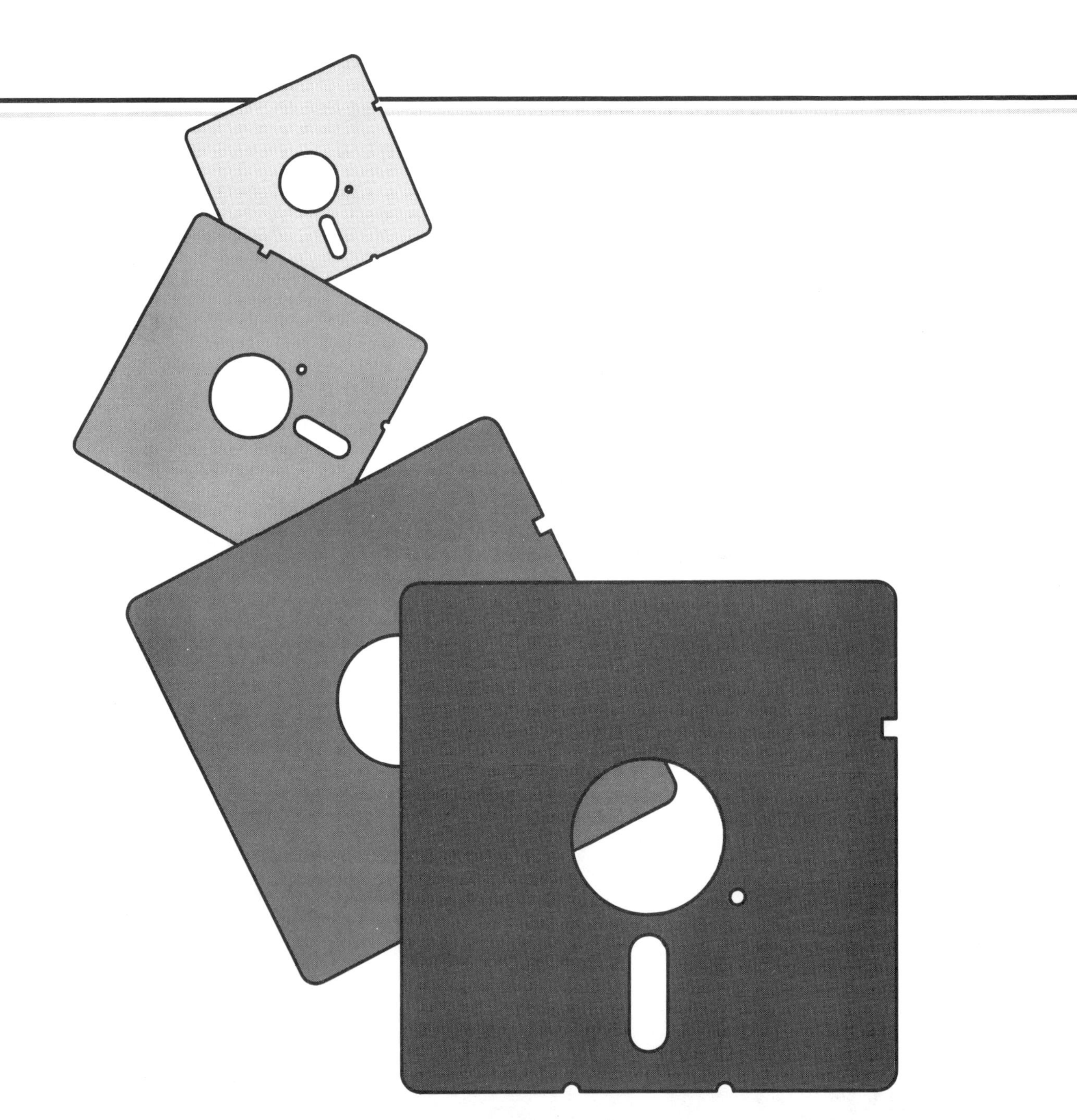

Chapter 19

Adding the Versatility of Other Programs to R:BASE

FAST TRACK

To convert R:BASE 5000 databases 556
to the new R:BASE format, use the CONVERT.EXE program that comes with your R:BASE package.

To use FileGateway, 559
R:BASE's import/export module, either select the Import/export option from the PBE *R:BASE and operating system utilities* menu, or enter the command **GATEWAY** from the R> prompt.

To export R:BASE tablc data 566
to word-processed form-letter files, use the *ASCII delimited* option in FileGateway.

To export R:BASE data to WordPerfect 570
for use as a secondary file, create an R:BASE report with special symbols at the end of each field and each record. Then use WordPerfect's Search and Replace feature to generate the required ^R and ^E characters.

To export R:BASE data to Microsoft Word 574
for use in mail-merge operations, create an ASCII-delimited data file and edit it to include field-name headers. Data locations in a Word form letter are marked with the << and >> symbols, created using Ctrl-[and Ctrl-], respectively.

To export dBASE files, 575
use the *ASCII delimited* option in FileGateway, and use the APPEND FROM <file name> DELIMITED command in dBASE to read in the ASCII file.

To import and export spreadsheet data, 581

use the specific FileGateway option, or set up intermediate ASCII files to interface with the spreadsheet package.

R:BASE INCLUDES MANY COMMANDS AND TWO programs—FileGateway and CONVERT.EXE—that can be used to transfer data to and from a variety of formats for interfacing with other software systems. In this chapter, we'll explore general techniques for creating and transferring ASCII-format files into and out of R:BASE, and we'll discuss the options available in the FileGateway program. First, we'll explain how to convert R:BASE 5000 data to the new R:BASE format using the CONVERT.EXE program.

R:BASE comes with two programs that can help you transfer data to and from other software systems. CONVERT.EXE is a small program that converts R:BASE 5000 databases to the R:BASE System V, R:BASE for DOS, or R:BASE for OS/2 database format. FileGateway lets you transfer data to and from other popular microcomputer software systems such as Lotus 1-2-3, dBASE, and WordStar.

You can also use the OUTPUT *file name* command to store copies of reports on disk files. These can then be embedded in word-processing documents. In this chapter we'll look at basic techniques for all types of data transfers.

CONVERTING R:BASE 5000 DATA TO CURRENT R:BASE FORMAT

If you have an R:BASE 5000 database that you wish to use with one of the new R:BASEs, you'll need to convert the original database to the new R:BASE format. Converting the database is simple, because R:BASE performs the conversion automatically with the CONVERT.EXE program. OS/2 users will have to run the CONVERT.EXE program under DOS.

Let's suppose that you have an R:BASE 5000 database named MyData that you want to convert to the new R:BASE format. Here are the steps necessary to make the conversion:

1. Use R:BASE 5000 to view all the column names and variable names in the original R:BASE 5000 database, and check to see if any of the column names (or variable names in reports) match any R:BASE *reserved words*. (Reserved words are listed in Table 1-7 in the R:BASE Fundamentals chapter of the

R:BASE *User's Manual.*) If you find any reserved words in the column names or variable names, change the names to non-reserved words in the R:BASE 5000 database.

2. Copy the entire R:BASE 5000 database to the subdirectory of your hard disk where you keep your R:BASE data files. The original database will be stored in three files, each with the file name you assigned followed by the number 1, 2, or 3. Each file will also have the extension .RBS, as in the examples below:

   ```
   MyData1.RBS
   MyData2.RBS
   MyData3.RBS
   ```

   To copy the files from a floppy disk in drive A to your hard disk, you could use R:BASE's COPY command at the R> prompt with the ? wild-card character, as follows:

   ```
   COPY A:MyData?.RBS
   ```

3. Verify that the CONVERT.EXE program is in the default subdirectory by typing

   ```
   DIR CONV*.*
   ```

   at the R> prompt. Then exit R:BASE and use the CD command, if necessary, to get into the subdirectory where the R:BASE 5000 database files and CONVERT.EXE program files are.

4. At the DOS C> prompt, enter the CONVERT command followed by the name of the file to convert. In this example, you would enter the command

   ```
   CONVERT MyData
   ```

   at the DOS C> prompt.

The converted files will be stored under the same file name, but with the extension .RBF, as below:

```
MyData1.RBF
MyData2.RBF
MyData3.RBF
```

The original files will still be stored under the original file names. To conserve disk space, you might want to erase the original .RBS files from your hard disk. However, only erase them once you're sure the conversion was successful.

If you do not have enough space left on your hard disk to convert the R:BASE 5000 databases, you can leave the R:BASE 5000 files in the floppy disk in drive A. With the CONVERT.EXE program on the hard disk and directory on which you normally store your R:BASE database files, enter the command

```
CONVERT A:MyData
```

(substituting the appropriate file name in place of *MyData*) at the DOS C> prompt. The original R:BASE 5000 files will still be stored on the floppy disks, and the converted R:BASE files will be stored on the hard disk.

Once the conversion is complete, you can use the R:BASE OPEN command to open the converted database, using the original database name (that is, **OPEN MyData** in this example).

To convert exceptionally large files, you can use the UNLOAD and LOAD techniques discussed below. The *Conversion Guide* section of the R:BASE utilities manual discusses additional techniques for converting large R:BASE files. The *Conversion Guide* also discusses techniques for converting applications written in R:BASE 5000 to the new R:BASEs. But in most cases, the application created in R:BASE 5000 will run well in R:BASE for DOS or R:BASE for OS/2 as long as you do the following:

1. Start Application EXPRESS and select option 2, *Modify an existing application.*
2. Choose the R:BASE 5000 application to update and without changing the application name, let R:BASE read the application files.

3. Press Esc and Enter to let R:BASE "rewrite" the application files.
4. Test your updated application to verify that it works with your updated database files.

USING FILEGATEWAY

The FileGateway program can copy data from tables to a variety of formats and can also import data from external formats into R:BASE tables. To run FileGateway, either select the Import/Export option from the PBE R:BASE and operating system utilities menu, or enter the command

```
GATEWAY
```

directly at the R> prompt. The FileGateway Main menu will appear on the screen, as in Figure 19.1. As the menu shows, you can import data, export data, get help on the screen, or exit FileGateway.

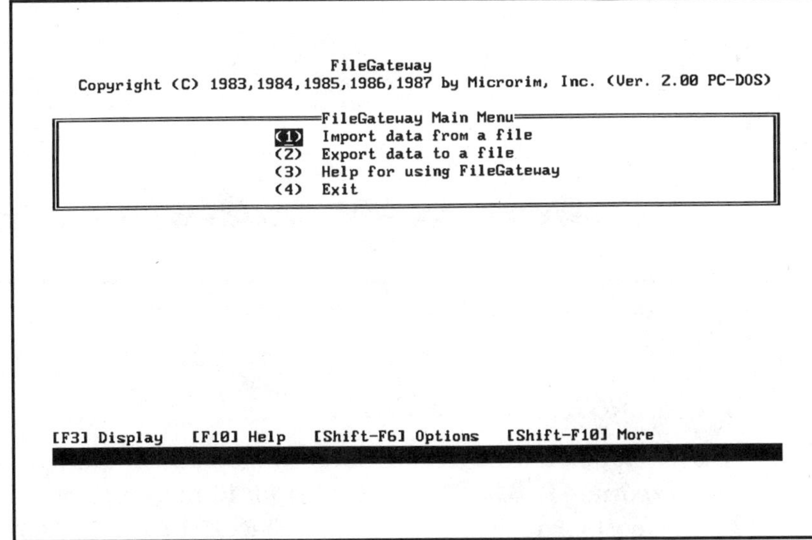

Figure 19.1: The FileGateway Main menu

GETTING HELP

If you need help while using FileGateway, select option 3, or press the F10 key at any time. After viewing the help screen, press Esc to return to FileGateway.

IMPORTING OPTIONS

Selecting option 1 from the FileGateway Main menu presents options for importing data into R:BASE tables. Figure 19.2 shows the Import menu options on the screen. We'll discuss some specific examples for importing data later in the chapter.

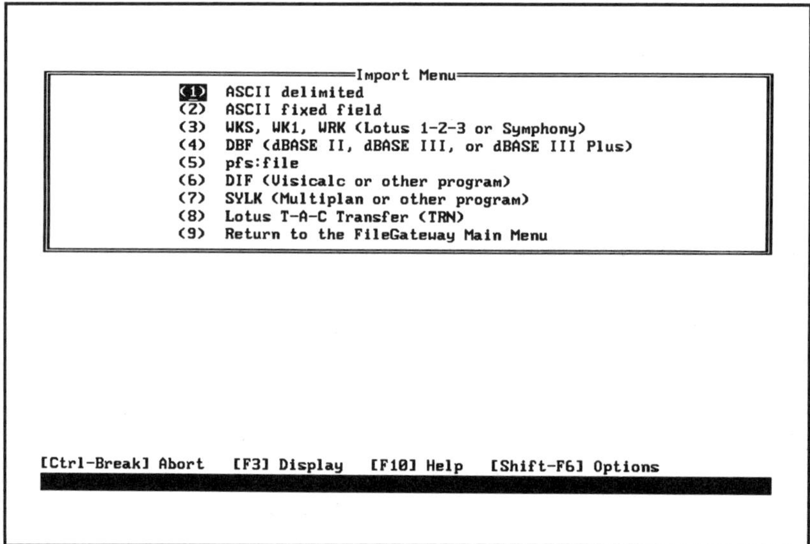

Figure 19.2: The options for importing data into R:BASE tables

EXPORTING OPTIONS

Option 2 from the FileGateway Main menu presents options for exporting R:BASE tables to other file formats. Figure 19.3 shows the Export menu option. (Again, we'll look at specific examples later in the chapter.)

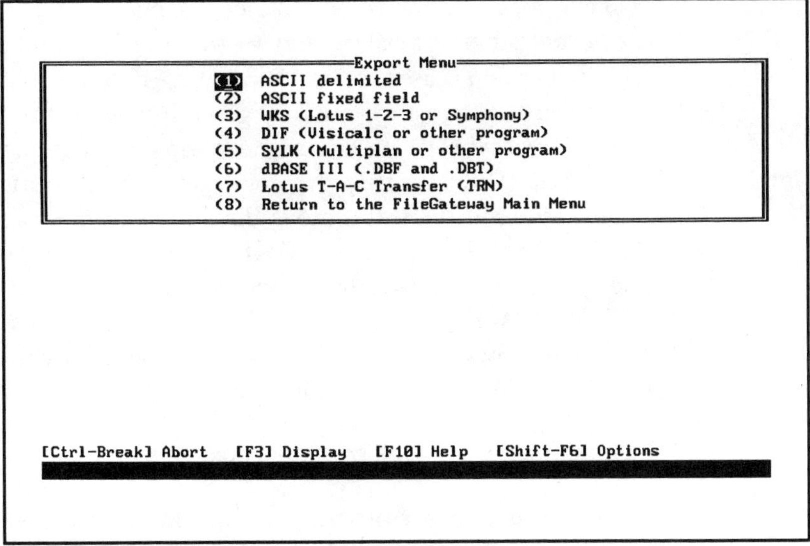

Figure 19.3: The options for exporting R:BASE tables

OTHER FILEGATEWAY OPTIONS

You can also call up the Options menu at any time while using FileGateway by pressing Shift-F6. This menu, shown in Figure 19.4,

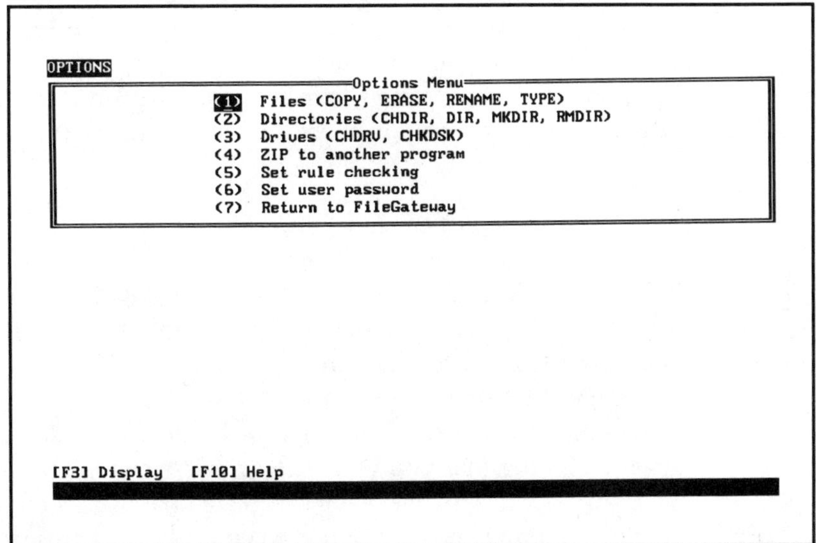

Figure 19.4: The Options menu

lets you perform basic file maintenance, change and view directories, run external programs (ZIP), and set rule checking and passwords.

The first option is used for basic operating system file maintenance such as copying, erasing, renaming, and viewing the contents of ASCII files with the TYPE command (a topic we'll discuss in the section on ASCII files in this chapter). The second option lets you change, create, view, and remove directories from your hard disk, using the basic CHDIR, DIR, MKDIR, and RMDIR commands. Option 3 lets you change drives and check the disk status with the CHDRV and CHKDSK commands.

Option 4 allows you to run an external program, memory permitting. When you select this option, the screen asks that you

```
Enter the name of the program to execute:
```

Type in the name of the program in the same way that you would to run the program from the C> prompt.

The external program will run only if it is small enough to fit into memory along with FileGateway. If not, you'll see the messages about "INSUFFICIENT MEMORY" for your program. You'll then be asked to "Press any key to continue" and be returned immediately to the Options menu.

If the external program does fit into memory, you can use it in the usual way. When you exit the program, you'll automatically be returned to the Options menu.

Option 5, *Set rule checking,* can be used when importing files into R:BASE tables. When you select this option from the Options menu, the screen asks whether to

```
Check data against entry rules?
```

If you select Yes, incoming data will be validated against whatever rules you defined for the table that is receiving the data. If you select No, all of the imported data from the external file will be imported, regardless of whether it meets the requirements of the rules.

Option 6 lets you enter the password necessary to add data to the table (assuming that you've created a password for the table). For now, suffice it to say that if you've created passwords for a database or table, you must use this option to enter the appropriate password before you can import or export table data.

In Chapter 16 we discussed techniques for recording and playing back keystrokes with Exec files. You can record and use Exec files in FileGateway using the same keys discussed earlier: Shift-F7 to start and stop recording keystrokes, and Shift-F8 to play back the keystrokes.

A NOTE ON ASCII FILES

Before discussing specific file transfer techniques, you should become familiar with basic ASCII file structures. Many software systems accept data that are stored in ASCII format. In fact, you can accomplish almost any data transfer imaginable, including many minicomputer and mainframe transfers, with some knowledge of ASCII file formats. Let's discuss those now.

ASCII (American Standard Code for Information Interchange) data files are generally stored in one of two formats: *delimited* or *structured.*

DELIMITED ASCII FILES

The most common format is the delimited ASCII file, also called the *sequential access* file. In this file, individual *fields* (columns) are separated by commas (or another delimiting character). Character (text) fields are usually surrounded by quotation marks. Many data files passed from minicomputers and mainframe computers to microcomputers are stored as delimited ASCII files. Figure 19.5 shows a sample delimited ASCII file.

STRUCTURED ASCII FILES

Structured ASCII files (also called *random-access* or *fixed-length* data files) store data with fixed *field* (column) and *record* (row) lengths, with no delimiting characters between the fields. Often, information captured from other computers via a modem is stored in the structured format. Figure 19.6 shows a sample structured data file.

ASCII files generally contain only data and delimiters, with no special formatting codes or header information. Therefore, if you use your operating system or the R:BASE TYPE command to view the file, you can quickly see the file displayed on the screen. When

```
1003,"Tape Backup",1.00,1250.00,"7/8/88"
1000,"Ram Disk",1.00,1100.00,"7/8/88"
1001,"Floppy Disks",10.00,2.11,"7/8/88"
1001,"Color Card",1.00,101.00,"7/8/88"
1001,"Video Cable",2.00,16.00,"7/8/88"
1001,"8 Mhz Clock",2.00,16.39,"7/8/88"
1001,"Ram Disk",1.00,1100.00,"7/8/88"
1002,"8 Mhz Clock",2.00,16.39,"7/8/88"
1002,"Ram Disk",1.00,1100.00,"7/8/88"
1003,"8 Mhz Clock",1.00,16.39,"7/8/88"
1003,"Tape Backup",1.00,1250.00,"7/8/88"
1003,"40 Meg. Disk",1.00,450.00,"7/8/88"
1003,"Floppy Disks",5.00,2.11,"7/8/88"
1003,"Color Card",1.00,101.00,"7/8/88"
1004,"Video Cable",10.00,16.00,"7/8/88"
1004,"8 Mhz Clock",1.00,16.39,"7/8/88"
1004,"Tape Backup",2.00,1250.00,"7/8/88"
```

Figure 19.5: A sample delimited ASCII file

importing an ASCII file, you need only use the TYPE command to see whether the file is structured or delimited. The TYPE command uses the following syntax:

TYPE *<d:> file name*

Hence, if you enter the command

TYPE NewData.DAT

at your operating system prompt or the R:BASE R> prompt, you'll see the contents of a file named NewData.DAT stored on the currently logged drive. The command

```
1000 Turbo Board      1     550.00   07/08/88
1000 Ram Disk         1    1100.00   07/08/88
1001 Floppy Disks    10       2.11   07/08/88
1001 Color Card       1     101.00   07/08/88
1001 Video Cable      2      16.00   07/08/88
1001 8 Mhz Clock      2      16.39   07/08/88
1001 Ram Disk         1    1100.00   07/08/88
1002 8 Mhz Clock      2      16.39   07/08/88
1002 Ram Disk         1    1100.00   07/08/88
1003 8 Mhz Clock      1      16.39   07/08/88
1003 Tape Backup      1    1250.00   07/08/88
1003 40 Meg. Disk     1     450.00   07/08/88
1003 Floppy Disks     5       2.11   07/08/88
1003 Color Card       1     101.00   07/08/88
1004 Video Cable     10      16.00   07/08/88
1004 8 Mhz Clock      1      16.39   07/08/88
1004 Tape Backup      2    1250.00   07/08/88
```

Figure 19.6: A structured data file

```
TYPE A:Transfer.DAT
```

displays the contents of a file named Transfer.DAT on drive A.

TECHNIQUES FOR TRANSFERRING FILES

The chapter called "FileGateway Guide," from the R:BASE *Utility Manual,* discusses all the details of transferring files using FileGateway. Rather than repeat all of that information here, we'll look at specific examples of transferring R:BASE table data. We'll look at some creative ways to perform transfers with ASCII files that are not discussed in the R:BASE manuals.

CREATING A WORDSTAR FORM-LETTER FILE

WordStar (like most other word processors) has a MailMerge option that allows you to print form letters using data stored in delimited ASCII data files. You can easily create such files from any R:BASE table using FileGateway.

For example, suppose you want to print form letters with WordStar using names and addresses from the Names table in the Mail database we created earlier in this book. Begin by starting FileGateway, and select 2, *Export data to a file,* from the Main menu. Select option 1, *ASCII delimited,* from the Export menu. When R:BASE asks for the name of the database to use, select Mail. When you are asked for the name of thc tablc to cxport, select Names.

Next, you'll be given the opportunity to select columns to export. For this example, you'll need only the following columns:

```
L:Name
F:Name
Company
Address
City
State
Zip
```

Press Esc after selecting the column names.

Next, select a sort order for the exported file. You can select any of the columns to sort on, although for bulk mailing, Zip would be the best choice. Select either Ascending or Descending order, and press Esc.

From the next screen, you can specify that only particular rows be exported, such as rows with CA in the State column, or rows with ZIP codes in the range 90000 to 99999. For this example, just press Esc to export all the rows. FileGateway will verify the request by asking

```
Export all rows?
```

For this example, you can select Yes.

Next the screen asks for the name of the file to export and suggests Names.DEL as the name. Let's enter a more descriptive name—WS.DAT. Press Enter to proceed.

Next the screen asks that you

```
Enter the character to separate fields in your output file:
```

In almost every situation, you'll want to use a comma to separate fields, so type in a comma and press Enter.

Next the screen asks

```
Add a carriage return/line feed at the end of each row?
```

Virtually all ASCII files need a carriage return/line feed at the end of each row, so you'll want to select Yes in response to this question.

At this point, FileGateway begins creating the ASCII file and displays its progress by displaying how many rows have been exported. (The original data in the Names table is left unchanged; the new file named WS.DAT will contain a copy of the table data in ASCII delimited format.) When exporting is complete, you can press any key to return to the FileGateway Main menu.

When the Import menu reappears, select option 8 to return to the Main menu, and select option 4 to exit from FileGateway.

To verify that the exportation was successful, you can enter the command

```
TYPE WS.DAT
```

at the R> prompt. The delimited ASCII file will appear on your screen as in Figure 19.7.

Next you'll want to make sure that the WS.DAT file is accessible to your word processor. You can either copy the word processor to the directory containing WS.DAT or copy WS.DAT to the directory containing your word processor, using the COPY command either from R:BASE or from your operating system.

Assuming that you are using WordStar as the word processor, run WordStar in the usual way. Create a document file by selecting D from the WordStar opening menu. Give it a file name, such as FORM.LET. Then type in the appropriate dot commands and the body of the letter, which is shown in Figure 19.8.

You use the .DF (data file) dot command to name the MailMerge file of names and addresses. The .RV (Read Variable) command assigns a name to each column in the data file. It is important

```
"Martin","Mary","Atomic Ovens","321 Microwave St.","Lassiter","OH","12121"
"Teasdale","Trudy","Atomic Ovens","321 Microwave St.","Lassiter","OH","12121"
"Miller","Monica","Acme Development","355 Torrey Pines St.","Newark","NJ""54821"
"Miller","Marie","Zeerox Inc.","234 C St.","Los Angeles","CA","91234"
"Adams","Bart","Dataspec Inc.","P.O. Box 2890","Malibu","CA","92111"
"Jones","Mindy","ABC Co.","123 A St.","San Diego","CA","92122"
"Baker","Robin","Peach Computers","2311 Coast Hwy","San Diego","CA","92122"
"Miller","Anne","Golden Gate Co.","2313 Sixth St.","Berkeley","CA","94711"
"Smith","Sandy","Hi Tech, Inc.","456 N. Rainbow Dr.","Berkeley","CA","94721"
```

Figure 19.7: An ASCII-delimited version of the Names table

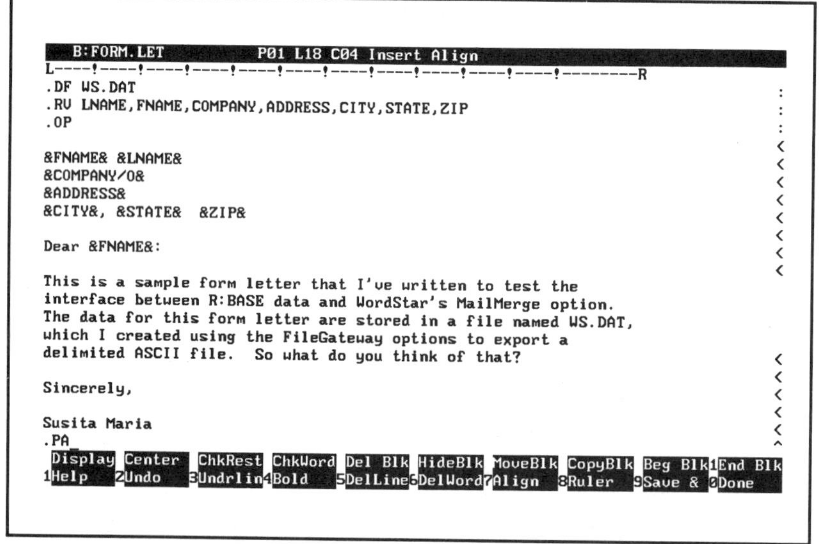

```
 B:FORM.LET            P01 L18 C04 Insert Align
L----!----!----!----!----!----!----!----!----!----!----!--------R
.DF WS.DAT                                                        :
.RV LNAME,FNAME,COMPANY,ADDRESS,CITY,STATE,ZIP                    :
.OP                                                               :
                                                                  <
&FNAME& &LNAME&                                                   <
&COMPANY/O&                                                       <
&ADDRESS&                                                         <
&CITY&, &STATE&  &ZIP&                                            <
                                                                  <
Dear &FNAME&:                                                     <
                                                                  <
This is a sample form letter that I've written to test the
interface between R:BASE data and WordStar's MailMerge option.
The data for this form letter are stored in a file named WS.DAT,
which I created using the FileGateway options to export a
delimited ASCII file.  So what do you think of that?              <
                                                                  <
Sincerely,                                                        <
                                                                  <
Susita Maria                                                      <
.PA                                                               ^
 Display  Center  ChkRest  ChkWord  Del Blk  HideBlk  MoveBlk  CopyBlk  Beg Blk  End Blk
1Help    2Undo   3Undrlin 4Bold    5DelLine 6DelWord 7Align   8Ruler   9Save &  0Done
```

Figure 19.8: The sample form letter created with WordStar Release 4

to assign a name to every column in the data file, even if you do not plan to use the column in your form letter. In this example, we've listed column names that match the columns we exported to the ASCII file. Note that, with WordStar Professional Release 4.0, you *must* separate the column names with commas. The .OP command omits page numbers, and .PA ensures that each form letter starts on a new page.

Variable names used within the letter are surrounded by ampersands, such as &LNAME& and &FNAME&. The /O option used with the &COMPANY/O& column tells WordStar to omit this line if there are no company data for an individual. This will ensure that a blank line doesn't appear between the name and the address if an individual does not have a company.

After you create and save the form letter using the WordStar Ctrl-KD command (hold down the Ctrl key and type K, then D), you need to merge print it using the Merge Print command. That is, select WordStar option M from the WordStar menu, and when it asks for the name of the file to merge print, type in the file name of the form-letter file (not FORM.LET, the WS.DAT data file). Accept the default answers to the printer questions by pressing Enter after each one. A letter for each individual in the Members database will then be printed.

OTHER TIPS FOR INTERFACING WITH WORDSTAR

You can send R:BASE reports to WordStar for further editing or inclusion in other documents. To do so, design a report format using Reports Express in R:BASE. Then, print the data using the syntax

OUTPUT *file name*

and

PRINT *report name*

Exit R:BASE and load WordStar to read in the text file.

The commands below, when entered at the R> prompt, will create an ASCII file named Transfer.TXT, which you can read directly into WordStar:

```
OPEN Mail
OUTPUT Transfer.TXT
PRINT Sales
```

```
OUTPUT Screen
EXIT
```

At this point, the Transfer.TXT file contains a copy of the data displayed by the Sales report format.

Now you can load WordStar. Let's say that you want to pull the R:BASE report into a document called MANUAL.TXT. At the operating system prompt, type in the command

```
WS MANUAL.TXT
```

When the document appears on the screen, position the cursor where you want the R:BASE report to appear. Then enter Ctrl-KR (hold down the Ctrl key and type K, then R). WordStar asks for the

```
NAME OF FILE TO READ?
```

Type in the name of the transfer file (**Transfer.TXT**, for this example), and press Enter. That's all there is to it.

You can also use WordStar to create and edit R:BASE command files. Just be sure to use the *nondocument* mode at all times when you're creating and editing the command file.

INTERFACING WITH WORDPERFECT

Many of you use WordPerfect and will want to know how to transfer R:BASE data into WordPerfect format. The technique we just described for sending R:BASE reports to a file for subsequent editing in WordStar works with WordPerfect as well, except that you'll need to type WP, rather than WS, to start WordPerfect. You'll use Ctrl-F5 and option 2 to read in the R:BASE report.

However, if you want to take advantage of WordPerfect's Merge feature for multiple mailings, things are a bit more complex. WordPerfect works well with ASCII-delimited files, but expects Ctrl-R's (^R) instead of commas as field delimiters, and Ctrl-E's (^E) instead of carriage returns to separate individual records.

The best approach to creating a WordPerfect Merge file is to create an R:BASE report, locating all the fields that will be needed in the WordPerfect form letter, and then output the report to a file.

Let's use the data from the Names table as we did with WordStar. Start Reports EXPRESS and create a new report called **GotoWP**. Establish the following expressions:

1: TEXT : RFulname = (F:Name & L:Name + "!")
2: TEXT : RCompany = (Company + "!")
2: TEXT : RCSZ = (City + "," & State & " " & Zip + "!")
3: TEXT : RAdd = (Address + "!")

Exit the Expression menu, select Edit mode, and enter report detail lines as shown in Figure 19.9.

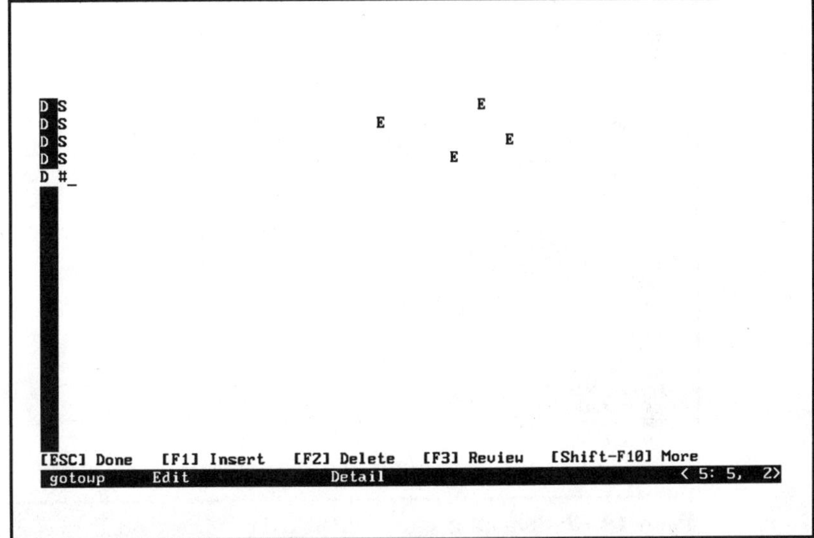

Figure 19.9: Report detail lines for the GotoWP report

The first SE pair corresponds to the variable RFulname, the second to Company, the third to RAdd, and the fourth pair to RCSZ. Don't forget to enter the pound sign (#) on the last detail line.

Why the exclamation mark (!) and pound sign (#) characters? Actually, you can choose any odd character not regularly used in your data or form letter. These will be used with WordPerfect's Search and Replace function to generate the required Ctrl-R's and Ctrl-E's.

Once the report is created, print the report with the output going to a file as you have done before:

```
OUTPUT WP.DAT
PRINT GotoWP
OUTPUT SCREEN
```

When this is completed, exit R:BASE, start WordPerfect and load in the GotoWP file for editing. You should see something similar to Figure 19.10.

```
Sandy Smith~
Hi Tech, Inc.~
456 N. Rainbow Dr.~
Berkeley, CA  94721~
!
Andy Jones~
ABC Co.~
123 A St.~
San Diego, CA  92122~
!
Marie Miller~
Zeerox Inc.~
234 C St.~
Los Angeles, CA  91234~
!
Bart Adams~
Dataspec Inc.~
P.O. Box 2890~
Malibu, CA  92111~
!
Anne Miller~
Golden Gate Co.~
2313 Sixth St.~
Berkeley, CA  94711~
A:\WP.DAT                                        Doc 1  Pg 1  Ln 1      Pos 10
```

Figure 19.10: Preparing to use R:BASE data for a WordPerfect mail merge

Now you need to use WordPerfect's Search and Replace feature to replace the exclamation point (!) and pound sign (#) characters with control codes. To do this, make sure the cursor is at the top of your document and press **Alt-F2**. You'll see a prompt at the bottom of the screen asking you

```
w/Confirm? (Y/N) N
```

Press Enter to let WordPerfect do an automatic search and replace without confirming each instance with you. The next prompt will ask you for the Search text as follows:

-> Srch:

Enter the exclamation point (!) character followed by a space and press **F2**. The next prompt will be

Replace with:

Now press the **F9** key to produce a ^R. This is a control code in WordPerfect that signifies an end of a field. Press **F2** again. After a few seconds, the file will have ^Rs where there were exclamation points.

Go back to the top of the document and repeat the Search and Replace process. This time enter the pound sign (#) and a space as the text to be searched for and replace it with a **Shift-F9** to generate the ^E symbol. The ^E code designates the end of a record in WordPerfect.

Save this file, since it will be the secondary file in WordPerfect's Merge routine. Now type in your form-letter template, or primary file, as in Figure 19.11.

```
^F1^
^F2^
^F3^
^F4^

Dear ^F1^:

This is a sample primary file that illustrates how R:BASE data
can be merged into a Word Perfect document.  The fields were
located by pressing Alt-F9, selecting F (for Field), and then
typing the number corresponding to the required data.  Since the
name is the first field, it was located by responding with a 1.
Do you see how it works?

Sincerely,


Susita Maria_




A:\FORM2.LET                                    Doc 1  Pg 1  Ln 18     Pos 22
```

Figure 19.11: Entering a primary file for WordPerfect's Merge routine

The codes ^F1^, ^F2^, ^F3^, and ^F4^ tell WordPerfect where to put the data that you are going to merge. ^F1^ tells WordPerfect where to locate the data for field one. In our example, the first field contains the full name of the addressee, so it will be located near the top of the letter. To locate these fields, press Alt-F9 at the appropriate location in the WordPerfect primary file. The following prompt appears:

^C; ^D; ^F; ^G; ^N; ^O; ^P; ^Q; ^S; ^T; ^U; ^V;

Type F (for field) and when asked for the

Field Number?

type in a 1, 2, 3, or 4 as appropriate. Continue locating each of the fields and then type in the body of the letter. Save this file as **Form2.LET**.

You're finally ready to merge the two documents together to create the letters. To do this type **Ctrl-F9** at the beginning of a clean document screen. The following menu appears:

1 Merge; 2 Sort; 3 Sorting Sequences: 0

Enter **1**, then type **Form2.LET** as the name of the primary file and **WP.DAT** as the name of the secondary file. After a few moments, the merged letters will appear on your screen. Save the merge file and print it at your convenience.

MAIL-MERGE WITH MICROSOFT WORD

Merging R:BASE data into Microsoft Word form letters is similar to performing mail-merge with WordStar. You need to create an ASCII-delimited data file (in fact, the file you generated for the WordStar example can be used again), but you need to edit it to include field-name headers. You also need to create a form letter template with field locations indicated by *field name*. Finally, you merge the two.

If you have Word and want to try your hand at using its merge feature, complete the following steps:

1. If you have created the WS.DAT file with FileGateway, make a copy of it called WORD.DAT. If you haven't, follow

the instructions in the section on "Creating a WordStar Form-Letter File" earlier in this chapter. Enter Word.DAT instead of WS.DAT as the export file name.

2. Start Word and load the file WORD.DAT. Adjust the margins so that all the data for each customer fits on one line. Type in a new first line containing the field names of the data, as shown in Figure 19.12.

3. Create the master form letter. Note that the name of the data file must be entered on the first line inside the "chevron" symbols. You create the left and right chevrons by entering Ctrl-[and Ctrl-], respectively. Then enter the field names, also within chevrons, at the desired locations, as shown in Figure 19.13.

4. Once you have completed these steps, select Print and then Merge.

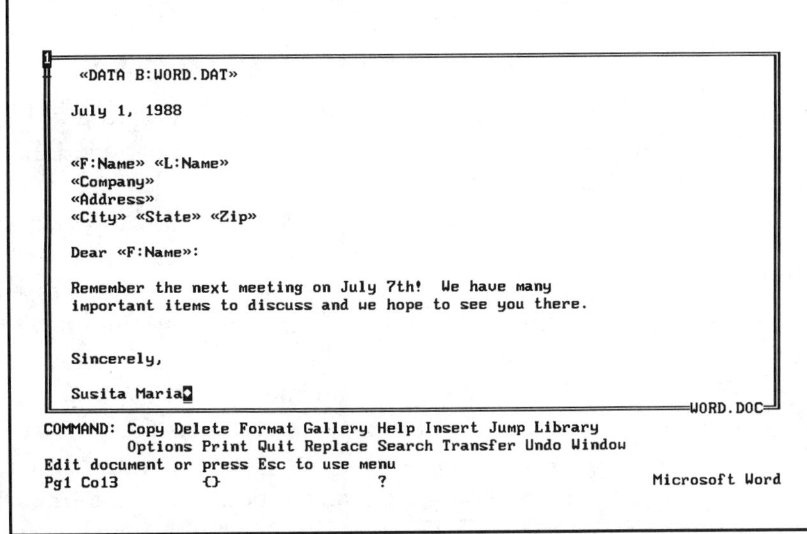

```
«DATA B:WORD.DAT»

July 1, 1988

«F:Name» «L:Name»
«Company»
«Address»
«City» «State» «Zip»

Dear «F:Name»:

Remember the next meeting on July 7th! We have many
important items to discuss and we hope to see you there.

Sincerely,

Susita Maria
                                                            WORD.DOC
COMMAND: Copy Delete Format Gallery Help Insert Jump Library
         Options Print Quit Replace Search Transfer Undo Window
Edit document or press Esc to use menu
Pg1 Co13          {}               ?                  Microsoft Word
```

Figure 19.12: The WORD.DAT file ready for use in a Word mail merge

dBASE INTERFACING

You can import data from dBASE data files into R:BASE tables, as well as export data from R:BASE tables to dBASE.

```
L:Name,F:Name,Company,Address,City,State,Zip
"Smith","Sandy","Hi Tech, Inc.","456 N. Rainbow Dr.","Berkeley","CA","94721"
"Jones","Andy","ABC Co.","123 A St.","San Diego","CA","92122"
"Miller","Marie","Zeerox Inc.","234 C St.","Los Angeles","CA","91234"
"Adams","Bart","Dataspec Inc.","P.O. Box 2890","Malibu","CA","92111"
"Miller","Anne","Golden Gate Co.","2313 Sixth St.","Berkeley","CA","94711"
"Baker","Robin","Peach Computers","2311 Coast Hwy","San Diego","CA","92122"
"Miller","Monica","Acme Development","355 Torrey Pines St.","Newark","NJ","5
"Teasdale","Trudy","Atomic Ovens","321 Microwave St.","Lassiter","OH","12121
"Martin","Mary","Atomic Ovens","321 Microwave St.","Lassiter","OH","12121"
::::::::::::::::::::::::::::::::::::::::::::::::::::::::::::::::::::::::::::::
◆

                                                                     WORD.DAT
COMMAND: Copy Delete Format Gallery Help Insert Jump Library
         Options Print Quit Replace Search Transfer Undo Window
Edit document or press Esc to use menu
Pg1 Co45          {}                  ?                          Microsoft Word
```

Figure 19.13: The master form letter for Microsoft Word

IMPORTING dBASE FILES INTO R:BASE

Importing dBASE files into R:BASE is a simple task. Figure 19.14 shows a dBASE III PLUS database named Sample.DBF that we'll import into R:BASE in this example.

First, you'll need to make a copy of the dBASE database available to FileGateway. The easiest way to do this is to copy the dBASE database to your R:BASE directory using your operating system's Copy command. (Remember that dBASE database files have the extension .DBF, so in this example you would want to use the file name Sample.DBF in the Copy command.)

When the file is on the same directory as FileGateway, run FileGateway in the usual way. Select option 1 from the FileGateway Main menu to import a file, and option 4 from the Import menu to import a DBF file. The screen will ask that you select the file to import. (In this example, let's assume that you want to import the file named Sample.DBF.)

Next, the screen asks that you specify the name of the R:BASE database in which to import the dBASE data. In lieu of importing the data into an existing database, you can select OTHER to have FileGateway create a new R:BASE database. Then you need to assign a name to the

Record#	PartNo	PartName	Qty	U_Price	Date
1	A-123	MicroProcessor	100	55.55	01/01/86
2	B-222	Laser Engine	2	1234.56	02/01/86
3	C-333	Color Terminal	5	400.00	02/01/86
4	D-444	Hard Disk	25	500.00	03/02/86
5	E-555	Disk Controller	50	200.00	04/15/86
6	F-666	Graphics Board	20	249.00	05/15/86
7	G-777	Modem	5	249.00	05/15/86
8	H-888	SemiDisk	25	600.00	06/15/86
9	A-123	MicroProcessor	10	55.55	07/30/86
10	B-222	Laser Engine	8	1234.56	07/31/86
11	A-123	MicroProcessor	10	55.00	08/30/86
12	E-555	Disk Controller	25	200.00	09/01/86
13	E-555	Disk Controller	100	180.00	10/01/86
14	F-666	Graphics Board	5	200.00	11/01/86
15	A-123	MicroProcessor	20	51.00	11/15/86
16	H-888	SemiDisk	15	600.00	12/15/86

Figure 19.14: A dBASE database named Sample.DBF

new database. In this example, type in the name **Sample.** (You don't need to add an extension to the R:BASE database name.)

The screen asks that you enter the name of the table to import the data into and suggests the name Sample. Press the Enter key to accept the suggested table name.

Next the screen asks if you want to

```
Import deleted records from dBASE file?
```

dBASE allows you to mark records for deletion without actually deleting them. If you want to exclude these records that are marked for deletion, select No. If you want to import all the records, select Yes.

Next, the screen shows a suggested structure for the table that will receive the imported data, as in Figure 19.15. You can use the suggested structure or change field names and data types. For this example, you'd want to change the data type for the U_PRICE column from DOUBLE to CURRENCY. Use the arrow keys to position the cursor to the data type for the U_PRICE column, and type in the new data type, CURRENCY. Press Enter after changing the data type; then press Esc when you are finished making changes on the screen.

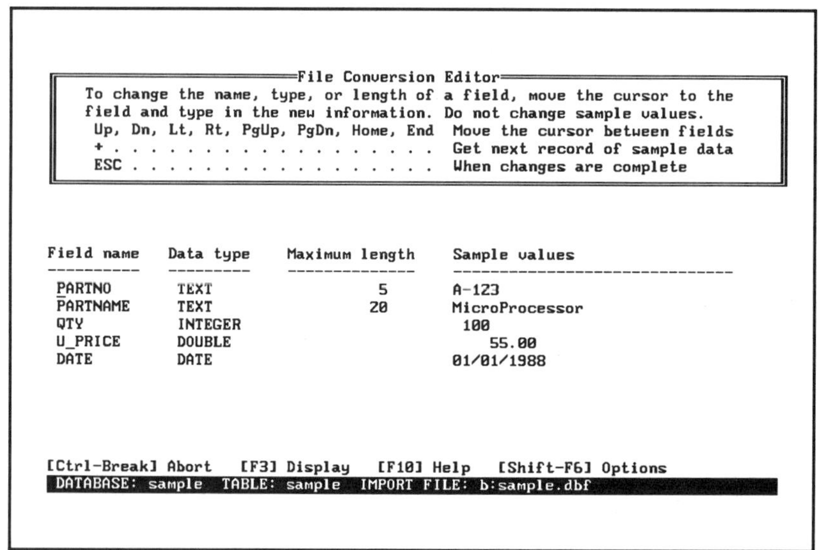

```
File Conversion Editor
To change the name, type, or length of a field, move the cursor to the
field and type in the new information. Do not change sample values.
 Up, Dn, Lt, Rt, PgUp, PgDn, Home, End  Move the cursor between fields
 + . . . . . . . . . . . . . . . . . .  Get next record of sample data
 ESC . . . . . . . . . . . . . . . . .  When changes are complete

Field name   Data type   Maximum length   Sample values
----------   ---------   --------------   ------------------------------
 PARTNO       TEXT              5         A-123
 PARTNAME     TEXT             20         MicroProcessor
 QTY          INTEGER                      100
 U_PRICE      DOUBLE                          55.00
 DATE         DATE                        01/01/1988

[Ctrl-Break] Abort   [F3] Display   [F10] Help   [Shift-F6] Options
 DATABASE: sample  TABLE: sample  IMPORT FILE: b:sample.dbf
```

Figure 19.15: The suggested default structure for new R:BASE table

Next you'll see the Data Loading menu. Select option 1 to load data into the database. If the file being imported contains dates, you'll see a screen presenting several possible formats for dates in the imported file. For dBASE, the suggested format (MM/DD/(YY)YY) is fine, so press Esc to use the suggested format.

Finally, FileGateway will begin importing data from the dBASE file, and it will present a counter to show its progress. When the importation is complete, you can press any key to proceed and then select menu options to exit FileGateway.

To verify that the data have been imported, run R:BASE to get to the R> prompt. Then open the database and select rows from the newly imported table. In this example, we named the new R:BASE database Sample, and we also assigned the name Sample to the new table. Therefore, to view the imported data, enter the commands

```
OPEN Sample
SELECT ALL FROM Sample
```

at the R:BASE R> prompt.

EXPORTING FILES TO dBASE

To send data from an R:BASE table to a dBASE database, you first need to create an ASCII delimited copy of the table data. To do so, use FileGateway and the same techniques we used to create the WordStar MailMerge file in the previous section.

Run dBASE and create a file with the same fields as the R:BASE table. The Names table has the following structure:

TABLE: NAMES

COLUMN DEFINITIONS

#	NAME	TYPE	LENGTH
1	CustNo	INTEGER	1 value(s)
2	L:Name	TEXT	15 characters
3	F:Name	TEXT	15 characters
4	Company	TEXT	25 characters
5	Address	TEXT	25 characters
6	City	TEXT	15 characters
7	State	TEXT	5 characters
8	Zip	TEXT	10 characters
9	Ent:Date	DATE	1 value(s)
10	Phone	TEXT	13 characters

In dBASE III, you would create a database with the following structure:

STRUCTURE FOR DATABASE : C:DBFILE.DBF

FIELD	FIELD NAME	TYPE	WIDTH	DEC
1	CUSTNO	Numeric	4	
2	LNAME	Character	20	

FIELD	FIELD NAME	TYPE	WIDTH	DEC
3	FNAME	Character	20	
4	COMPANY	Character	25	
5	ADDRESS	Character	25	
6	CITY	Character	15	
7	STATE	Character	5	
8	ZIP	Character	10	
9	ENT_DATE	Date	8	
10	PHONE	Character	13	

In dBASE II, you could create a database with the structure below:

STRUCTURE FOR FILE: C:DBFILE .DBF

FLD	NAME	TYPE	WIDTH	DEC
001	CUSTNO	N	004	
002	LNAME	C	020	
003	FNAME	C	020	
004	COMPANY	C	025	
005	ADDRESS	C	025	
006	CITY	C	015	
007	STATE	C	005	
008	ZIP	C	010	
009	ENT:DATE	C	008	
010	PHONE	C	013	

In either case, you would then use the database you created and enter the command

```
APPEND FROM RbtoDB.DAT DELIMITED
```

After the dot prompt reappears, use the LIST command to verify the accuracy of the transfer.

INTERFACING WITH SPREADSHEETS

FileGateway includes options for directly transferring data to and from Lotus 1-2-3 (Versions A or 2.01), Symphony, Multiplan SYLK files, and VisiCalc DIF files. (These file formats are also often used by other packages.) Keep in mind, however, that databases store tables in a fixed column and row format, while spreadsheets allow you to place data randomly around the screen. Therefore, when importing data from spreadsheets, you'll need to import only those areas that are stored in a fixed tabular format (columns and rows), such as with 1-2-3 and Symphony databases.

Remember also, that if you want to export data for Lotus for use in Lotus' database, you'll need to have the column names in a row along the top of the worksheet. Let's see how it works.

Assume that we want to transfer the data from the Charges table into Lotus. First, start FileGateway and select option 2, *Export data*, from the FileGateway Main menu. Then, from the Export Options menu, select option 3, WKS. When prompted for your database and table names, choose Mail and Charges. Tell FileGateway you want to export all columns, and press Esc twice to bypass sorting and qualifying statements.

When FileGateway asks if you want to sort all the rows, press Enter to accept the default of Yes. Similarly, accept the default filename, Charges.WKS, unless you already have a worksheet with that name. If you are exporting to Lotus 2.01 or Symphony, you may want to modify the file-name extension at this time.

FileGateway should now be asking you if you want field (column) names to be exported also. Since Lotus' database requires column names for most of its activities, enter a **1** so that the field names will go in row 1.

Finally, you'll be asked for the address of the upper-left cell to receive the data. Since row 1 is already being used, enter A2. That's it! Exit FileGateway, copy the new worksheet file into your Lotus subdirectory, and type **/FR Charges**. Your screen should look like Figure 19.16. Asterisks in the P:Date column indicate that the column needs to be wider to accommodate the data.

There are many ways to move data to and from worksheets. As an alternative to using the options for directly importing and exporting spreadsheet data, you can use intermediate ASCII files to help with

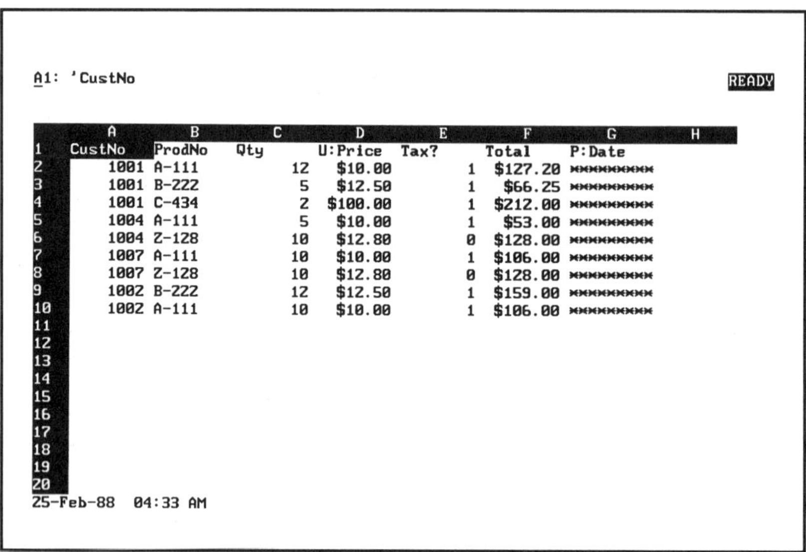

	A	B	C	D	E	F	G	H
1	CustNo	ProdNo	Qty	U:Price	Tax?	Total	P:Date	
2	1001	A-111	12	$10.00	1	$127.20	**********	
3	1001	B-222	5	$12.50	1	$66.25	**********	
4	1001	C-434	2	$100.00	1	$212.00	**********	
5	1004	A-111	5	$10.00	1	$53.00	**********	
6	1004	Z-128	10	$12.80	0	$128.00	**********	
7	1007	A-111	10	$10.00	1	$106.00	**********	
8	1007	Z-128	10	$12.80	0	$128.00	**********	
9	1002	B-222	12	$12.50	1	$159.00	**********	
10	1002	A-111	10	$10.00	1	$106.00	**********	
11								
12								
13								
14								
15								
16								
17								
18								
19								
20								

Figure 19.16: Data exported from the Charges table into Lotus 1-2-3

the conversion (although you may never need to). For example, you can use FileGateway to create a delimited ASCII file from an R:BASE table and assign a file name to the exported file with the extension .PRN. Then, you can use the /FIN (File Import Numbers) options in Lotus 1-2-3 to read the ASCII file directly into a spreadsheet.

For example, copy the WS.DAT file you created for WordStar into your Lotus subdirectory as WS.PRN. Start Lotus, type **/FIN** and select WS.PRN as the file.

You can export ASCII fixed-field files from almost any spreadsheet. For example, the /PF (Print File) options will allow you to highlight any portion of a Lotus 1-2-3 spreadsheet and write that portion of the spreadsheet to an ASCII file. Then, you can use FileGateway to import the ASCII fixed-field file into a new or existing R:BASE table.

WHERE DO I GO FROM HERE?

R:BASE is a large and powerful database-management system for microcomputers. A single book on the subject can hardly do justice to its many capabilities. However, we've covered the basic concepts using practical examples, and I hope that these examples have helped you to understand the basic workings of R:BASE and enabled you to manage your own databases.

If you bought this book because the manuals that came with R:BASE seemed too technical or too abstract, this tutorial text should have given you sufficient practical background to make the more technical material in the manuals understandable. The *User's Manual* that came with the R:BASE package should be particularly helpful in expanding your knowledge and skills in using R:BASE.

I should mention that, as I finish this book, I'm already preparing to write a companion book entitled *Advanced Techniques in R:BASE,* which will continue where this book left off and present examples of more complex business applications. That book will also be published by SYBEX.

But perhaps the most important element in fully mastering any software package, including R:BASE, is practice. Hands-on experimentation (with some printed reference material nearby to back you up) will provide the experience that leads to complete mastery. Experimenting and working in a comfortable place will make your learning experience enjoyable and productive.

Appendix

Installing R:BASE

When you set out to install R:BASE on your computer for the first time, the most obvious source of information will be your R:BASE documentation. You'll find the R:BASE for DOS *Single-User & Multi-User Installation & Start-up Guide* and R:BASE for OS/2 *Single-User Installation & Start-up Guide/Multi-User Guide* very helpful; take the time to read through them.

However, for those of you who are allergic to manuals, here is a quick overview of the installation process, as well as some tips and techniques for customizing R:BASE to meet your needs.

SETTING UP A BATCH FILE

If you are using R:BASE for DOS, you can make life easier for yourself by creating a batch file similar to the one below. You can call it RB.BAT:

```
PATH C:\;C:\RBFILES;C:\DOS
CD C:\DBFILES
RBASE
CD\
```

Note: R:BASE for OS/2 users should create a batch file with a name such as SRTRBASE.CMD and add R:BASE to OS/2's Program Selector. There's nothing magic about the SrtRBASE file name—you can use any legal file name—but be sure to remember to use .CMD rather than .BAT for its file-name extension. Your batch file will probably look like this:

```
PATH C:\;C:\OS2;C:\RBFILES
DPATH C:\;C:\OS2;C:\DBFILES
CD \DBFILES
RBASE
CD\
```

Both R:BASE for DOS and R:BASE for OS/2 also make use of a number of add-on parameters, which are inserted to the right of the word RBASE in the batch file. These parameters are listed in Table

A.1. Tables A.2 and A.3 show the codes for setting background and foreground screen colors, respectively.

Table A.1: Add-In Parameters

PARAMETER	ACTION
–C	Bypasses PBE and leaves you at the R> prompt.
–P	Starts R:BASE in PBE mode (default setting).
–R	Bypasses the Microrim logo screen.
–B*n*	Sets the default background color (see Table A.2).
–F*n*	Sets the default foreground color (see Table A.3).
–M*n*	With systems with CGA card and monochrome display, use –M1 for a clearer screen display.
–T*n*	Specifies a type of monitor for R:BASE for DOS users. –T0 indicates color, –T1 indicates monochrome, and –T2 is used for some compatibles such as Tandy.

Table A.2: Background Color Codes

CODE	COLOR
0	Black
1	Blue
2	Green
3	Cyan
4	Red
5	Magenta
6	Brown
7	Light grey

Table A.3: Foreground Color Codes

CODE	COLOR
0	Black
1	Blue
2	Green
3	Cyan
4	Red
5	Magenta
6	Brown
7	Light grey
8	Grey
9	Light blue
10	Light green
11	Light cyan
12	Light red
13	Light magenta
14	Yellow
15	White

Using these parameters, the following batch file would start R:BASE with a blue background and a yellow foreground, bypass the Microrim logo, and leave you at the R> prompt:

```
PATH C:\;C:\RBFILES;C:\DOS
CD C:\DBFILES
RBASE -F14 -B1 -C -R
CD\
```

SETTING UP THE SYSTEM MENU

Those readers who are R:BASE System V users probably miss the RBSYSTEM.ASC file that came with previous versions of R:BASE. However, you can create your own file in R:BASE that serves the same purpose; it must be called RBASE.MNU. RBASE.MNU is the file R:BASE uses in place of RBSYSTEM.ASC to determine the textual information that is displayed on the system menu, its order, the colors used in individual modules, and whether or not to suppress the Microrim logo. In addition, you can use RBASE.MNU to specify an initial command file for R:BASE and initial exec files for the other modules, whether or not you want R:BASE to start in PBE.

An RBASE.MNU file might look something like the file shown in Figure A.1. The digits 0–8 shown in the first column of the menu are significant here. Although you can arrange up to fifteen menu items in any order you wish, the number 5 must always be associated with R:BASE, 3 with Forms EXPRESS, and so on as shown. Keep in mind that you don't have to use all the standard options (0–8) if you don't want to. Any options other than the standard nine, however, must have integer codes between 100 and 255 to identify them. You select a 3-digit integer code for any programs you want to run besides the ones associated with the codes 0 through 8. If you create the menu using RBASE.MNU, you'll see a screen like the one shown in Figure A.2 when you start R:BASE.

```
5 "Custom Application"  "RBASE    -R -F7  -B1 cmdfile"
5 R:BASE                "RBASE    -R -F15 -B5 -C"
1 "Definition EXPRESS   "RBDEFINE -R -C"
2 "Application EXPRESS  "EXPRESS  -R -F7  -B1"
4 "Reports EXPRESS"     "REPORTS  -R -F7  -B1"
3 "Forms EXPRESS        "FORMS    -R -F7  -B1"
7 FileGateway           "GATEWAY  -R"
8 CodeLock              "CODELOCK -R -F12 -B1"
6 RBEDIT                "RBEDIT   -R -F7  -B1"
101 RCOMP               "RCOMP    -R -F14 -B1"
102 RRUN                "RRUN     -R -F14 -B1"
103 "Batch file"        "COMMAND /C batfile.BAT"    *(OS/2:  "CMD /C batfile.CMD")
0 "Operating system"
```

Figure A.1: A sample RBASE.MNU file

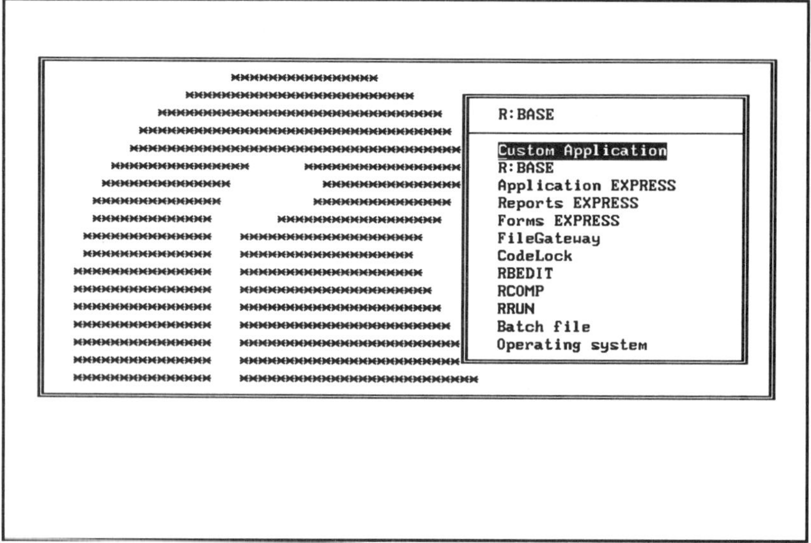

Figure A.2: Starting R:BASE with a custom RBASE.MNU file

TROUBLESHOOTING YOUR INSTALLATION

If you've installed R:BASE, but can't get it to work, check the following points:

- In order to run R:BASE for DOS, your system should have about 400K RAM available after DOS and any memory resident utilities have been loaded. R:BASE for OS/2 requires about 1MB of RAM after OS/2 has been loaded.
- Check your CONFIG.SYS file. It should be in the root directory. It should also have been modified automatically to include the statements BUFFERS = 16 and FILES = 20, unless it already had BUFFERS and FILES statements with higher numbers, or you specified higher numbers during installation. Sooner or later, you'll see ominous messages such as "Out of file handles" or "Not enough buffers" if your CONFIG.SYS file isn't set up properly. If you want to use your mouse, your CONFIG.SYS file should also list the

device driver for the mouse, and the mouse driver file should be in the root directory.

- Make sure you have a subdirectory for your database files. The recommended directory name is \DBFILES.
- If you have an RBASE.MNU file, make sure the numbers to the left of the modules follow Microrim's rules (see "Setting Up the System Menu" earlier in this appendix). If they don't, you'll be selecting one option and ending up in another (or just be cycled back to the menu).
- If you are using R:BASE for OS/2 and nothing happens when you want to print, modify your CONFIG.SYS file to delete the line

```
RUN = C:/OS2/SPOOL.EXE /D: LPT1 /O:LPT1
```

OS/2 automatically puts this line in its CONFIG.SYS file. This line directs all printer output to the spooler, which prints only when you exit R:BASE.

- Check to see whether you have a file called RBASE.DAT in either of your R:BASE subdirectories. The contents of any RBASE.DAT file will be interpreted by R:BASE as startup instructions. If R:BASE always starts by running an application, and you don't want it to, erase the R:BASE.DAT file.
- Don't use any R:BASE command names or reserved words as names for your columns, tables, variables, reports, forms, views, and passwords. The words to avoid are listed in Table A.4.
- If you're trying to do multitasking under OS/2, but it isn't working, remember that R:BASE needs to have access to two files: SERVER.SY5 and USER.SY5. These should have been generated automatically when you installed R:BASE and indicated that you wanted to add network concurrency. If you don't remember running the BUMP and ADDUSER programs to add networking and identify the work-station to the screen, reinstall R:BASE. If you're trying to use multitasking on a single database (run two different applications concurrently), remember that you

Table A.4: Words to Be Avoided as Names in R:BASE

#DATE	EXP	LAST	RTIME
#PAGE	FLOAT	LIMIT	SFIL
#PI	FOR	LIST	SGET
#TIME	FORMS	LJS	SIGN
=	FROM	LOG	SIN
ABS	FV1	LOG10	SINH
ACOS	FV2	LUC	SLEN
AINT	HELP	MAX	SLOC
ALL	ICAP1	MIN	SMOVE
AND	ICAP2	MOD	SORTED BY
AND_OR	ICHAR	NEWPAGE	SPUC
ANINT	IDAT	NINT	SQRT
ASIN	IDWK	NOT	STRIM
ATAN	IFEQ	OR	TAN
ATAN2	IFGT	PMT1	TANH
AVE	IFLT	PMT2	TDWL
CHAR	IHR	PV1	TERMS1
COMPCOLS	IMIN	PV2	TERM2
COS	IMON	PROMPT	TERM3
COSH	IN	RATE1	TMON
COUNT	INY	RATE2	ULC
CTR	ISEC	RATE3	VARIABLES
CTXT	IYR	RDATE	WHERE
DIM	JDATE	RJS	

must use the

```
SET MULTI ON
```

command, either at the R> prompt, or more permanently by changing the DEFAULT.ASC file discussed below.

- If you need to convert an old R:BASE 4000 or R:BASE 5000 database and/or application into R:BASE for OS/2 format, you'll need to run the CONVERT program under DOS.

CUSTOMIZING THE DEFAULT.ASC FILE

Most users won't need to (and shouldn't) modify the DEFAULT.ASC file. DEFAULT.ASC is the file R:BASE uses in deciding case equivalence (a = A if case is turned off) and sorting order for nonnumeric data. Network users and OS/2 users who want to be able to do multitasking on a single database, however, probably will want to modify this file, because it contains the main "switch" that will put R:BASE in multi-user mode.

DEFAULT.ASC, as the name implies, is an ASCII file, which can be edited by RBEDIT or most word processing packages. The first few lines of the file contain the lines

```
;MULTI-USER SWITCH
OFF
;
```

For network or single-database multitasking use, the OFF should be changed to an ON. R:BASE doesn't use the ASCII file directly, however. Once the file has been edited, you should run DEFGEN to generate a machine-readable version of it, called DEFAULT.MSG.

What else can you customize in DEFAULT.ASC? The rest of the file contains character equivalences (called the *case folding table*) that R:BASE uses for sorting, displaying, and printing. We recommend you leave this part of the file alone unless you have strong reasons to change it. Characters are listed in their ASCII form, so you will see double columns of numbers when you view this portion of the file.

For example, the first group of numbers contains pairs such as 97 65, which equates A with a. R:BASE uses the equivalences established in this table (assuming CASE is SET OFF) to evaluate IF and WHILE conditions and WHERE clauses.

Assume you have a table that includes the last names anderson, Anderson, and Azizi and that case is set off. If you issue the command

```
SELECT ALL FROM table name WHERE L:Name = anderson
```

R:BASE will display both Andersons. If, on the other hand, CASE is SET ON, this command displays only the lowercase anderson.

The next group of numbers in the DEFAULT.ASC file corresponds to the *collating* (sorting) *table*, which determines how efficiently R:BASE performs when sorting the inequality testing. The SET CASE switch has no effect on these commands. Whether the switch is on or off, the command

```
SELECT ALL FROM table name SORTED BY last name
```

will result in anderson coming before Azizi. If you need to sort in true ASCII order, you should consider modifying this table.

The next portion of the file contains a line directing R:BASE to use another ASCII file, PRINTER.ASC, which contains the *printer table*. This file contains codes that allow your printer to print accents on letters, and can be edited as well.

The final table in DEFAULT.ASC is identified as the *expansion character* table, and includes additional (mainly foreign language) equivalences for R:BASE's use in evaluating ORDER BY and WHERE clauses and IF and WHILE conditions.

CUSTOMIZING THE PROMPT MODE

R:BASE gives you the ability to modify its PROMPT.MSG file. This is the file R:BASE uses when you are in PBE mode. You can modify the message displayed in PBE or even add new prompts by changing the PROMPT.MSG file. However, you need to understand R:BASE programming (discussed in Chapter 16) in order to do this. Refer to the chapter on "Customizing R:BASE" in your *User's Manual* for details about this process.

INSTALLING R:BASE IN MULTI-USER MODE

There is no special, separate multi-user version of R:BASE; if you've purchased R:BASE, you can use it either in single- or multi-user mode. As of press time, R:BASE for OS/2 users will have to run R:BASE for OS/2 in multi-user mode to do multitasking, since no OS/2 local-area networks (LANs) are yet available.

SYSTEM REQUIREMENTS

R:BASE for DOS works with most major network hardware and software, and the list of supported networks is constantly growing. You should check with Microrim to find out if R:BASE will work with your configuration. Microrim currently supports multi-user versions of R:BASE with the following network configurations:

- 3Com EtherLink, EtherLink Plus, or EtherLink Plus running either 3Com 3 +, version 1.0 or higher, or Novell Advanced Netware 86/E, version 1.02, 2.0a + +, or 286 2.0a + +.
- IBM PC Network with IBM PC Network Program, version 1.0 or higher, or Novell Advanced Netware 86/PCN, version 1.02, 2.0a + +, or 286 2.0 + +.
- IBM Token Ring running IBM PC LAN program, version 1.10 or higher, or 3Com 3 +, version 1.01 or higher.
- Ungermann-Bass Net/One using Ungermann-Bass Personal Connection, version 1.0, IBM PC Network Program, version 1.0 or higher, or Microsoft Networks, version 1.0 or higher.

In addition to having DOS 3.1 or higher, the network server must have at least 640K of available memory. Work-stations must have at least 512K of available RAM to run R:BASE.

WHAT A NETWORK VERSION DOES

People generally install local-area networks to share both tangible (laser printers) and intangible (data) resources. On a network, R:BASE lets users share databases. It allows more than one user access to both the same R:BASE program (legally, you only have to buy one copy) and the same database files. To prevent users from trying to change the same data at the same time, R:BASE features automatic *concurrency control* at the item level. "What's that?", you're probably wondering.

Assume two users are editing the same field in the same record at the same time. R:BASE's automatic checking will accept the changes entered by the first user and alert the second user to them. At that point, the second user can either abandon his or her efforts or continue. Although R:BASE's default for concurrency control is column checking—that is, two users can be working on the same record as long as they don't try to change the same column—you can use the SET VERIFY command to have R:BASE check all values in the row during updating.

To further ensure data integrity, R:BASE supports database, table, and user-defined locking. For example, if a user is in the process of changing the database structure, the database will automatically be *locked* until the changes are made. Similarly, R:BASE will allow only one person at a time to work on a given application file with Application EXPRESS, RBEDIT, RCOMPILE, Definition EXPRESS, and CodeLock. Users can also use the SET LOCK command to set locks on tables. The SET WAIT command can be used to tailor the number of seconds R:BASE waits when encountering a lock before halting execution of the command that encountered the lock.

See Table A.5 for a summary of R:BASE's multi-user features.

INSTALLING A NETWORK VERSION

The following list outlines the basic steps you need to take to install R:BASE in a network environment:

1. Make the R:BASE program files available to network users either by installing them on the network server or by having

Table A.5: R:BASE's Multi-User Features

FEATURE	**DESCRIPTION**	**COMMANDS AFFECTED**
Concurrency control	Automatically provided for other users and items unless a table lock is issued.	EDIT USING ENTER [USING]
Concurrency control and table lock.	Issuance of a table lock interrupts concurrency control while data is modified. Table lock automatic for existing Reports and Forms tables.	APPEND CHANGE DELETE ROWS
Table lock	When set, excludes other table locks issued after it. Cannot be set if concurrency control is in effect for any part of table. Database lock will preempt table lock for new Forms, Reports, and Views tables.	EDIT ALL ENTER...FROM *filespec* LOAD FORMS REPORTS SET LOCK ON UNLOAD FOR *table name* VIEW
Database lock	Locks all tables. Cannot be set while concurrency control or table locks are in effect, and won't allow other locks to be set while it's in effect.	DEFINE EXPAND RELOAD REDEFINE REMOVE REMOVE COLUMN UNLOAD
Table/database combination locks	While a database's structure is being modified, a database lock is issued. Once the changes are made, table lock(s) replace the database lock.	BUILD FORMS INTERSECT JOIN PROJECT RENAME REPORTS SUBTRACT UNION VIEW

them at each work-station. If the files are to be on the network server, be sure to provide users with network read, write, and create access rights. You'll probably want to install the R:BASE program files at the individual work-stations, though, to enhance performance.

2. Put the database and application files in a directory to which users have network read, write, and create access rights. Use R:BASE to establish read only and read/write passwords for any of the database tables when appropriate. Use the utilities on the Network Administrator Disk to keep the list of authorized users current.

3. Edit DEFAULT.ASC to include the SET MULTI ON command if you want network users to share R:BASE databases. This will ensure automatic concurrency control and locking, make the SET VERIFY, SHOW VERIFY, SET LOCK, SET LOCK OFF, SET WAIT, and SHOW WAIT commands available, and preclude the SET CLEAR and PACK commands. After editing the file, compile it by running DEFGEN to create a new DEFAULT.MSG file. Make sure the new DEFAULT.MSG file is in the same directory as the R:BASE program files. If your network users will be running R:BASE off their own hard disks, the new DEFAULT.MSG file needs to be on each of their hard disks.

4. Set up a CONFIG.SYS file at each of the work-stations containing at least the statement FILES = 20. Also create appropriate batch files for each work-station; it is crucial that these include the DOS PATH command.

5. Establish a procedure for database backup. The PACK command will not work when R:BASE is running in multi-user mode. You will either have to SET MULTI OFF or use an alternative method for backing up your multi-user database.

Index

Selections from The SYBEX Library

SPREADSHEETS AND INTEGRATED SOFTWARE

The ABC's of 1-2-3 (Second Edition)

Chris Gilbert/Laurie Williams

245pp. Ref. 355-4

Online Today recommends it as "an easy and comfortable way to get started with the program." An essential tutorial for novices, it will remain on your desk as a valuable source of ongoing reference and support. For Release 2.

Mastering 1-2-3 (Second Edition)

Carolyn Jorgensen

500pp. Ref. 528-X

Get the most from 1-2-3 Release 2 with this step-by-step guide emphasizing advanced features and practical uses. Topics include data sharing, macros, spreadsheet security, expanded memory, and graphics enhancements.

Lotus 1-2-3 Desktop Companion (SYBEX Ready Reference Series)

Greg Harvey

976pp. Ref. 501-8

A full-time consultant, right on your desk. Hundreds of self-contained entries cover every 1-2-3 feature, organized by topic, indexed and cross-referenced, and supplemented by tips, macros and working examples. For Release 2.

Power User's Guide to Lotus 1-2-3

Peter Antoniak/E. Michael Lunsford

368pp. Ref. 421-6

This guide for experienced users focuses on advanced functions, and techniques for designing menu-driven applications using macros and the Release 2 command language. Interfacing techniques and add-on products are also considered.

Lotus 1-2-3 Instant Reference SYBEX Prompter Series

Greg Harvey/Kay Yarborough Nelson

296pp. Ref. 475-5; 4 3/4x8

Organized information at a glance. When you don't have time to hunt through hundreds of pages of manuals, turn here for a quick reminder: the right key sequence, a brief explanation of a command, or the correct syntax for a specialized function.

Mastering Lotus HAL

Mary V. Campbell

342pp. Ref. 422-4

A complete guide to using HAL "natural language" requests to communicate with 1-2-3—for new and experienced users. Covers all the basics, plus advanced HAL features such as worksheet linking and auditing, macro recording, and more.

Simpson's 1-2-3 Macro Library

Alan Simpson

298pp. Ref. 314-7

Increase productivity instantly with macros for custom menus, graphics, consolidating worksheets, interfacing with mainframes and more. With a tutorial on macro creation and details on Release 2 commands.

Mastering Symphony (Fourth Edition)

Douglas Cobb

875pp. Ref. 494-1

Thoroughly revised to cover all aspects of the major upgrade of Symphony Version 2, this Fourth Edition of Doug Cobb's classic is still "the Symphony bible" to this complex but even more powerful package. All the new features are discussed and placed in context with prior versions so that both new and previous users will benefit from Cobb's insights.

Focus on Symphony Macros
Alan Simpson

239pp. Ref. 351-1

An in-depth tutorial guide to creating, using, and debugging Symphony macros, including developing custom menus and automated systems, with an extensive library of useful ready-made macros for every Symphony module.

Focus on Symphony Databases
Alan Simpson/Donna M. Mosich

398pp. Ref. 336-8

Master every feature of this complex system by building real-life applications from the ground up—for mailing lists, inventory and accounts receivable. Everything from creating a first database to reporting, macros, and custom menus.

Better Symphony Spreadsheets
Carl Townsend

287pp. Ref. 339-2

Complete, in-depth treatment of the Symphony spreadsheet, stressing maximum power and efficiency. Topics include installation, worksheet design, data entry, formatting and printing, graphics, windows, and macros.

Mastering Quattro
Alan Simpson

400pp. Ref. 514-X

This tutorial covers not only all of Quattro's classic spreadsheet features, but also its added capabilities including extended graphing, modifiable menus, and the macro debugging environment. Simpson brings out how to use all of Quattro's new-generation-spreadsheet capabilities.

Mastering Framework II
Douglas Hergert/Jonathan Kamin

509pp. Ref. 390-2

This business-minded tutorial includes a complete introduction to idea processing, "frames," and software integration, along with its comprehensive treatment of word processing, spreadsheet, and database management with Framework.

Advanced Techniques in Framework: Programming in FRED
Alan Simpson

320pp. Ref. 246-9

This introduction to the FRED programming language is for experienced Framework users who need to expand their word processing, spreadsheet, graphics, and database management skills.

Mastering Excel on the IBM PC
Carl Townsend

550pp. Ref. 403-8

A complete Excel handbook with step-by-step tutorials, sample applications and an extensive reference section. Topics include worksheet fundamentals, formulas and windows, graphics, database techniques, special features, macros and more.

Mastering Enable
Keith D. Bishop

350pp. Ref. 440-2

A comprehensive, practical, hands-on guide to Enable 2.0—integrated word processing, spreadsheet, database management, graphics, and communications—from basic concepts to custom menus, macros and the Enable Procedural Language.

Mastering Q & A
Greg Harvey

399pp. Ref. 356-2

This hands-on tutorial explores the Q & A Write, File, and Report modules, and the Intelligent Assistant. English-language command processor, macro creation, interfacing with other software, and more, using practical business examples.

Mastering SuperCalc 4
Greg Harvey

311pp. Ref. 419-4

A guided tour of this spreadsheet, database and graphics package shows how and why it adds up to a powerful business planning tool. Step-by-step lessons and real-life examples cover every aspect of the program.

Understanding Javelin PLUS

John R. Levine
Margaret Levine Young
Jordan M. Young

558pp. Ref. 358-9

This detailed guide to Javelin's latest release includes a concise introduction to business modeling, from profit-and-loss analysis to manufacturing studies. Readers build sample models and produce multiple reports and graphs, to master Javelin's unique features.

DATABASE MANAGEMENT

Mastering Paradox (Third Edition)

Alan Simpson

600pp. Ref. 490-9

Paradox is given authoritative, comprehensive explanation in Simpson's up-to-date new edition which goes from database basics to command-file programming with PAL. Topics include multiuser networking, the Personal Programmer Application Generator, the Data-Entry Toolkit, and more.

Mastering Reflex

Robert Ericson/Ann Moskol

336pp. Ref. 348-1

A complete introduction to Reflex: The Analyst, with hands-on tutorials and sample applications for management, finance, and technical uses. Special emphasis on its unique capabilities for crosstabbing, graphics, reporting, and more.

dBASE III PLUS Programmer's Reference Guide (SYBEX Ready Reference Series)

Alan Simpson

1056pp. Ref. 508-5

Programmers will save untold hours and effort using this comprehensive, well-organized dBASE encyclopedia. Complete technical details on commands and functions, plus scores of often-needed algorithms.

The ABC's of dBASE III PLUS

Robert Cowart

264pp. Ref. 379-1

The most efficient way to get beginners up and running with dBASE. Every 'how' and 'why' of database management is demonstrated through tutorials and practical dBASE III PLUS applications.

Mastering dBASE III PLUS: A Structured Approach

Carl Townsend

342pp. Ref. 372-4

In-depth treatment of structured programming for custom dBASE solutions. An ideal study and reference guide for applications developers, new and experienced users with an interest in efficient programming.

Also:

Mastering dBASE III: A Structured Approach

Carl Townsend

338pp. Ref. 301-5

Understanding dBASE III PLUS

Alan Simpson

415pp. Ref. 349-X

A solid sourcebook of training and ongoing support. Everything from creating a first database to command file programming is presented in working examples, with tips and techniques you won't find anywhere else.

Also:

Understanding dBASE III

Alan Simpson

300pp. Ref. 267-1

Understanding dBASE II

Alan Simpson

260pp. Ref. 147-0

Advanced Techniques in dBASE III PLUS

Alan Simpson

454pp. Ref. 369-4

A full course in database design and structured programming, with routines for inventory control, accounts receivable, system management, and integrated databases.

Also:

Advanced Techniques in dBASE III
Alan Simpson
505pp. Ref.282-5

Advanced Techniques in dBASE II
Alan Simpson
395pp. Ref. 228-0

Simpson's dBASE Tips and Tricks (For dBASE III PLUS)
Alan Simpson
420pp. Ref. 383-X
A unique library of techniques and programs shows how creative use of built-in features can solve all your needs – without expensive add-on products or external languages. Spreadsheet functions, graphics, and much more.

Expert dBASE III PLUS
Judd Robbins/Ken Braly
423pp. Ref. 404-6
Experienced dBASE programmers learn scores of advanced techniques for maximizing performance and efficiency in program design, development and testing, database design, indexing, input and output, using compilers, and much more.

dBASE Instant Reference SYBEX Prompter Series
Alan Simpson
471pp. Ref. 484-4; 4 3/4x8
Comprehensive information at a glance: a brief explanation of syntax and usage for every dBASE command, with step-by-step instructions and exact keystroke sequences. Commands are grouped by function in twenty precise categories.

Understanding R:BASE System V
Alan Simpson
499pp. Ref. 394-5
This complete tutorial guide covers every R:BASE function, while exploring and illustrating the principles of efficient database design. Examples include inventory management, mailing list handling, and much more.

Also:
Understanding R:BASE 5000
Alan Simpson
413pp. Ref. 302-3

GENERAL UTILITIES

The ABC's of the IBM PC
Joan Lasselle/Carol Ramsay
143pp. Ref. 102-0
Hands-on experience – without technical detail – for first-time users. Step-by-step tutorials show how to use essential commands, handle disks, use applications programs, and harness the PC's special capabilities.

Mastering ThinkTank on the IBM PC
Jonathan Kamin
350pp. Ref. 327-9
A business-minded tutorial on "idea processing" with ThinkTank – from first outlines to advanced features. Examples include logging sales calls, maintaining a resume, and creating a marketing plan. With complete reference sections.

COMPUTER-AIDED DESIGN AND DRAFTING

The ABC's of AutoCAD
Alan R. Miller
350pp. Ref. 498-4
This brief but effective introduction to AutoCAD quickly gets users drafting and designing with this complex CADD package. The essential operations and capabilities of AutoCAD are neatly detailed, using a proven, step-by-step method that is tailored to the results-oriented beginner.

Understanding *R:BASE*

Sample Programs Available on Disk

If you'd like to use the database command files and forms in this book but don't want to type them in yourself, you can send for a disk containing all the examples in the book. To obtain this disk, complete the order form and return it along with a check or money order for $40.00. California residents add 6½% sales tax.

SMS Software
P.O. Box 2802
La Jolla, CA 92038-2802

Name____________________________________

Company________________________________

Address_________________________________

City/State/Zip____________________________

Enclosed is my check or money order.
(Make check payable to *SMS Software*.)
Understanding R:BASE

SYBEX is not affiliated with SMS Software *and assumes no responsibility for any defect in the disk or program.*

SYBEX Computer Books are different.

Here is why . . .

At SYBEX, each book is designed with you in mind. Every manuscript is carefully selected and supervised by our editors, who are themselves computer experts. We publish the best authors, whose technical expertise is matched by an ability to write clearly and to communicate effectively. Programs are thoroughly tested for accuracy by our technical staff. Our computerized production department goes to great lengths to make sure that each book is well-designed.

In the pursuit of timeliness, SYBEX has achieved many publishing firsts. SYBEX was among the first to integrate personal computers used by authors and staff into the publishing process. SYBEX was the first to publish books on the CP/M operating system, microprocessor interfacing techniques, word processing, and many more topics.

Expertise in computers and dedication to the highest quality product have made SYBEX a world leader in computer book publishing. Translated into fourteen languages, SYBEX books have helped millions of people around the world to get the most from their computers. We hope we have helped you, too.

For a complete catalog of our publications:

TASK/TOPIC	PBE MENU SELECTIONS	R> COMMAND	PAGES
Edit data	(5)/EDIT	EDIT	52
Edit data through a form	(5)/EDIT/Form Edit	EDIT USING	201
Eject printer page		NEWPAGE	167
Embedded searches	(6)/Look at data	...CONTAINS...	105
Enhanced print			169
Exit to operating system		ZIP	137
Exit R:BASE	(9)	EXIT	35
Export data	(8)/ImportExport/GATEWAY/(2)	GATEWAY	560
Form for two tables			249
Form letters			399
Format dates	(8)/Environment/Keywords	SET DATE	132
Format reports	(2)/REPORTS/(1)	REPORTS	155
Format times	(8)/Environment/Keywords	SET TIME	135
Frequency distribution	(6)/Look at data/TALLY	TALLY	142
Functions			295
Help	F10 *key*	F10	28
Highest value	(6)/Look at data/COMPUTE	COMPUTE MAX	291
Import foreign data	(8)/ImportExport/GATEWAY/(1)	GATEWAY	560
Join two tables	(1)/R:BASE commands/Combine/JOIN	JOIN	387
Lowest value	(6)/Look at data/COMPUTE	COMPUTE MIN	291
Macro substitution		&	294
Mailing labels	(8)/3Labels		175
Math functions			298
Merge two tables	(1)/R:BASE commands/Combine	INTERSECT, UNION	379
Multiple tables (view)	(1)/RBDEFINE/(2)/(2)/(1)	RBDEFINE, VIEW	392
Open a database	(3)	OPEN	40
OR searches	(6)/Look at data	...OR...	104
Page length	(8)/Environment/SET/Keywords	SET LINES	128
Page width	(8)/Environment/Keywords	SET WIDTH	128
Password protection	(1)/RBDEFINE/(2)/(3)		29
PBE (prompt by example)		PROMPT	40
Print data		OUTPUT PRINTER	124
Print reports	(6)/Print data	PRINT	167
Print single sheets	(6)/Print data/PRINTER/SCREEN	OUTPUT PRINTER WITH SCREEN	168
Prompt by example		PROMPT	40